Contributions to Economics

The series *Contributions to Economics* provides an outlet for innovative research in all areas of economics. Books published in the series are primarily monographs and multiple author works that present new research results on a clearly defined topic, but contributed volumes and conference proceedings are also considered. All books are published in print and ebook and disseminated and promoted globally. The series and the volumes published in it are indexed by Scopus and ISI (selected volumes).

Gilberto Seravalli

Collective Action in the Age of Polycrisis

From Stalemate to Success

Springer

Gilberto Seravalli
University of Parma
Parma, Italy

ISSN 1431-1933 ISSN 2197-7178 (electronic)
Contributions to Economics
ISBN 978-3-032-12652-8 ISBN 978-3-032-12653-5 (eBook)
https://doi.org/10.1007/978-3-032-12653-5

This Springer imprint is published by the registered company Springer Nature Switzerland AG
The registered company address is: Gewerbestrasse 11, 6330 Cham, Switzerland

Preface

In "Essence of Nihilism", the great philosopher Emanuele Severino wrote half a century ago: "The West is a sinking ship". Decades later, that judgment seems prophetic and is remembered by the many who now publish essays with titles such as "The West is sick" or "The disease of the West". The widespread malaise is truly alarming, intertwined with a crisis of political and social institutions; a malaise and crisis which contrast greatly with the growing well-being of the first 40 years after the end of the Second World War, then accompanied by the sure functionality of the democratic organization. In Chapters 1 and 2, the book presents data and considerations that demonstrate this involution at the basis of true failures of the State and the Market. It then illustrates how difficult it is to imagine a way out while the authoritarian solution is at the door. Since "égalité" has been seriously damaged and inequality has eroded "liberté", the authoritarian path will eliminate it by not having planned corrections in the distribution of income, wealth and opportunities. Closing the long historical cycle that began with the French Revolution, the contradiction will be overcome with a tragic regression.

What is to be done? Chapter 3 begins by proposing the "top-down" solution that institutions and ruling classes could adopt to stem the widespread malaise. Although they are now far from this perspective, those who believe it to be realistic think that sooner or later institutions and the ruling classes will be forced to do so in order to regain the indispensable consensus. They will try, as they do now, to promise, spread propaganda, and lie. But when expedients are no longer enough, they will have to use policies capable of re-establishing a certain degree of equality, even with the main instrument indicated by experience in the phases in which inequality was contained: a progressive tax system and a consistent guaranteed minimum wage. However, according to a now strong current of thought, this solution is rather unlikely if one remains in the liberal individualistic conception of citizenship. A communitarian version would be needed in which participation is an essential element of freedom. It is the solution "from below" that, on the grounds of hope, should impose itself judging by the number of analysts from the most diverse disciplines who, after having explored the crisis of the system, call for the direct participation of citizens, associations, the third sector, self-help, in short, the collective action of the citizens themselves for the common good. And yet, in all these appeals there is little space, often no space, for the explanation of how to do it. The chapter therefore continues by presenting an overview of "dilemmas" of collective action and answers that are not lacking in the specialized literature. They are answers that configure the authentic aspect of inclusive and innovative collective action as a sophisticated process, continually open to possibilities and risks; with the problem of its unpredictability, meritorious character but also fragility. Now, faced with such a demanding perspective, there is the sad cultural reality of the contemporary world which dictates its unpopularity in the face of "combative cynicism". The widespread simplifications, false and vain verbalizations in all areas of information, politics, and civil society, call into question the way out of the contradiction for which the same reality in crisis, which would require difficult remedies, prevents them by favoring landings of combative cynicism and "imbecility", as a philosopher wrote. Combative cynicism, by considering what goes beyond the known and well-known useless and ridiculous, rises violently against those who laboriously search and explore.

However, there is help offered by "transindividualist" thought, which sees a profound human reality in which the collective and individual determine themselves together and not in opposition. At this depth there would therefore not be the dilemmas of collective action as a systematic contrast between individual good and common good to overcome which one must overcome the dilemmas thus arriving at the sophisticated path that clashes with combative cynicism. But not only that. Transindividualist thought maintains that this profound human reality has come to the surface precisely because of neoliberal degeneration. The exploration of this thought allows one to reach an interesting result: using inclusion against conservation and innovation against exclusion, using faith against science and science against faith. Faith, according to Dante Alighieri's definition: "substance of things hoped for and argument of the non-appearing"; science in the sense of knowledge learned through study and experience. This "formula" is then illustrated and tested with reference to examples taken from the very origins of Western culture.

In Chapters 4, 5, and 6, modern examples are also presented: one of capitalism at the origins of Silicon Valley; the other of the alternative proletarian culture between the nineteenth and twentieth centuries in the construction of a singular device, "the people's house". In the examples, the complicated processes that led to these achievements really saw the use of the formula faith against science and science against faith demonstrating its realism. They also allow it to be better specified. The example of the laborious elaboration of an alternative proletarian culture at the service of collective action during the Industrial Revolution suggests the "local rootedness" that could return as a lever for the collective action of social groups, while it was the factory in the Taylorist-Fordist system. The example also suggests that social groups should build something, some artifact, some device, perhaps even the recovery of some surviving people's houses, and set themselves concrete goals for the solution of specific problems affecting workers. From that experience came the proletarian counter-power that was, after the Second World War, at the base of the welfare state. That is, a general progressive project came from it. Yet this experience warns that it is necessary to accept, indeed cultivate, a double ambiguity. Ambiguity as a reference to tradition, today to that same proletarian experience, may appear to be a degraded and passive myth while there is tension toward the original and the active. And ambiguity also as a formal inconsistency that despite this was then recomposed into "unity" in a general reform project. It could be like this today too: the local initiative recomposed for a project of new citizenship, even digital, for the socialization of Capital, today above all Cloud Capital, for policies to overcome inequalities.

Gilberto Seravalli
University of Parma
Parma, Italy

Acknowledgments I would like to thank Alba Bonelli, Alberto Schena, Sergio Manghi for the invaluable help they provided, as well as the students at University of Parma to whom I presented some parts of the work in the lectures I held in March 2024 and 2025. Their reactions and comments have been truly helpful.

Competing Interests The author has no competing interests to declare that are relevant to the content of this manuscript.

Contents

Chapter 1
The Illness of the West

1.1 Collapse of the Middle Class

The term collapse is not an exaggeration. The middle class of Western countries, their backbone supported by upward social mobility after the Second World War, has been hit precisely in this essential foundation. [1]The condition of many wage earners who had experienced notable progress compared to their parents is documented, while now their children are slipping behind and their grandchildren even more so. According to an OECD report, a share of two-thirds to three-quarters of the entire Western population still thinks they belong to the middle class, but since the 1980s this has no longer been true. "Middle-class lifestyle is typically associated with

[1] Emanuele Severino writes about the sinking ship in two passages. The first is this: "The 'problems of humanity' are the superficial aspect of the fundamental problem of the West, which still escapes our awareness. The great international and national organizations and the forces of culture are treating a disease they do not know. A crowd of carpenters and workers who repair the furnis1972/1982hings of a sinking ship, without knowing if there is and where the leak is. On the sinking earth, technology can multiply its wonders infinitely, but only the truth of being can save the earth". (Severino, p. 191) The second is: "We are beginning to discover the deadly disease. But who cares? The West is a sinking ship, where everyone ignores the leak and works assiduously to make navigation ever more comfortable, and where, therefore, one only wants to discuss immediate problems, and one recognizes a meaning to problems only if one already glimpses the specific resolution techniques. But doesn't true health come about because one is capable of discovering true illness?". (Severino 1972/1982, p. 263) For Severino, the true disease of the West is not the one denounced today and considered also in this book, which is perhaps one of the ways in which the "true" disease manifests itself. For Severino, this was the abandonment, at the origin of Western thought, of the Parmenidean idea of being "that cannot not be and of non-being that is not". "The West is the civilization that grows within the horizon opened by the sense that Greek thought assigns to the being-thing of things. This sense progressively unifies [...] the boundless multiplicity of events that we call the history of the West [...]. For some time now my writings have indicated the Western [...] sense of the thing: the thing (a thing, everything) is, as a thing, nothing [...] that is, it appears as that of which it must be said that it is, but that it was not and will not be. That is, it appears as that which, totally or partially, comes out of nothing and returns to it". (Severino 1972/1982, p. 418)

G. Seravalli, *Collective Action in the Age of Polycrisis*, Contributions to Economics,
https://doi.org/10.1007/978-3-032-12653-5_1

certain goods and services and certain living conditions, such as decent housing, good education and good and accessible health services. However, the prices of core consumption goods and services such as health, education and housing have risen well above inflation, while middle incomes have been lagging behind". (OECD 2019, p. 23) Comparing the progress of per capita income by class at a global level, one sees that since 1980 the middle class of Western countries has suffered very significant relative losses (Fig. 1.1).

At the basis of these losses of income of the middle class was the reduction of the wage share in the functional distribution of income (see the data on the "decoupling" between wages and productivity below). The connection between the wage share and inequality has long been noted empirically, confirmed by recent research, and explained theoretically. Although other circumstances also influence it, the most decisive is that the inequality between those who only earn income from work is lower than that between those who earn other incomes, as documented by Branko Milanovic (2017) and Iñaki Erauskin (2020). If the wage share decreases, the weight of those with more egalitarian incomes decreases and therefore inequality increases. From the end of the Second World War to the 1980s, the opposite occurred: with a high wage share, inequality was contained.

But the middle class has also suffered serious losses due to the deterioration of the supply of social services. High health and education indices, correlated with

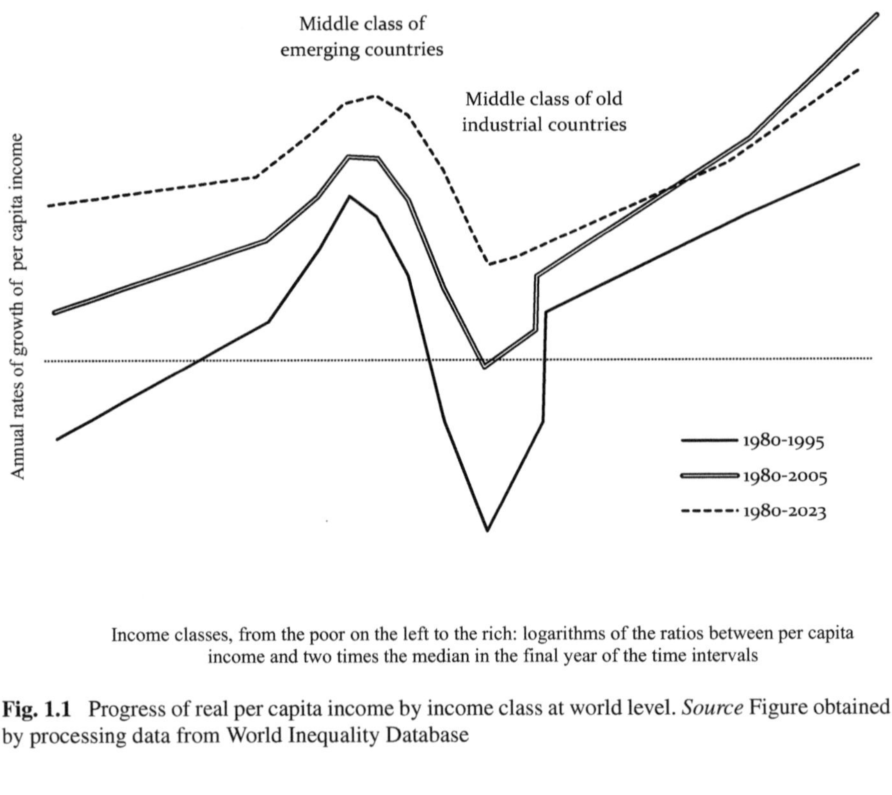

Fig. 1.1 Progress of real per capita income by income class at world level. *Source* Figure obtained by processing data from World Inequality Database

per capita income, were characteristic of developed countries. But from the 1980s onwards the scenarios began to change. The following graph shows that in upper-middle income countries the correlation between income and health-education has disappeared, while it has remained in lower-middle income countries. This means that in Western countries, the public services underlying the health-education index have very often lagged behind the growth of resources indicated by GDP per capita. The middle class has thus been penalized twice: in terms of income *and* social services, as highlighted in the 2019 OECD Report (Fig. 1.2).

Considering the available research, it is not easy to establish what the will to finance school and health services at a level adequate to the available resources depends on: in different countries there are very different situations and mechanisms

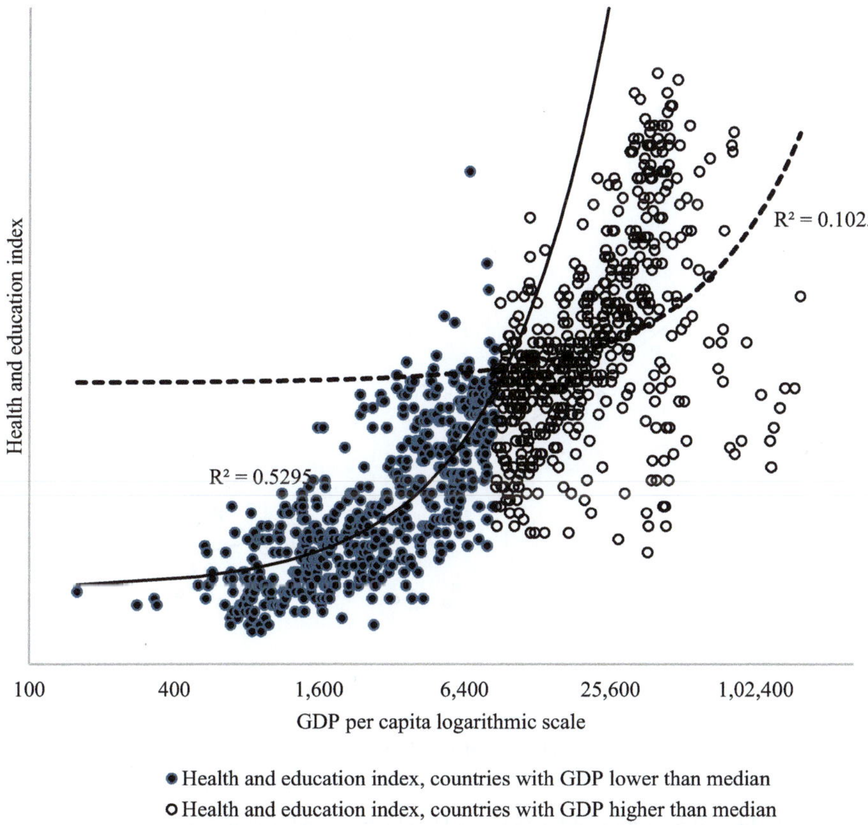

Fig. 1.2 Health and education index (Human Development Index minus income component) in relation to GDP per capita in purchasing power parity (PPP) international dollars constant prices 2015; country-year observations from 1985 to 2020 in five-year intervals, 153 countries divided into two groups: per capita GDP lower and higher than the median. *Source* Figure obtained by processing data from Ourworldindata statistics. *Note* R squared, coefficient of determination, is a measure of the proportion of variance explained by the interpolant

as well as many variables that intervene. For this reason, it is important to note that one of the most influential variables concerns the distribution of income itself. In this way there is a perverse circuit: the middle class of Western countries, already penalized on the income side, has also been penalized on the social services side precisely because it has lost position in income distribution. It is interesting to observe the health-education index compared with the shares of national income belonging to the richest 1% of the population. For 68 countries with reference to 2020, the correlation is significant and negative: the greater the wealth of the richest individuals, the worse the health and education index of the country (Fig. 1.3).

> "Inequality reduces [...] health and education so that the intergenerational transmission of inequality is strengthened [...] because the rich, individually or in associations [...] can exert political pressure to further increase their share of existing wealth through regulatory capture and by influencing the formulation and application of laws to their advantage. Such behavior makes social policies that promote investment in areas such as education, health and social protection much more difficult". (ONU 2013, pp. 22, 71)

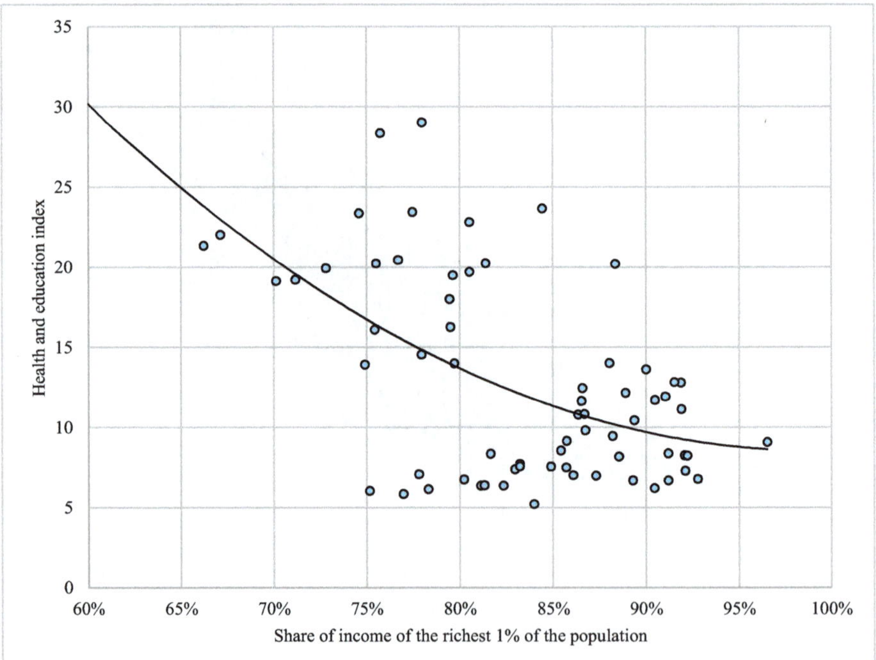

Fig. 1.3 Health and education index (Human Development Index minus income component) in relation to the percentage share of income belonging to the richest 1% of the population, 2020, 68 countries. *Source* Figure obtained by processing data from UN database

1.2 Arrest of Social Mobility and Crisis of Hegemony of the Ruling Class

In Western countries, the collapse of the middle class and the increase in inequality are linked to the crisis of upward social mobility. The clear increase in upward social mobility that occurred after the Second World War, accompanied by a reduction in inequality, was then reversed with an increase in inequality. This correlation makes inequality unbearable because it violates what Roland Bénabou and Ok (2001) have called the "prospect of upward mobility hypothesis", the idea that those with lower incomes are not strong advocates of redistributive policies "because of the belief that they, or in the least their children, are likely to climb the income ladder. However, an emerging body of evidence suggests that more inequality of incomes in the present is likely to make family background play a stronger role in determining the adult outcomes of young people, with their own hard work playing a commensurately weaker role". (Corak 2013, p. 1) But the crisis of social mobility has even more serious consequences because it delegitimizes the system as a crisis of hegemony of the ruling class.

1.2.1 Negative Correlation Between Social Mobility and Inequality

Miles Corak (2013), with data on the 1990–1995 income of children born in the years 1960–1965 in comparison with the income of their parents, and inequality in the distribution of income 1985 (Gini index), had demonstrated the negative correlation between social mobility and inequality for 11 major high-income countries. Scandinavian countries had the highest social mobility and the lowest inequality. Italy, the United Kingdom, and the United States had the lowest social mobility and the highest inequality. In an intermediate position were Germany, Canada, and Japan. For Miles Corak this demonstration was decisive because it denied the belief in the "American dream". His essay began with these sentences:

> The "American Dream" is a very broad concept with many meanings and certainly broader than any single statistic can measure. However, when the Economic Mobility Project, supported by the Pew Charitable Trust, conducted a nationally representative poll that asked Americans what they understood this phrase to mean, some typical answers included: [...] being able to succeed regardless of the economic circumstances in which you were born. These meanings have historically not only made the American Dream a defining metaphor of the country, they are also likely a reason why Americans have been willing to tolerate a good deal more inequality of outcomes than citizens of many other rich countries (Corak 2013, p. 1).

In the same countries, comparing inequality 1990–1995 and mobility, as the higher income of children born in the 1970s compared to that of their parents, the same negative but even more significant correlation is found (World Economic Forum 2020) (Fig. 1.4).

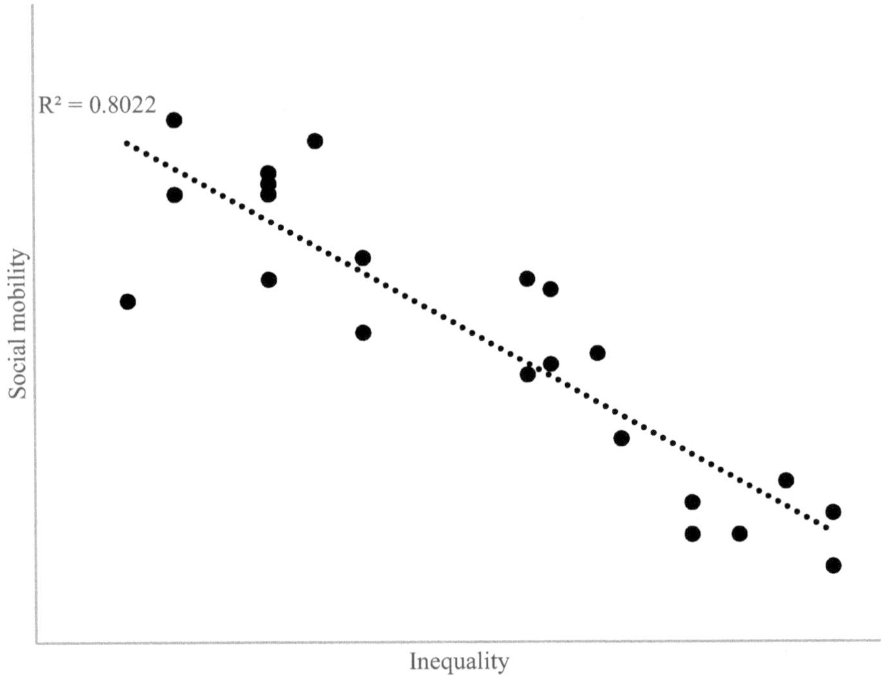

Fig. 1.4 Finland, Norway, Denmark, Sweden, Germany, Canada, Japan, France, Italy, the United Kingdom, and the United States. Inequality (Gini coefficient) of disposable income 1985 and 1990–1995 and social mobility as income superiority compared to fathers of children born in the years 1960–1965 and 1970–1980. *Note* The mobility indices are calculated in the same way for the two periods: one less elasticity of fathers' income compared to that of children. Given the distribution of fathers' and children's income, taking the variation of one percent of children's income, the elasticity of fathers' income is equal to the corresponding percentage increase in their income. A high elasticity implies that children are richer if fathers were richer. A low elasticity implies that children are richer even if fathers were not richer or were richer to a modest extent. *Source* Figure obtained by processing data from Corak (2013, p. 3) and World Economic Forum (2020, p. 10)

1.2.2 Increase and Then Decrease in Social Mobility

Remarkable data on the trend of social mobility are distributed as an attachment to the publication "IZA Institute of Labor Economics", the result of the work of 14 researchers (Manduca et al. 2020). It contains the differences in income of children at age 30 compared to their parents when they were the same age for cohorts born from 1964 to 1984 with reference to current income from 1994 to 2014. In this way, the incomes of children and parents a quarter of a century apart are compared. For the growth of average per capita income, one would expect that all children would have earned more than their parents, with limited random exceptions. This is probably the case in Norway: at a substantially constant rate of around 74%, those born from 1964 to 1984 earned more at age 30 than their parents did at the same age. This is the highest share among all Western countries considered in the IZA research. For other countries, a measure of upward social mobility in terms of income can then be calculated as a reduction in the difference compared to Norway, and downward mobility as an increase in the difference. It can thus be seen that on average in Northern European countries, upward mobility occurred until the early 2000s (born up to the early 1970s). Then there was downward mobility. The difference compared to Norway in the share of children with higher income than their parents went from minus 9% to minus 2% and then to minus 12%. In the United States, the difference was even greater, going from minus 13% to minus 9% and then to minus 27%. The researchers also calculated the trends in social mobility with reference to the age of 40 to ascertain whether its fall since the 2000s was only due to an extension of the time to reach good job positions. The result shows that this has occurred, but only in the Scandinavian countries, not in the United States and Great Britain. They then ran further tests to determine whether changes in family size, the number of adults per family, and activity rates had an impact. It turned out that these circumstances had an impact but without significantly changing the trends (Fig. 1.5).

In another important piece of research for the United States (Songa et al. 2019) indicators of social mobility were constructed not in terms of income but of *status* for a large sample of people born from 1900 to 1980 in ten-year intervals. The status is obtained by classifying 70 professional positions for prestige scores gradually

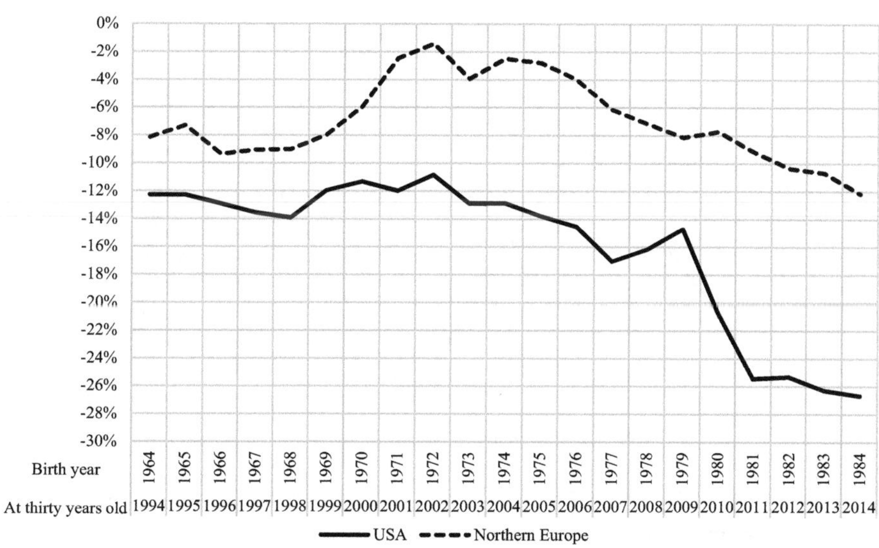

Fig. 1.5 Upward mobility deficit compared to Norway (tending to be constant at the highest level). Percentage points of difference from the Norwegian figure for shares of births per year whose real household income at age 30 was higher than the parents' household income at age 30. Northern Europe refers to the United Kingdom (complete data), Sweden (1984 missing), Denmark (1964–1965 missing), and Finland (1964 missing). *Source* Figure obtained by processing data from Manduca et al. (2020)

adjusted to reflect changes in common perception. For example, the scores of the clerical positions decreased as the "executive" positions characterized by greater autonomy and responsibility spread. Consequently, the status of a clerical son went backward even if his father was a clerical son like him. Considering the transition matrices children-parents at about 35 years between quintiles of the distribution of scores, together with the social mobility in terms of income already considered, for the years of birth from 1940 to 1980, the following graph was obtained (Fig. 1.6).

In the United States, upward mobility also followed a parabolic trajectory, first increasing for those born between 1940 and 1960 and then decreasing. For those born between the end of the 1950s and the beginning of the 1960s, upward mobility was not only high, but downward mobility was also singularly limited. Upward mobility in terms of income continued for those born throughout the 1960s even when status mobility had begun to decline. This delay in the reduction of income mobility compared to status mobility was probably due to the growth in the general level of education. The prestige of various professions was decreasing, as in the case of clerks, while the wages of graduates increased, especially in the period 1995–2005. As David Autor (2014) has found, in real terms and net of the cost of attending university, the difference between the remuneration of graduates and young people

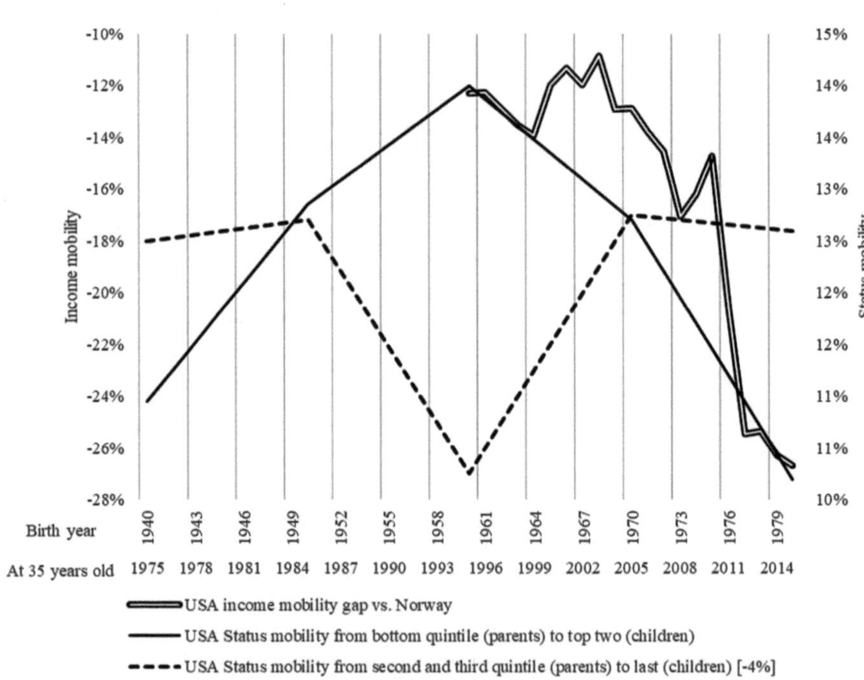

Fig. 1.6 The United States, income and status mobility. *Source* Figure obtained by processing data from Manduca et al. (2020), Songa, et al. (2019, Table S15 Mobility Transition Matrix Estimates Based on Occupational Quintiles, p. 98-99 Supporting Information for Long-Term Decline in Intergenerational Mobility in the U.S. Since the 1850s)

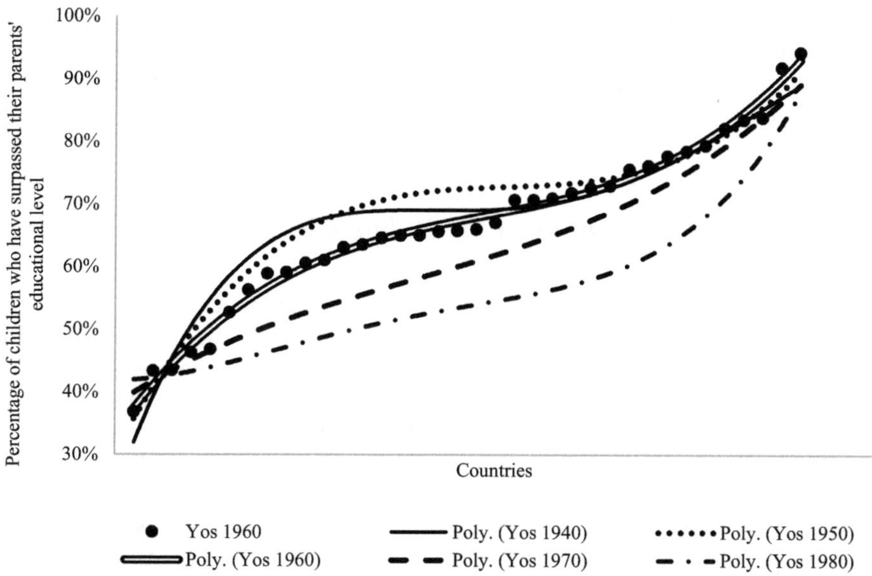

Fig. 1.7 36 high-income countries. Percentage of children who have surpassed the highest level of education of either parent (Yos) by decade of birth from the 1940s to the 1980s, polynomial interpolations (Polin). *Source* Figure obtained by processing data from World Bank data, Global Database on Intergenerational Mobility

with only a high school diploma increased between 1995 and 2005 from 9500 dollars (2009 prices) per year on average for a 42-year career, to 14,000, then remaining at that level in subsequent years (Autor 2014, p. 847). This was for men; for women, the increase was from 7000 to 9500 dollars.

Finally, the data on social mobility measured in terms of education (GDIM—Global Database on Intergenerational Mobility) can be considered.[2] For 36 high-income countries, years of birth of children from 1940 to 1980 by decades, highest educational level of one or the other parent, percentage of children who have exceeded the highest educational level of their parents (surveys from 1999 to 2017), the following graph can be constructed (Fig. 1.7).

These data show that: (1) in countries at the extremes of the distribution of measures of social mobility in terms of education it has not changed over time (at the lowest level, Switzerland and New Zealand; at the highest level, Spain and Ireland); (2) in countries with medium-high mobility it has remained stable for those

[2] This measure is justified because "there are several reasons for the focus on education. Firstly, human capital is a key aspect of economic well-being. Secondly, intergenerational data on education is more widely available than on income. Thirdly, the estimation of educational mobility involves fewer methodological challenges. Unlike income, the level of education, once acquired, does not vary across an individual's lifecycle. Fourthly, individuals can report their parents' education level with a high degree of precision, whereas the same is not true for income, making it possible to study mobility in education without panel data". (Van der Weide et al. 2021, p. 3)

born from the 1940s to the 1960s and then decreased for those born in the 1970s and 1980s; (3) in countries with medium-low mobility it remained at relatively high levels for those born in the 1940s and 1950s and then decreased for those born from the 1960s onwards.

1.2.3 *Crisis of Hegemony of the Ruling Class*

The reality described by the figures examined has caused much alarm. "The study of social mobility can be traced back to around 100 years. But up until the turn of the Millennium it remained largely an academic topic, studied by sociologists focused on intergenerational shifts in social class. While a few seminal papers on income mobility had been published in the 1990s, 2005 signaled a new wave of social mobility studies that have proliferated over the last two decades". (Eyles et al. 2022, p. 6) (Fig. 1.8)

The alarm is fully justified if one considers the importance of social mobility: from the point of view of the interests of the majority of the population, but also for the hegemony of the ruling class, as conceived by Antonio Gramsci, in which social mobility acquires central importance. The political leader and philosopher Gramsci, who along with Benedetto Croce was among the greatest Italian thinkers

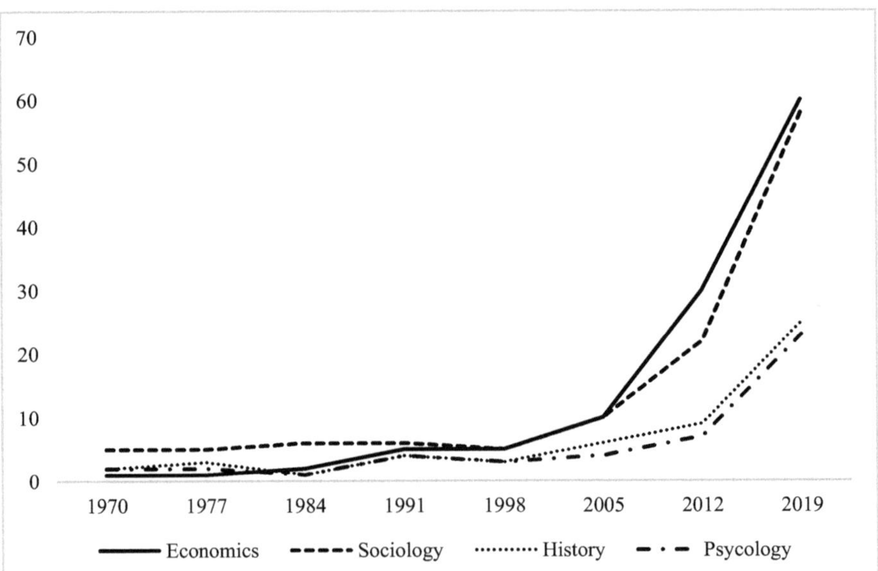

Fig. 1.8 The United Kingdom: Social mobility academic articles, narrow topic search by subject (data are taken from the Web of Science Core Collection via a topic search for the terms "social mobility" or "intergenerational mobility". *Source* Figure obtained by processing data from Eyles, Elliot Major, Machin (2022, p. 10)

of the twentieth century, is known throughout the world precisely for his reflection on hegemony. "Much has been written on the concept of hegemony in Gramsci, indeed a great deal: of the little less than sixteen thousand texts listed in the online Gramscian bibliography edited by John Cammett and collaborators [today there are 21,550] almost a thousand [today 1400] contain this key word". (Cospito 2008, p. 187)

Social mobility was not part of the primitive concept of hegemony that is traced back to Greek historians who

> conceive hegemony as a military leadership of an alliance against a common enemy [...]. Hegemony [...] presupposes that the allies are independent subjects [...] and presupposes an inequality of capabilities [...]: material power [is] a necessary element for an ally to be able to lead the others in the common struggle. [...]. One must be "worthy" of assuming supreme military command [...]; military value and strategic effectiveness are indisputable elements that make one worthy of being recognized as hegemons [...but] also non-military qualities such as [...] cultural excellence are [...] included among the bases that make the recognition of hegemonic leadership possible (Clementi 2018, pp. 354-359).

This concept, with its double meaning of *strength* and *prestige* to lead a coalition of independent subjects, underwent a first twist in the eighteenth century, moving from the finalization against a common enemy to that of the ordering of nations, often in the throes of struggles for the prevalence of one over the others.

> The concept of hegemony was used extensively since the eighteenth century, not only in ancient history but also in the politics of the European powers of the time [...] in the sense of an attempt by one nation to gain supremacy over others. In this sense, it is also widely found in the nineteenth century, as, for example, in the works of Pierre Joseph Proudhon and Ernest Renan. But the most significant use in this century is found in the writings on the events of Germany and Italy, both divided into several sovereign states, some of which aspired to hegemony over others (Di Meo 2016, p. 2).

A further twisting of the concept of hegemony, "from horizontal (geographical, international) to vertical (political, social)" (Di Meo 2016, p.20), was certainly widespread in France before 1872. In the history of the Paris Commune reported in the appendix of volume IX, "Encyclopedic Yearbook" (Encyclopédie du XIX Siècle 1869–1871), published in 1872, paragraph VII is devoted to the "Social and political doctrines of the central committee and the Commune - Role of the International - Hegemony of the workers". (pp. 2254–2269) But the meaning is that of absolute domination through the annihilation of every other social component. In the text, after having explained that the very divided revolutionaries of 18 March, had found common ground in the federalist perspective between proletarian communes to be spread throughout France, the hegemony of the proletariat is understood as "elimination from society of the classes that have arrived [...] at fortune, comfort, well-being and intellectual culture. [...]. Making the whole of France a Nation of proletarians" (p. 2258). If the hegemony of the ancients was the guide of several independents, this appears, on the contrary, to be domination through annihilation. It could then be said that the concept of the hegemony of the proletariat of Vladimir Il′ič Ul'janov (Lenin) was placed in an intermediate position between these two extremes. The hegemony of the proletariat could and should be exercised in an alliance of different social components that did not disappear. Which would have acted for a common goal leaning on the proletariat that would have therefore led them rather than simply guided them as advanced representatives of all the exploited. For the far from obvious discovery of the working class as a preeminent class, Gregory Zinoviev's reconstruction can be valid.

> In the Russian Revolution, the founders of the idea of the hegemony of the proletariat were Plekhanov and Lenin. [...]. Lenin first formulated the idea of the hegemony of the proletariat in the Russian Revolution in 1894 [...]. The working class, the factory proletariat, is nothing but the advanced representative of all the exploited, that is, even of the landless peasants. Therefore, the working class must place itself at the head of all the exploited, that is, it must assume hegemony in the struggle for emancipation. [...] At the Congress of the Second International (Paris, 1889), Plekhanov, then the undisputed leader of all revolutionary Marxists in Russia and the intellectual ruler of the then Marxist intelligentsia, uttered the historical truth: «The Russian revolution will either conquer as a revolution of the working class, or it will not conquer at all». [...]. In the period preceding Plekhanov's historic declaration [...] the popularly inspired intelligentsia relied on the "people", that is, on the "peasants". [...] the working class existed at most as an auxiliary force. [...]. [On the other hand,] on one point the Mensheviks never doubted for a minute [...], that the next day, after the victory, the working class would have to offer power to the liberal bourgeoisie (Zinoviev 1923, pp. 267-268).

According to Lenin's writings of 1905, the function of leadership is: "support" which "can and must be given to every liberalism exactly to the extent that it acts in concrete terms in fighting against autocracy. Precisely this support of the only democrat consistent to the end, that is, the proletariat, to all the inconsistent democrats (that is, bourgeois), realizes the idea of hegemony [... which] belongs to the one whose words correspond to the deeds, to the one who is therefore the ideological leader of democracy". (Lenin 1905/1961, p. 66) When the proletariat then conquered power and had to begin the construction of a socialist society, Lenin did not propose the term hegemony again. The importance of the peasants as "productive forces" required an agreement based on incentives rather than on constraints. But now the proletarian power had been acquired, and the consent of the peasants was due. The term hegemony would have been ambiguous, implying free adhesion. Lenin instead used the terms alliance with the peasants and dictatorship of the proletariat.

> The poor peasants (proletarians and semi-proletarians) have, in many cases, transformed themselves into middle peasants. The small-proprietor, petty-bourgeois element has therefore strengthened. [...] On the other hand, the production and storage of grain, the storage and transportation of fuel cannot be increased unless the conditions of the peasants are improved, their productive forces are increased. [...] The dictatorship of the proletariat is the political leadership of the proletariat. The proletariat, as the ruling, dominant class, must be able to orient politics in such a way as to solve first the most urgent [...] task. Today the most urgent thing is constituted by measures that can immediately increase the productive forces of the peasant economy. Only by this means can we succeed both in improving the conditions of the workers and in strengthening the alliance of the workers with the peasants, in strengthening the dictatorship of the proletariat (Lenin 1921/1967, pp. 320-321).

It was Gregory Zinoviev who would later make the distinction disappear to dictate the official history of Bolshevism as the realization of hegemony, at least until 1924: "The whole history of Bolshevism is nothing but a struggle for the realization of the idea of the hegemony of the proletariat. Bolshevism has always waged the same struggle, from the time of the Friends of the People (1894) to the present day. And all this time the struggle has been led by V.I. Lenin". (Zinoviev 1923, p. 268) And it was Iosif Vissarionovič Džugašvili (Stalin) from 1924 who would reduce hegemony to a historical precondition for the dictatorship of the proletariat[3] repositioning the peasants in the role of their "reserve".[4] And then arriving, with the turning point of 1927, at the doctrine of class against class (VI Congress of the Communist International, Moscow July–September 1928) and forced industrialization, to the proletarianization of all the peasants with unheard of massacres and deportations leading to famine in Russia, and especially Ukraine, with millions of deaths from starvation.[5]

---

[3] "The characteristic feature of this period [1905 - February 1917] is the liberation of the peasantry from the influence of the liberal bourgeoisie [...], the turn of the peasantry towards the proletariat, towards the Bolshevik Party [...]. The period of the four Dumas was a lesson [...] for the peasantry [...]. It showed that they would receive neither land nor freedom from the hands of the Cadets, that the tsar was entirely obedient to the landowners and the Cadets supported the tsar, that the only force on whose support the peasantry could count was the workers of the cities, the proletariat. The imperialist war [...] made the peasantry's detachment from the bourgeoisie complete, for the war years showed how vain, how illusory was the hope of obtaining peace from the tsar and his bourgeois allies. Without the political lessons of the Duma period, the hegemony of the proletariat would have been impossible. [...]. Thus was achieved the hegemony (leadership) of the proletariat in the common struggle for the overthrow of tsarism, a hegemony that led to the February Revolution of 1917". (Stalin 1924/1952, p. 155)

[4] Stalin clarifies what he means by reserve in the following sentence that precedes the chapter on the peasants: "Tsarist Russia was an immense reserve of Western imperialism not only in the sense that it gave free access to foreign capital, which held in its grip decisive sectors of the Russian economy, such as fuel and metallurgy, but also in the sense that it could put millions of soldiers at the service of the imperialists of the West". (Stalin 1924/1952., p. 98) Reserve, therefore, as a passive resource at their disposal. In this sense the peasants must be conceived as a reserve: "The question is posed as follows: [...] is there a hope [...] of making the peasants, of their exploited majority, no longer a reserve of the bourgeoisie, as they were during the bourgeois revolutions of the West and as they continue to be today, but a reserve of the proletariat, its ally? Leninism answers this question affirmatively, that is, in the sense of recognizing the existence of revolutionary capacities in the majority of the peasants, and in the sense of considering it possible to use these capacities in the interests of the proletarian dictatorship. The history of three revolutions in Russia fully confirms the conclusions of Leninism in this respect. [...] This does not mean, of course, that the proletariat must support any peasant movement. It is a question of supporting that movement and that struggle of the peasants which, directly or indirectly, facilitate the emancipation movement of the proletariat, which in one way or another bring water to the mill of the proletarian revolution, which contribute to making the peasantry a reserve and an ally of the working class". (Stalin 1924/1952, pp. 154–155)

[5] "The [...] result was a catastrophic decline in agricultural output [...]. The government's reaction was to base its requirements for delivery from the collective farms not on actual production but on [...] the estimated size of the crop [...] 40 percent higher than the reality. [...]. The grain requisitions [...] were ruthlessly enforced by activist squads (and, in Bukharin's view this experience contributed greatly to the brutalization of the Party). Such action left peasants with [...] non-existent surplus on which to live. As a result, over winter of 1932–33 major famine swept the grain-growing areas. Some 4 to five million died in Ukraine, and another 2 to three million in the North Caucasus and Lower Volga area". (Conquest 2000, pp. 95–96) Other estimates indicate four million 500 thousand losses in Ukraine from 1926 to 1939, of which one million deportees, two million 500 thousand deaths, one million fewer births (Vallin et al. 2002).

Antonio Gramsci used the term hegemony for the first time in an article in "Ordine Nuovo" in March 1924 in which he endorsed Zinoviev's interpretation.

> In 1903 the second Congress of the Russian Socialist Party met. The theses put forward by Lenin [...] led to the split. The minority [...] believed that the workers could not defeat the Tsar and the landowners, in whose hands the government of Russia was, except by allying themselves with the bourgeoisie [...]. The majority, the Bolsheviks, maintained that such a coalition would be deadly for the workers' movement and that the worker could have only one ally, the poor peasant. The majority wanted a strongly organised and centralised party [...]. The minority did not want centralisation [...]. With the split the tenacious struggle between Bolsheviks and Mensheviks began. Bolshevism became [...] the independent party of the working class [...]. What does its political originality consist in [...]? Bolshevism is the first, in the international history of classes, to have developed the idea of the hegemony of the proletariat and to have practically posed the main revolutionary problems that Marx and Engels had theoretically raised. The idea of the hegemony of the proletariat, precisely because it was conceived historically and concretely, brought with it the need to seek an ally for the working class: Bolshevism found this ally in the mass of poor peasants (Gramsci 1924, p. 3).

Gramsci wrote this article at the age of 33, when he had been a member of the executive of the Socialist International for a year and was still in Moscow. Elected deputy (6 April 1924), he returned to Italy in May 1924, two years and seven months before his arrest (8 November 1926) in total violation of parliamentary immunity. After 10 years spent in prison, suffering, studying, and thinking, in 1934 he wrote in paragraph 24 of Notebook 19 the definition of hegemony, always reported by interpreters, which could seem to be that of Lenin-Zinoviev without substantial differences: "A social group can and indeed must be a leader before conquering government power (this is one of the main conditions for the conquest of power itself); afterwards, when it exercises power and even if it holds it firmly in its grip, it becomes dominant but must also continue to be a leader" (Gramsci 1934/1977, p. 2011). This definition must be read in the context of the paragraph from which it is taken, which does not concern the proletarian revolution at all, but the Italian Risorgimento during which the "moderates" were the hegemonic group, "related and allied" groups were the Action Party, while the groups loyal to the Austria of the Restoration were the "adversaries". It is also significant to note that this definition from 1934 and the passage from which it is taken already appear in the first Notebook § 44 composed in February–March 1930 and are repeated as is in Notebook 19 § 24 of 1934: "The problem of political direction in the formation and development of the Nation and the modern State in Italy".

> The whole problem of the connection between the various political currents of the Risorgimento, that is, of their mutual relations and of their relations with homogeneous or subordinate social groups [...], boils down to this fundamental fact: the moderates represented a relatively homogeneous social group, so their direction underwent relatively limited oscillations [...] while the so-called Action Party did not rely specifically on any historical class and the oscillations undergone by its governing bodies were ultimately composed according to the interests of the moderates: that is, historically the Action Party was led by the moderates [...]. The methodological criterion on which one must base one's examination is this: that the supremacy of a social group manifests itself in two ways, as domination and as intellectual and moral direction. A social group is dominant over opposing groups that it

> tends to "liquidate" or subdue even with armed force and is the leader of similar and allied groups. A social group can and indeed must be the leader before conquering governmental power (this is one of the main conditions for the conquest of power itself); later, when he exercises power and even if he holds it firmly in his grip, he becomes dominant but must also continue to be a leader. The moderates continued to lead the Action Party even after 1870 and 1876 and the so-called "transformism" was nothing but the parliamentary expression of this intellectual, moral and political hegemonic action (Gramsci 1930/1977, pp. 40-41).

By transferring the concept of hegemony to the Italian Risorgimento, attributing it to the moderate component, considering the revolutionary component subordinate, Gramsci had achieved a complete re-conceptualization of hegemony, while maintaining the 1924 definition as a necessary combination of domination and direction. In the 10 years between 1924 and 1934 Gramsci had reached the conviction that: (1) the hegemonic process, inevitably *dynamic*, is *general*, inherent in the conquest and exercise of power, and therefore there are always conflicts between *alternative hegemonic projects*; (2) a hegemonic project prevails on the basis of its capacity to *include the subaltern* by the ruling class (social mobility); (3) in this way it is, however, *contradictory*: by promoting the emancipation of the subaltern classes it threatens the same dominant classes who must therefore combine in a problematic way *inclusion and control* which becomes a central aspect of the hegemonic process; (4) the way out of the contradiction by *blocking social mobility* is equivalent to a *crisis of hegemony*.

1.2.3.1 Hegemonic Processes in Conflict

In Notebook 3, paragraph 14 ("History of the ruling class and history of the subordinate classes") written in June 1930 (this and subsequent dating are taken from Cospito 2011, Appendix), then taken up again in Notebook 25, paragraph 2 ("Methodological criteria") written between July 1934 and the first months of 1935 one reads:

> The history of subaltern social groups[6] it is necessarily disintegrated and episodic. There is no doubt that in the historical activity of these groups there is a tendency towards unification, even if on provisional levels, but this tendency is continually broken by the initiative of the dominant groups and therefore can only be demonstrated once the historical cycle is complete, if it ends with a success. The subordinate groups always suffer the initiative of the dominant groups, even when they rebel and rise: only "permanent" victory breaks, and not immediately, subordination. Even when they appear triumphant, the subordinate groups are only in a state of alarmed defence (this truth can be demonstrated with the history of the French Revolution up to 1830 at least). Every trace of autonomous initiative on the part of subaltern groups should therefore be of inestimable value to the integral historian (Gramsci 1930/1977b, pp. 299-300; Gramsci 1935/1977, pp. 2283-2284).

[6] This is the first time Gramsci uses the expression subaltern social groups in his prison work. They are "intended both as marginal social groups [...] and as fundamental classes that are not yet hegemonic. [...] It should be emphasized that with the hegemonic/subaltern couple Gramsci offers broader and more comprehensive categories than the classical Marxist ones (bourgeois/proletarians), since they better intertwine social location and subjectivity, structural data and cultural and ideological data". (Liguori 2015, p. 48)

As Fabio Frosini has underlined, “the adjective autonomous has a precise, clear meaning in Gramsci: it indicates the capacity of a social class to direct itself as a class [...]. If emancipation is the premise of autonomy, autonomy is the premise of hegemony”. (Frosini 2016, p. 128) The sentences reported therefore indicate processes (premises that give rise to outcomes[7]), on the one hand, implemented by the dominant groups to maintain their hegemony and the subordination of the dominated groups, on the other hand, by the latter to gain emancipation-autonomy with a view to an ever-possible overthrow of the hegemony.

1.2.3.2 Hegemony and Social Mobility

The active and dynamic connection between the process of hegemony of the dominant class and upward social mobility of parts of the subaltern can be reconstructed in Gramsci’s reflection starting from Notebook 1 paragraph 44 “Political direction of the class before and after the move to government”. (February–March 1930) The paragraph opens with the passage already cited which begins with the words “the whole problem of the connection between the various political currents of the Risorgimento”; after a few pages it continues with the illustration of the inability of the Action Party to become hegemonic unlike the Jacobins in France.

> Regarding Jacobinism and the Action Party, one element to remember is that the Jacobins conquered their role as the leading party through struggle: they imposed themselves on the French bourgeoisie, leading it to a much more advanced position than the bourgeoisie would have wanted “spontaneously” and much more advanced than the historical premises should have allowed [...]. This trait [...] of forcing the situation [...] by kicking the bourgeois class forward [...], by a group of extremely energetic and resolute men can be schematized as follows: the third estate was the least homogeneous [...] the bourgeoisie constituted the most advanced part culturally and economically [...] which initially raised the questions [... of] its [...] immediate and selfish interests [...]; the precursors of the revolution were moderate reformists, who spoke out loudly but in reality asked for very little. This advanced part gradually loses its “corporate” characteristics and becomes the ruling class due to the action of two factors: the resistance of the old classes and the political activity of the Jacobins. The old classes do not want to give up anything and if they give up something they do so with the intention of gaining time and preparing the counteroffensive; the bourgeoisie would have fallen into these successive “traps” without the energetic action of the Jacobins, who oppose every intermediate stop and send to the guillotine not only the representatives of the old classes, but also the revolutionaries of yesterday who have become reactionaries today. The Jacobins, therefore, represent the only party of the revolution, in that they not only see the immediate interests [...] of the French bourgeoisie, but they also see the interests of tomorrow and not only of those specific physical persons, but of the other social strata of the third estate who tomorrow will become bourgeois (Gramsci 1930/1977, pp. 50-51).

[7] Note that for Gramsci such processes from premises to outcomes are never “automatic” but always depend on the human factor. “The historical ‘automatism’ of certain premises (the existence of certain objective conditions) is politically strengthened by parties and capable men: their absence or deficiency (quantitative and qualitative) makes the ‘automatism’ itself sterile (which therefore is not automatism): the premises are abstractly there, but the consequences are not realised because the human factor is missing”. (Gramsci 1932–33/1977b, p. 1627)

Gramsci, in the same notebook, completed the connection between bourgeois-Jacobin hegemony and social mobility in the long phase of parliamentarism up to the First World War. The central passage is the following, then taken up again in a more organic arrangement in notebook 13 (Notes on French national life) § 37 (May 1932–November 1933).

> The development of Jacobinism (of content) [...] found its legal-constitutional perfection in the parliamentary regime, which achieves, in the period richest in private energy in society, the permanent hegemony of the urban class over the entire population, [...] progressively through a complete process, in which propaganda and practical activity (economic, political-juridical) alternate: the economic base, for industrial and commercial development, is continually broadened and deepened, from the lower classes the social elements richest in energy and entrepreneurial spirit rise up to the ruling classes, the entire society is in a continuous process of formation and dissolution followed by more complex formations rich in possibilities; this lasts, in general, until the era of imperialism and culminates in the world war (Gramsci 1932b-33/1977, pp. 1636-1637).

1.2.3.3 Inclusion and Control

The process of hegemonic construction through the assimilation of parts of the subaltern social groups, that is, of their upward social mobility, and of its contradictory nature whereby its history is also the history of the forms in which inclusion and control are articulated, recalled several times in the Notebooks, is finally effectively outlined in the aforementioned Notebook 25 "History of the subaltern social groups" paragraph 2 "Methodological criteria" July 1934—first months of 1935.

> It is necessary to study: 1) the objective formation of subaltern social groups, due to the development and upheavals that occur in the world of economic production, their quantitative diffusion and their origin from pre-existing social groups, of which they retain for a certain time the mentality, ideology and aims; 2) their active or passive adhesion to the dominant political formations, the attempts to influence the programs of these formations to impose their own demands and the consequences that such attempts have in determining processes of decomposition and renewal or neoformation; 3) the birth of new parties of the dominant groups to maintain the consensus and control of the subaltern groups; 4) the formations proper to the subaltern groups for claims of a restricted and partial nature; 5) the new formations that affirm the autonomy of the subaltern groups but within the old frameworks; 6) the formations that affirm integral autonomy (Gramsci 1935/1977, p. 2288).

1.2.3.4 Arrest of Social Mobility and Crisis of Hegemony

In November 1931, in Notebook 8 "Scattered notes and notes for a history of Italian intellectuals" paragraph 2 "The State and the conception of law" the connection between bourgeois hegemony and social mobility is still found not only in one direction but in both, the constructive and the deconstructive one.

> The previous ruling classes were essentially conservative in the sense that they did not tend to elaborate an organic passage from the other classes to their own, that is, to broaden their class sphere technically and ideologically: the concept of a closed caste. The bourgeois class presents itself as an organism in continuous movement, capable of absorbing all of

> society, assimilating it to its cultural and economic level: the entire function of the State is transformed: the State becomes an "educator", etc. How a stop occurs, and one returns to the concept of the State as pure force, etc. The bourgeois class is "saturated": not only does it not spread, but it disintegrates; not only does it not assimilate new elements, but it disassimilates a part of itself or at least the disassimilations are enormously more numerous than the assimilations (Gramsci 1931/1977, p. 937).

The "return to the conception of the State as pure force", that is to domination without direction is nothing other than a crisis of hegemony, which would necessarily imply domination *with* direction. The crisis occurs when the bourgeois class no longer spreads but, on the contrary, disintegrates; when there has been a halt in the upward social mobility of the subordinate social groups and a downward social mobility: the bourgeois class "disassimilates a part of itself".

The application to the current situation of this "model" of the crisis of hegemony of the ruling class (and consequent authoritarian involutions) as a crisis of social mobility seems to be quite direct. It should be noted, however, that it is not usual as it is not usual to attribute to Gramsci a concept of hegemony with social mobility at its center, except for some specialists, especially those who have studied the Gramscian connection between subalternity and the educational question in the context of the theory of praxis (Baldacci 2017). Although it is clear that, the texts reported leave no doubts in this regard, the reception of the Gramscian concept often appears reduced to that (well known and certainly present in the Quaderni), of hegemony as political-cultural, moral, and ideological leadership of the ruling class; and this is especially true in the contributions that have proposed and discussed applications to the current crisis. With the result of arriving at interpretations that, on the one hand, can identify elements neglected by Gramsci, such as for example the formation or imposition of "habits" (Beasley-Murray 2003) with all the largely unresolved questions that this opens up.[8] On the other hand, with the risk of reducing the current perspective to a mere opposition between "narratives", for which the neoliberal one would remain hegemonic despite everything and/or destined to "catastrophic" ends. It would remain hegemonic, for example, in Owen Worth's analysis of Europe after the 2008 crisis:

> the legitimacy of the neoliberal system is upheld through a set of narratives that have looked to normalise the role of austerity and crisis and presented as necessary processes that occur in everyday economic life [...]. None of the alternative positions [...] have managed to rid themselves of the tag of 'extremist', especially in the realm of the popular media. As a result, opposition to policies such as austerity is presented as unrealistic, utopian and, in some cases, dangerous (Worth 2016, pp. 133, 139)

It would be destined to have (potentially) catastrophic outcomes for Andrea Sau.

[8] "There are [...] some interesting and unexplored questions that this debate has undoubtedly raised for critical theory and the notion of hegemony. First, how can we conceptualise Gramsci's 'extensive' notion of hegemony? If we argue that habit is also an element within said notion, what exactly is its role in the formation of 'consent'? What is the 'place' of ideology vis-à-vis habit as a potential mechanism through which consent is achieved? [...] has the problem of the 'lack of trust' changed its role within the broader notion of hegemony? If so, should our research focus more on habit rather than ideology?". (Sau 2025, p. 102)

> Populists can explain problems rooted in capitalism and neoliberal economic policies as being caused by 'evil elites' controlling the state. This allows populist actors to harvest both workers' anger and their distrust against the order they represent. […]. The theatrical 'performance of crisis' and the blaming of political adversaries through allegations of conspiracy are the logics that determine the populist narrative. […] During our current 'populist wave', we are witnessing unpredictable and chaotic political actors. While their antiestablishment attitude does not displace the hegemony of neoliberalism (indeed it embraces it), their opportunist and arbitrary critique of institutions and structures make their effect on the socioeconomic order unpredictable and potentially catastrophic (Sau 2025, p. 119)

A scenario in which the crisis of hegemony of the ruling class and neoliberalism has, of course, political-cultural, moral and ideological contours, but anchored to a material basis in the arrest and inversion of social mobility, appears very different. In this case, the counter-hegemonic space opens on the concrete terrain of an effective reduction of inequalities and not only on that of counter-narratives. From the point of view of empirical evidence, it will be said shortly, with Diogo Ferrari, that the crisis of democracy as a consensus to right-wing populism hostile to its institutions and rituals is not so much due to "perceptions" as to the worsening of the actual conditions of families that justifies and accentuates them.

1.3 Crisis of Economic and Social Equilibrium

The economic and social equilibrium at the heart of the Western capitalist system had been established for a period but then it fell apart. This trend can be seen by defining this equilibrium on the basis of three indicators: (1) growth of productive capital per worker, or the rate of capital accumulation on which labor productivity and growth of per capita income depend; (2) growth of unit wages per worker minus the interest rate, which measures the real remuneration of labor; and (3) "frictional" rate of unemployment minus effective rate of unemployment, which measures the degree of approximation to full employment. The data for the United States shown in the following figure demonstrate that after the Great Depression, a happy season of economic and social equilibrium began that lasted from the 1940s until the early 1970s. Subsequently, it was lost with a particularly sharp fall in indicators in the 1980s. According to analysts (Snower and Henry 1997; Pasimeni 2018; Paternesi and Stirati 2022), other Western countries have followed the same path, even if all the data necessary to calculate exactly the same indices shown in the figure are not available (Fig. 1.9).

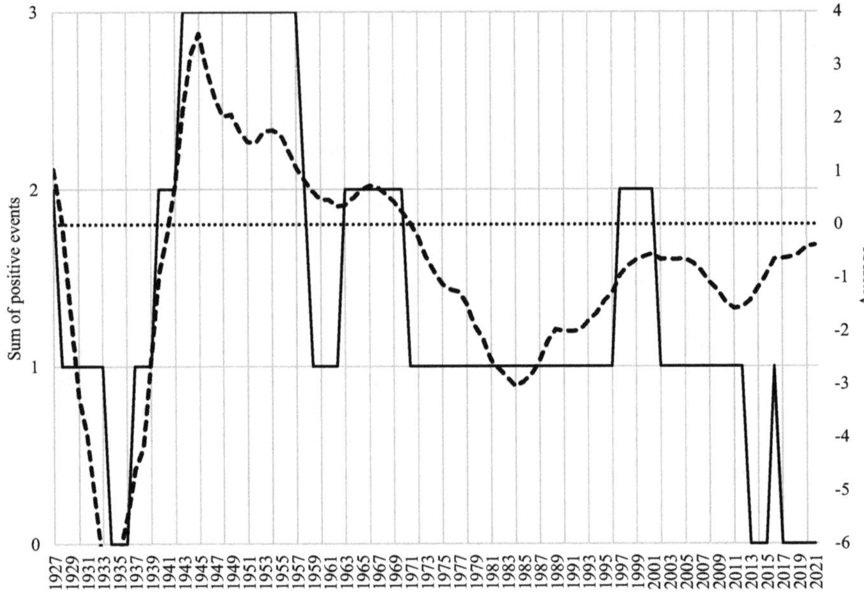

Fig. 1.9 The United States: left scale continuous line sum of positive events = 3 if all three indicators are greater than zero, 2 if only two are, 1 if only one, zero if none; right scale dotted line, arithmetic mean of the value of the three indicators. *Source* Figure obtained by processing data from BEA data - US Bureau of Economic Analysis, Fred - Federal Reserve Bank of St. Louis, US Historical Statistics

1.4 Accumulation Mechanism Faults

Not only has the economic-social balance been lost, but the central mechanism of accumulation has also broken down, as can be seen by considering the processes that determine the trend of the profit rate. The profit rate has been constant. But since the 1980s this reassuring trend has been obtained through a contradictory process.

It is known that the statistics of the United Kingdom from 1830 to today demonstrate a tendency for the rate of profit to fall. If this were the long-term trend of the capitalist system, it would be doomed, as Marx believed, because the rate of profit is at the heart of the system, and if there is a "law" that causes it to fall, capitalism will collapse by itself. But considering the data of the United Kingdom from 1830 to today as representative for the capitalist system is not correct. In doing so, two very different phases of the British economy are considered together: that of hegemony over global capitalism, with high profits, but also the subsequent one, since the First World War, with lower profits due to the exhaustion of this hegemony. The fall in the rate of profit is obtained only for this. In the first phase and in the second separately, this rate has tended to be constant.

In the case of the United States, the rate of profit would be increasing considering together the periods in which they were the semi-periphery and those in which they became the center of the World-System. But it is constant considering only the second period. Therefore, the right data must be used from the point of view of the time period considered. Furthermore, data referring to the entire economy must not be used. Defining a profit for the public sector is incorrect and in the financial sector profits are to a considerable extent speculative and therefore very uncertain. The right data are those of the private non-financial sector, central to the system of accumulation of productive fixed capital and for the creation of the surplus (Fig. 1.10).

For the economy as a whole the values are unrealistically high and unstable with an increasing long-term trend. For the non-financial private sector the trend is constant and the values are much more reasonable, just above 6% (Piketty's estimates for global capitalism as a whole and in the very long term are around 5%). It is useful to consider, then, the data on the profits of US non-financial corporations since 1913, since the beginning of their hegemony. The Wavelet analysis shows frequent oscillations of the profit rate but only a weak very low frequency cycle, which—once

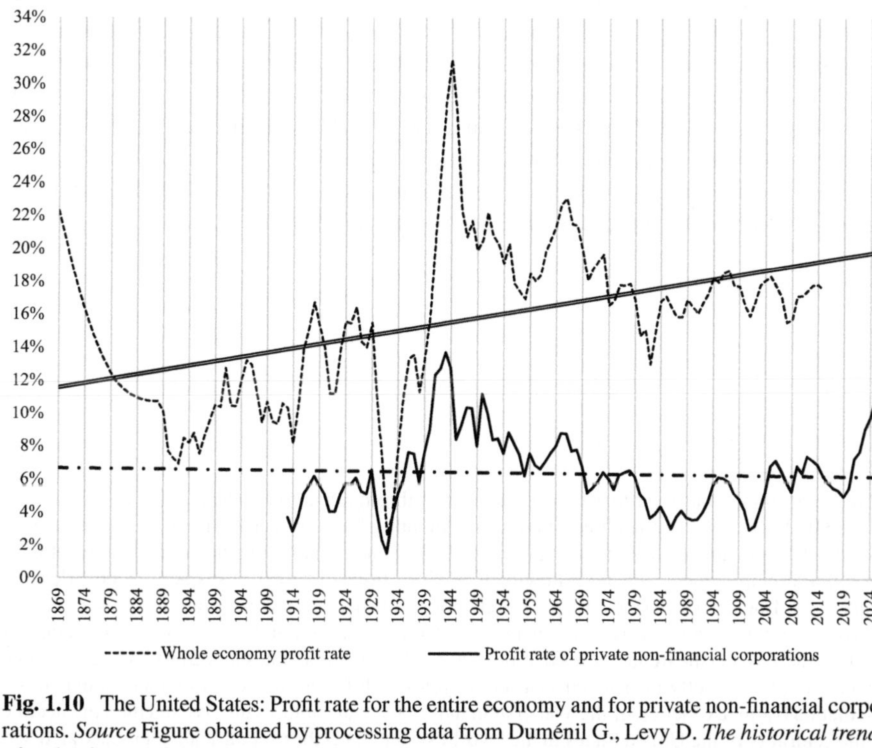

Fig. 1.10 The United States: Profit rate for the entire economy and for private non-financial corporations. *Source* Figure obtained by processing data from Duménil G., Levy D. *The historical trends of technology and distribution in the U.S. economy since 1869: Data and Figures*, CEPREMAP September 2016; Fred data from 1929 to 2024—the previous data (1913–1929) are estimated on the basis of stock returns (Fred) which are correlated with the profit rate until the Second World War

extracted—does not reveal overlaps with the GDP cycles. The profit rate cycle is too long to be Kondrat'ev and too short to be Wallerstein.[9]

It is therefore necessary to understand how, after the phases of reduction, the phases of increase in the rate of profit were obtained, which determined its long-term constancy. It is not enough to consider the trend of the rate of profit and conclude that, by being constant, the capitalist system has denied the prophecies that predicted its self-destruction. Nor can it be said that its fluctuations are explainable by cycles. The fluctuations of the rate of profit have occurred according to their own mechanisms. And it is by examining these mechanisms that a malfunction of the accumulation process at the heart of world capitalism since the 1980s can be found. The rate of profit can increase in two ways: by increasing the productivity of capital or by reducing the share of wages. With the first way, an increase in productivity, the "pie" increases to the advantage of all; with the second, a reduction in the share of wages, the "pie" remains the same and the share of profits increases to the detriment of wages. As can be seen in the following figure, in a long phase the wage share in the United States remained constant and then increased in the 1960s and 1970s. The profit rate first increased with the war, then decreased in the 1950s–1970s due to the increase in the wage share while productivity stabilized at high levels. From the 1980s, the recovery of the profit rate was achieved by reducing the wage share. Capital productivity remained high until 2009 but then began to decline. These trends were accompanied by rising unemployment and financialization (Fig. 1.11).

These are the failures in the accumulation mechanism: not a fall in the profit rate but a reduction in the wage share to keep it constant (Fig. 1.12).

[9] This is an important point that I have ascertained through a a comprehensive study of the data of the GDP per capita of the United States on a monthly basis from 1889 to 2025 (sources: from 1889 to 1946 monthly data estimated starting from the annuals and using the monthly index of non-agricultural employment; for the following The U.S. Bureau of the Census and Federal Reserve Bank of St. Louis). For reasons of space, I cannot report here all the elaborations. To summarize, I have been able to demonstrate that using the Wavelet analysis and much relevant literature, it clearly emerges: (1) the trend of the GDP per capita of the United States in the last 135 years can be effectively and correctly interpreted as a set of cycles at different frequencies with residual erratic fluctuations, after extraction of the Wallerstein half-wave that captures the rise and then the decline of the centrality of the United States in the "world system"; (2) these empirically demonstrated and theoretically justified cycles are: technical—Kondrat'ev (50 years), real estate—Kuznets (19 years), credit—Juglar (13 years—significant in the central years from 1920 to 1970), stocks—Kitchin (6 years), electoral (4 years with a marked attenuation between the late 1930s and the early 1970s); (3) the set of these systematic fluctuations are able to explain the timing and amplitude of NBER certified recessions, minus 9 out of 25, which can be considered a share not too low nor too high; furthermore, all the causes of missed recessions have specific and exceptional characteristics, so that this result validates the correctness of the extraction of the cycles.

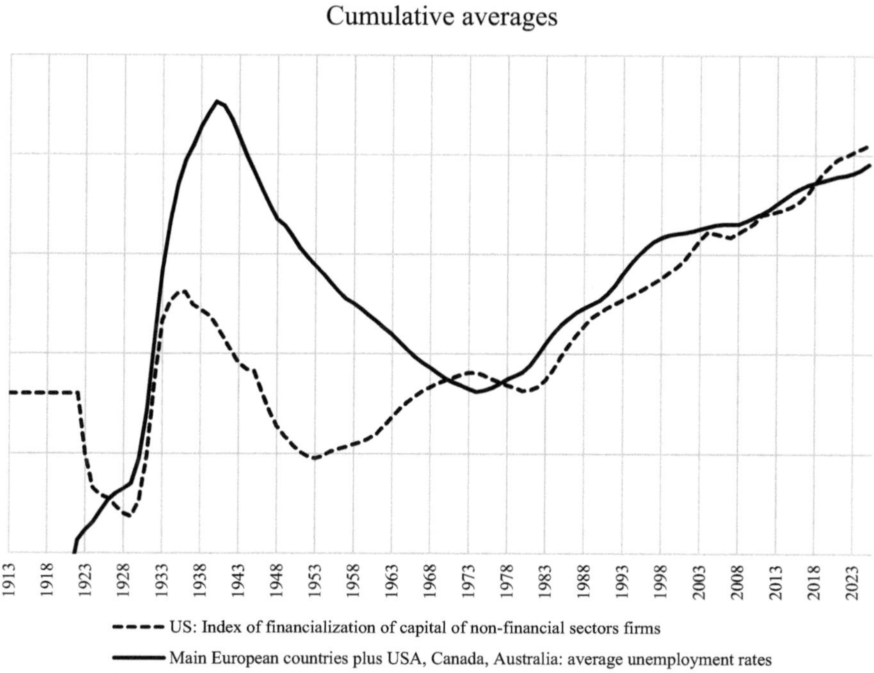

Fig. 1.11 Financialization and unemployment. *Source*: Figure obtained by processing data from Federal Reserve Bank of St. Louis and reported directly by Erik Hegelund and Josef Taalbi. Financialization as the difference in the ratios of gross value added of depreciation allowed on total capital less inventories, and actual depreciation on productive fixed capital

1.5 Crumbing of Motivation at Work

To complete the clinical picture of the sick West, there is the crumbling of motivation to work and the erosion of the foundations of democracy.[10] For the breakdown of work motivation, TFP (Total Factor Productivity), which is a measure of growth factors other than hours worked, education and training of workers, stock and average age of capital, is considered. TFP, therefore, as a measure of a complex of factors, especially innovation and motivation to work of employees, as demonstrated by the Nobel Prize winner for economics Edmund Phelps. His book, published in 2020 with three other co-authors significantly from extreme corners of the world

[10] These are serious and evident syndromes highlighted in three books that appeared in a few months, from November 2022 to February 2023. Yet, the authors Martin Wolf Krishnan Nayar Ian Greer have very different skills: Wolf is a journalist with an honorary degree from the London School of Economics, Nayar deals with international affairs and world history, Greer is a labor economist and directs a research laboratory at Cornell University. They also have very different conceptions of the democracy-capitalism nexus. For Wolf it is a spontaneous and indispensable nexus, for Nayar it was imposed by the fear of the communist international (while it existed), for Greer it is differentiated in the various “models” of capitalism.

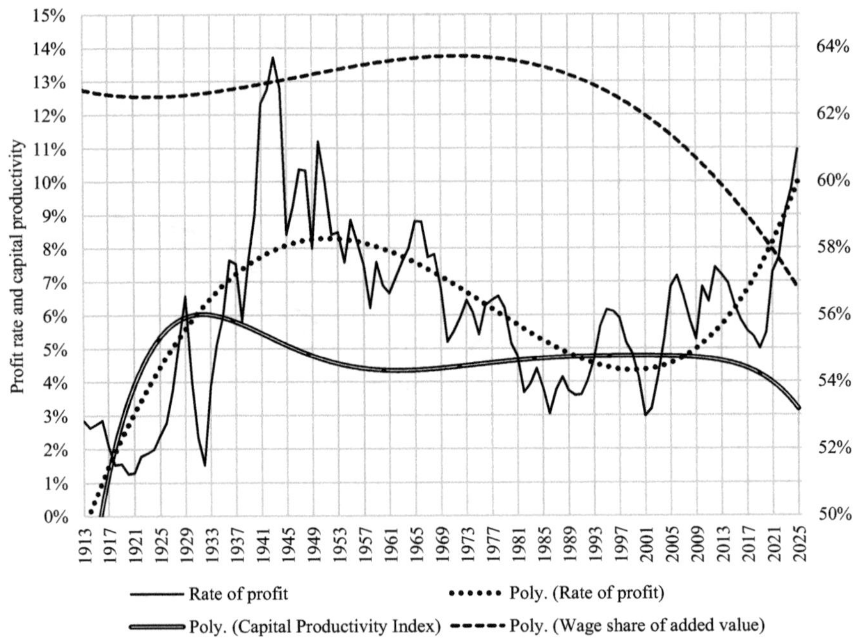

Fig. 1.12 The United States: Capital productivity, profit rate, and wage share of private non-financial corporations. *Source*: Figure obtained by processing data from Fred, Charpe M., Bridji S., McAdam P. *Labor Share and Growth in the Long Run*, European Central Bank Woking Paper 2021; and Stock Market Data Used in *Irrational Exuberance* Princeton University Press, 2000, 2005, 2015, updated by Robert J. Shiller

(Raicho Bojilov—University of Chile, Hian Teck Hoon—University of Singapore, Gylfi Zoega—University of Iceland), has an explicit title: "Dynamism - the values that support innovation, job satisfaction and economic growth". (Phelps et al. 2020)

> According to the standard theory […] the source of innovation […] is in the application by the astute entrepreneur of technical-scientific discoveries. […]. But another hypothesis has long existed […]: having acquired know-how […], all operators have the ability to conceive and put into practice new methods and new things. Moreover, if the nation possesses the necessary values, then people also have the desire to develop these new methods and new things. […]. The result will be satisfaction in work and the joy given by the exploitation of the new possibilities from which economic progress arises. The purpose of this book is to test this different theory. […]. We have found that low levels of innovation […] and TFP […] are accompanied by low degrees of satisfaction at work(Phelps et al.2020, pp. x-xi, 25)

Well, the following graph clearly demonstrates the strong reduction of the TFP component starting from the 1980s both in the United States and in the Euro area (Fig. 1.13).

But one may ask what the mechanism is that led to the crumbling of work motivation and the reduction of the TFP component. According to Greer (2022), it was a paradigm shift with the decline of the "voice" method in favor of the "exit" method. With the first, agents promoted their interests by dialogically trying to assert the

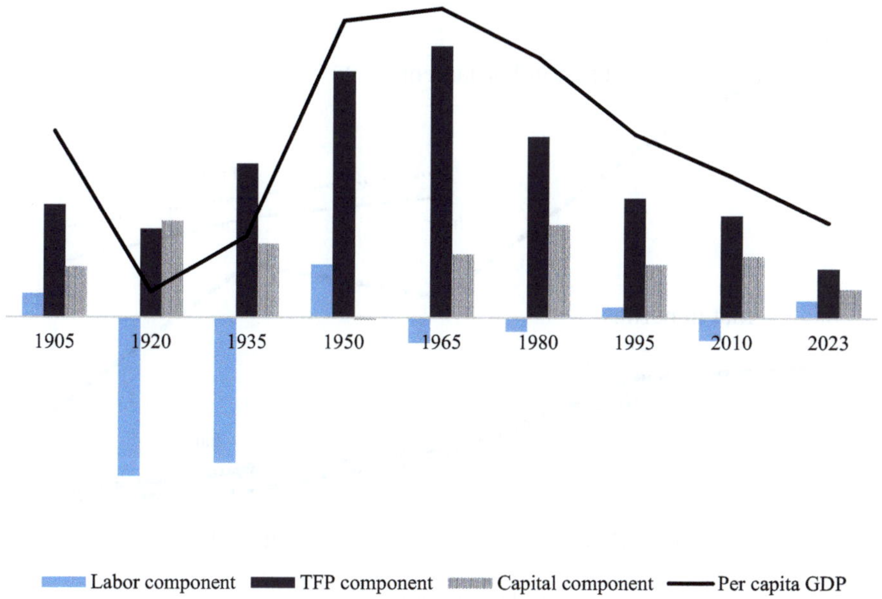

Fig. 1.13 The United States and Euro Area: GDP per capita growth for 15-year intervals and growth components. *Source* Figure obtained by processing data from Bergeaud A., Cette G., Lecat R.: Productivity Trends in Advanced Countries between 1890 and 2012 *Review of Income and Wealth* 2016 62(3): 420–444

good foundation of their reasons. With the second, agents do not argue but express themselves only by accepting or abandoning a relationship, a relation, a transaction, a place. In the use of labor, the paradigm shift has translated into the replacement of high-productivity, high-cost guaranteed work with low-cost, low-productivity precarious work. Being careful has disappeared, while waste has increased: a product, a service, a relationship, a place is no longer fixed; they are abandoned, thrown away, others are taken. The result has been the devaluation of any real assumption of responsibility and of work well done, the compression of remuneration, and the fall in job satisfaction.

1.6 Erosion of the Democratic System

Finally, there has been an erosion of democracy, the signs of which are many: for example, the almost complete disappearance of trust in political parties and the collapse of trust even in Parliament, earlier and to a greater extent than the more recent and still limited (until yesterday) degradation of the democratic character of political deliberation (Fig. 1.14).

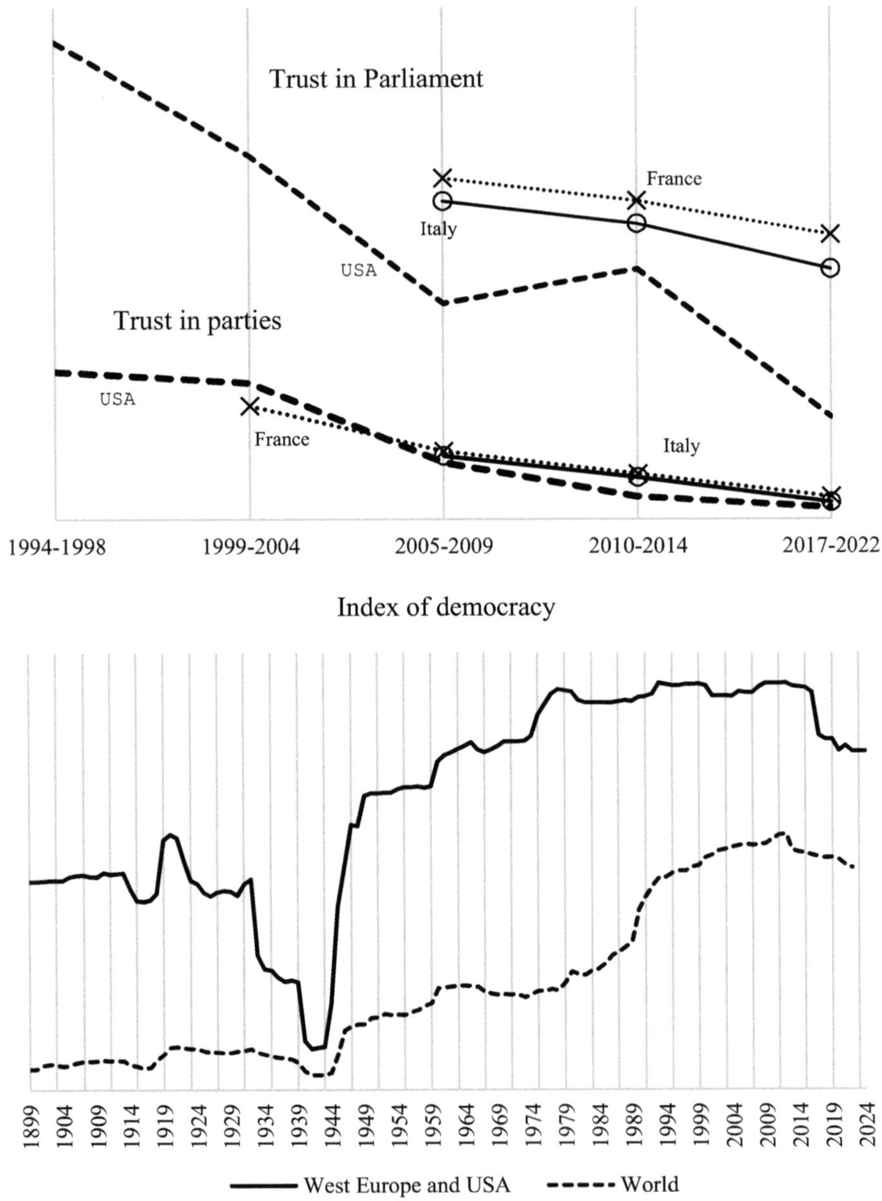

Fig. 1.14 Trust in Parliament and parties and index of democracy from a deliberative point of view. The index with value 1 = perfect democracy 0 = no democracy, refers to the principle according to which political decisions oriented toward the public good should come from a dialectical comparison respectful of all positions, rather than from emotional appeals, reasons of belonging, corporate interests, coercion. The index is the result of analysis of the principal components on five sub-indexes which in turn are synthesis of different variables: reasoned justification, justification for the common good, respect for counterarguments, frequency of consultation, involvement of civil society. *Source* Figure obtained by processing data from the World Values Survey and V-Dem Project

Other unmistakable worrying signs are found by considering three variables that move together in a surprising way: increasing economic inequality, disaffection toward the institutions of democracy, alarm of analysts (Fig. 1.15).

Diogo Ferrari demonstrated the logic of this multiple correlation, contradicting previous analysts who had argued that there were only emotions, beliefs, and perceptions at the base of the growing consensus for right-wing populism which is at the same time the effect and cause of the crisis of democratic institutions (perceived as such by analysts, which explains the increase in the usage of terms like crisis and democracy). Indeed, much literature has denied that the actual condition of families and the level of economic and social inequality had an influence on it, since the weight of these variables lost significance when considered together with those of the perception of being culturally and economically threatened by immigrants and of

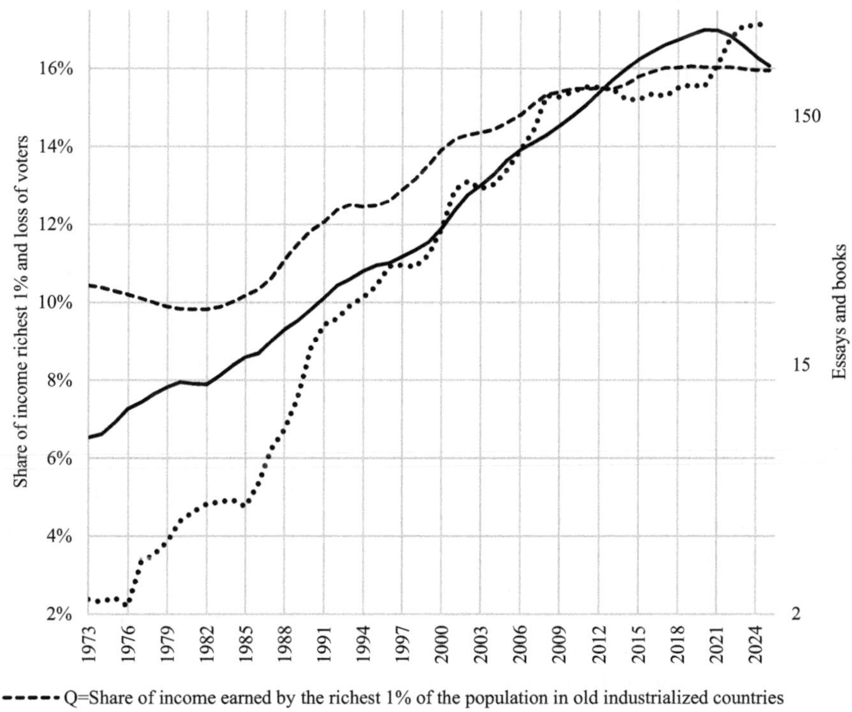

----- Q=Share of income earned by the richest 1% of the population in old industrialized countries

•••••• Loss of voters for Parliament from the maximum recorded in the period 1948-68 - old industrialized countries

—— S=Essays and books containing both the words "democracy" and "crisis" in the title or summary, geometric mean of year-by-year records in the scientific publication databases Jstore and Google Scholar (logarithmic scale, right)

Fig. 1.15 Economic inequality, disaffection for democratic institutions, analysts' alarm. *Source* Figure obtained by processing data from IDEA database International Institute for Democracy and Electoral Assistance, World Inequality Data Base, my research on Google and Jstore an uncertain environment, including dissatisfaction with, distrust of, and resentment toward the political elites, and established institutions. Ferrari demonstrated that this loss of significance was entirely due to the data processing methods since the actual conditions function as “mediators”.

> Using the ESS [a cross-country academically driven survey that measures attitudes, beliefs, and behavior of populations across Europe and the UK] data from 2002 to 2018, this article shows that, on average, around 55% of the effect of families’ income on the propensity to vote for right-wing populist parties is mediated by the effect of the former on feelings of resentment at the status quo and perceptions of being culturally and economically threatened by immigrants. In other words, 55% of the effect of families’ income on populist vote occurs because income affects resentment and perceptions. (Ferrari 2021, p. 275)

1.7 The Causes

The “wage issue” has appeared several times in the clinical examination. The reduction in the share of wages in national income has been seen to have had an impact on the loss of income of the middle class, which was also a determining factor in the breakdown of the accumulation mechanism. The reduction in the rate of growth of real wages has had an impact on the end of the economic and social equilibrium; the substitution of precarious work, paid less, for stable work that was paid more has had an impact on the crumbling of motivation to work; inequality and the reduction in the share of wages has had an impact on the erosion of the democratic system. Now, the basis of the wage issue is the “decoupling” that has occurred between the trend of wages and productivity. In all the industrialized countries, the traditional coupling whereby wages tended to grow in line with productivity has failed. This tendency has been serious, and efforts have been made to try to disprove it by discussing the data used and the definitions of wages and productivity. The conclusion of the long debate confirmed this without a shadow of a doubt (Paternesi and Stirati 2022). In parallel, a specific literature has grown that has tried to explain the causes of decoupling, rightly imagined to be very different. A short list includes at least five: (1) change in technologies: labor-saving information technologies have caused the prices of investment goods to fall and have increased the elasticity of substitution, thus reducing the relative demand for labor and wages in relation to productivity; (2) globalization: the entry into the international market of a gigantic supply of low-cost manufactured goods has penalized the wages of manual labor in the countries of ancient industrialization in competition with the low-paid labor of emerging countries; (3) financialization: by moving companies from long-term to short-term objectives and from profits to financial income, financialization has reduced the relative demand for labor and greatly reduced the strategic weight of workers; (4) unemployment: unemployment and lack of employment have penalized the bargaining power of workers which has also affected economic, monetary and fiscal policies which have become “antisocial”; (5) labor market institutions: deregulation for “flexibility” has increased precarious, low-paid work and reduced stable work which was paid more, the fall in the unionization rate has depressed wages.

The empirical results obtained in many analyses are quite different but there is a convergence on some aspects. New technologies as such have had modest effects. Globalization was not a main factor in the start of decoupling, but contributed subsequently, together with financialization, less than the most influential factors. These were: the fall in unionization, deregulation of the labor market, unemployment, dismantling of social policies. For a panel of 22 high-income economies from 1970 to 2018, Paternesi and Stirati were able to verify that

> a greater weakness of the labor market and the weakening of pro-labor institutions seem to have played an important role as factors of wage compression: all the variables representing these two dimensions are consistently significant [...] and have contributed, respectively, for -0.55 and -0.45 percentage points per year to hindering the growth of real wages. The process of increasing commercial and financial globalization, which has translated into increasing trade openness and capital mobility (foreign direct investments), has also contributed to the slowdown of average wages (-0.3 and -0.13 percentage points respectively) (Paternesi and Stirati 2022, p. 454).

For the United States, the following graph can be considered, in which the decoupling is evident, compared with the trend of unionization and imports from China as an indicator of globalization. The decoupling between wages and productivity began in 1980, while imports from China became significant only 15–20 years later. It is from 1980, however, that the decline (which had begun even earlier) of the unionization rate accelerated due to the deregulation of the labor market, the introduction of anti-union laws, a real class struggle that was engaged in and subsequently won by the employers; the same thing happened in other Western countries (Fig. 1.16).

In the 1980s there was the neoliberal turn, which can be seen in the following figure using indicators of economic and social policy. In the first long phase leading up to the Great Crisis, a non-interventionist economic policy was dominant: very low public spending, around 10% of GDP, and a modest share of social spending on public spending. Everything changed from the 1930s, during and after the Second World War, when the system turned toward the welfare state. Public spending increased, reaching 50% of GDP, social spending on public spending reached almost 60%, while effective interest rates were kept very low. Much changed again with the neoliberal turn. And not so much on the side of public spending, which, despite the proclamations, remained just under 50% of GDP, but on the side of social spending, which lost 10 percentage points on public spending. But above all, monetary policy changed with interest rates that recorded very high peaks for a long time, on average three times higher than during the welfare state era. High interest rates depressed productive investments, hence, unemployment and a real "antisocial" State. (The second chapter will return to the strange coupling between the reduction of the interest rate and the increase in unemployment after 2008) (Fig. 1.17).

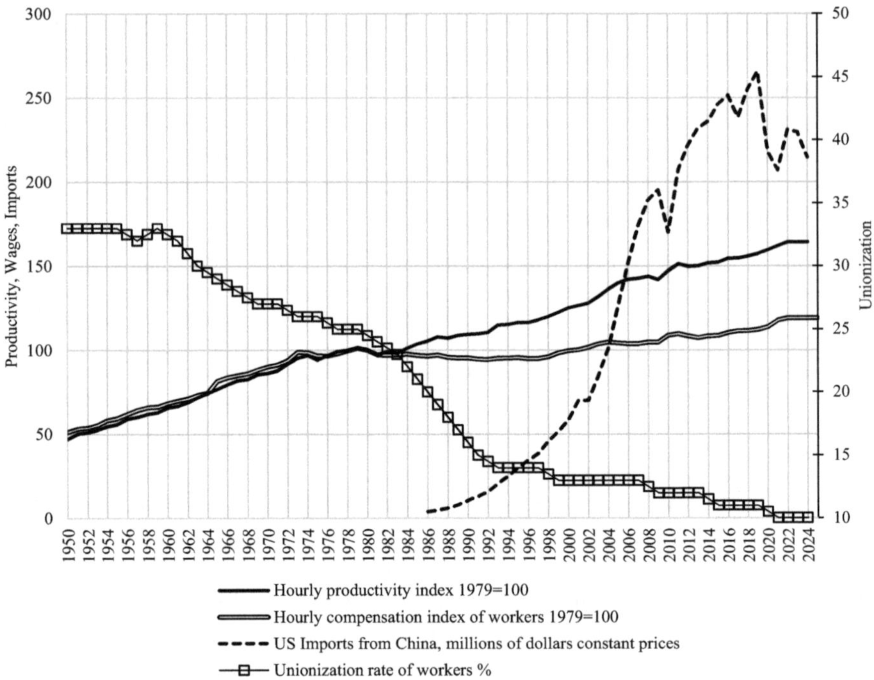

Fig. 1.16 The United States: productivity, wages, unionization, globalization. *Source* Figure obtained by processing data from the Economic Policy Institute, US Census Bureau, US Bureau of Labor Statistics

1.8 Conclusion

The disease of the West began in the late 1970s: the start of the collapse of the middle class, the end of the economic-social equilibrium, the breakdown of the accumulation mechanism, the crumbling of motivation to work, the erosion of the basis of democracy. At the heart of this "polycrisis" was the decoupling between wages and productivity due to the weakening of workers, which in turn was linked to unemployment and the precariousness of work, and to a complex of forces that operated for this weakening. The symptoms and causes of the disease indicate that it was a failure of the State-Market system (Welfare State) which had recorded great successes from the end of the war to the 1970s.

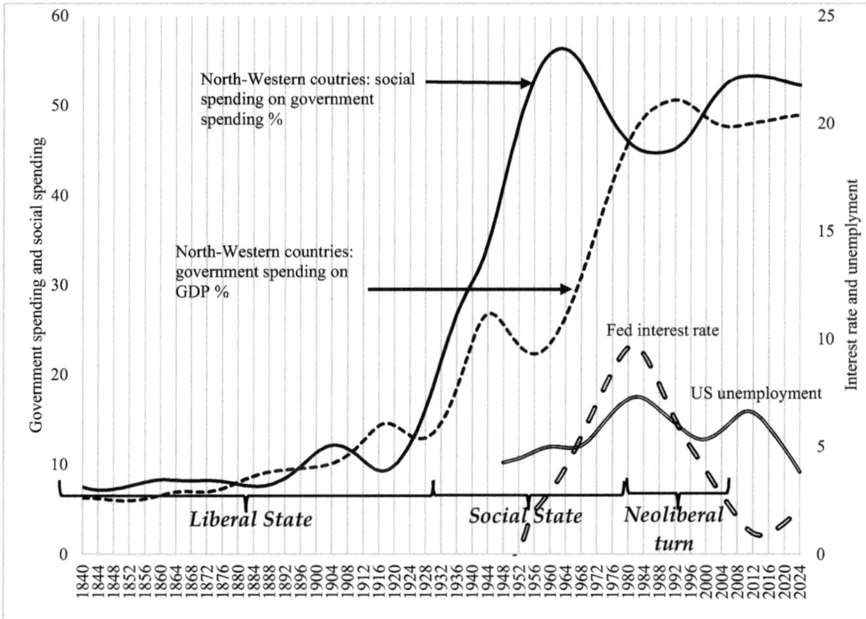

Fig. 1.17 North-Western countries: government spending on GDP %, social spending on government spending %, effective interest rate of the FED %; U.S. unemployment rate %. *Source* Figure obtained by processing data from Peter Flora: *State, Economy, and Society in Western Europe, 1815–1975* Vol.1; in: *The Growth of Mass Democracies and Welfare States: A Data Handbook in Two Volumes*. New York: Palgrave Macmillan 1983; updates and completions on data from Fred and the World Bank

References

Autor, D. H. (2014). Skills, education, and the rise of earnings inequality among the other 99 percent. *Science, 344*(6186), 843–850.

Baldacci, M. (2017). *Oltre la subalternità - Praxis e educazione in Gramsci.* Carocci.

Beasley-Murray, J. (2003). On posthegemony. *Bulletin of Latin American Research, 22*(1), 117–125.

Bénabou, R., & Ok, E. A. (2001). Social mobility and the demand for redistribution: The Poum hypothesis. *Quarterly Journal of Economics, 116*(2), 447–487.

Clementi, M. (2018). Il declino degli Stati Uniti e la Grecia classica. *Quaderni di Scienza Politica, xxv*, 349–369.

Conquest, R. (2000). *Reflections on a ravaged century.* W.W. Norton & Company.

Corak M. (2013). Income inequality, equality of opportunity, and intergenerational mobility. *IZA discussion paper* 7520.

Cospito G. (2008). Genesi e sviluppo del concetto di egemonia nei Quaderni del carcere. In d'Orsi A (a cura di) *Egemonie.*.Dante & Descartes (pp. 187–207).

Cospito, G. (2011). Verso l'edizione critica e integrale dei Quaderni del Carcere. *Studi Storici, 52*(4), 881–904.

Di Meo A. (2016). Dizionario dell'egemonia - Da Gioberti a Gramsci. www.filosofia-italiana.net, aprile: 1–32.

Encyclopédie du XIX Siècle 1869-1871 (1872). *Annuarie Encyclopédique vol.* IX.

Erauskin, I. (2020). The labor share and income inequality: Some empirical evidence for the period 1990-2015. *Applied Economic Analysis, 28*(84), 173–195.
Eyles, A., Elliot, M. L., & Machin, S. (2022). *Social mobility past, present and future - the state of play in social mobility, on the 25th anniversary of the Sutton trust.* The Sutton Trust.
Ferrari, D. (2021). Perceptions, resentment, economic distress, and support for RightWing populist parties in Europe. *Politics and Governance, 9*(3), 274–287.
Frosini, F. (2016). L'egemonia e i subalterni: utopia religione democrazia. *International Gramsci Journal, 2*(1), 126–166.
Gramsci A. (1924). Vladimiro Ilic Ulianov. *Ordine Nuovo*, Terza serie 1 (1 marzo), 1–10.
Gramsci A. (1930a). Quaderno 1 § 44: Direzione politica di classe prima e dopo l'andata al governo. In Gerratana V. (a cura) *Quaderni del Carcere vol. 1.*Einaudi, 1977.
Gramsci A. (1931/1977). Quaderno 8 § 2: Lo Stato e la concezione del diritto. In Gerratana V. (a cura) *Quaderni del Carcere vol. 2.* Einaudi, 1977b.
Gramsci A (1932b-33/1977b). Quaderno 13 § 31: Il teorema delle proporzioni definite. In Gerratana V. (a cura) *Quaderni del Carcere vol. 3.* Torino: Einaudi, 1977.
Gramsci A. (1934/1977). Quaderno 19 § 24: Il problema della direzione politica nella formazione e nello sviluppo della Nazione e dello Stato moderno in Italia. In Gerratana V. (a cura) *Quaderni del Carcere vol. 3.* : Einaudi, 1977.
Gramsci A. (1935/1977). Quaderno 25 § 2: Criteri metodologici. In Gerratana V. (a cura) *Quaderni del Carcere vol. 3.* Einaudi, 1977.
Greer, I. (2022). *Marketization: How capitalist exchange disciplines workers and subverts democracy (autonomy and automation).* Bloomsbury Publishing PLC.
Lenin V.I. (1905/1961) Democrazia operaia e democrazia borghese. *Vperiod* 3(24 gennaio 1905). In *Lenin V.I. Opere Complete VIII*. 1961.
Lenin V.I. (1921/1967). Sull'imposta in natura. In *Lenin V.I. Opere Complete XXXII*. Roma: Editori Riuniti, 1967.
Liguori, G. (2015). Classi subalterne marginali e classi subalterne fondamentali in Gramsci. *Critica Marxista, 4*, 41–48.
Manduca, R., Hell, M., Adermon, A., Blanden, J., Bratberg, E., Gielen, A. C., Van Kippersluis, H., Lee, K. B., Machin, S., Munk, M. D., Nybom, M., Ostrovsky, Y., Rahman, S., & Sirniö, O. (2020). *Trends in absolute income mobility in North America and Europe. IZA discussion paper series* (p. 13456).
Milanovic, B. (2017). Increasing capital income share and its effect on personal income inequality. In H. B. DeLong, J. Bradford, & S. Marshall (Eds.), *After Piketty - the agenda for economics and inequality.* Harvard University Press.
Oecd. (2019). *Under pressure: The squeezed middle class.* Oecd Publishing.
ONU. (2013). *Inequality matters - report of the world social situation.* United Nations Department of Economic and Social Affair.
Pasimeni, P. (2018). The relation between productivity and compensation in Europe. *UE Commission Discussion Paper, 079.*
Paternesi, M. W., & Stirati, A. (2022). The decoupling between labour compensation and productivity in high-income countries: Why is the nexus broken? *BJIR An International Journal of Employment Relations*, 425–463.
Phelps, E., Bojilov, R., Hoon, H. T., & Zoega, G. (2020). *Dynamism: The values that drive innovation, job satisfaction, and economic growth.* Harvard University Press.
Sau, A. (2025). Hegemony and crisis: An analysis of habit and ideology as mechanisms for achieving 'consent'. *Capital & Class, 49*(1), 101–121.
Severino, E. (1972/1982). *L'essenza del nichilismo. Milano: Adelphi Edizioni. First edition Brescia: Padeia*, 1972.
Snower, D. J., & Henry, S. G. B. (1997). *Economic policies and unemployment dynamics in Europe.* International Monetary Fund.

Songa, X., Masseyb, C. G., Rolfc, K. A., Ferried, J. P., Rothbaume, J. L., & Xief, Y. (2019). Long-term decline in intergenerational mobility in the United States since the 1850s. *Proceedings of the National Academy of Sciences, 117*(1), 1–109.

Stalin J. (1924/1952). Principi del Leninismo. In Stalin J. *Opere Complete vol 6.* Roma: Edizioni Rinascita 1952. First publication: *Pravda* April–May 1924.

Vallin, J., Meslé, F., Adamets, S., & Pyrozhkov, S. (2002). A new estimate of Ukrainian population losses during the crises of the 1930s and 1940s. *Population Studies, 56*(3), 249–264.

Van der Weide, R., Lakner, C., Mahler, D. G., Narayan, A., & Ramasubbaiah, R. (2021). Intergenerational mobility around the world. In *Policy research working paper 9707*. World Bank.

World Economic Forum. (2020). *The global social mobility report 2020 equality, opportunity and a new economic imperative.* WEF.

Worth, O. (2016). The battle for hegemony: Resistance and neoliberal restructuring in post-crisis Europe. *Comparative European Politics, 16*(1), 126–142.

Zinoviev, G. (1923). The Bolsheviks and the hegemony of the proletariat. *International Press Correspondence, 3*(32, 14), 267–268.

References

Chapter 2
State and Market Failures

2.1 Genealogies and Definitions

The failure of the welfare state and the advent of the state of neoliberal competition (state with a lowercase letter indicates a complex of devices that includes the State, but not only) marked the turning point of the 1980s, but these terms require clarification. The expression welfare state was rarely used before the end of the 1940s and appeared in the 1930s in England only in newspaper reports on Germany. It was the translation of the German *wohlfahrtsstaat*,

> combining the German words for welfare and state [that] was coined by Carl Nauwerck[1] in 1844 to describe a vision of a state that would "satisfy all societal needs". Thirty years later, the term was taken up by the economist Adolph Wagner, who used it to describe the growing public sector associated with the social reform-oriented state then emerging in Germany and by Lorenz von Stein, the founder of public administration, who defined it as "a compulsory institution promoting the well-being of the people" (Garland, 2022, pp. 136–137).

The term welfare state does not come from Great Britain, but from Germany, and was coined by attributing to welfare the strong meaning of "all social needs", and to the State a demanding responsibility to support market capitalism by remedying its shortcomings. (It will be demonstrated shortly that the term "neoliberalism" was also born in Germany, used for the first time by Alexander Rüstow, even if the concept came from the United States). In England the welfare state in this strong sense was born almost fortuitously. On the one hand, it was implemented before being theorized, on the other, it required a kind of stratagem on the part of its inventor. The British political, institutional, and cultural environment was not prepared to believe in social reforms, certainly on the right, but also on the left. Left-wing intellectuals and politicians were convinced that English conservatism was incapable of accepting

[1] Ludewig Gottlieb Carl Nauwerck (1810–1891) was a journalist, orientalist, and member of the Frankfurt Parliament. In 1844 he became a member of the "Central Association for the Welfare of the Working Classes", and in the same year he was banned from teaching because of his liberal views.

G. Seravalli, *Collective Action in the Age of Polycrisis*, Contributions to Economics,
https://doi.org/10.1007/978-3-032-12653-5_2

such a demanding role for the State. Even though they were committed to obtaining a change of direction, skepticism about social reforms remained. Thus, the reforms were implemented before being theorized.

> What came to be known as the welfare state was [...] enacted before it was theorized and without having been kitted out with a developed ideological rationale. On the 'Appointed Day' (5 July 1948), when the National Health Service (NHS), National Insurance, and National Assistance came into operation, the political meaning of these reforms was still quite inchoate. It was not until a few months later that the Labour Party retrospectively named its creation "the welfare state". And although the welfare state would later come to be sanctified by the British labour movement as its most important progressive achievement, during the late 1940s and 1950s, the concept was viewed with considerable scepticism both by Left intellectuals such as Michael Young and by social policy experts close to the Labour Party such as Richard Titmuss and Peter Townsend (Garland, 2022, p. 135).

It all began on 3 December 1942 with the publication of the "Report to the Parliament on Social Insurance and Allied Services". The war was at a turning point after the Allied landing in North Africa (8 November) and the looming defeat of Germany at Stalingrad (21 November). The Report helped to turn the page and over 600,000 copies were printed. It had been written by the economist William Henry Beveridge as Chairman of the Inter-Ministerial Committee, which had been given a modest exploratory mandate on social security systems. Beveridge used the stratagem of signing the Report only personally to be able to go beyond the mandate without having to submit to the qualms that came from the Committee. He thus proposed a revolutionary model: all citizens would pay a periodic contribution to a national body that would provide insurance "from cradle to grave" against the "great evils: infirmity, ignorance, impoverishment, unemployment", as the Report states. The proposals flowed into the reform programs of the Labour government that took over from Churchill's coalition government in the summer of 1945. In a short time, social insurance was expanded, gaps in the social security system were filled, and in 1948 the National Health Service began operating: all reforms that went hand in hand with planning and nationalization programs. The Beveridge Plan influenced the adoption of similar policies throughout Europe. In the United States it had a wide resonance for its emotional and intellectual force due to its simplicity and lucidity: a system of contributions and fixed benefits regardless of income for the entire population as a right of citizenship. Economist Eveline Mabel Richardson Burns, Roosevelt's adviser on the Social Security Act of 1935, wrote that there was some anticipation that a similar system of social security would be adopted in the United States, but that it was not done because a system that treated African-Americans in the South equally with workers and employees in the industrial North would simply be laughed at in the halls of Congress (Zdencanovic, 2021).

The results were significant, although assessed in very different ways. Using the traditional definition of absolute poverty (the minimum necessary for a person to maintain a state of physical health), Benjamin Seebohm Rowntree (a sociologist, industrial leader, and Minister of Munitions during the First World War) conducted his third poverty survey in the city of York in 1950. He found that the deprivation documented in the two previous surveys of 1889 and 1936 had almost completely disappeared, an improvement that Rowntree attributed to the interventions of the new welfare state (Gazeley et al., 2016, p. 3). Using the same real poverty line as in 1936, the 1950 survey found that only 4.6% of working-class families could be considered poor, compared with 31.1% in 1936. Rowntree also calculated that if welfare measures had been the same in 1950 as in 1936, 24.7% of working-class families would have been in poverty. However, using a modern concept of relative poverty, introduced by Peter Townsend in 1954, the reality was much less rosy. Considering poor the population that did not have the resources to live and participate in social activities according to standards considered normal in their social context, Abel-Smith and Peter Townsend (1965) found that in the whole country poor families were 10% in 1953–54 and increased to reach 18% in 1960: the poor in the United Kingdom had thus gone from 4 million to 7.5 million. This confirmed their left-wing skepticism about the government's social reforms. But it was at least partly a prejudice. Townsend and Abel-Smith had processed the data with a little too much interpretative freedom. Thanks to the recent digitalization of the results of that ancient survey, Gazeley et al. (2016) have redone the calculations finding that poor families were actually slightly fewer and that above all from 1953–1954 to 1960 they increased by only one percentage point: from 9 to 10%. The truth is that after the end of the Second World War, capitalism throughout the West had entered an extraordinarily favorable season, as shown when discussing the economic-social equilibrium. Thus, there were enough economic and political resources to support the public services, much greater than those that left-wing intellectuals had imagined.

Turning to the term neoliberalism, according to unanimous indications one must refer to the famous "Lippmann Colloquium" organized by the French philosopher Louis Rougier in August 1938 in Paris to discuss the book by the American journalist Walter Lippmann, which had been published the previous year with the title "An Enquiry into the Principles of the Good Society" and translated into French with the title "La Cité libre". It was during this conference that the well-known German economist and sociologist Alexander Rüstow used the term neoliberalism for the first time, to indicate the new emerging perspective that distanced itself from the old *laissez-faire* liberalism. Then, on 10 April 1947, an association was born initially called the Acton-Tocqueville Society and then the Mont Pèlerin Society, it was founded during a meeting in the Mont Pèlerin spa in Switzerland by the same intellectuals who had participated in the Lippman Colloquium. This association is considered fundamental for the development and diffusion of neoliberalism. Its program was: analysis of the crisis of liberal thought; redefinition of the role of the State; fight against the use of history for purposes hostile to liberalism; reformulation of laws for the protection of private rights from groups and individuals who threaten them; promotion of minimum standards not hostile to the functioning of the free market; and creation of an international order that safeguards peace, freedom, and international economic relations. Neoliberalism was born with extraordinary timing, even anticipating the implementation of the Beveridge Plan by a year. The National Health Service began operating in England on 5 July 1948 and on 10 April 1947 the Acton-Tocqueville Society was born. The Welfare State spread simultaneously with the growth of the prestige of the neoliberal association. Eight Nobel

Prizes were awarded to its members, including Friedrich von Hayek (Nobel 1974) and Milton Friedman (Nobel 1976). Several members and supporters assumed key roles in various Western governments. Of Reagan's 76 economic advisers, 22 were members of the Mont Pèlerin Society.

Right from the beginning, therefore, two very different ideas, the welfare state and the neoliberal state, were in opposition, a decisive element for the analysis of the failures of the welfare state. Even for this reason alone, one can doubt that a general theory of the State can be useful. This implies an approach to the question of the State that is distant from the textbooks. In microeconomics textbooks, for example, the chapter that deals with the failures of the State follows the one dedicated to the failures of the Market, which—it is stated—require public intervention, which in turn encounters failures for which it is not possible to reach Pareto optimal states (moving from which the condition of a single subject cannot improve without worsening that of others). And just as the cases of Market failure are listed as a violation of the conditions required for it to operate as a general mechanism of optimal allocation (public goods,[2] natural monopoly,[3] externalities,[4] asymmetric information,[5] incomplete markets[6]), State failures are also identified as violations of the conditions required by an abstract State model. State failure is said to occur when the benefits of its intervention are lower than the costs and the causes are listed. Following, for example, the taxonomy of Charles Wolf (1988): disjunction between

[2] Non-excludable goods and services (once made it is impossible or very expensive to exclude someone from using them) and non-rival (if one uses them, it does not mean that another cannot use them) that no one individually has an interest in producing. Common goods (existing, that do not need to be made) can be considered public goods if they require conservation and maintenance.

[3] A natural monopoly exists when, for unavoidable technical reasons, there cannot be more than one producer, who therefore obtains excess profits and produces less than would happen under a competitive regime. In this case, the activity should be taken over by the State as an agent in the interests of all consumers.

[4] Externalities occur when negative or positive effects of an economic activity occur on subjects who have no way of being paid for the damage or of remunerating the advantage through contractual means. The intervention of the State is intended to force the person responsible for the externalities to pay this cost or to collect this advantage, for example with taxation and with the payment of incentives, or by taking on the task of realizing what generates externalities.

[5] Information asymmetries occur when in a contractual relationship one party has more complete information than the other. The former can exploit the greater information after the contract by behaving opportunistically (moral hazard: for example, a company that has obtained a bank loan exposes itself to excessive risks); or before the contract to stipulate conditions to its advantage (adverse selection: for example, riskier customers are more interested in insuring themselves than less risky ones). State intervention will be aimed at producing greater and more reliable information for all agents or at directly providing goods and services that involve greater information asymmetries, as for example in the case of the health sector.

[6] Every agent decides today to do something that will have future consequences. With a full set of contracts available, they can protect themselves from unwanted or negative outcomes by paying a price today for an indemnity tomorrow to cover such events. When a market is incomplete, such contracts do not exist for all possible contingencies. In this case, competition is unable to produce the optimal allocation of resources, which must then be achieved by the State.

costs and revenues,[7] internalities,[8] derived externalities,[9] distributive inequities.[10] The early historical opposition between conceptions of the State that are in many ways opposed suggests abandoning these schemes with the advantage of also being able to account for post-neoliberal developments, as underlined by William Davies and Nicholas Gane (2021), Philip Mirowski and Dieter Plehwe (2009) who recognize Foucault's thought as having a major role also for the new reflection on neoliberalism after the 2008 crisis. Mirowski and Dieter Plehwe have underlined the importance of Foucault's thought to also place the ordoliberal version that came back into vogue after 2008 within neoliberalism. "It is curious to note how many crucial historical contributions to the formation of neoliberal thought have not been recognized by subsequent generations. In Germany, for example, most scholars would raise their eyebrows if the ordoliberal inspirations of the social market economy were denigrated as neoliberal. But contrary to many [...], Foucault suggested that ordoliberalism has a legitimate claim to the title neoliberal" (Mirowski & Plehwe, 2009, pp. 1–2).

2.2 Governmentality

From 1970 until the eve of his death in 1984, at the age of only 58, Foucault held a Laboratory at the "Collège de France" in Paris, the most prestigious French academic institution. For a long time, only partial audio recordings of the lectures circulated, while the complete texts, also reconstructed from his notes, were published by Seuil/Gallimard rather late, from 1997 to 2015[11] contributing to their new, more accurate and widespread, reception. The lectures that concern this topic are "Security, Territory, Population" and "Birth of Biopolitics" (Foucault, 2005a, 2005b). Other texts

[7] This disjunction occurs because the tax revenues that cover the costs of public intervention are imposed regardless of the extent of the utility of such intervention. They can therefore be too high and, furthermore, there are few incentives to reduce costs by increasing the efficiency of the intervention.

[8] Internality occurs when, in the absence of direct, inexpensive, and effective ways to measure the results of public intervention, objectives dictated within the state organization prevail, in the interest of its components rather than in the collective interest of the population.

[9] Derivative externalities occur when the State is unable to evaluate all the consequences of its interventions, some of which may be undesirable, especially in the long term.

[10] Distributive inequity occurs when public intervention creates "winners and losers" in a socially undesirable way beyond the formally declared intentions and on the basis of which explicit decisions were made.

[11] 1970–1971: *Leçons sur la volonté de savoir*, Gallimard 2011; 1971–1972: *Théories et Institutions pénales*, Seuil 2015; 1972–1973: *La société punitive*, Gallimard 2013; 1973–1974: *Le Pouvoir psychiatrique*, Gallimard 2003; 1974–1975: *Les Anormaux*, Gallimard 1999; 1975–1976: *Il faut défendre la société*, Gallimard 1997; 1977–1978: *Sécurité, territoire, population*, Gallimard 2004; 1978–1979: *Naissance de la biopolitique*, Gallimard 2004; 1979–1980: *Du gouvernement des vivants*, Seuil 2012; 1980–1981: *Subjectivité et vérité*, Seuil 2014; 1981–1982: *L'Herméneutique du sujet*, Gallimard 2001; 1982–1983: *Le Gouvernement de soi et des autres I*, Gallimard 2008; 1983–1984: *Le Gouvernement de soi et des autres II - Le Courage de la vérité*, Gallimard 2009.

will also be useful, which together will allow the foundation of an interpretation of the failures of the State and the Market starting from the concepts of governmentality, modern governmentality, the "securititarian" welfare state and, in opposition, the "liberal" competition state.

The term governmentality is introduced by Foucault to mean government and rationality, a broader concept of "government". "We must leave this term the very broad meaning it had in the sixteenth century. It did not refer only to the structures of politics and the management of States but designated the way of conducting the conduct of individuals or groups [...]. To govern, in this sense, is to structure the field of action of others" (Foucault, 2001a). In this way he did not start from sovereignty, from the State, from civil society, but he arrived there.

> I would like to [...] determine how the scope of the practice of government has been established, its different objects, its general rules, its overall objectives, in order to govern in the best possible way. [...]. This involves a choice of method [...]: not to consider as a primary, original, already given object, [...] notions such as [...] those of sovereign, sovereignty, people, subjects, State, civil society [...]. I would like to do exactly the opposite, and take as a starting point this practice of government as it is given, but also as it reflects on itself and tries to give itself a rationality, to see how, from a certain moment on, certain things, whose status we will have to question ourselves, can effectively be constituted: the state and society (Foucault, 2005b, pp. 14–15).

Governmentality is a concept and a practice that Foucault sees as being born in Europe between the seventeenth and eighteenth centuries in a break with the ancien régime. "In the medieval and Renaissance tradition, a good government, a well-ordered kingdom was part of a world order, which was willed by God. [...]. With respect to this natural order, reason of state [... introduced] a fracture [...]. Absence of naturalness, absolute artificiality [...], which had also provoked accusations of atheism. Artificialism of governmentality, artificialism of reason of state" (Foucault, 2005a, pp. 253–254). Another break occurred in the second half of the eighteenth century, starting from France, due to the emergence of new ways of thinking about wealth due to changes in the social structure. During the long reign of Louis XIV (1661–1715), the desperate need for funds had induced the monarchy to sell the nobility patents to wealthy bourgeois who had purchased land from bankrupt aristocrats. As the "Director of Finance" Jacques Necker noted in 1796: "the nobility [...] was no longer the same after an endless aggregation of new nobility [...] introduced because of the needs of the state. [...]. I have no doubt that about half of the order of nobles is [... now] composed of nobility [...]: counselors, auditors, correctors, accountants, [...], treasurers, secretaries [...], military men, [...] simple bourgeois" (Necker, 1821, pp. 122–123). They, who had become the most faithful "king's men", had quickly acquired aristocratic customs, but remained bourgeois in the claim that the land should guarantee a surplus to be accumulated and not only the means for a sumptuous existence, as the now supplanted nobles had always understood. Thus, the fundamental concept and objective of the surplus changed nature also at the macro level. Conceived by the mercantilism of Jean-Baptiste Colbert, finance minister of Louis XIV from 1661 to 1683, as the growth of the gold and silver circulating corresponding to an active balance of payments, to be obtained through aggressive trade policies, the surplus was now conceived as the result of the internal economic system, and in particular of agriculture capable of providing an annual product exceeding production costs, if well conducted and without interference from the State to disturb the "natural" movement of prices. These ideas were placed at the center of an advanced analytical construction—the "Tableau Économique"—by François Quesnay (1694–1774), doctor to Madame de Pompadour at the court of Louis XV and leader of the physiocrats, the "economists" as they called themselves, with the aim of promoting economic development based on agricultural progress. This was thought to be stimulated by eliminating all controls on the price of wheat, a price controlled by mercantilism to contain monetary wages and therefore the cost of production of manufactures whose products constituted the most significant and stable part of exports. The wealth of the nation, therefore, and the consequent wealth of the State fuelled by taxes, was no longer to be conceived as an inherently s provisional and uncertain result of competition with other countries, but as a sure result of competition within producers of the "grande culture" compared to the "petite culture", by a larger size of agricultural companies operating with more capital-intensive techniques, by greater investments stimulated by adequate profitability. Physiocratic ideas encountered strong opposition even among contemporary Enlightenment thinkers. A great historian of economic thought wrote (Ware, 1931, p. 617):

> This constant identification of the interests of the class they represented with those of the nation succeeded in blinding the eyes of the Physiocrats to the palpable fact that an increase in income is of little importance to a person who has no income to increase. Linguet, Galiani, Graslin, Voltaire, and Rousseau all launched the same accusation of class interest against the Physiocrats. [...]. And the Physiocrats themselves offered the best proof of their class point of view. In answer to the accusation that the people suffered from the high price of bread, Quesnay replied: «It is important that the common people should work hard under pressure from necessity. In the last century when wheat was sold much dearer, the people had become accustomed to it and earned in proportion by being more industrious because they were more constrained. It is therefore a grave mistake to accustom the people to buy their wheat at a low price; they become less industrious, they feed themselves with little difficulty and so become parasites and arrogant; it is difficult to find workers and servants, and one is very poorly served in the years of plenty» (Daire, 1846, p. 302).

The list of critical Illuminists is very significant. The French jurist Simon-Nicolas Linguet, the Neapolitan economist Ferdinando Galiani (the abbot Galiani), the French economist Jean-Joseph-Louis Graslin are mentioned, alongside the philosophers François-Marie Arouet (known as Voltaire) and Jean-Jacques Rousseau. It is significant because they all criticized the class interest of the physiocrats despite having very different positions toward the "physiocratic revolution": Linguet and the economists were completely critical, but the philosophers were partly in favor.

"It is important that the common people work hard, pressed by necessity", this is the short sentence with which Quesnay in 1759 specified what Capitalism was and what its problem is. It is not capital, which had always been there. Capitalism is *command* over the source of its accumulation, over work; command that is obtained only if workers are forced to work hard, as happens in the "grande culture" that employs wage earners without their own means of production. The physiocrats had understood that the surplus is disposable wealth that its owner sells but has not bought and that depends on the power of command. For this reason, Marx will judge Quesnay's "Tableau économique" "an extremely ingenious idea, indisputably the most ingenious that political economy has so far been responsible for" (Marx, 1863/1979, p. 363). The problem of governmentality descends consequently. Whether to give enough income (enough grain) so that people have the possibility and the interest to increase it, as the critical Illuminists wanted, or—as the physiocrats wanted—leave them at the mercy of need so that they will be very busy. So, at its very birth, modern governmentality is conceived as an opposition between its two poles; *both of which are, however, constitutive* because ultimately there were always sufficient reasons to think that one or the other alternative was preferable. Foucault says that "the development of the state of competition [...] and the development of the state of wohlfahrt [...] are the two principles that [...] the rational art of government must be able to *coordinate*" (Foucault, 2005a, p. 268). But the two poles remain opposite as security on one side and liberalism on the other. In fact,

> Freedom is not a given, a pre-constituted sphere that one would simply have to respect [...]. Freedom is something that is manufactured at every moment [...] with all the problems of cost that this manufacturing entails. What will be, then, the criterion for calculating the cost of producing freedom? It will be [...] security. Which means that the art of governing will find itself forced to determine in what exact proportions, and within what limits, the different individual interests [...] can become a danger to the interests of all. The problem of security is therefore that of protecting the collective interest against individual interests. The same thing happens in the opposite direction: it will be necessary to defend individual interests against everything that could appear in relation to them as an usurpation deriving from the collective interest (Foucault, 2005b, pp. 67–68).

Furthermore, "the political problem of the population begins to emerge [...]. This is not conceived as a collection of "subjects by law", nor as a group of arms destined for work, but is analyzed as [...] support for concerted interventions through laws, but also through changes in attitudes, ways of doing and living" (Foucault, 2005a, p. 268). This last passage on the population and on attitudes, ways of doing and living, clarifies that the opposition is between entire systems of relationships that are established in consistent ways, becoming ideological, capable of exhibiting a mutually provocative integralism. Ideological, not in the sense of descending from false consciousness about the world, but from its modeling.[12] Systems, as cohesive networks of power and knowledge relations. Individual collaboration and complicity

[12] "If our concept of ideology remains the classical one in which illusion is found in knowledge, then today's society undoubtedly appears post-ideological: the prevailing position is one of cynicism; people no longer believe in ideological truth; they do not take ideological proposals seriously. But fundamentally, ideology is not an illusion which masks the real state of things, but rather a fantasy [....] which structures our very social reality. And at this level, we are obviously far from being a post-ideological society. Cynical distance is just one way – one of the many ways – to blind us to the structuring power of ideological fantasy: even if we maintain an ironic distance, we are still exercising it" (Žižek 1989, p. 30).

are involved,[13] the whole society is permeated by it,[14] the production of specific knowledge comes from this,[15] localized episodes are relevant only for their effects on the network.[16]

2.3 Polarization

From all this, there is a definition and two corollaries. Definition: governmentality as artificial production and reproduction of the social order is structured in modern governmentality as coordination between two opposite poles: welfare state (security) and competition state (liberal). Where state with a lowercase initial is understood as the political-social condition of the population, which derives from the procedures and mechanisms of power and resistance to power that run through it entirely and in which individual subjectivities are active even if conditioned by a variable field of forces structured by and in cultural, political, economic, and social devices. First corollary: the opposition between welfare state and competition state is essentially consistent and becomes ideological because it is also opposition between security and freedom; the cause-effect logics are opposed, on one side competition through security welfare, on the other welfare through freedom-competition; the related power relations are pervasive "concerted interventions through laws, but also through changes in attitudes, ways of doing and living", tendentially coherent and alternative forms of "networks of power relations and knowledge". Second corollary: the opposition is also of the regulatory mechanisms, protection- imposition on the side of the security welfare state, autonomy-competition on the side of the free-market competition state ("it is the game of the interests of private individuals in competition with each other, who seek maximum profit, that allows [...] the entire population to pocket [...] the benefits of their conduct" (Foucault, 2005a, p. 251).

---

[13] "The sovereign [...] exercised his right over life [...] by implementing his right to kill, or by abstaining from it. That is, he made his power over life manifest only through the death he was able to demand. [...] The West has known a very profound transformation of these mechanisms of power since the classical age [the seventeenth century] The 'levy' tends to no longer be the principal form, but only one element among others that have functions of incitement, reinforcement, control, surveillance, empowerment, and organization [...]: a power destined to produce forces, to make them grow and to sort them rather than to block, bend or destroy them" (Foucault 1978, pp. 120–121).

[14] "State power is part of a network of relations «not as a superstructure alongside or above the relations of production [...]; [on the contrary] the mechanisms of power are intrinsic to all these relations" (Foucault 2005a, p. 13).

[15] "The analysis of these power relations can [...] set in motion a [...] global analysis of a society. [...] the analysis must show the effects of knowledge produced in our society by the struggles, clashes, conflicts that take place there and by the power tactics that are the elements of this struggle" (Foucault 2005a., p. 14).

[16] "The study of this microphysics of power relations [...] supposes that the power exercised there is not conceived as a property but as a strategy [...and that] none of its localized episodes can be inscribed in history except through the effects it induces in the entire network in which it is caught" (Foucault 1976, pp. 30–31).

Fig. 2.1 Outline: first part

Fig. 2.2 Friedrich von Hayek's triangle

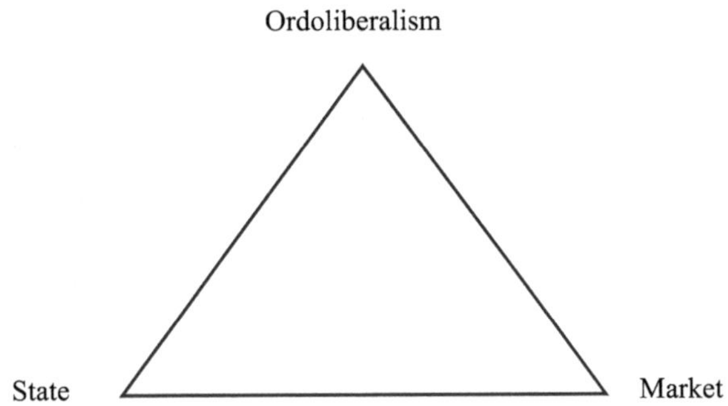

In this way there is the first part of a scheme that will be gradually completed (Fig. 2.1).

The line between the two opposite poles, the welfare state of security—the state of free-market competition, is not obvious and innocent. The line excludes the prospect of a third vertex, that is, a triangle, which has sometimes been drawn for ordoliberalism (as a third pole or third way), in particular by Friedrich Von Hayek (Fig. 2.2).

The exclusion of the triangle and the third pole comes from Foucault. As previously mentioned, "contrary to many […] Foucault suggested that ordoliberalism has a legitimate claim to the title neoliberal" (Mirowski & Plehwe, 2009, p.2). Furthermore, the principles to be coordinated by the art of government are two: "development of the competition state […] and development of the welfare state". In the end, even Friedrich von Hayek himself dropped the triangle:

> Hayek [1960, 343–355] argued that it is wrong to understand socialism, liberalism and conservatism as positions along a single line from socialism on the left to conservatism on the right, instead drawing these political positions as different corners of a triangle […]. Hayek's position, however, changed […] from the 1960s onwards. […]. Hayek then moved away from the project […] of redefining the logic of government and the state […] seeking instead to break the state's monopoly […] to strengthen individual liberties (Davies & Gane, 2021, pp. 8–9).

The processes of subjectivation introduce the dynamics. For Foucault, the subject is constituted on imposed or at least conditioned ways of being. However, it is also constituted in its own singularity.

> Power is only exercised over free subjects because they are free – we mean […] individual or collective subjects who have before them a field of possibilities in which multiple conducts,

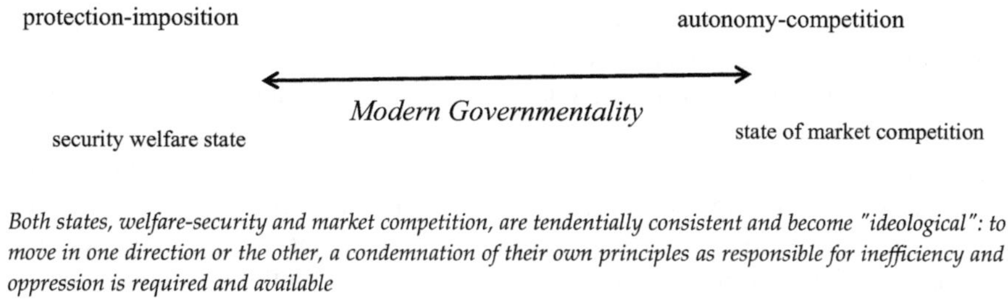

Fig. 2.3 The outline, first part: statics and dynamics

> multiple reactions and different ways of behaving can take place. Where determinations are saturated there is no power relationship: slavery is not a power relationship; when man is in chains it is a question of physical constraint [...]. There is therefore no face to face between power and freedom, with a relationship of exclusion between them (wherever power is, freedom disappears); but a much more complex game: in this game freedom will appear as a condition of existence [...], because there must be freedom for power to be exercised, and it is its permanent support because if freedom were to disappear because of the power that is exercised over it, the latter would disappear ipso facto [...]; it thus appears as that which cannot but oppose an exercise of power (Foucault, 2001a, p. 1056).

It follows that, since the two poles that "the rational art of government must be able to coordinate" do not coordinate spontaneously, on both sides the intersection between being subjectivized and subjectivizing always gives rise to resistance, protest, centrifugal forces. When forces that feel penalized by the current order, inevitably unbalanced to one side or the other, want to contest it and move toward the other pole, they can always find a basis for consensus and, since this form also constitutes itself as ideology, they must and can use the weapon of total condemnation of the principles of the current order to weaken it and attempt to overcome it: condemnation of the principles as responsible for the inefficiency and perverse nature of performance. The outline therefore becomes (Fig. 2.3).

2.4 Welfare State

It was the condemnation of the principles of the free-market state of competition that led to the configuration of the welfare state in the post-war period: Keynesian interventionism, state enterprises, planning, industrial policy, general public services such as schools, health care, pensions and social insurance, housing programs, strong unionization, labor law, limited distributive inequality, culture of solidarity. But signs of such condemnation at the level of government ideas and practices had been seen since the 1880s. After the crisis of 1873[17] and the consequent "Long Depression",

[17] The crisis began with the collapse of the Vienna Stock Exchange on 8 May 1873, and the New York Stock Exchange on 18 September. The depression continued in some countries for five, in others for six years as in the Austro-Hungarian Empire. For the first time, both in agriculture and

protectionist policies, already partly practiced as a consequence of the reduction of transport costs and the connected increase in international competition, were adopted more widely violating the liberal credo. Just as it was violated by the adoption of interventions for the "social question". "The nineteenth-century social question [...] was posed in these terms: [...] how can disorders be averted in a society that wants to enjoy the benefits deriving from the exploitation of a large class of poorly paid and [...] discontented people? The response of the European states [...] with the adoption of social policies was given without considering almost nothing of contemporary theories [...] of economic liberalism" (Judt, 1997, p. 103). The fact is that that large "class of discontented people" despite a thousand difficulties grew in awareness and demanded ever more satisfaction, otherwise threatening the established order.

As would later happen in the neoliberal revolt against the welfare state, the change of state was a rapid process, but long prepared, even if this preparation was little noticed and only became clear with hindsight. It struck the anti-liberal criticism, but only when it became an avalanche in the 1930s, due to the disappointments and resentments of the post-war period and the Great Depression which, neglecting the more complex reasons that emerge in the analysis of the cycles,[18] was attributed to the democratic-liberal order itself. This was condemned en bloc, leading Europe to the collapse of parliamentary democracies and the affirmation of National Socialism and Fascism, while in the United States the New Deal was conceived and launched to avoid the same authoritarian turn[19] as John Maynard Keynes attested in an open letter to President Roosevelt published in the New York Times on 31 December 1933: "You remain to me the eminent statesman whose general outlook and attitude to the tasks of government [...] make you the only one in the world who sees the necessity for a profound change of methods and is attempting to do it without intolerance, tyranny or destruction" (Keynes, 2013, p. 295).[20]

---

in industry, the crisis was due to overproduction, that is, to a lack of demand due to the failure to adjust wages to the increase in productivity, as well as to the entry into the international market of new producers such as Germany and the United States.

[18] The analysis of the cycles already mentioned in the first chapter has demonstrated that: (1) all the cycles contributed negatively to the great crisis of '29, this observation is of particular importance as it allows that crisis to be placed in the right perspective, often neglected in interpretations that have often insisted on a single cause; (2) in the 1976–1997 crisis, since it was longer, the inventory cycle and the electoral cycle had counterbalancing effects, while the negative Kodrat'ev effect (false start of new technologies) was accentuated; (3) the crisis of the years 2007–2013 had peculiar characteristics, in addition to the effects of the inversion of the real estate and inventory cycle; (4) in the central phase of great development (1943–1973), all the cycles contributed positively except, but only at the beginning, the inventory cycle and in the 1960s the credit cycle; (5) in the next 7–8 years in the United States there will probably be another rather serious crisis since the large cycles are in a negative phase and the positive phases of the short cycles are running out.

[19] "Throughout the 1930s, many European observers also predicted a fascist future for the United States. Given the crisis of democracy, they believed that the world had only two alternatives, socialism or fascism; since the United States had proven unsuitable for communism, fascist observers, like Marxist theorists, deduced that corporatism, a third way between capitalism and socialism, was inevitable" (Sedda 1999, pp. 245–246).

[20] Keynes met Roosevelt at the White House on 28 May 1934, five months after the December 1933 open letter, and the meeting was not warm. According to the memoirs of Labor Secretary Frances

At the end of the 1970s, the condemnation of the principles hit the welfare state, as Foucault recalled in the lecture of 31 January 1979 using the expression "state phobia".

> You are certainly all familiar with Berenson, the art historian. He was almost a hundred years old, and therefore not too far from death, when he made a statement like this: «God only knows how much I fear the destruction of the world by the atomic bomb, but there is at least one thing that I fear as much, and that is the invasion of humanity by the State». It seems to me that here is expressed, in the purest and most praised form, a real phobia of the State [...] which has drawn nourishment from various sources; from the Soviet experience starting in the 1920s, from the German experience of Nazism, from post-war English planning [... and] which has had numerous agents and supporters; from professors of political economy inspired by Austrian neo-marginalism to political exiles (Foucault, 2005b, pp. 73–74).

These are the sentences with which he began the series of lectures of 1979 with the analysis of nascent neoliberalism, which from German ordoliberalism to the version of the "Chicago School", to Thatcherism and Reaganism, he lashed out against Keynesian interventionism and Beveridge's system of universal social security. The "phobia of the state" spread in political circles and among cultural elites. If one remembers especially that of the leaders, it is only to underline its strong consequences in terms of styles of government. Margaret Thatcher did not represent alone "the guiding spirit of the age" (Davies et al., 2023, p. 100). In any case, an article in the "Guardian" on 28 December 2012 (by Alan Trevis) revealed that on the basis of documents released after the regulatory 30 years of secrecy, Thatcher in 1982 had presented to the Council of Ministers a plan with many measures to reduce social spending, including the sale of clinics and hospitals to private individuals and the privatization of doctors' and nurses' contracts. And the plan states: "this obviously means the end of the National Health Service". This part of the measure was not implemented due to a revolt within the Conservative government itself, but it expresses very well what the real furious intention of the English Prime Minister was. The same anti-statist anger spread to the United States, where the watchword became: "starve the beast", meaning that the hated public spending was cut by cutting taxes. The expression was circulating among White House officials during the Reagan era (Bartlett, 2007), as evidenced by a 1985 Wall Street Journal article. Ronald Reagan, in his inaugural address in 1981, had said, "In the present crisis, government is not the solution; government is the problem" (Reagan, 1981). The theoretical background had been clarified by Milton Friedman as early as 1978.

Perkins, Roosevelt did not appreciate his arrival with "a slew of figures". Considering Keynes' subsequent open letter of 10 June 1934, less than a month and a half after the meeting, he had brought "figures" to show him that U.S. government spending should have been higher: \$5–6 billion in the 1934–1935 fiscal year, instead of the \$3.4 billion that was actually spent because Roosevelt feared it would trigger inflation. Keynes was right about the state of the economy. Consumer prices had fallen by 10% in 1932 and by 5% in 1933. On average from 1934 to 1937 they increased by a modest 2.7% and fell again in 1938 and 1939. The reduction in prices is a serious sign of a permanent crisis: if prices fall, purchases are postponed and there is no way out of the crisis. But Roosevelt's concerns were politically founded because he had to deal with the opposition of conservatives, while he nurtured the ambition of tearing the progressives from the Republican Party and founding a movement or a real progressive party.

> There is an important point that needs to be explained to conservatives. By focusing on the wrong thing, the deficit, rather than the right thing, government spending, conservatives have been the handmaidens of the big spenders. […]. The big spenders pass laws that increase government spending. A deficit emerges. The conservatives worry: My God, this is terrible; we must do something about that deficit. So they collaborate with the big spenders to raise taxes. As soon as the new taxes are in place, the big spenders start spending again, there is another explosion of spending and another deficit (Friedman, 1978, p. 11).

The accusation of excessive spending was not unfounded, as will be demonstrated shortly. In this way, the criticism of the right was added to that of the left, which in the 1968 movement accused the state apparatus, but also the big factory, the big union, the big party, the traditional school of having trampled on, as Herbert Marcuse had already written,

> self-determination, [which] will be real to the extent that the masses have dissolved into individuals free from all propaganda, indoctrination and manipulation, capable of knowing and understanding the facts and evaluating the alternatives. In other words, society would be rational and free to the extent that it was organized, supported, and reproduced by an essentially new historical Subject. In the current state of development of advanced industrial societies, both the material system and the cultural system reject this requirement (Marcuse 1964–1967, p. 261).

There was also the accusation of perverse incentives, which would educate people to live on providence. The idea is at least as old as the moral condemnation of poverty, dating back to the mid-seventeenth century when the poor ceased to be regarded with benevolence for their "mortification" and for the charity of the rich. It was then that they began to be interned as idlers together with all the irregulars or those suffering from "shameful" diseases or madmen. Internment took place in hospitals without medical functions where there was instead compulsory labor, against the "immorality of idleness and laziness" considered the father and mother of all immoralities. Foucault places the beginning of internment in 1656 (the date of the opening of the "Hôpital Général" in Paris), which was widespread throughout Europe. Once leprosy had disappeared, leper colonies were filled with the poor and other outcasts, in an impressive proportion. "In Paris, for the entire century and a half up to the threshold of the Revolution, one percent of the entire population was interned" (Foucault, 1962–1972, p. 64).

The accusation of perverse incentives, which was always trumpeted, was, in reality, rather weak. Many lived on welfare, but a distinction is necessary between those who took advantage of it and those who were forced to do so because they had no alternatives. There was no lack of empirical research capable of demonstrating the absence of statistically significant effects of welfare programs on the reduction of the labor supply and on the spread of "professionals of the subsidy", while "it is always talked about in the media, where the considerable research available on the subject is completely ignored" (Moffitt, 1992, p. 3). Living on welfare is unbearable for dignity. This is indirectly demonstrated by the most recent invention of workfare to reduce welfare. Workfare uses the idea of dignity by warning: we give you temporary support only on condition that you demonstrate that you are actively committed to getting rid of it, "so we can help you not to lose your dignity" (Lu,

2021, p. 15). “By the time of the federal welfare reform in 1996, New York City was already a laboratory for punitive workfare [...]. New York Mayor Rudy Giuliani trumpeted the conditionality of workfare by comparing it to the “dignity” of the then widely respected New Deal WPA programs” (Lu, 2021, p.15). The comparison was inappropriate. The well-deserving WPA (Works Progress Administration) programs were designed to alleviate unemployment with socially useful work organized and financed by the State, while workfare demands proof that the recipient is committed to finding a job on his or her own. The objection is obvious: if dignity is an argument, it means that those who live on subsidies simply cannot do without them. The wholesale condemnation of one system to support another therefore also uses unfounded criticism, demonstrating that they are ideological systems. For the welfare state, one should write “failures” in quotation marks, since they are less real than those denounced. On the other hand, a singular contradiction must be noted. That “phobia of the State” and the related change of an economic, political and cultural system should have decisively reduced the weight of the State in the economy. But the reduction, which did take place, turned out to be rather modest. So much so that Cornelius Castoriadis was able to write:

> The inconsistency – indeed, the blatant deception – of contemporary “liberalism” in this respect defies the imagination. [...]. When, as happens everywhere today, half of the national product passes in one way or another through the central and local public sector [...]; when between half and two-thirds of goods and services [...] that enter into final national expenditure are in one way or another [...] influenced by state policy, and when one notes that all this is irreversible (ten years of Thatcher and Reagan have brought no substantial changes), it becomes clear what neoliberal discourse is: a crude farce intended for imbeciles (Castoriadis, 1997, p. 410).

There are no time series data for all aspects of the influence of the State. One must make do with statistics on public spending, as three well-known economists did for the essay “The Size of Government” in the manual on “Public Sector Efficiency”. From their statistics it is possible to draw the following graph, which shows that a significant reduction in public spending occurred only in the United Kingdom, but largely corrected from 2000 to 2017. The reduction was modest and only able to interrupt its growth in Germany, the United States and in the average value of Austria, Belgium, France, Germany, Italy, the Netherlands, Sweden, the United Kingdom, and the United States. Taking into account this profile of public spending on GDP, as a demonstration of the “farce” of the downsizing of the State, the failures of the welfare state denounced by neoliberalism must be put in quotation marks also for this reason: not only because the denunciation used poorly justified arguments, such as that of perverse incentives, but also because it wanted to enslave the State and not downsize it as it vaunted (Figs. 2.4, 2.5).

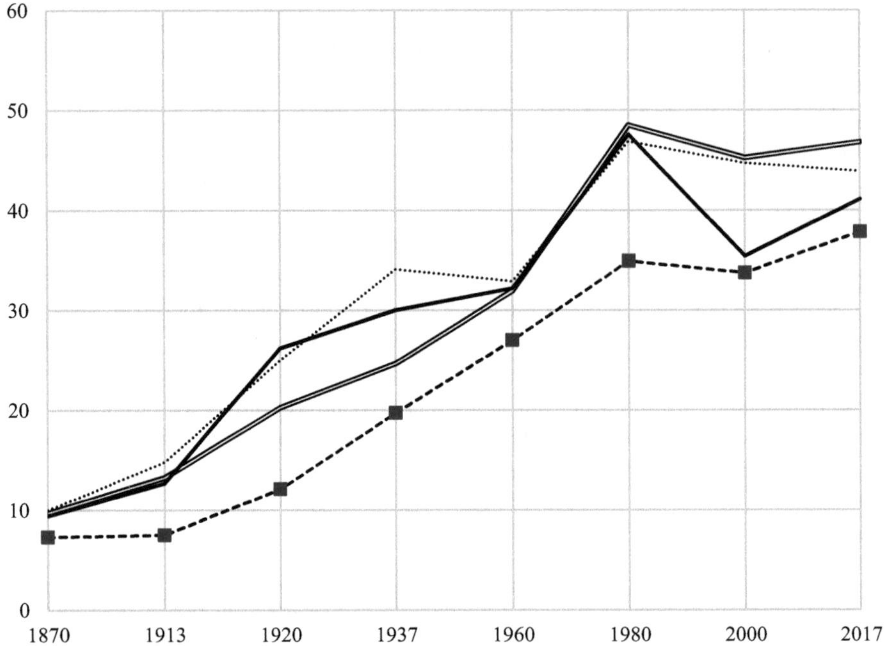

Fig. 2.4 Public spending on GDP %: central government and local governments. Germany—dots, the United Kingdom—solid line, the United States—squares, Average—double line (Austria Belgium, France, Germany, Italy, Netherlands, the United Kingdom, and the United States) *Source* Figure obtained by processing data from Afonso, Schuknecht, Tanzi (2023)

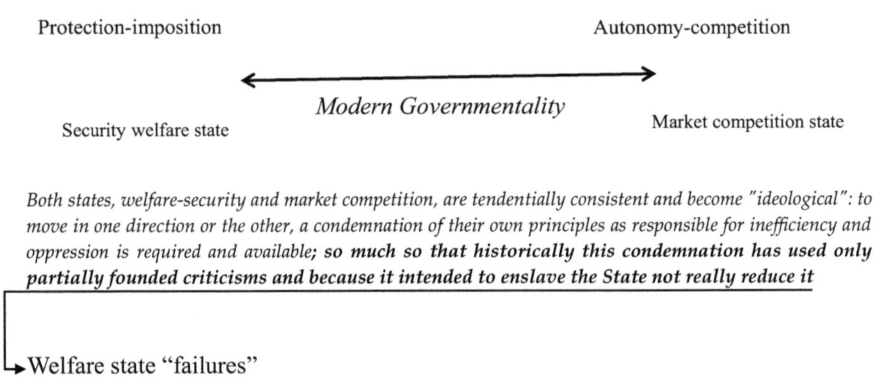

Fig. 2.5 Outline: first part and beginning of the second

2.5 Welfare State Failures

In two respects, however, there was a *real failure* of the welfare state. The first was the excess of administrative costs: although with significant differences, in all the main Western countries social spending increased from the 1950s to the 1970s, but the incidence of the cost of public administration personnel increased more (Fig. 2.6).

The sharp increase in administrative costs was itself a source of criticism. Added to this was the accusation of a perverse use of "concertation" to increase taxes by making them appear inevitable since all parties agreed, just as Milton Friedman had written in 1978. But Foucault, politically at the antipodes, said something similar the following year, in a more general and therefore even more significant version. "The criticism advanced in the name of economic liberalism leverages the danger represented by this inevitable sequence: economic interventionism, inflation of government apparatuses, excess of administration, bureaucracy and stiffening of all mechanisms of power that cause new economic distortions inducing in turn other interventions" (Foucault, 2005b, p. 266). In the case of the United States, inter-party concertation has been measured (Andris et al., 2015) (Fig. 2.7).

The significant growth in personnel costs anticipated by 5–6 years a similar significant growth in concertation between Democrats and Republicans, whose index,

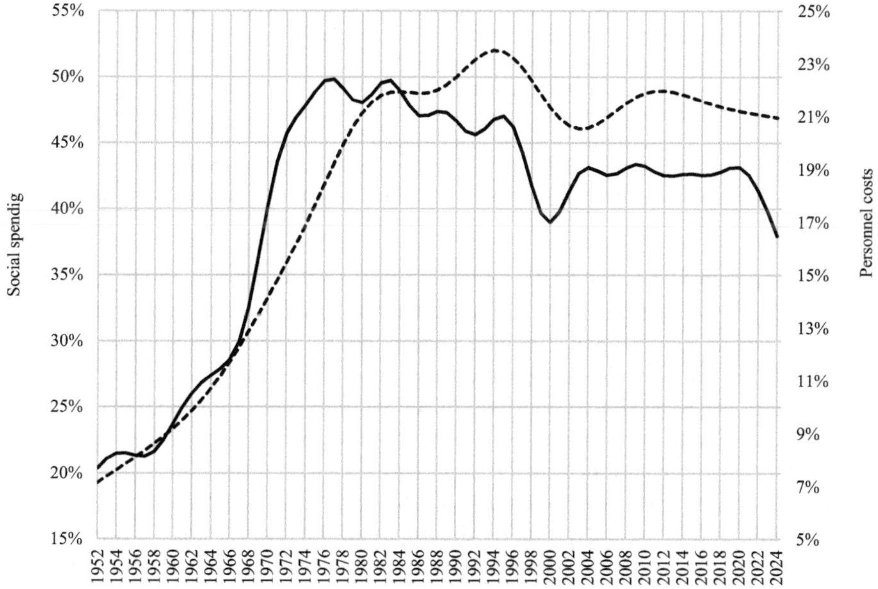

Fig. 2.6 Main Western countries: "structural" state social spending on GDP (dotted line) and personnel costs on public spending (solid line) *Source* Figure obtained by processing data from Fred, OECD, Eurostat data. *Note* Countries considered: the United States, Canada, the United Kingdom, Germany, France, Spain, Italy, Denmark, Sweden, Norway. "Structural" social spending = social spending weighted by the unemployment rate in order to remove the cyclical effect

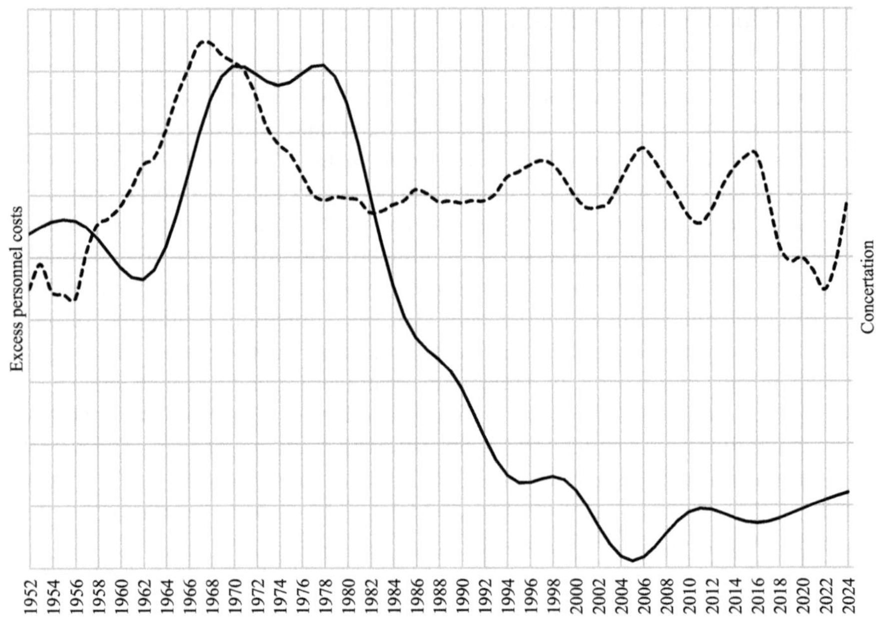

Fig. 2.7 The United States: Excess State Personnel Cost (dotted line) and Index of Inter-Party Concertation (solid line) *Source* Figure obtained by processing data from Andris et al. (2015) and as in Fig. 2.6. *Note* The excess State Personnel Cost is calculated as the percentage ratio between the cost of State personnel (central and local government) and social spending; Concertation: having constructed all possible pairs of representatives (5,663,723) from 1949 to 2012, Andris, et al. counted in the roll-call votes the votes that agreed with each other (yes, yes or no, no), and those that disagreed (yes, no), distinguishing the pairs formed by two representatives of the same party or by a Republican and a Democrat. They processed the results and calculated a frequency of agreements in pairs of different parties, obtaining an index that shows the reported trends

doubled between 1962 and 1970, remained high also in the following decade and began to decline only from 1980. On the other side of the Atlantic, a new party form was born, which Richard Katz and Peter Mair (1995) called “cartel”, characterized, also in Europe, by collusion between competitors. Concertation could be judged in two opposite ways: as shared approval of the welfare state, or as a statist “conspiracy”. The neoliberal fury obviously judged it in the second way. If the suspicion of an ever excessive interference by the State was flaunted [“criticism is permeated by this principle: one always governs too much, or at least one must always suspect it” (Foucault, 2005b, p. 262)], that burdening of administrative costs without objections from the parties demonstrated that the suspicion was well founded, that the statist conspiracy covered the repeated impotent attempts of the State to govern the economy.

> Homo juridicus says to the sovereign: I have rights, I have entrusted you with some, and you must not touch the others […]. Homo economicus does not say this. Of course, he also says to the State you must not, but he says it in this way: you must not because you cannot […]. And why are you impotent, you cannot? You cannot because you do not know and

> cannot know. [... thus] the theory of the invisible hand [...] essentially has the function of discrediting the political sovereign [...] of disqualifying a political reason anchored to the State and its sovereignty (Foucault, 2005b, p. 232).

This was the basis for the campaign of denigration of the State that aimed to form a common sense convinced of its inefficiency; a campaign organized by "numerous agents and supporters; from professors of political economy inspired by neo-marginalism [...] to political exiles" (Foucault, 2005b, p. 232), but above all to the many cultural operations financed by capitalists in the long anti-statist crusade. Naomi Oreskes and Erik Conway (2023) in the book "The Big Myth: How American Business Taught Us to Loathe Government and Love the Free Market" present an impressive documentation on "market fundamentalism" as a triumph of organized propaganda aimed at convincing the public that the government takes away freedom and the market guarantees it. Textbooks, scientific and popular articles oriented in this direction financed by business groups, shows and television programs, invented stories made to be believed true about individual self-sufficiency, a huge film production on the hero who wins against the wickedness of the government multiplied. It was a campaign all the more insidious and effective because it appealed directly to public opinion without traditional mediation and accused of being co-responsible for the "conspiracy". This denigration had two consequences. It contributed to the very inefficiency from which it originated; it strengthened the prospect of individual protagonism leading to the "identity obsession" that is today among the causes of the failure, and also paradoxically, of the resilience of the neoliberal project. The second consequence will be discussed later. First, it is necessary to consider how the inefficiency of the State as an excess of administrative costs justified the denigration of the State that contributed to its inefficiency.

2.5.1 Denigration and Inefficiency of the State

This little-noticed but powerful cumulative circuit is found following a reasoning suggested by considerations of Joseph Stiglitz and Douglas North which date back to the end of the 1980s, thus placing itself in the midst of the neoliberal turning point: (1) the State is essentially "for everyone and forever", therefore it has strong coercive powers[21] while its results are difficult to ascertain[22]; (2) it needs a trust

[21] "Our objective is to identify the differences between the State [...] and other organizations and to draw conclusions from these differences about the appropriate role of the State [...]. I am inclined to argue that there are two particular characteristics of the State, from which most of the other differences derive [...]: the State is [..] the organization to which membership is universal, and the State has a coercive power which is not granted to any other organization" (Stiglitz 1989, pp. 36–37).

[22] "The State must honor for itself and for all contracts entered into with unknown parties through time [forever]. In other words, the State cannot use, like other organizations, especially if they are "small", the defense offered by a certain knowledge of the counterparties' choices, limited timeframes for commitments, and timely verification of results" (North 1989, p. 134).

agreement[23] but this constrains it from the side of discretionary spending and the formal demonstration of fairness[24]; 3) given these two circumstances, the ability and integrity of elected officials and managers are decisive for the results[25]; (4) but they are not appointed on the basis of honesty and competence which remain largely unknown to those who choose them[26]; (5) their quality ends up depending on who proposes themselves and how they will be motivated, (6) the best offer themselves and are motivated only if that job is generally considered prestigious[27]; (7) denigrating the State, therefore, produces the effect of making mediocre managers and officials flow into it who will also be demotivated and will give rise to inefficiencies that will justify such denigration.

This is the thesis that can be supported considering: what that prestige depends on, its effect on those who enters the public administration, its effect on motivation. The prestige of work in the public sector depends on how much the idea is shared that the State is truly at the service of the common good conceived as conditions that guarantee human dignity and the defense of future generations while the respectability of the government is thought to be appreciated in the international context (Jørgensen & Bozeman, 2007). That work is considered not very prestigious if, instead, the opinion is widespread that the public sector serves mainly partisan and short-term interests, considered dominant in society, while it is believed that in the international context economic and military strength count, regardless of the quality of the government. On motivation, the research that has explored the theme of "strategic human resources

23 "The second consequence of the […] distinctive characteristics of the State […] is that, since revenues must be realized through the imposition of a fiscal obligation, there exists a special fiduciary responsibility of the State" (Stiglitz 1989, p. 43).

24 The State cannot pay (political and administrative) officials at will, it must implement policies according to procedures which ensure fairness, at least formally. This results in structural inefficiencies because the best officials cannot be rewarded and bureaucratic burdens become inevitable, given that the fairness of public action must be formally demonstrated. (Stiglitz 1989, p. 43).

25 "It is true that good institutions in the sense of rules and norms can direct incentives […] however, the truth is that the cost of controlling elected officials and employees […] offers them great opportunities for opportunistic behavior if the rules are not supported by their good spontaneous behavior" (North 1989, p. 135).

26 "The Public Administration […] is a public asset. […] Everyone benefits from it [therefore …] private incentives to acquire information [on who runs for office] are limited [because] individual votes have little effect and […] the gain that individuals would have from selecting candidates well is only an insignificant fraction of the total social gain. […]. If individuals believe that their vote does not count, they can let ideology prevail over reason, apparently without cost to themselves and to society" Stiglitz, 1989, p. 42). On the other hand, managers and officials in public administration are often asked above all for loyalty, even at the expense of competence and efficiency: "the more a politician is elected for ideological reasons, the more jobs in the public sector are assigned to consolidate the politician's electoral position" (Peters & Bianchi 2020, p. 230).

27 "The crucial element of the proposed model [which specifies the variables influencing public sector outcomes] is the variable in the ways of thinking prevalent in the population. These play multiple roles. First, as objectives or guiding principles of managerial intentions and as criteria for evaluating behavior. Second, as constraints and facilitators during the process of creating public added value […] including the satisfaction of operators and their diligence" (Vandenabeele et al.,2013, p. 49).

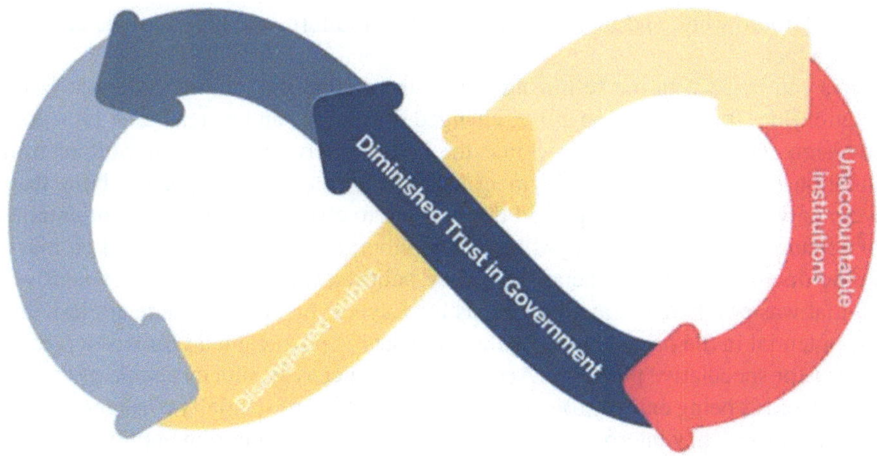

Fig. 2.8 The perverse cumulative cycle of distrust in government *Source* Hitlin and Shutava (2022, 8)

management" in public administration has something remarkable to say. Boselie et al. (2021) selected 77 pieces of research published in the period 2000–2016, finding two main themes: the definition and the attempt to measure the value of such management, its remodeling focused on contexts. Although the first theme appears dominant with 56 publications, the second (21 publications) is significant and more frequent in recent times. The importance of contexts has emerged as an influence exerted on motivation by administrative traditions specific to each country and by the methods of cuts in personnel spending that have occurred everywhere, but above all "by the evolution of social values" (Boselie et al., 2021, p. 492). The motivation of public administration staff depends greatly on the value attributed to the State by the widespread way of thinking.

In conclusion, the inefficiency of the State justifies its denigration which produces the effect of making mediocre and unmotivated managers and officials flow into it, from which inefficiencies will confirm the basis of the denigration. "The lack of trust in the government is an obstacle to its ability to meet collective needs, providing modern, equitable solutions and accessible services. Distrust dissuades young talents from entering the public service […] and has an impact on the will and capacity of its staff" (Hitlin & Shutava, 2022, p. 8) (Fig. 2.8).

2.5.2 *Unfulfilled Promises*

The unfulfilled promises were *the second real failure* of the welfare state. It may seem strange that there were unfulfilled promises after seeing the great results of the welfare state so contrasting with the miseries that occurred after the neoliberal turn.

Instead, there were, and they truly represented a failure, and here too one can start from a fact.

As can be seen in the following figure, from 1968 the inflation-unemployment relationship, traditionally negative, changed drastically, and instead took on a positive sign. The change was shocking: the balance between losses of welfare from inflation and gains from employment and vice versa had disappeared. Now there were only losses. This change had the strength to change the prevailing orientation of economists and those responsible for economic policy who converted en masse to the doctrine of the "monetarists". They believed that existing employment was all that was possible, not at all given, as for Keynes, by effective demand, less than the potential in the presence of significant means of payment held back as a precaution or for speculative purposes. According to monetarists, money should always be considered as being entirely used for exchanges with a substantially constant velocity of circulation. They interpreted the negatively sloping inflation-unemployment relationship as a short-term relationship, as Milton Friedman explained in his lecture "Inflation and Unemployment", which he gave when he received the Nobel Prize in 1976. According to monetarists, Keynesian economic policy had shifted this relationship upward (dotted lines in the figure), fuelling inflation which, due to the increased resulting uncertainty, had depressed productive activity (Fig. 2.9).

Monetarist theses are highly debatable. However, stagflation can actually be considered a failure of the welfare state as will now be demonstrated.

As one can imagine, this new phenomenon has been one of the most studied, on a par with the Great Crisis, but the most lucid analysis remains that of Salvatore Biasco (1979). The great inflation of the 1970s intervened on the side of international liquidity as a permissive condition, of costs, and of a particular transmission mechanism, which depressed production activity and caused high unemployment due to the reduction of the international competitiveness of Western countries. There were four interacting factors: (1) rapid transition from scarce to abundant international liquidity due to the deterioration of the stop and go mechanism for correcting balance of payments imbalances following the increased bargaining power of workers,[28] imbalances which, not corrected, were necessarily financed; (2) relevance of the basic deficit of the United States in feeding international liquidity[29]; (3) effects on

[28] "The rules of the game [...] required that immediate and drastic corrections in employment would promptly put an end to payment difficulties [...]. This presupposed [...] that collective acceptance of that pressure that keeps all social groups within the norms set by the dominant group would be maintained. Instead, this pressure weakened and [...] the strength of the subordinate social groups grew, taking away flexibility from the system. It is difficult to speak of flexibility [...] when each group administers some parameter [...] and restores its share of income whenever other groups manage to reduce it" (Biasco 1979, p. 47).

[29] The "basic" balance of payments includes the current account balance (exports minus imports of goods and services and net unilateral transfers, income of residents abroad minus income of foreigners in the country, remittances from emigrants, and in general payments and receipts without counterpart), to which is added the balance of long-term public and private capital movements that are not compensatory, that is, not from discretionary activities of the Central Bank and banks to compensate for private financial and commercial choices. The basic balance of payments of the United States is the "machine" that produces liquidity in dollars. With a deficit balance, the United

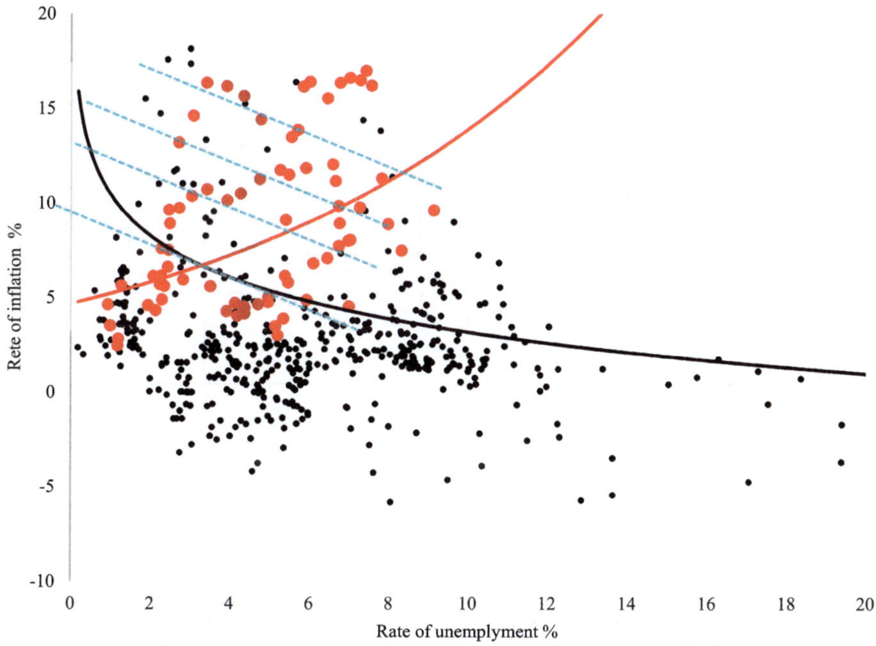

Fig. 2.9 Germany, France, Italy, the United Kingdom, the United States: Inflation and unemployment rate by year. The black dots correspond to the values of the variables minus the period 1968–1982 (black solid line as interpolation)) whose values are indicated by the red dots (red solid line as interpolation). Dotted lines as short-term interpolations moving upward *Source* Figure obtained by processing data from (inflation) Alvaredo et al. (2016) for the United States, the United Kingdom, France, and Germany from 1870 to 2015; Mitchell (1998) for Italy from 1938 to 1958, OECD data from 1959 to 2015; (unemployment) the United States from 1870 to 2015 EPI analysis of data from the BEA and BLS, other countries, Galenson and Zellner (1957), Boyer and Hatton (2002), Chelini and Prat (2011), OECD. *Note* For Germany the years of hyperinflation have been excluded

the prices of primary goods of international liquidity, of the devaluation of the dollar, of the long previous period of deterioration in the terms of trade between raw materials and industrial manufacturing in contradiction with the continuity of the increase in demand for primary goods which increased the bargaining power of the producing countries; (4) transmission of external inflation within individual countries and of

States borrows from the rest of the world and issues promises to pay in dollars. Up to a certain point, this debt is sustainable because the dollar is the currency of international trade, that is, it has an exchange value that tends to fluctuate less than other currencies. This was also guaranteed within the Bretton Woods system by specific rules that provided for basically fixed exchange rates anchored to the dollar, which in turn was anchored to convertibility into gold for central banks. On 15 August 1971, the U.S. government declared that it no longer guaranteed convertibility. In the new conditions, everything depends on expectations. The limit of sustainability of U.S. international debt in dollars is exceeded when operators begin to think that there are too many dollars in circulation and that its value may become unstable. They then begin to sell dollars and its value decreases compared to other currencies and compared to the goods traded on the global market whose prices in dollars increase.

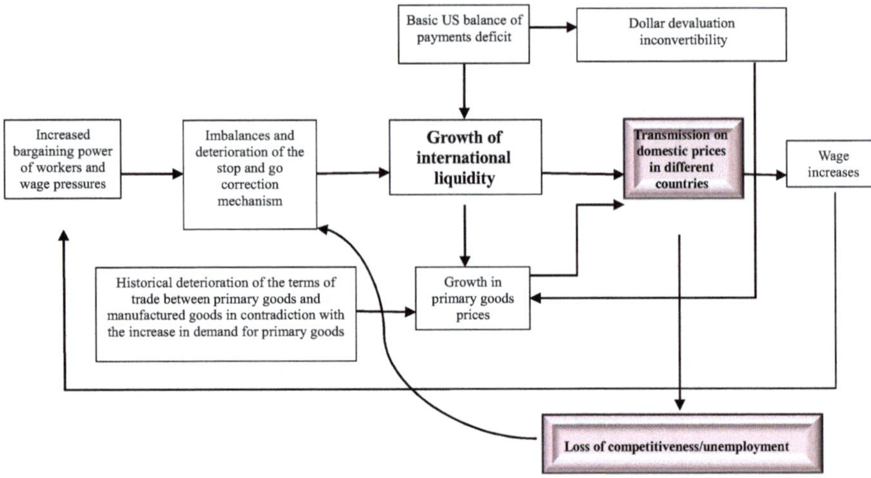

Fig. 2.10 Mechanisms underlying stagflation *Source* Figure obtained by processing data from Biasco (1979)

this to wage increases, losses of competitiveness, unemployment, increase in balance of payments imbalances, thus forming a self-feeding circle (Fig. 2.10).

In this explanation, the failure of the welfare state lies in the contradiction between the increased bargaining power of workers and producers of raw materials and the conditions that would be necessary to sustain it. The conditions could be, alternatively or together: *a stronger increase in productivity* and/or the acceptance by the dominant groups and countries of a *reduction in their share of income and power*. In the absence of these conditions, it can be said that the welfare state ended up in the long run being a promise that could not or would not be kept. On the other hand, the governance of the global system did not help because of the excessively high cost imposed by the center, namely the United States, which accumulated an excessively high deficit in the balance of payments due to the extraordinary expenses of the war in Vietnam, for international aid and for investments abroad.

2.6 Neoliberal Project

Neoliberalism, as a reaction and alternative to the welfare state, was conceived as a "biopolitical" project involving all aspects of social and personal life, as Margaret Thatcher also said in the famous interview given to Ronald Butt of the Sunday Times on 3 May 1981. After having answered on the state of the British economy and the policies implemented by the government, to the last question on the prospects she replied with a certain embarrassment that the economic recovery was slow in coming but added that her program went well beyond the economy.

> What's irritated me about the whole direction of politics in the last 30 years is that it's always been towards the collectivist society. People have forgotten about the personal society. And they say: do I count, do I matter? To which the short answer is, yes. And therefore, it isn't that I set out on economic policies; it's that I set out really to change the approach, and changing the economics is the means of changing that approach. If you change the approach, you really are after the heart and soul of the nation. Economics are the method; the object is to change the heart and soul (Sunday Times, 3 May 1981).

Michel Foucault had clarified that neoliberalism, as a systematic suspicion of government, is not a doctrine of the pure and simple retreat of the State. It is in fact interventionist albeit in a particular sense. The State must intervene with regulatory, educational, cultural, and political means to "generalize the form of enterprise within the body or the social fabric [...], to ensure that the very life of the individual [...] makes him [...] a kind of enterprise" (Foucault, 2005b, p. 197). The neoliberal homo economicus "is rather an entrepreneur, the entrepreneur of himself, who as such is his own capital [...], human capital" (Foucault, 2005b, p. 186). In short, the bold operation that the neoliberal project intended to achieve is clearly stated here. In the capitalism of physical capital, command over work had to be exercised by the capitalist with the problem of which lever to use: the stick of necessity or the carrot of opportunity, as Quesnay had already written. In human capital capitalism, the burden of commanding labor performance was assumed by the worker who, as an entrepreneur of himself, provided for his *self-discipline.* The complementary physical capital and manual labor did not disappear but remained under the command of the capitalist. In this way, that self-discipline became self-exploitation. The combination of self-entrepreneur and human capital could also ensure the dynamics of the system through innovation. Innovation that, "if it occurs, [...] if new things are found, [...] new forms of productivity, [...] technological inventions, all this represents nothing other than the income of a certain capital, human capital, that is, the set of investments that have been made in relation to man as such" (Foucault, 2005b, p. 192). The denigration of the security of the welfare state was in this way also a condemnation of the "losing" personal aversion to risk and exaltation of the personal "winning" bet on innovation, that is, the propensity to risk. There was, however, an obvious *problem.* The problem of how one could simultaneously sustain investments in human capital, which each was called upon to make by renouncing consumption, and the propensity for risk that was all the more difficult the greater those investments were. The response consistent with neoliberal ideology did not consider devices or levers or mechanisms of an institutional or collective nature. It responded with mass therapeutic action to convince each of the entrepreneurs to consider *self-esteem* as important above all else.

In the United States, the "therapeutic turn" had its manifesto in the Report "Toward a State of Self-Esteem" written by experts commissioned by the State of California and published in 1980. The success and diffusion of the Report were enormous despite the fact that "extolling self-esteem without being able to define what is estimable, and without being able to establish a distinction between better and worse forms of behavior, seemed to many an undertaking [...] absurd" (Fukuyama, 2018, pp. 116, 119). Therapeutic activity increased rapidly in the major American cities.

"The number of mental health professionals quadrupled between 1970 and 1990" (Fukuyama, 2018, p. 119). In 1963, the number of graduates enrolled in doctoral courses in clinical psychology was 3,340 but reached 25,973 in 2006, almost ten times as many (Grus, 2011, p. 150), while the "American Psychological Association" estimated that in 2000 there were 250,000 active therapists (88 per 100,000 inhabitants). According to a survey by "Psychology Today" in 2004, 30 million Americans (14.3% of the entire population) had resorted to some psychological therapy in the previous two years (Marks, 2017, p. 5). In Europe, according to data from the World Health Organization, on average in the years from 2013 to 2017, the number of people working in psychological care services (psychiatrists, psychologists, auxiliary staff) was even greater than in the United States (with the exception of Sweden): out of 100,000 inhabitants, 105 in the United States, 160 in France, 106 in Germany, 144 in the Netherlands, 220 in Switzerland, and 70 in Sweden.

The results of the mass action for self-esteem were extraordinary. In the United States, "modern adolescents were more likely respond true to items such as "I am an important person". […] This item was endorsed as true by only about 12% of the Hathaway and Monachesi (1963) sample. In contrast, this item was endorsed as true by 77% (girls) to 80% (boys) of contemporary adolescents" (Rutledge Newsom et al. 2003, p. 80). "Almost two-thirds of recent college students are above the mean 1979–1985 narcissism score, a 30% increase. The results complement previous studies finding increases in other individualistic traits such as assertiveness, agency, self-esteem, and extraversion" (Twenge et al., 2008, p. 875). As regards the related approval of the meritocratic idea that was still condemned in 1958 by Michael Dunlop Young in his work "The Rise of the Meritocracy", a recent challenging empirical work that, using data from The Fraser Institute for 160 countries from 1970 to 2019, has demonstrated that (Fig. 2.11):

> at a broad level, our analysis suggests that equity beliefs and distributive justice more generally should be understood with respect to the socioeconomic context and the ideological hegemony of the era within which they are studied and not merely by resorting to universalistic notions of distributive justice. Neoliberal systems have been instrumental in promoting equity-based distributive beliefs, shifting the emphasis from the equality principle to the merit principle. […] Meritocracy as a descriptive belief and an equity-based distributive rule has been identified as the main contributor to the success of neoliberalism […]. In turn, neoliberalism undermines solidarity and redistribution by promoting competitive individualism and the narrative of meritocracy (Goudarzi et al., 2022, pp. 1444, 1446).

2.7 Neoliberal Failure

Therapeutic services, initially developed to nurture self-esteem, have increasingly found themselves treating disorders of the capacity for self-regulation of self-esteem in the face of widespread personal failures caused by the increasing distance between a few very rich people and the relatively impoverished masses. The services have found themselves treating more or less serious forms of "narcissistic wound",

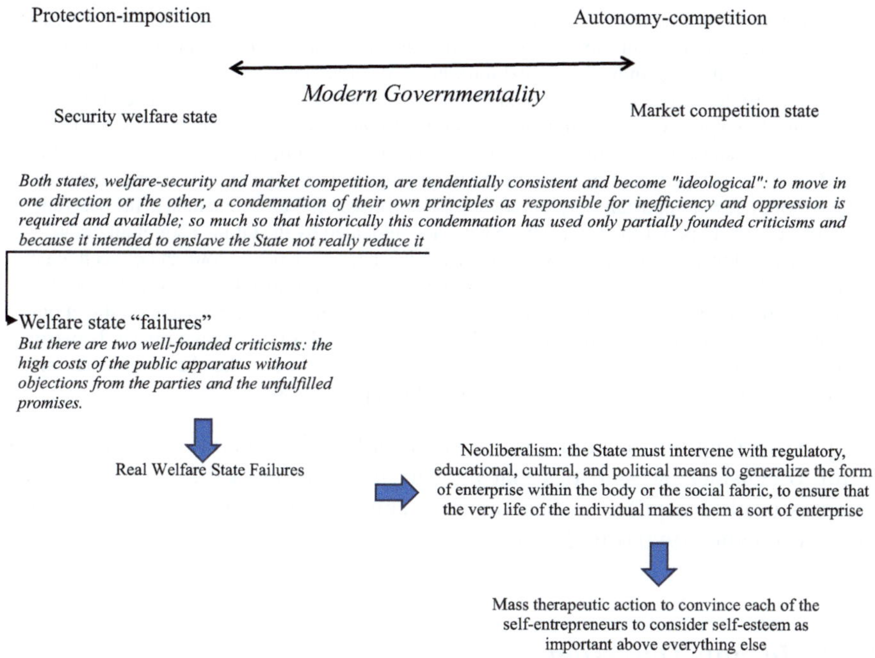

Fig. 2.11 Outline: first and second part

> a multifaceted pathology that has a dimensional continuum of severity and functionality and which manifests itself in various clinical forms - even quite different from each other from a categorical point of view - all characterized by a disturbance in the ability to self-regulate one's self-esteem which manifests itself mainly, even if not exclusively, in interpersonal relationships, through more or less serious and harmful dysfunctional behaviors (Fabj, 2022, p. 7).

2.7.1 Shame

There is no lack of data to authorize the expression "narcissistic epidemic" (Twenge & Campbell, 2009). A book by Christopher Lasch, who in 1979 had already raised the problem, in the 1980s was famous more for the criticisms than for the teachings imparted, but today it is being rediscovered: "Forty years after Lasch, [...] in my clinical practice I am struck by the private, hidden but pervasive character of the experiences of failure and inadequacy of the people [...] who turn to me [...]. And the abject self, the shame, is the emotional state that accompanies [...] the narcissistic wound" (Hoggett, 2017, pp. 365, 372). This corresponds to what Shady Dell'Amico—who has compiled a review of studies following Lasch's book—concludes.

> The idea of a "cultural narcissism" is closely associated with a highly successful book by Christopher Lasch, The Culture of Narcissism, 1979. [...]. However, the concept is

> not lacking in ambiguity. [...] In light of what has been exposed in this article, we can conclude some significant aspects. First of all, how the so-called "age of narcissism" is [...] an age of defensive grandiosity, of exhibitionism as a reaction to a strong self-evaluation, to a deep-rooted sense of sadness and shame. [...] the growth of social expectations, of glowing stereotypes of affirmation and omnipotent fantasies of achievement, has occurred, in recent decades, along with progressive social impoverishment, a loss of power of the middle class and a gradual increase in the unemployment rate in major Western countries. Less money, fewer opportunities, less capacity for professional fulfilment than in the past (and also much less hope for the future) have been accompanied by the taking root of an imagery characterized by a strong grandiosity. The result has been a source of conflict between what one is called to be and the re-sources available, between promised success and a limited capacity for action. It is from this contrast that emerges the synthesis, so characteristic of our time, between the lack of self-esteem and the defensive cult of one's own image, between the demand to be looked at in one's own artificial perfection and the shame of what one perceives oneself to be in reality (Dell'Amico, 2022, pp. 38–39).

By associating this form of narcissistic disorder with an *anxiety syndrome*, it is useful to consider the statistics that indicate its widespread diffusion in Western countries (with exceptions in Scandinavian countries and Canada) and its notable growth even after 1990 (Fig. 2.12).

2.7.2 *Identity Obsession*

The process that led the narcissistic epidemic to shame and then to identity obsession occurred because of the widespread desperate need for security caused by mass narcissism itself in the face of the collapse of the middle class and the frustration of many people who feel they "didn't make it". It is "social withdrawal as a maladaptive response to the fear of being overwhelmed by shame for one's inadequacy, [...] the myth of identity is a product of this impoverishment. [...]. We cling to identity as something that illusorily gives us security: an illusory security, a fallacious and dangerous myth" (Remotti, 2011, p. 18). That it is a myth, Francesco Remotti explains by clarifying how one cannot confuse difference (which implies similarity) and identity which implies otherness. It is a fallacious and dangerous myth because the identity obsession does not provide the security that one would expect within the neoliberal system: its program was conceived in contrast with the security welfare state. It is no coincidence that the identity myth grows together with authoritarian involutions, betraying the same neoliberal statutes of the origins. Therefore, and in conclusion, this is a real failure of the neoliberal project.

2.7.3 *An Alternative Explanation: The "Complexity"*

One might doubt this interpretation by objecting that it looks at the gears and not at the machine. An alternative interpretation has been proposed, "from above", as the

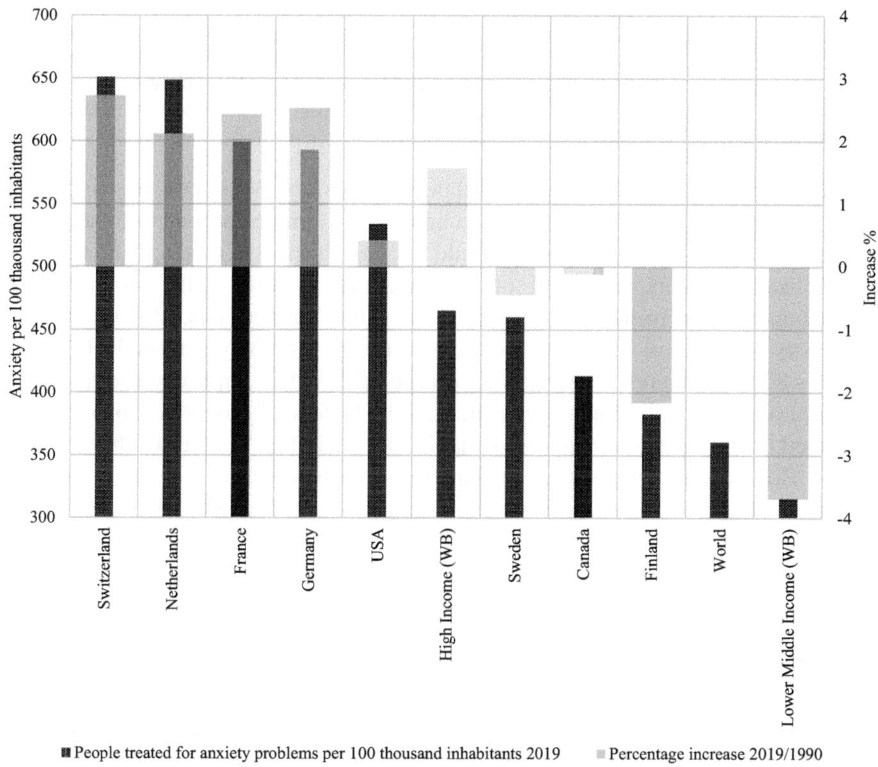

Fig. 2.12 People treated for anxiety problems per 100,000 inhabitants and percentage increases in different countries and in the world 1990–2019 *Source* Figure obtained by processing data from Our World in Data

incapacity of the institutions. According to this interpretation, the true origin of the polycrisis would be in the increase in economic, social, environmental, technological complexity; complexity that has exceeded the capacity of the democratic institutions to understand and govern. The origins of this idea can be found in studies on the failures of development in backward countries. Sheri Berman, one of the most famous supporters of the interpretation from above, wrote:

> [These] explanations locate the main cause of populism in the decline of responsiveness and effectiveness of political institutions, which has made many citizens willing to vote for politicians and parties with antiestablishment, anti–status quo messages. These types of explanations have become popular in recent years among scholars of the advanced industrial world, but they have a long history among students of the developing world, dating back at least to Samuel Huntington's seminal *Political Order in Changing Societies* (1968). Huntington argued that political disorder stemmed from a disjuncture between the challenges countries faced and the strength of their political institutions. As he put it, «The primary problem of politics…is the lag in the development of political institutions behind social and economic change» (Huntington 1968, p. 5). The larger, more complex, more complicated and diverse the demands emanating from society, the more political stability becomes dependent on the existence of strong political institutions capable of responding to them (p. 6).

> [...] Huntington observed that the same challenges that were easily handled in countries with strong and responsive political institutions—e.g., ensuring employment opportunities for an increasingly educated populace, providing avenues of political participation for newly mobilized social groups—caused political disorder and even violence in countries lacking them (Berman, 2021, p. 78).

The same thing would have happened in the developed West in the post-industrial era. Its institutions would have remained behind, too simple compared to the greatly increased complexity to which they would not have been able to adapt and respond.

As always happens, one could find good reasons for either of the two interpretations from above or from below. But one can note the "strange" case of Peter Turchin, University of Connecticut, research director at the "Complexity Science Hub" which includes 80 full-time researchers. The Institute deals with complexity and responses to complexity. His wide-ranging research on the history of crises has obviously not neglected the explanation from above that is specific to the "statute" of the Research Center. However, he arrives at an explanation from below after "the analysis of the dynamics of large-scale human societies organised as states showing that they all experience recurrent waves of political crisis, such as the one we face today. My research team built a database of hundreds of societies across the past 10,000 years to determine what causes them".

> We found that the precise mix of events that leads to crisis varies, but two drivers of instability loom large. The first is popular immiseration—when the economic well-being of broad swathes of a population decline, resulting in wide-spread feelings of discontent and a loss of legitimacy of state institutions. The second [...] factor is elite overproduction—when a society produces too many wealth-holders and people with advanced degrees, and not enough elite positions to satisfy their ambitions. These forces have played a key role in the current crisis in the US. In the past several decades, despite overall economic growth, the quality of life for most Americans has declined. The wealthy have become wealthier, while the incomes and wages of the median American family have stagnated. As a result, our social pyramid has become top-heavy. At the same time, the US began overproducing graduates with advanced degrees. More and more people aspiring to positions of power began fighting over a relatively fixed number of spots. The competition among them has corroded the social norms and institutions that govern society. The US has gone through such crises twice before. The first time ended in civil war. But the second one, which unfolded during the Progressive and New Deal eras, led to a period of unusually broad-based prosperity. Both offer lessons about today's dysfunction and, more importantly, how to fix it. Integrative/disintegrative dynamics in Europe were similar. (https://csh.ac.at/news/from-inequality-to-instability/)

One could therefore discuss at length the merits and demerits of the two alternative explanations of the current crisis. The clear impression, supported by the experience of the "Complexity Science Hub", which by statute should privilege the one from above, is instead that the most well-founded is the one from below (Fig. 2.13).

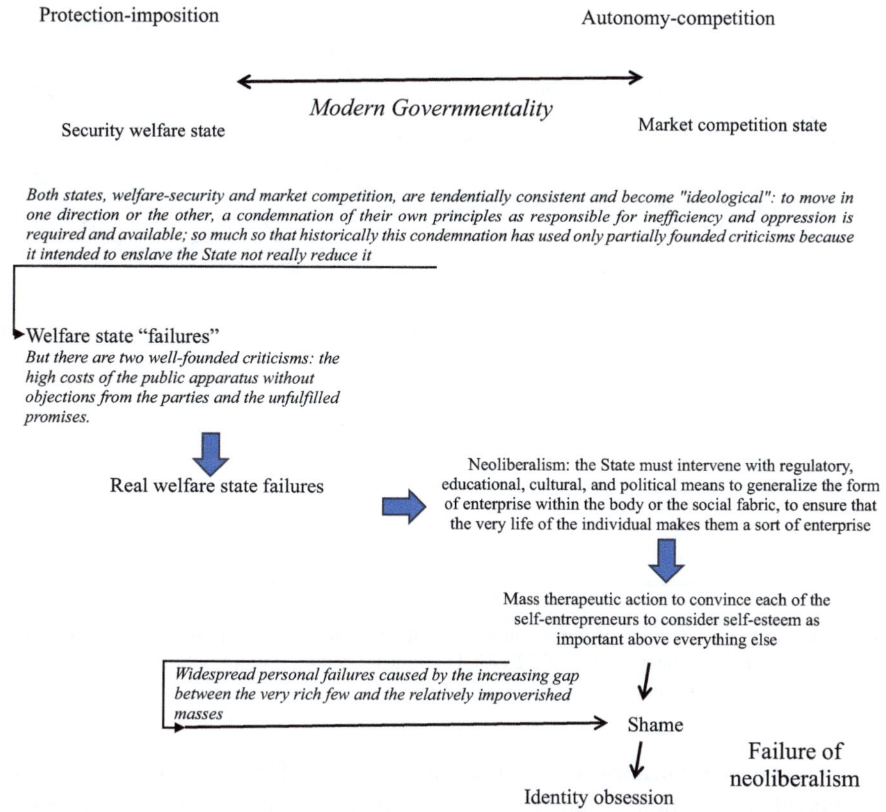

Fig. 2.13 Outline: first, second part, and beginning of the third

2.8 Neoliberal Strengthening and the Crisis of Democracy

If neoliberalism has failed, how is it possible to explain "the paradox of this neoliberalism [...] whose damages, tensions, weaknesses, inconsistencies and omissions are in some ways a source of strength?" (Kiely, 2018, p. 6). As demonstrated, according to the facts, the neoliberal project failed because it betrayed its promises and is paradoxically strengthening itself while democracy is in serious trouble.

2.8.1 *Too Weak Opposition Forces*

One answer is that the forces capable of contesting the neoliberal system are too weak due to the distortion (or "betrayal") of the parties and organizations of the left. The ever-latent contestation of one of the poles of governmentality, that of the neoliberal state, remains disarmed because those who suffer from it and would like to change

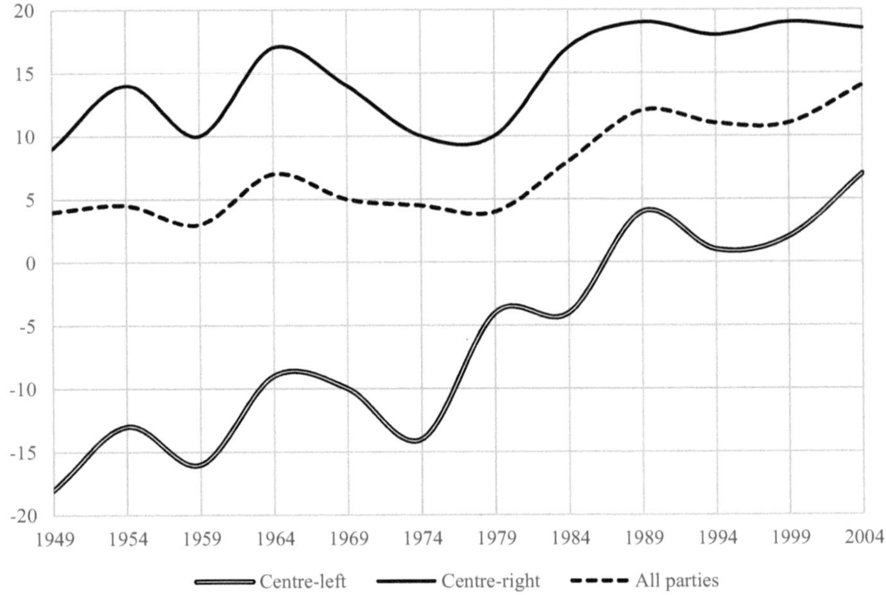

Fig. 2.14 Values of the index of importance of neoliberal contents in the political discourse of the parties on average for the complex of 22 OECD countries *Source* Figure obtained by processing data from Mudge (2018, p. 64)

cannot find the organizational tools to do so. One reason for this disarmament of the anti-liberal contestation would be, according to various reconstructions, the adoption of right-wing programs by the parties and organizations of the left starting from the end of the 1960s. In the remarkable book by the Berkeley sociologist Stephanie Mudge (2018), neoliberal content in public discourse of the parties in OECD countries from 1949 to 2004 are reported.[30] Overall, there has been an increase in the weight of neoliberal content since the end of the 1960s. But the contribution of the center-right parties to this growth has been modest. On the contrary, the contribution of the center-left parties has been decisive, moreover, the timing of this change has been singular if one considers the common belief that the "fall of the Berlin Wall" would have had the greatest impact. If this had been the case, the rightward turn of the left-wing parties should have occurred only from the end of the 1980s; instead, it occurred 20 years earlier (Fig. 2.14).

[30] "I characterise neoliberal politics using a composite index that takes into account emphasis [...] on the discourse of opportunity rather than equality [...], on law and order and militarism rather than welfare state and pacifism [...], on efficiency, subsidiarity, free market orthodoxy, productivity and trade openness [...], on representation of the financial professions and white-collar workers rather than [...] the working classes [...] and trade unions" (Mudge 2018, p. 381). Stephanie Mudge used a database that she had developed with an impressive documentation effort, extracting the parties' positions on 113 categories of political discourse taken from election manifestos and official declarations on the occasion of votes of confidence in governments (Mudge 2018, p. 379).

Stephanie Mudge also presents data referring to three content items indicated as: finance and white collar, law-order and market, anti-Keynesianism. The following graphs are obtained which may suggest some explanation for the surprising temporal profile of the rightward turn of the left parties (Fig. 2.15).

In the discourse of the center-left parties, the importance of "finance and white-collar workers" has grown a little but only since the 1990s when it declined in the discourse of the center-right. The importance of "law and order" has grown much more so as not to fall behind the center-right. But above all, anti-Keynesianism has grown, which has not been growing in the center-right: therefore, an autonomous and specific choice of the center-left. Furthermore, it is precisely this growth of anti-Keynesianism that has determined the timing of the center-left parties' turn to the right since the end of the 1960s, so clearly in advance of the fall of the Berlin Wall. It is for this reason, strengthened by the study of the biographies of many representative personalities, that Stephanie Mudge has proposed an interpretation centered on the reciprocal influences between political personnel and economists in the left-wing parties. Until the 1940s, even in the phases in which left-wing parties were in government, the training of managers, who often came from journalism, remained the traditional historical-literary type, and so did that of managers who took on roles in economic ministries. After the war, and for the first time in the history of left-wing parties, leaders and staff began to study economics and economists began to become leaders and staff. In the Keynesian era, it was, in fact, essential to develop the economic policy agenda to respond to social demands. Since then, these relationships between politics and economic studies have always remained strong. But from the end of the 1960s, the paradigm of economic disciplines changed in an anti-Keynesian direction. Young economists and the most influential economics schools began to conceive of another task: no longer that of responding to social demands, but that of influencing these demands to adapt them to the "laws of the market system".

This explanation of the persistence of neoliberalism despite its failures due to the involution of left-wing parties, which have adopted the anti-Keynesian agenda and thus lost any anti-neoliberal challenging force, has its truth but is not exhaustive. The left-wing parties have had a long history and were complex organizations that responded to many internal and external influences and needs. One may wonder what was behind this drastic simplification whereby they changed projects and nature because several leaders and staff had studied the neoclassical paradigm and had adhered to it. Furthermore, the neoliberal project did not only involve the parties. The question is what caused the weakening of the challenging force throughout the social system. On this deeper and broader level, the explanations available are essentially that: there would be no alternative; the neoliberal system uses the same collective resources that it is fighting; its crisis fuels defensive and compensatory reactions capable of sustaining it even at the cost of distorting its statutes in an authoritarian sense; and even if unnoticed, the system has actually already changed into something worse.

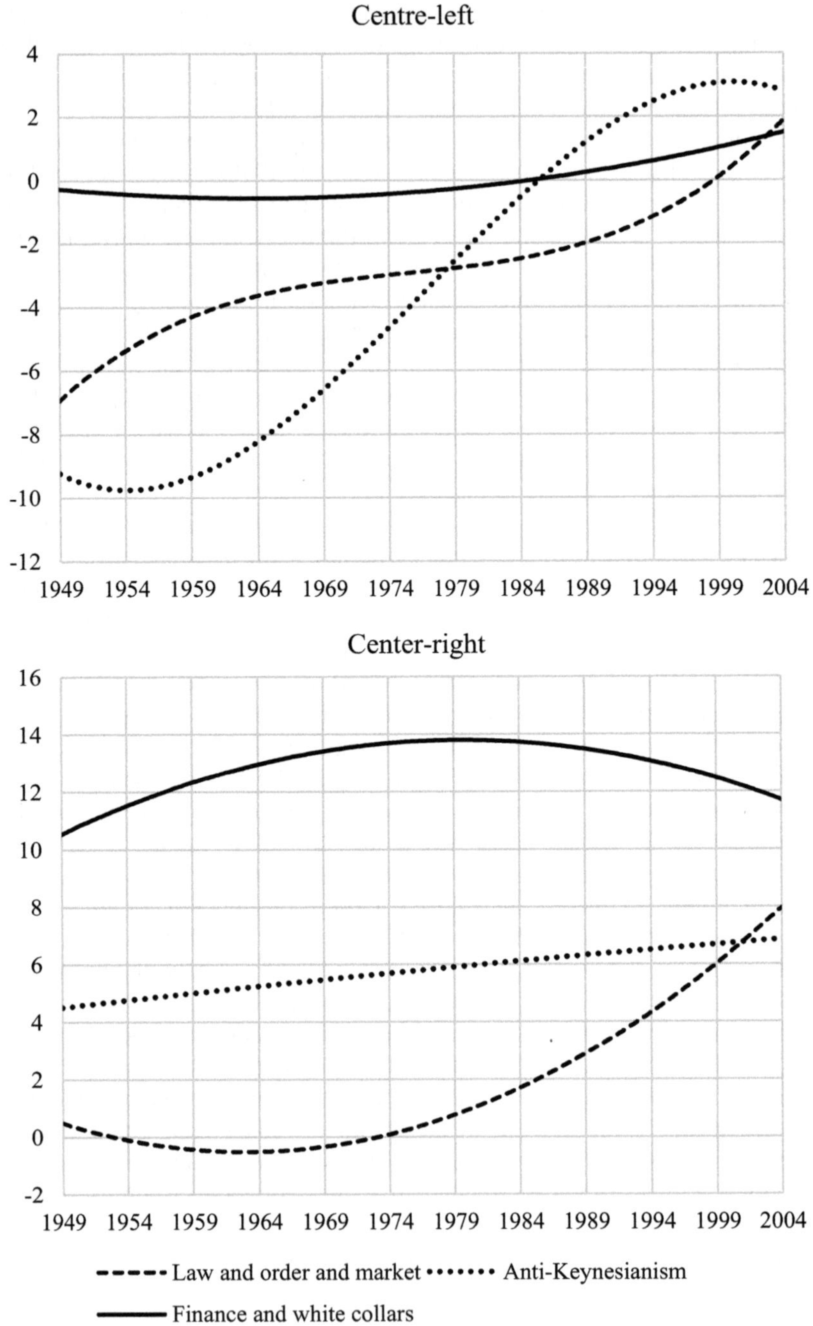

Fig. 2.15 Trends in the values of the importance index of three types of neoliberal content in the political discourse of parties on average for the set of 22 OECD countries *Source* Figure obtained by processing data from Mudge (2018, p. 65)

2.8.2 There Is No Alternative

There is no alternative is the expression that was often used and became an acronym: TINA. Justified by the failures of planning, the statement is also based on the fact that the neoclassical economic theory underlying neoliberalism has indeed been stripped of its foundation by the "heterodox" critique (for being based on chimerical assumptions such as perfectly rational agents, complete markets, perfect competition, and an inadequate theory of capital), but without it being possible to formulate an equally general alternative theory. This was written by Luigi Pasinetti (2007), one of the protagonists of the "Cambridge School", who produced the most advanced critique of neoclassical theory. Alternatives exist, but on the terrain of the "art of government" that goes beyond economic theory. Giorgio Lunghini wrote commenting on Pasinetti's book:

> In Pasinetti's view, the task of institutions is to create and maintain that "natural" configuration of the economic system that ensures full employment, closing its degrees of freedom with all the procedures, rules and laws necessary for this purpose. Pasinetti's "natural" system is not, as the terminology might suggest, a mode of production governed by inviolable laws of nature; on the contrary, by difference it shows the negative specificities of the monetary economies of production in which we live, and indicates the ways in which they could be conformed to the "natural" system [...] which, due to its properties, should be conceived and pursued, through institutions, as an ideal system. There is a reversal with respect to Quesnay's terminology, which called ordre naturel the order imposed by nature and ordre positif the order imposed by society; so that while Quesnay invoked laissez faire, Pasinetti distances himself from it. Needless to say, the institutional level of the discourse is no longer pure economic theory, but opens historical, sociological and political perspectives. On the other hand, good political economy, according to Keynes, is a careful mix of economic theory and the art of government (Lunghini, 2008, p. 117).

But economic thought has made significant progress in recent years. Dani Rodrik, Suresh Naidu, and Gabriel Zucmann, have claimed the progress made and those in progress in light of which it cannot be argued that economic studies have stopped at the neoclassical paradigm: "Contemporary economics is finally freeing itself from its market fetishism, offering numerous tools that we can use to make society more inclusive" (Rodrik et al., 2019, p. 1). The art of government will have to be dealt with later, but as far as economic theory is concerned, it is significant to remember that there are steps forward even on the central question that remained unresolved according to Pasinetti, that of the regime to adopt for productive capital.[31]

[31] "While there is no difficulty in producing arguments in favor of private ownership of consumer goods, private ownership of the means of production is a more controversial issue, simply because, in an industrial system, every decision on the use of capital goods has consequences that affect society as a whole. The problem is, however, rather thorny and complex on an institutional level. In a free society, the source of ownership of capital goods and the source of ownership of consumer goods appear to be the same. If we consider it legitimate for each individual to decide to dispose of his savings in the way he prefers, or to accumulate them, for example, in the form of gold bars, why should one object, or interfere, in the face of their accumulation in the form of capital goods? A clear and non-controversial answer to this question – which emerges from a typically new institutional problem, generated by the Industrial Revolution – has not yet been found" (Pasinetti 2007, p. 17).

> The Coase theorem[32] suggests it does not matter for efficiency how property rights are allocated as long as transaction costs are zero. But the caveat does a lot of work here: transaction costs matter greatly. So, we must make choices. Should a job belong to a company, a worker, or a combination? Perhaps the company itself should be owned by a third party—a local government entity, say—and simply ensure incentive compatibility for managers and workers. That might sound crazy to most Americans, but China has eked unprecedented rates of economic growth out of such a property-rights regime. Perhaps employers should have property rights (for a fixed period) only over new assets they create, with existing assets distributed among other claimants. That too sounds crazy, unless we realize that is exactly what the patent system does, giving innovators temporary ownership over new "intellectual property." Perhaps the government, on behalf of the general public, should retain part ownership of new technologies since so much of innovation relies on public infrastructure (public R&D and subsidies, higher education, the legal regime, etc.). The choices that need to be made must consider distributional concerns and depend both on our ultimate objectives and the potential fit with local context (Rodrik et al., 2019).

These advances raise doubts that there is no alternative. But few know about the progress of the "heterodox" economics. Above all, whether there is an alternative in the abstract or not, it is certain that it is not permitted by the large multinational economic forces. Terry Hathaway wrote:

> Big business was powerful even before the neoliberal period, but the particular institutional constructions of neoliberalism around the world have repeatedly favored increasing the size of businesses, broadening the scope of their activity, granting them new rights, enabling new forms of corporate organization, and decreasing their responsibilities, while at the same time speaking of freedom, consumer choice, and a cosmopolitan global system. In this way, neoliberalism has fundamentally functioned in the interests of multinational corporate power (Hathaway, 2020, p. 332).

In fact, multinational companies have aimed directly and explicitly at increasing their power. The case of Amazon is emblematic. It has achieved a turnover close to the GDP of an entire country like Greece, controls 50% of all electronics trade in the United States, has increased its size exponentially by pushing tens of thousands of merchants out of the market, and all this while showing relative disinterest in profits (Fig. 2.16).

Following this dominant role assumed by multinationals thanks to neoliberalism that has favored them, has hidden and hides their power, it is obvious that they use it to defend neoliberalism. "The literature on neoliberalism has noted, but not adequately explored, the power of corporations. Likewise, the literature on corporate power has rarely connected it to neoliberalism" (Hathaway, 2020, p. 315).

---

[32] Ronald Coase, Nobel Prize winner for economics in 1991, published the "theorem" (which later had countless reinterpretations and elaborations) in an article in 1960 (The Problem of Social Cost, *The Journal of Law and Economics* 3, 1960, pp. 1–44). Transaction costs are payments or lost earnings due to the search for a partner for the exchange and the necessary information, to the purchase of the means and supports to reach the agreement, to enforce it, and to execute it.

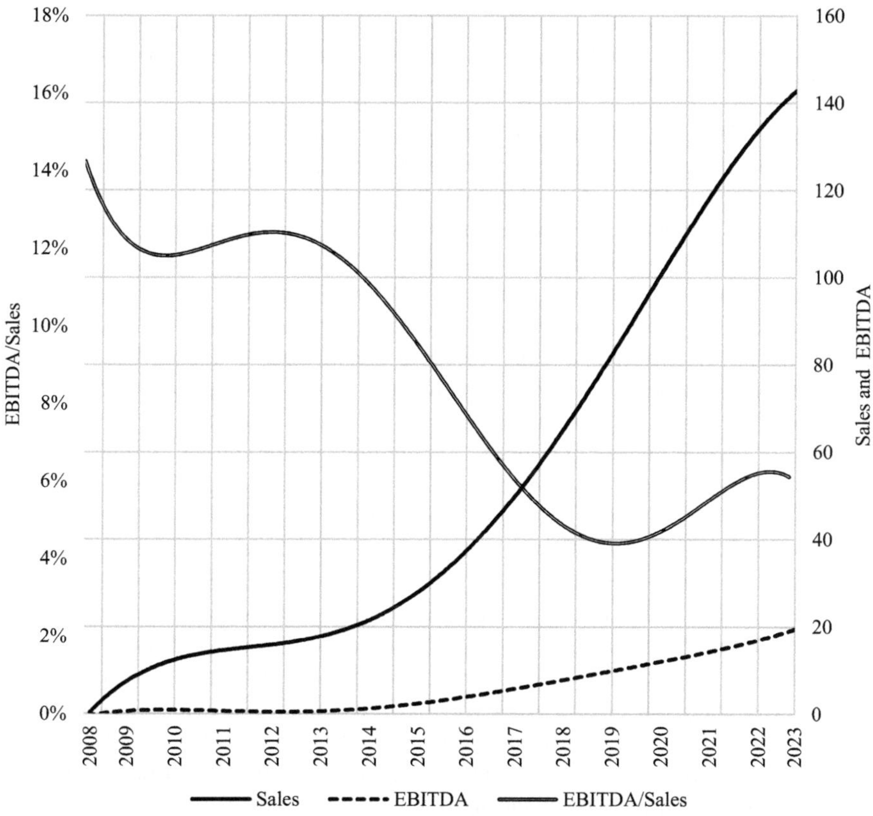

Fig. 2.16 Amazon: Sales and EBITDA (Earnings Before Interest Taxes Depreciation and Amortization), billions of dollars; EBITDA/Sales ratio %, tendencies *Source* Figure obtained by processing data from https://www.macrotrends.net/stocks/charts

2.8.3 Exploitation of Persecuted Collective Resources

The second explanation is suggested by observing characteristic neoliberal contradictions that are also paradoxically elements of strength. There is the one denounced by Castoriadis for public spending, which neoliberalism was supposed to reduce but was cut very relatively. The ideology and practice of denigration of the government and the vaunted intentions of "starving the beast" were, in reality, aimed at freeing the public budget from traditional controls to put it under the control of emerging forces. Another contradiction-instrumentalization is added, reported by Pierre Bourdieu. According to the French sociologist:

> Despite the growing volume of the population in danger and the extraordinary mass of suffering produced by this type of political-economic regime, the social order does not dissolve into chaos because of the continuity or survival of those same institutions and representations of the old order that are the target of the neoliberal process of dismantling:

> all the work of all categories of social workers, all forms of solidarity in the institutions, family and beyond the family [...], the reserves of social capital that [...] is destined to be extinguished, but not in the short term (Bourdieu 1998, p. 3).

If the few data available are considered over long periods of time, surprising facts emerge. Robert Putnam managed to collect information for 32 large civic organizations in the United States throughout the last century, from 1900 to 2000. And he calculated the percentages of participation in relation to the reference population: for example, the share of all Jewish women in America enrolled in Hadassah (a Jewish feminist association), the share of Catholic men belonging to the Knights of Columbus, the share of adult men belonging to one of the various clubs such as the Lions, the Moose, the Elks. Keeping the number of these civic organizations constant over time, the trends in membership rates correspond to the profile of other indices (Putnam & Garret, 2020) such as "prevalence of we over I", "social cohesion", "mutual respect in politics", "economic egalitarianism". Undergoing the neoliberal turn, the profile is one of growth from the beginning of the century until the 1960s and 1970s, then of sharp decline (Putnam, 2001, p. 48). But there is other evidence of a completely different trend. In the "World Values Survey" one question was: are you an active member of charitable or humanitarian organizations? For the United States, in 1981 6.6% of the interviewees (a representative sample of the adult population) had answered yes. But the share had risen to a sensational 18% in 2022. Another question (for which answers are available over a shorter time frame) was: do you carry out unpaid work for services to help the elderly, the poor, the disabled? The frequency of affirmative answers was 3% in 1989 but 8% in 2004, again in the United States. In the Swedish sample (the only one in Europe): 6% and 11%. According to these data, what Bourdieu wrote is confirmed. Neoliberalism has depressed participation in large traditional civic organizations, but at the same time has caused a significant increase in voluntary work in "grassroots welfare" activities.

2.8.4 Personal Defensive Reactions and the Crisis of Democracy

These explanations of neoliberal persistence despite failures are useful, but they are not enough. Those who suffer from them, especially the impoverished middle class, cannot be content to blame the parties of the left, nor the fact that there is no alternative—a narrative mainly of the rich—and to depend on precisely what is threatened: public assistance and social solidarity. They should rebel and fight. If they do not do so, if they blame democratic institutions and look for scapegoats, it must be because their "heart and soul" have been corrupted to the point that they are no longer capable. The explanation that considers reinforcements of the neoliberal system generated by its own failure at the level of consciousness is therefore important. The explanation seems to be this: "The inability of people to achieve neoliberal narcissistic fulfilment [...] generates defensive and compensatory reactions that root the logic of neoliberalism and [...] manifest themselves in what Kohut[33] has defined narcissistic anger" (Gammon, 2017, p. 1).

The mechanism starts from shame due to the perception of being inadequate, which is different from guilt. "Both guilt and shame derive from the work of an [...] internal judge, but while in guilt the judge deals with what one does, in shame he deals with who one is. [...]. Most analysts agree that anxiety [...] from shame concerns the loss of self, abandonment, rejection, exclusion" (Hogget 2017, p. 373). Some data on anxiety have already been seen. It can be added that the widespread diffusion of states of shame in Western countries, although systematically hidden to the point of being qualified by experts as a kind of taboo[34] is evidenced by the increasing number of writings by therapists who have elaborated their experience with patients. "There has been an increase in clinical interest in shame in the psychotherapeutic literature and many of the problems related to anxiety have now been reconceptualized as problems of shame" (Sinha, 2017, p. 251). If one frees oneself from guilt by repairing the damage or attributing it to reasons of force majeure, freeing oneself from shame is impossible, and it pushes one to establish violently separate identities between oneself and others. "By looking at others with contempt, some of the tears in one's fragile sense of self can be temporarily repaired. [...]. Scheler defines the delusion of resentment as the process by which the experience of impotence is transformed into its opposite, a feeling of superiority, through a devaluation of the qualities of the other (Scheler, 1992, p. 126); this is exactly what Lansky means by projection and inversion of shame (Lansky, 1999) and others call humiliated fury" (Hogget, 2017, p. 374). Humiliated fury is the widespread feeling among the impoverished middle class who have suffered economic losses and above all losses of dignity.

The progressive left as a whole, and not only the parties, has not been able to respond to this discomfort. "The response [...] has often been contemptuous. How could they be so stupid as to vote, like turkeys, for Christmas? But by insulting the intelligence of the class [...] left behind [...], the left contributes to the shame of this social group" (Hogget 2017, p. 376). The progressive forces and the new educated workforce have thus ended up reconfirming neoliberal subjectivation, authorizing even more investment in it and falling deeper into its contradictions. "Addressing the

---

[33] Heinz Kohut (1913–1981), an Austrian physician and psychoanalyst naturalized in the United States, was, with Otto Friedmann Kernberg, one of the main psychodynamic theorists of narcissistic disorder. Kohut and Kernberg present very different models, for some completely incompatible so as to leave the subject of NPD (narcissistic personality disorder) in complete confusion. For others, their two approaches are complementary, Kohut dealing mainly with "hypervigilant" (and less serious) narcissism and Kernberg with "grandiose" (and more serious) narcissism, thus giving more importance to one or the other typology of a disorder that presents itself as extremely varied. The passage from Kohut to which Gammon refers is this: "Narcissistic rage presents itself in many forms; all, however, share a specific psychology that gives them a distinct position within the vast field of human aggression. The need for revenge, to right a wrong, to mend a wound by any means, and the deeply rooted and relentless drive in the pursuit of these goals gives no respite to those who have suffered narcissistic damage" (Kohut 1972, p. 364).

[34] "Shame [...] becomes invisible even for most social and behavioral researchers. In the numerous studies on the subject, a taboo is implicit, so much so that often the forbidden word is not used at all. Similar terms are used" (Scheff 2014, p. 116).

anger induced by neoliberal subjectivation with counter-aggression proves unproductive. [...]. It would be necessary to create the necessary conditions for an empathetic reactivity with those who are trapped in its logic. [...Instead] hoping for a catharsis resulting [...] from further investment in neoliberal subjectivities [...] could create traumatic situations of frustration, resulting in even harsher manifestations of neoliberal anger" (Gammon, 2017, p. 28). In turn, this anger, which cannot blame the system of competition, attributes all its ills to the weaknesses of democracy for which it seeks solutions based on leaders, up to the point of new forms of fascism. "Mass frustration intensifies, fueling discontent, which leaders address by fueling new resentments and conflicts. They cannot stop or their popularity decreases because they cannot solve real problems [...]. It follows that authoritarian neoliberalism is intrinsically unstable and its dynamics, perhaps unintentionally, will offer increasing importance and scope to the emergence of modern forms of fascism" (Bonanno, 2019, p. 22).

These authoritarian forms are already consistent with the ongoing transformations of neoliberalism, which also resists through distortions of its statutes. Unfortunately, the world is not going in the direction hoped for by the "willing" like Rodrik, Naidu, and Zucmann, who, as seen, rely on developments in economic theory toward forms of socialization of property rights. These distortions go in exactly the opposite direction.

> Since 2008, critiques [...] of neoliberalism [...] have come to focus [...] on the sovereignty of property rights [...]. And some leading figures on the right [...] no longer see competition as a force [...] for the good of all, but something that "losers" believe in [...]. The task [...] would now be to capture "final values" by building monopolies. [...]. In such a world, the values of democracy, equality and tolerance have come under renewed attack from new forms of authoritarian government [...] and the game of corporate big power (Davies & Gane, 2021, pp. 22–23).

2.8.5 *This Is Already Another System*

These considerations by Davies and Gane resonate with those of Yanis Varoufakis who sees a transformation of the system, which began after the 2007–2008 crisis. In the book "Technofeudalism: What Killed Capitalism" Varoufakis (2023) argues that it is no longer even a question of the "construction of monopolies" that the existence of the market would imply, but of the liquidation of the market itself, since the digital platform with which transactions are increasingly made establishes everything for everyone: what is shown, how, what is offered, at what price, at what time. The platform and the algorithm concentrate in themselves the power and the function of matching the single buyer with the single seller.

> It is not even some form of hypercapitalist digital market. Even the ugliest markets are meeting places where people can interact and exchange information reasonably freely. In fact, it is even worse than a totally monopolized market – there, at least, buyers can talk to each other, form associations, perhaps organize a consumer boycott to force the monopolist to reduce the price or improve the quality. The same is not true in the realm of Jeff [the fictional character who controls the algorithm that presides over the exchanges], where everything

> and everyone is intermediated not by the disinterested invisible hand of the market, but by an algorithm that works for Jeff's bottom line and dances exclusively to his music (Varoufakis, 2023, p. 104).

The second transformation concerns the accumulation of capital, which no longer occurs only through the extraction of surplus value in the wage relationship, but increasingly through the unpaid labor of all users of digital communication devices, given that the capital that counts is increasingly Cloud Capital, the means of production of value obtained through the privatization of the Internet, which consists in the accumulation of Big Data and its exploitation through artificial intelligence algorithms.

The progressive reduction of the extraction of surplus value through the wage relationship

> is unprecedented. Workers employed by General Electric, ExxonMobil, General Motors, or any other large corporation rake in, in terms of wages and salaries, roughly 80% of the company's revenue. This proportion becomes larger at smaller companies. Big Tech workers, by contrast, rake in less than 1% of their companies' revenue. The reason is that paid labor does only a fraction of the work that Big Tech relies on. Most of the work is done for free by billions of people (Varoufakis, 2023, p. 102).

Other data can be added. For example, on average over the last 10 years, the ratio between capitalization in billions of dollars (market value of shares) and employees has been equal to 1 for Volkswagen, but 109 for Nvidia, the second largest U.S. company and world leader in artificial intelligence applications (it produces graphics processors for the video game and professional market, modules for smartphones and for the automotive industry). The ratio is 22 and 14 for Apple and Microsoft, the first and third largest U.S. companies. It is also 22 for Meta Platforms (Facebook), the seventh largest U.S. company. A similar ratio in traditional sector companies is found only in large oil companies that thrive on extractive revenue, such as Saudi Arabian Oil Co. As for Cloud Capital:

> By using neural networks to process gargantuan amounts of data, reinforcement-learning algorithms could do things that Don Draper couldn't have imagined. By observing the reactions of millions of people to their suggestions billions of times every hour, they could train at lightning speed not only to influence us, but also to perform the new and fascinating trick [...]: to be influenced by the way they influence us; to influence themselves in light of the way they influence humans (Varoufakis, 2023, p. 96).

Value and unpaid work:

> The algorithm is in the business of selling things to us, while it sells our attention to others. Then something deeper comes into play that gives the owners of the algorithm immense power – to predict our behavior, to guide our preferences, to influence our decisions, to change our minds, thus reducing us to their unpaid servants, whose job is to provide our information, our attention, our identity and above all the behavioral patterns that train their algorithms (Varoufakis, 2023 p. 96).

Finally, the third transformation necessarily connected to the first two, is that the system is supported by the money issued by the Central Bank. The income extracted by Cloud Capital from the value circuit, that is, from profits and wages of the traditional sector, erodes the self-financing of investments and consumption that must be financed by debt from banks that rely on the central bank. But cloud capitalists are the most capable of grabbing the liquidity that is continually created. The circle therefore becomes cumulative, pushing up the share value of Cloud Capital, and depressing consumption and investments.

The process has already been seen. It started after the financial crisis of 2007–2008 and continued, changing scale with the pandemic. On the morning of 12 August 2020, the media in England reported that GDP had fallen quarter-on-quarter by 20.4%, the worst reduction in the history of data, more than in the United States (−11%), France (−14%), Italy (−13%), Germany (−10%), and Japan (−7%). Since the expectation was for a reduction that was indeed heavy but at most 15%, it was logical to expect a stock market crash. But 15 min later, another piece of news broke: the London stock exchange had risen by 2.3%. "This is what made 12 August 2020, so bizarre: news far worse than expected had caused the stock market to rise. Nothing like this had ever happened before" (Varoufakis, 2023, p. 111).

> What had happened? The news [...] was so bad that City traders in London had realised this: when things are this bad, the Bank of England panics. And what have panicked central banks been doing since the crash of 2008? They print money and give it to us. And what do we do with all the money [...] the central bank issues? We buy stocks, driving up their price. And if prices are going to go up, only a fool would miss out. [...]. And they bought, causing the City to buck the gravitational laws of capitalism. The trend was not limited to London. When the pandemic began to hit [...], authorities on both sides of the Atlantic, in Japan and elsewhere, responded by doing much more than they had done [...] in 2008: they printed money and gave it to financiers at zero cost in the hope that it would support investment in businesses, thereby generating stable jobs and preventing the economy from collapsing. It didn't. Fearing that ordinary companies would not be able to repay them, financiers lent the central bank money only to big business. And that [...] invested only in cloud capital. [...]. Conglomerates based on traditional capital, such as General Electric and Volkswagen, refused to invest the central bank money [...] because [...] they saw the same thing the bankers had seen: masses of ordinary people condemned to low wages, shitty jobs and diminished prospects – a sea of people unable to afford new high-value products. So why invest in this? Instead, they would have made a profitable operation with zero risk and stress: they would have used it to buy back the shares of their own company, driving up the price and, with it, their bonuses (Varoufakis, 2023, pp. 111–112).

This experience taught capitalists one thing: when central banks print money and lend it at very low rates to support the economy and, to avoid inflation and instability, governments reduce public spending (austerity), there are great prospects of gains by choosing to invest not in the traditional production process but in Cloud Capital that increases power over everything. This explains the strange coupling between the reduction of the interest rate and the increase in unemployment that we have already seen in Fig. 1.17. Furthermore, the system works as a self-reproducing process.

> Poisoned money flowed freely, but not for serious investment, good jobs, or anything that would revive the lost spirit of capitalism. Instead, shareholders and executives bought up land, empty warehouses, works of art, chalets in Switzerland, entire villages in Italy, and even islands in Greece, the Caribbean, and the Pacific. They collected soccer teams, superyachts, and, at some point, they started buying digital assets like Bitcoin or things called NFTs [Non-Fungible Tokens, a digital asset, often a piece of art, music, or a collectible, that is

> unique, a digital certificate of ownership for a unique item, stored on a blockchain] that they didn't understand what they were or what to do with. This is how socialism for bankers and austerity for the rest of us stymied the dynamism of capitalism, pushing it into a state of golden stagnation. [...] Cloud capital was the only pulsating force that benefited from the poisoning of money. (Varoufakis, 2023, pp. 121–122).

All this would explain the enormous growth of the stock market in the United States driven by technology stocks regardless of returns. There is a purely speculative explanation, but Varoufakis' seems more credible. Capitalism has already become something else (Fig. 2.17).

"Cloud rent" means how much you pay to use the Cloud in addition to what you would pay if it were a public good set equal to the minimum cost necessary for its production, in turn equal to the yield or utility in its use. If the Cloud were a public good it would remain included in the Capital of the traditional sector and the system would remain as in the traditional capitalist sector part. The subtractions and the need for re-injections occur because Cloud Capital collects rents that do not correspond to production costs. To remedy the "subtractions" of investments due to the rents paid to Cloud Capital, the Central Bank operates re-injections to support them with credit. But a significant part of the added credit is captured by cloudists who use it to purchase, in addition to "luxury" goods (outside the represented circuit), their own shares and those of other cloudists, to corrupt politics, to put ever larger segments of the traditional capitalist sector under control. The financial system prefers to lend

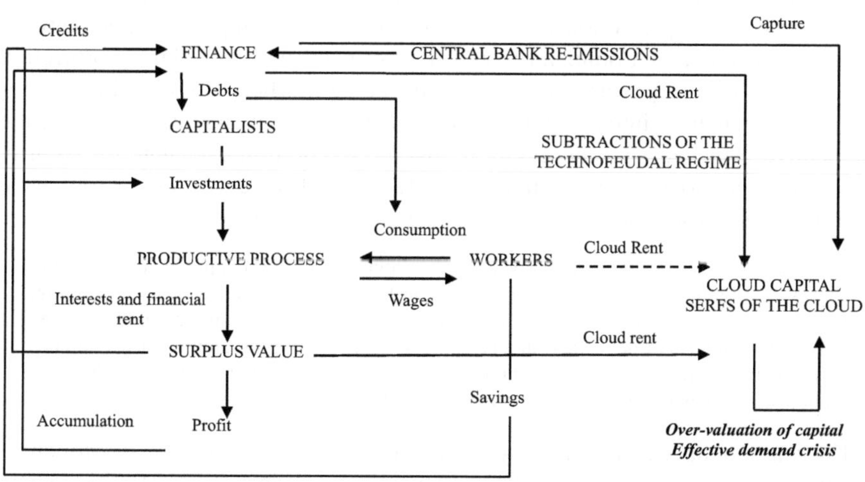

Fig. 2.17 Technofeudal System "model" *Source* Figure obtained by processing data from Varoufakis (2023). *Note* "financial rent" means the cost paid by the companies of the "Production Process" for the loans from the banks, in addition to the "Interest" which also includes the operating costs of the "Finance" system equipment. The dotted line under the "Cloud rent" of the employees represents the fact that their explicit payments for IT services are modest in relation to what other operators pay. By far the most significant contribution of the employees is the unpaid hidden work they do as "Cloud serfs".

to those who earn secure incomes rather than those who earn unstable profits and wages. This capture requires new injections that are also captured and so on. The result is a continuous growth of cloud securities, chronic lack of effective demand, increased frequency, and severity of crises. Adding the public sector (not represented in the figure for simplicity), the result does not change. The public sector also suffers subtractions: less revenue since taxpayers pay the cloud rent, less public consumption and investment because the State also pays the cloud rent. The external sector remains in which there will be a hardening of the fight for markets, and consequently an increase in military spending, another subtraction, and a relaunch of imperialism (which is already evident).

The result would therefore lie outside of capitalism, characterized by the market and accumulation through wage relations. Neoliberalism persists as an ideology that approves the winners and condemns the losers regardless of the means used to win or the lack of means of the losers. But the new system is not one of "autonomy and competition". And, obviously, not even of "protection-imposition". It would be a hierarchical authoritarian system of general self-oppression, maintained by the fact that everyone voluntarily serves it without even realizing it.

2.9 An Entirely "Panoptic" System

Post-neoliberalism would thus solve the problem of modern governmentality as an oscillation between protection-imposition and autonomy-competition, and between security and freedom. Command would impose itself without offering protection in exchange because people suffer it without seeing it. There is no need to pay for autonomy by entering into competition because the algorithm has already solved the competitive game. It is not necessary to give up freedom in exchange for security because the network gives all the freedom and security desired by deciding for people what they want. The system would become a gigantic Panopticon.

> The Panopticon is a machine for dissociating the seeing-being seen couple: in the peripheral ring one is totally seen, without ever seeing; in the central tower, one sees everything, without ever being seen. An important device, because it automates and de-individualizes power. This finds its principle less in a person than in a certain programmed distribution of bodies, surfaces, lights, glances; in an apparatus whose internal mechanisms produce the relationship in which individuals are caught (Foucault, 1976, pp. 93–94).

The Panopticon was invented by Jeremy Bentham (1748–1832), an economist and philosopher. During his travels, he arrived in 1787 in southern Russia, where his brother Samuel, an engineer and inventor, had been called since 1780 by Prince Grigory Aleksandrovich Potemkin and where, in the autumn of the previous year, he had designed a particular industrial plant, circular in shape with a tower in the center from which the very undisciplined English technicians recruited by the prince could be constantly monitored. He had called it Inspection House, and later Panopticon from pân "all" and optikón "visible".

> The Panopticon was conceived in the autumn of 1786 at the Krichev estate in the southern Mogilev province of White Russia [...] under the name of "Inspection House" [...]. The estate belonged to Prince Grigorii Potemkin, the most influential of Catherine II's favourites during the 1780s. It had about a thousand square miles, with five towns and more than a hundred villages. By 1784, Potemkin had built numerous manufactories for his own profit [...]. The local workforce never gave Bentham any particular problems with discipline. [...]. On the contrary, by the summer of 1786, the English technicians became increasingly difficult to control. [...]. John Debraw [...] appointed for the purpose [...] presented a report to Bentham in September 1786, condemning the lack of discipline among the English [...]. He listed laziness, theft, quarrels, drinking [...]. It seems [...] then, that the specific problem of poor discipline among these English people was the immediate reason for the design of the Panopticon. [...]. However, while plans were being made to build it, the project failed to materialize. Prince Potemkin sold his estate in May 1787 and Samuel Bentham was forced to leave (Werrett, 1999, pp. 3–5).

The machine for dissociating seeing and being seen was born in the feudal regime, to make the power of control and discipline as efficient and inexpensive as possible, indecipherable, and hidden. "Potemkin owned a thousand square miles with five towns and more than a hundred villages", he also owned all the people who lived there and had no problems of discipline from them. The English who came to work were undisciplined, free men, and for them the Panopticon was made, so as to be able to discipline them silently, secretly, so as to make them obedient like the serfs who had always been living on the land and in the villages of the master. The Panopticon also presents another characteristic. By solving in a machine every problem of discipline, abolishing for governability every problematic conciliation between opposite poles, it evokes and indeed suggests only one way out: an "anti-panoptic" system. Thus, there is the completion of the outline (Fig. 2.18).

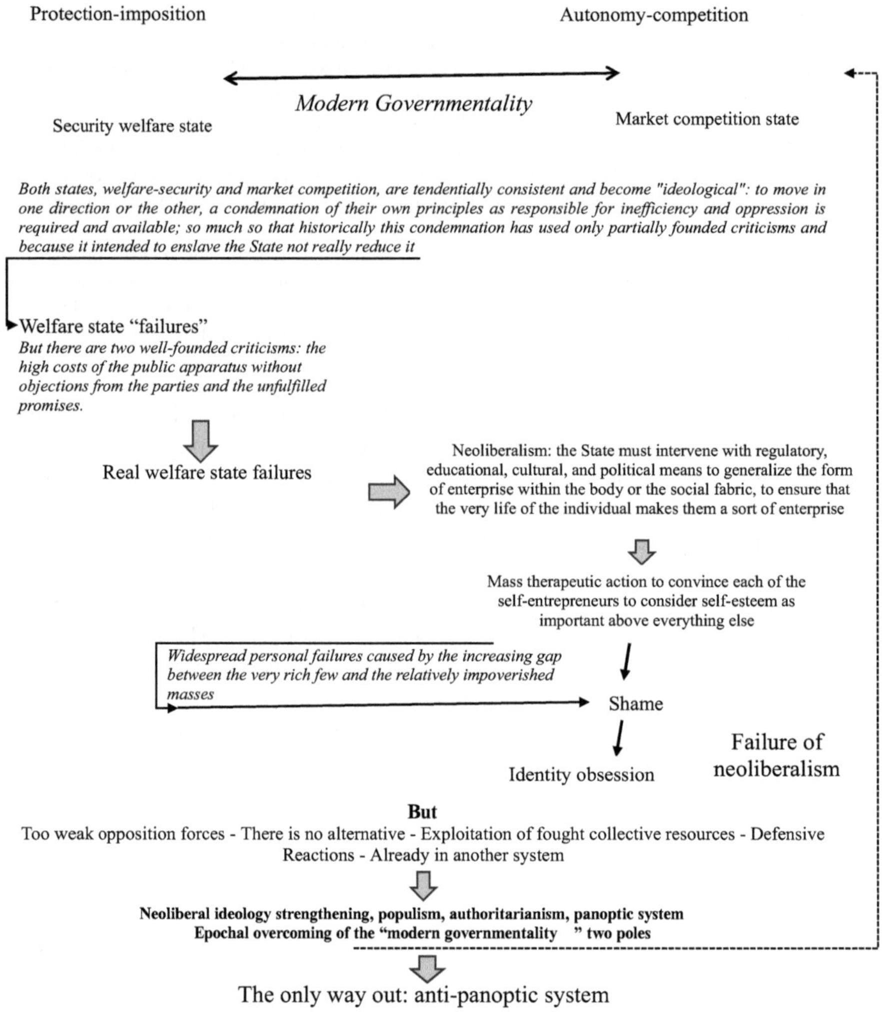

Fig. 2.18 Outline completed

References

Abel-Smith B., & Townsend, P. (1965). The Poor and the Poorest, A New Analysis of the Ministry of Labour's Family Expenditure Surveys of 1953–54 and 1960. *LSE Occasional Papers on Social Administration* (p. 17). G. Bell and Sons.

Afonso, A., Schuknecht, L., & Tanzi, V. (2023). The Size of Government. In A. Afonso, J. T. Jalles, & A. Venâncio (Eds.), *Handbook on Public Sector Efficiency*. Cheltenham: Edward Elgar Publishing.

Alvaredo F., Atkinson T., Piketty T., Saez E., Zucman G. (2016). *The World Wealth and Income Database*. http://www.wid.world.

Amos Bianchi A. (2013–2014). Che cos'è un dispositivo. *AdVersuS* X(25).

Andris, C., Lee, D., Hamilton, M. J., Martino, M., Gunning, C. E., & Selden, J. A. (2015). The Rise of Partisanship and Super Cooperators in the U.S. House of Representatives. *Plos-One, 10*(4), e0123507.

Bartlett, B. (2007). 'Starve the Beast' Origins and Development of a Budgetary Metaphor. *The Independent Review, 12*(1), 5–26.

Berman, S. (2021). The Causes of Populism in the West. *Annual Review of Political Science, 24*, 71–88.

Biasco, S. (1979). *L'inflazione nei paesi capitalistici industrializzati—Il ruolo della loro interdipendenza 1968–1978*. Feltrinelli.

Bonanno, A. (2019). Crisis of Neoliberalism, Populist Reaction, and the Rise of Authoritarian Capitalism. *International Review of Modern Sociology, 45*(1), 9–26.

Boselie, P., Van Harten, J., & Veld, M. (2021). A human resource management review on public management and public administration research: Stop right there... before we go any further. *Public Management Review, 23*(4), 483–500.

Boyer, G. R., & Hatton, T. J. (2002). New Estimates of British Unemployment 1870–1913. *The Journal of Economic History, 62*(3), 643–667.

Castoriadis, C. (1997). *The Castoriadis Reader*. Blackwell.

Chan, C. K., & Bowpitt, G. (2005). *Human Dignity and Welfare Systems*. The Policy Press.

Chelini, M.P. & Prat, G. (2011). Cliométrie du chômage et des salaires en France 1950–2008. *AFC Working Papers* 8.

Daire, E. (1846). *Physiocrates : Quesnay, Dupont de Nemours, Mercier de la Rivière, l'Abbé Bandeau, Le Trosne, avec une Introduction sur la doctrine des physiocrates, des commentaires et des notices historiques, par Eugène Daire*. Librairie de Guillaumin.

Davies, A., Freeman, J., & Pemberton, H. (2023). Thatcher's Policy Unit and the 'Neoliberal Vision.' *Journal of British Studies, 62*(1), 77–103.

Davies, W., & Gane, N. (2021). Post neoliberalism? An introduction. *Theory, Culture & Society, 38*(6), 3–28.

Dell'Amico, S. (2022). Discontent and its Civilizations - What is Cultural Narcissism? *International Journal of Psychoanalysis and Education: Subject, Action, & Society, 2*(1), 29–44.

Fabj, L. V. (2022). *Il narcisismo patologico*. Giunti.

Foucault, M. (1962–1972). *Folie et déraison: Histoire de la folie à l'âge classique*. Libraire Plon 1962. Edition Gallimard 1972.

Foucault, M. (1976). *Sorvegliare e Punire*. Einaudi.

Foucault, M. (1978). *La volontà di sapere*. Feltrinelli.

Foucault, M. (2001a). Il soggetto e il potere. In *Dits et Écrits, vol. 2 1976–1988*. Quarto Gallimard.

Foucault, M. (2001b). *Fearless Speech*. Edited by Josep Pearson. Los Angeles: Semiotext(e).

Foucault, M. (2005a). *Sicurezza, territorio, popolazione*. Feltrinelli.

Foucault, M. (2005b). *Nascita della biopolitica*. Feltrinelli.

Friedman, M. (1978). The Limitations of Tax Limitation. *Policy Review*, Summer, 7–14.

Fukuyama, F. (2018). *Identity: The Demand for Dignity and the Politics of Resentment*. Farrar Straus & Giroux.

Galenson, W., & Zellner, A. (1957). International Comparison of Unemployment Rates. *NBER: The Measurement and Behavior of Unemployment* (pp. 439–584). National Bureau of Economic Research.

Gammon E. (2017). Narcissistic rage and neoliberal reproduction. *University of Sussex Working Paper.*

Garland, D. (2022). The emergence of the idea of 'the welfare state' in British political discourse. *History of the Human Sciences, 35*(1), 132–157.

Gazeley, I., Gutierrez, R., Newell, H., Reynolds, K., & Searle R. (2016). The Poor and the Poorest, fifty years on: Evidence from British Household Expenditure Surveys of the 1950s and 1960s. *University of Sussex Working Paper Series* 93.

Goudarzi, S., Badaan, V., & Knowles, E. D. (2022). Neoliberalism and the Ideological Construction of Equity Beliefs. *Perspectives on Psychological Science, 17*(5), 1431–1451.

Grus, C. L. (2011). Training Credentialing and the New Roles in Clinical Psychology Emerging Trends. In D. H. Barlow (Ed.), *The Oxford Handbook of Clinical Psychology.* Oxford University Pres.

Hathaway, T. (2020). Neoliberalism as Corporate Power. *Competition & Change, 24*(3–4), 315–337.

Hayek, F. (1960). *The Constitution of Liberty.* Routledge.

Hitlin, P., & Shutava, N. (2022). *Trust in Government: A Close Look at Public Perceptions of the Federal Government and its Employees.* Freedman Consulting.

Hoggett, P. (2017). Shame and performativity: Thoughts on the psychology of neoliberalism. *Psychoanalysis, Culture & Society, 22*(4), 364–382.

Jørgensen, T. B., & Bozeman, B. (2007). Public Values: An Inventory. *Administration & Society, 39*(3), 354–381.

Judt, T. (1997). The Social Question Redivivus. *Foreign Affairs, 76*(5), 103–104.

Katz, R. S., & Mair, P. (1995). Changing Models of Party Organizations and Party Democracy: The Emergence of the Cartel Party. *Party Politics, 1*, 5–28.

Keynes, J. M. (2013). World Crises and Policies in Britain and America. In D. Moggridge (Ed.), *The Collected Writings, Volume XXI Activities* (pp. 1931–1939). Cambridge University Press.

Kiely, R. (2018). *The Neoliberal Paradox.* Edward Elgar Publishing Limited.

Kohut, H. (1972). Thoughts on Narcissism and Narcissistic Rage. *The Psychoanalytic Study of the Child, 27*(11), 360–400.

Lansky, M. R. (1999). Shame and the idea of a central affect. *Psychoanalytic Inquiry, 19*(3), 347–361.

Lasch, C. (1979). *The Culture of Narcissism - American Life in an Age of Diminishing Expectations.* W.W. Norton.

Lu, L. D. (2021). *From Stigma to Dignity?* Transforming Workfare with Universal Basic Income and a Federal Job Guarantee.

Lunghini, G. (2008). Una rivoluzione incompiuta e un programma di ricerca - Pasinetti su Keynes (e Sraffa). *Rivista di Storia Economica, 1*, 103–117.

Marcuse, H. (1964–1967). *L'uomo a una dimensione—l'ideologia della società industriale avanzata.* Torino: Einaudi, 1967. First edition: *One-dimensional man - Studies in the ideology of advanced industrial society.* Beacon Press, 1964.

Marks, S. (2017). Psychotherapy in historical perspective. *History of the Human Sciences, 30*(2), 1–22.

Marx, K. (1863/1979). Teorie sul plusvalore 1. In C. Pennavaja e G. Giorgetti (Eds.), *Marx-Engels, Opere complete* (Vol. 34). Editori Riuniti.

Mirowski, P., & Plehwe, D. (2009). *The Road from Mont Pelerin: The Making of the Neoliberal Thought Collective.* Harvard University Press.

Mitchell, B. R. (1998). Prices. In *International Historical Statistics.* Palgrave Macmillan.

Moffitt, R. (1992). Incentive Effects of the US Welfare System: A Review. *Journal of Economic Literature, 30*, 1–61.

Necker, J. (1821). De La Revolution Françoise. In *Œuvres Complètes de M. Necker* (Vol. IX). Treuttel et Würzt.

North D. (1989). Comment. In Joseph Stiglitz: *The Economic Role of the State.* Oxford: Blackwell (pp. 127–136).

Oreskes, N., & Conway, E. M. (2023). *The Big Myth: How American Business Taught Us to Loathe Government and Love the Free Market.* Bloomsbury Pub Plc USA.

Pasinetti, L. (2007). *Keynes and the Cambridge Keynesians - A 'Revolution in Economics' to be Accomplished.* Cambridge University Press.

Peters, G., & Bianchi, C. (2020). Patronage and the Public Service: A Dynamic Performance Governance Perspective. In C. Bianchi, L. F. Luna-Reyes, & E. Riche (Eds.), *Enabling Collaborative Governance through Systems Modeling Methods Public Policy Design and Implementation* (pp. 215–236). New York: Springer.

Putnam, R. D. (2001). Social Capital: Measurement and Consequences. *Isuma Canadian Journal of Policy Research, 2*, 41–51.

Putnam, R. D., & Garrett, R. S. (2020). *The Upswing: How We Came Together a Century Ago and How We Can Do It Again.* Simon & Schuster.

Reagan, R. (1981). *Inaugural Address - January 20.* Simi Valley: Ronald Reagan Foundation.

Remotti, F. (2011). L'ossessione identitaria. *Rivista Italiana di Gruppoanalisi, 25*, 9–29.

Rodrik D., Naidu S., Zucmann G. (2019). Economics After Neoliberalism. *Boston Review Forum*, February 27.

Rutledge, N. C., Archer, R. P., Trumbetta, S. L., & Gottesman, I. (2003). Changes in adolescent response patterns on the MMPI/MMPI-A across four decades. *Journal of Personality Assessment, 81*(1), 74–84.

Scheff, T. (2014). Goffman on Emotions: The Pride-Shame System. *Symbolic Interaction, 37*(1), 108–121.

Scheler, M. (1992). *On Feeling, Knowing and Valuing.* H. Bershady.

Sedda, M. (1999). Il New Deal della pubblicistica politica italiana dal 1933 al 1938. *Il Politico, 64*, 241–275.

Seravalli, G. (1986). *Gli effetti delle integrazioni salariali sulla mobilità del lavoro.* Franco Angeli.

Sinha, M. (2017). Shame and psychotherapy: Theory, method and practice. In E. Vanderheiden & C.-H. Mayer (Eds.), *The value of shame: Exploring a health resource in cultural contexts.* Springer International Publishing.

Stiglitz, J. (1989). *The Economic Role of the State.* Blackwell.

Twenge, J. M., Konrath, S., Foster, J., Campbell, W. K., & Bushman, B. (2008). Egos Inflating Over Time: A Cross-Temporal Meta-Analysis of the Narcissistic Personality Inventory. *Journal of Personality, 7*, 875–902.

Twenge, J. M., & Campbell, W. K. (2009). *The narcissism epidemic: Living in the age of entitlement.* Free Press.

Vandenabeele, W., Leisink, P., & Knies, E. (2013). Public value creation and strategic human resource management: public service motivation as a linking mechanism. In P. Leisink, P. Boselie, D. M. Hosking, & M. van Bottenburg (Eds.), *Managing Social Issues: A Public Values Perspective.* Edward Elgar Publishing Limited.

Varoufakis, Y. (2023). *Technofeudalism: What Killed Capitalism.* Bodley Head.

Ware, N. J. (1931). The Physiocrats: A Study in Economic Rationalization. *The American Economic Review, 21*(4), 617–618.

Werrett, S. (1999). Potemkin and the Panopticon: Samuel Bentham and the Architecture of Absolutism in Eighteenth Century Russia. *Journal of Bentham Studies, 2*(1), 1–25.

Wolf, C. (1988). *Markets or Governments - Choosing Between Imperfect Alternatives.* MIT Press.

Zdencanovic B. (2021). *The Gentleman We're All Talking About: William Beveridge and the Idea of Postwar Social Planning in the United States during World War II.* Rockefeller Archive Centre Research Report.

Žižek, S. (1989). *The Sublime Object of Ideology.* Verso Books.

Chapter 3
What Is to Be Done? (Liberté Égalité Fraternité)

3.1 Liberté, Égalitè

It is hard but urgent to imagine a way out while the authoritarian solution is already here. Since "égalité" has been seriously eroded and inequality has eroded "liberté", the authoritarian way will do away with it by not accepting any correction in the distribution of income. The contradiction will be overcome by closing the long historical cycle opened with the French Revolution, and it will be overcome with a tragic regression. Hence, the question of what can be done is repeated. One option is to resist by fighting to re-establish a certain degree of equality, for example through the main instrument indicated by experience, having been at the center of the phases in which inequality was contained: a tax system for which the rich must pay proportionally more than the poor.[1] This would require a progressive tax on income and capital, and a tax structure with a significant weight of taxes on income and capital and a limited weight of indirect taxes and social contributions which are regressive levies: the complete opposite of what has happened since the 1980s in almost all Western countries (Fig. 3.1).

For tax rates, the data presented by Thomas Piketty and Emmanuel Saez for the United States are considered. In the following graph, the strong reduction in the tax burden on the very rich is evident: from the very high levels of the 1970s, close to 80%, it had fallen to 30% already in 2007. In comparison, the burden of direct taxes on the middle class has remained essentially constant at 20% (Fig. 3.2).

On the spending side, other tools for rebalancing distribution could be those of social services (school, health care, pensions), illness and unemployment insurance; and on the labor market regulation side, rules to protect against arbitrary dismissals, and measures useful for supporting workers' bargaining power. The question, however, is where to start to have a progressive tax reform and better social

[1] In Italy it would be enough to apply the Constitution which in Article 53 says: "Everyone is required to contribute to public spending in proportion to their ability to contribute. The tax system is based on criteria of progressivity".

G. Seravalli, *Collective Action in the Age of Polycrisis*, Contributions to Economics,
https://doi.org/10.1007/978-3-032-12653-5_3

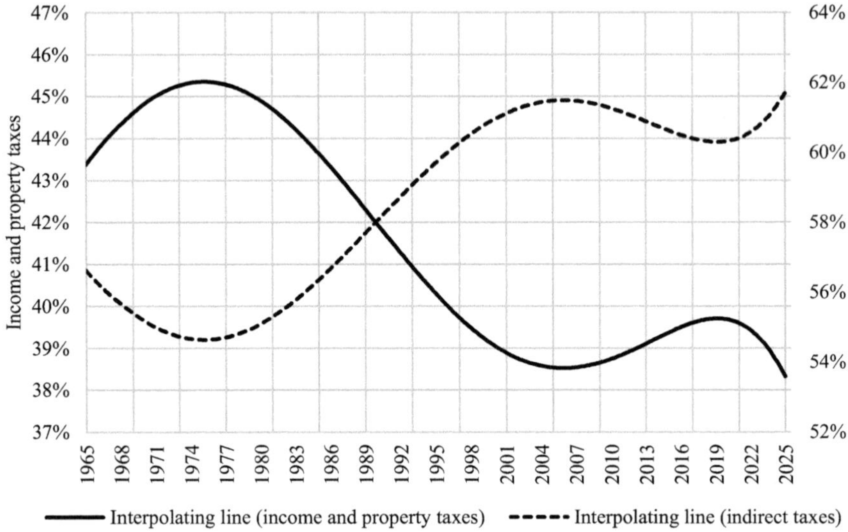

Fig. 3.1 OECD countries: trends in the share of total tax revenues of income and property taxes and indirect taxes (social contributions included) *Source* Figure obtained by processing data from OECD Database data—Tax revenue trends

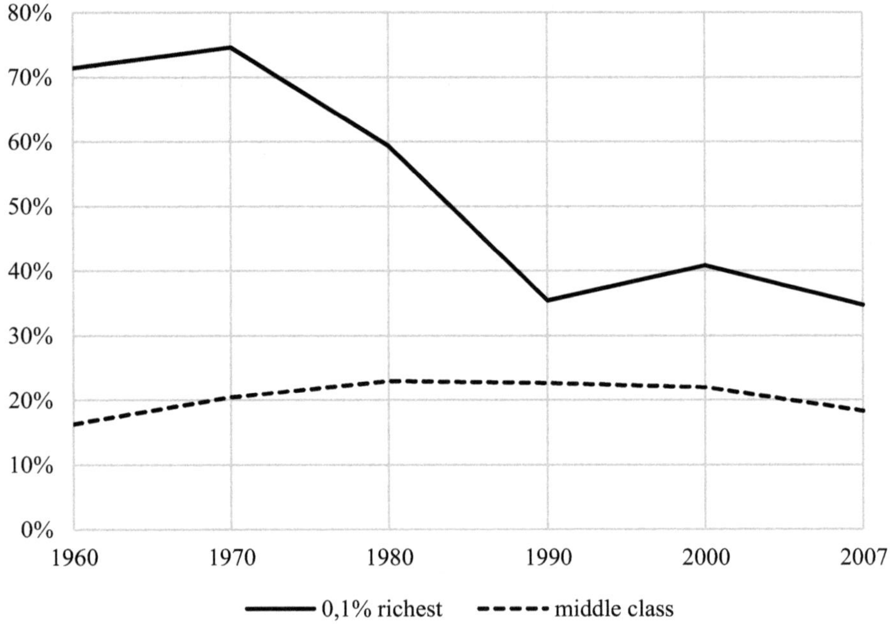

Fig. 3.2 United States: Income and property tax rates for two income classes, the top 0.1 percent of the population and the middle class between 40 and 80 percent in the distribution of the population by increasing income *Source* Figure obtained by processing data from page 13 of Thomas Piketty and Emmanuel Saez (2007, p. 13)

policies, if neoliberalism fights them and the right-wing populism program includes something else, such as to weaken the division of powers, further privatize schools and health care, and fight immigration.

The answer can come once again from above or from below. The answer from above claims that the ruling classes, the parties, the parliament, the government "must" change course due to widespread discontent, since they will have to do something to regain the indispensable consensus. A clue that this path could be taken comes from the "Piketty case", from the reception of his book "Capital in the Twenty-First Century" (Piketty, 2014). One can discuss the approximations that he had to and wanted to adopt to arrive at his demonstration of the "very long-run law of capitalism", according to which a constant rate of profit (around 5%) and a tendentially lower economic growth (around 2%) have inevitably led to the tendential increase in social inequality (growth of profits greater than that of wages), except in some exceptional phases in which growth exceeded the rate of profit, such as from the end of the Second World War to the 1970s. But this demonstration has led Piketty to affirm that now it is necessary to reform historical capitalism through two interventions that become structural, permanent, constitutionalized: an epochal and paradigm shift or else capitalism will end. These are the progressive tax system and the guaranteed good minimum wage. Well, while "economic historians are surprisingly silent about Thomas Piketty's fundamental book [...with little] attention and criticism [...] about his theory of capital", his proposal has "led to a "Piketty Panic" among the rich and among the journalists at their service [...while] the left is affected by "Piketty Envy" (Hesse, 2014, p. 500). The French economist thus seems to have achieved his goal if instead of mobilizing economic historians he has sown panic among the rich and envy among the left. This gives the impression that he has hit the mark. Perhaps he has grasped the epochal change that many now fear or hope for, or in any case consider inevitable under penalty of disaster. It is something of this kind that Piketty keeps repeating in all his interviews, public debates, hearings at public institutions.

But on a couple of these occasions, Piketty met publicly and exchanged views with Michael Sandel, a philosopher at Harvard, one of the preeminent supporters of the other response, the one from below. During these discussions, Sandel argued that, remaining within the liberal individualistic conception of citizenship, such incisive social policies are very unlikely. They would be more likely in a communitarian version of citizenship in which participation is an essential element of freedom. The "fraternité" should come into play. According to the philosopher, the right things can only be done after, together, what is right has been established. And this is also true in emergency conditions. Sandel does not believe, in other words, that institutions can implement incisive social policies only driven by the emergency of a lack of consensus. For many analysts, inequality is objectively at the root of this void, but for some scholars who insist on the thesis of "complexity" and for a mass of people, inequality has less to do with it than the ignorance, inefficiency, corruption of politicians and public officials, less than globalization, new technologies, immigrants, the failed European project, the Russians, the Americans, the Chinese, and more. In short, according to Sandel, to address the polycrisis the task of first agreeing on the causes and on the remedies cannot be avoided. However, this can only be done by introducing a community spirit that has long since been lost or perhaps never existed.[2]

3.2 Fraternité

In the modern history of the West, "fraternité" has always been left in the shadows: perhaps because Robespierre had mentioned it during the Terror (the motto at the time was "fraternity or death"). Surely because it seemed to be in contrast with the idea of progress, openness, expansion of individuals and societies. Being fraternal means being linked to each other through mutual obligations and commitments, which seemed to be a limitation. Ernest Barker, the first holder of the chair of political science at Cambridge University from 1928 to 1939, wrote in his 1952 Treatise that fraternity has a lower status than liberty and equality.[3] In fact, there has been a continuous oscillation between more equality arousing the accusation of violating liberty, or more liberty arousing the accusation of violating equality. The issue of the criterion to be established "fraternally", communally, about how much freedom and how much equality has been put on the back burner. And it must now be forcefully taken up. It is the solution that, on the ground of hopes, should impose itself judging by the number of analysts from the most diverse disciplines who, after having explored the polycrisis, call for the direct participation of citizens, associations, the third sector, self-help, in short, collective action from below for the common good. Even Varoufakis, arguing that capitalism itself is in an advanced stage of overcoming, evokes self-management in companies and reforms capable of guaranteeing an economic

---

[2] Sandel's celebrated Harvard course on "Justice", attended by thousands of students, begins with the story of a trial held in London on 9 December 1884: "The Queen v. Dudley and Stephens". The two sailors were accused of murder because, on a boat without provisions after the ship had foundered 1,600 miles from land, they had killed the cabin boy in a precarious state of health and eaten him in order to survive. The question was whether it was murder or the only justified means for two to survive on the sensible assumption that otherwise all three would have died. Sandel presents the documents of the trial during which the two positions were carefully presented and scrupulously examined. It is clear from those documents that, in one way or another, neither position could be sustained without relying on an a priori criterion of justice. The idea of the apparently rational lesser evil did not hold because if the two sailors had not been rescued, that criterion would have led them, after killing the cabin boy, to fight to the death one on one. So, they applied the "natural law" of the strongest. And they were condemned because the rule established by the national community of the United Kingdom, rejecting the law of the strongest (among Englishmen), allowed killing only in legitimate proportionate defense, and there was no way to decide if not by applying it even in an extreme case like the one under discussion. Conclusion: the distribution of resources (life in the case of sailors) can be left to nature or chance, but if someone wants to intervene, they must first develop a criterion together to do so.

[3] "The principle of Fraternity is a more difficult matter than the principles of Liberty and Equality. [...]. All of us individually need liberty and equality for ourselves. [...]. Fraternity in its strict sense is an emotion rather than a principle, and in that sense, it cannot be said to be in pari materia with the principles of liberty and equality" (Barker, 1952, p. 142).

and digital citizenship with active participation. Yet, in all these appeals there is little space, often no space, for the explanation of how to ensure that it remains not only a logical and desirable solution, but also a realistic one. If the Panopticon only admits an Anti-panopticon, the problem of how to do it is even more difficult than that of what to do.

3.3 Communitarianism

In the United States, a "communitarian resurgence" is actually underway, led by well-known cultural figures, who hope for the transition from the self to the community, from personal desire to desire for the common good t which is achieved through the fulfillment of social obligations (Collier & Kay, 2020). They hope for this by recalling that American society, individualistic at the end of the nineteenth century as it is now, was able to find the sense of sharing that supported it for a long period until the 1970s (Putnam & Romney Garrett, 2020). Even a well-known financial economist has denounced the exaggerated dependence on the State and the Market, hoping for the growth of the "third missing pillar, that is, the community" (Rajan, 2019). In the United States, communitarianism as a movement and as a historical practical experience supports the philosophical one, that is, the appeal addressed to consciences to give greater weight to the common good. This appeal, however, does not overcome the ambiguities that surround communitarianism which is caught between right and left. The current struggle waged by conservative centers in political, social, and cultural institutions against multiculturalism often uses the appeal to community, and it is true that both "conservatism and communitarianism rely on the community and its traditions to determine their value system as opposed to the liberal approach that bases it on rational elaboration" (Young, 2020, p. 61).

In Europe, philosophical communitarianism has no followers because, as a movement and as experiences, it had already had its season, its glories and woes and its exhaustion. In Germany, during the years of the First World War, the communitarian theses of Ferdinand Tönnies (1887) had a wide circulation even in non-academic circles. In the 1920s and 1930s, they were partly swept away by the Nazis, but partly merged into that same "nationalsozialismus" thus becoming unpresentable after the Second World War. Just as the traditionalist positions of the protagonists of the German "Konservative Revolution" of the first post-war period were considered largely unpresentable (De Benoist, 2014), as not extraneous to the construction of the ideological bases of the same Nazism (Harris, 1942). Hannah Arendt wrote:

> The terms sworn brothers, sworn comrades, sworn community, etc., are repeated ad nauseam throughout Nazi literature, partly because of their appeal to juvenile romanticism which was widespread in the German youth movement. It was mainly Himmler who used these terms in a more definite sense, introduced them into the central watchword of the SS («Thus we have fallen in line and march forward to a distant future following the unchangeable laws as a National Socialist order of Nordic men and as a sworn community of their tribes» [...] and

gave them their articulate meaning of «absolute hostility» against all others. (Arendt, 1958, p. 377)

The absolutely presentable "communitarian personalism" proposed since the 1930s, albeit in different ways, by Emmanuel Mounier (1932) and Jacques Maritain (1936) had greater success in other European countries. It influenced the constitutional dictate in Italy through the contribution of the "Dossettiani" who recognized themselves in it (Giuseppe Dossetti, Giuseppe Lazzati, Amintore Fanfani, Giorgio La Pira, Paolo Taviani, and Aldo Moro), but also of Alcide De Gasperi, although oscillating between personalism and ordoliberalism and certainly oriented more toward the latter than the former. There was also a communitarian in the true sense in Italy, the enlightened entrepreneur Adriano Olivetti who during the war developed a complete project of a communitarian Constitution (Olivetti, 1945). Unfortunately, the Constituent Assembly ignored it while it could have been usefully used in the construction of an efficient political-administrative decentralization of the Republic, avoiding the ramshackle version adopted, which was at the basis of the failure of the regional institution. Personalist communitarianism contributed in France to the Constitution of 1946 and to most attempts at socialist and trade union renewal. It contributed, albeit in a minority, to the construction of Europe (Papini, 1981) and even to the Second Vatican Council (Curcio & Papini, 2016). Yet, having already disappointed in the generous pacifist commitment during the civil war in Spain crushed by the strongest logic of radical oppositions, it was defeated by Gaullism in France and by Christian Democrat centrism in Italy. It was nevertheless defeated on the same conceptual ground, according to Paul Ricœur, who began one of his essays by writing: "the younger generations than mine are repugnant even to use the term personalism" (Ricœur, 1983, p. 113). Having "left itself or wanted to place itself on the terrain of competition between systems", personalist communitarianism did not hold up first in the face of "the exceptional complexity of a thought like that of Gramsci and Althusser", and then "in the Sixties, in the face of the powerful wave of structuralism" (Ricœur, 1983, p. 114).

In Scotland, Robert Owen had implemented bold social reforms in his large textile factory in New Lanark and had presented his "Report to the County of Lanark" on 1 May 1820, a real communitarian plan for "relieving public distress, and removing discontent by giving permanent, productive employment to the poor and working classes; under arrangements which will essentially improve their character and ameliorate their condition; diminish the costs of production and consumption and create markets co-extensive with production" (Owen, 1827, p. 1). The influence of Owen's example and thought was decisive for the birth of English socialism, as Marx and Engels recognized in the Communist Manifesto of 1848, and for communitarianism itself, a term used for the first time in 1841 by John Goodwyn Barmby, founder of the "Universal Communitarian Association". Communitarianism had a long political and cultural history in Great Britain, in which John Macmurray (1891–1976) was a protagonist. The Canadian Ronald Beiner, the Scotsman Alasdair MacIntyre, the Americans Michael Sandel and Michael Walzer, considered among the most important contemporary communitarian philosophers, were inspired by him. It was Tony

Blair who buried communitarianism, and precisely with his insistent references to Macmurray, but instrumentally, to insist on social duties in order to scale down rights (Hale, 2004). At the same time, German ordoliberalism, then European, had and has also represented in England a third way considered superior to the communitarian perspectives (Dyson, 2021).

All this weighs on the weak hold of philosophical communitarianism in Europe. But the practical call to participation and collective action from below is striking, which, nevertheless, is evoked to avoid populism and authoritarianism and for a way out of the crisis of democracy. "Welfare from below" is included in these appeals, while taking into account the neoliberal instrumentalization as reported by Bourdieu. In this regard, I take up a passage from the lecture that I presented to the GSSI "Gran Sasso Science Institute" called to discuss the Report on the research "The fullness of the void, study and analysis of the practices of mutualism solidarity of the Rete dei Numeri Pari". The research was conducted between 2020 and 2022 by PhD students of the "Phd program in Regional Science and Economic Geography" and protagonists of the Network on a stratified sample of 91 associative realities engaged in active citizenship initiatives, practices of solidarity and mutual support, summarized with the term "mutualism". I wrote in that report commenting on the results of the research:

> In the current political-social condition, initiatives of participation and collective action from below find little room in principle, which are often tolerated with annoyance, unlike the "charitable" ones, as the research has highlighted. At the same time, the "system" cannot hide the growing social needs that it leaves unanswered and for which it is also ready to leave room for substitute actions. The research has highlighted this well in the complicated relationship of mutualistic initiatives with public institutions. On the one hand, the institutions recognize them, use them and support them in situations of emergency, on the other, outside from the extraordinary, the active associations perceive the institutions as latent, if not absent, in terms of listening and involvement in the design and construction of fundamental policies, services and infrastructures (https://lapienezzadelvuoto.it/i-risultati/#download).

But the call for collective action from below does not stop at mutualism. In fact, there are many voices that underline its urgency for broader objectives: movements that serve to monitor the exercise of power (Rosanvallon, 2006), to restore strength to democracy by fighting the resignations of "post-democracy" (Crouch, 2020),[4] for an "urgent" response to the current "simultaneous growth of hubris, ressentiment, and studied complacency in contemporary politics" (Connolly, 2013, p. 19), as the only

[4] "Fear and hate are the most powerful human emotions: even more essential than love and cooperation for the primary needs of the species [...]. This does not change the fact that, in the context of the complex activities that characterize today's society, survival requires cooperation: innovation and resourcefulness depend on the willingness to experiment with cultures and to collaborate with outsiders; and a satisfying life requires care and love. [...] It is quite clear that we cannot live without recognizing that we depend on each other. [...]. For democracy to regain strength, these alternatives must find a way to deploy their great capacity for motivation. On the one hand, we must emphasize the virtues of positive values and, on the other, we must decisively show the way" (Crouch, 2020, p. 161).

way to combat the "mystifying Corporate Mindfulness Culture" and the "toxic institutions" of neoliberalism,[5] to connect autonomy in work and democracy (Honneth, 2024, pp. 136–138). Considering all these hopes, the perspective should be that of the discovery or rediscovery of a community spirit, which could then also serve to form an adequate consensus for general policies of greater equality and effective citizenship. This discovery or rediscovery should occur through increasingly widespread and consistent concrete practices of collective action in work, for self-help purposes, welfare from below, control of the exercise of power, the vast range of possible cultural, political, entertainment activities, and others that create public assets and are training grounds for democracy. It is noteworthy, however, to observe that all these calls for collective action from below are almost never accompanied by indications on how to do it, perhaps because it is believed that what counts most is the drive and intention or perhaps because of an implicit reference to the abundant specialist literature on the subject. It is therefore a question of filling this gap and making these calls explicit.

3.4 "Traps" of Collective Action

From a critical realist perspective, collective action is not only the decision of several individual subjects to provide together for a need or for a common interest. It is not even limited to their concretely coming together and then acting as a unitary subject, nor even to remaining together despite conflicts between individual and collective interests. If one reads what one of the greatest scholars of collective action of the twentieth century, Charles Tilly (1985), wrote 40 years ago, one understands that the paradigm at the time was precisely that, and it was lacking on the dynamic side. Deciding, coming together, doing and remaining together imply an explicit or implicit assumption of given needs, given individuals, a given collective. It is a static perspective. Since then, studies have made substantial progress in the direction of a dynamic perspective and today there is sufficient theory and empirical research to conceive the modalities and conditions of a collective action understood as "praxis" (Musté, 2018). This does not leave the actors substantially unchanged while they operate so that they can be considered defined at the beginning once and for all in terms of interests, values, knowledge, resources, objectives of individuals and of the collective. Models and applications are able today to suggest a fairly detailed grid

[5] "Corporate spirituality, whether generic warm-fuzziness, Eastern meditation inspired, or Christian infused, all function to turn worker discontent inward so that the worker focuses on improving herself rather than seeking change within the corporation or finding solidarity and solutions in collective action. The corporation is thereby able to transform job insecurity, economic precarity, and other workplace dysfunctions into therapeutic opportunities for self-enhancement. Mindfulness in all its forms mystifies institutional context. Material reality is rendered as epiphenomenal. Stress and distress are rendered as atomistic and individual. A post-neoliberal future lies in the rejection of extreme individualism, in embracing collective action, and in challenging those institutions that rely on the narrative of the self to veil the machinations of neoliberalism" (Wrenn, 2022, p. 168).

of methods and results of collective action when the transformation it brings about concerns its object but also its subjects. Collective action thus appears to be truly "work" (capable of transforming both things and those who are doing it) as György Lukács once said in "The Ontologie of Social Being" (Lukàcs, 1973/1981, p. 55). This definition can be proposed.

Collective action is the process in which a social group is formed, maintained and transformed by acting for collective and individual good objectives with the use of material and immaterial resources, on the basis of explicit and implicit rules on values, knowledge, interests, boundaries, external relations, methods of action, distribution of costs and results, evolution of the rules themselves, thus resolving conflicts in a procedural way and avoiding in a non-authoritarian manner opportunism (behaviors that take advantage of opportunities to act for a private gain by damaging the collective interest) and strategic behaviors (aimed at influencing the decisions of others in order to gain an individual advantage).

For collective action as defined, the specialist literature suggests a whole series of dilemmas that are encountered in theory and in practice. A logical-factual path is drawn from this in which "traps" are encountered that must be overcome in sequence: a difficult path. One could say that the historical prevalence of command and competition has been an "easy" way to avoid the difficult community concertation and collective action from below. The titles of the following sections indicate the traps: exclusion and conservation, arduous evaluation of outcomes, rhetoric, fundamental contradiction, unpopularity in the face of combative cynicism. Starting from the "construction site", one falls into the first trap when one adopts the least problematic configuration, capable of excluding the main reasons for uncertainty. The trust in reciprocity that supports this form of collective action translates into a trap of exclusion and conservation. If designed to avoid uncertainty, collective action would work easily but would make little sense in relation to the emerging demand that requires innovative and inclusive responses. This, of its manifest mistaken objective, is a sufficient lever to escape from the first trap: the error would be quite evident. Having escaped from this trap, one falls into that of the arduous but indispensable evaluation of outcome, from which one tries in vain to escape with rhetoric. Against which, the evaluation "at the margin" is valid, which admits and indeed requires sensible but circumscribed narratives. At this point the conservation-exclusion trap reappears, which seems to nullify the path taken by being brought back to the starting point: a fundamental contradiction. The way out is in a formula: using innovation to fight exclusion and inclusion to fight conservation. A sensible formula, but far from easy to put into practice. Such a complex path, which leads to such a demanding program, can be considered, finally, completely unfeasible in a world like the current one, which wants simplifications, loves banalities, does not tolerate long speeches, is suspicious of what is not immediately accessible or already known or that at least echoes common sense, increasingly armed with the presumption of already knowing everything and at the same time completely impotent. So then working for and with inclusive and innovative collective action could be an adventure worth living, but which requires, in addition to good will and commitment, the awareness of a difficult job and of leading a battle of civilization. Which implies being "idiots" (as Gilles

Deleuze wrote), that is, being incapable and inexperienced in the approved ways of being and thinking: being idiots in order to fight against "imbecility" (as René Scheu wrote). Unless, as will be seen, it is possible to count on another perspective, the "transindividual" one.

3.4.1 Esclusion and Conservation

Collective action requires free inter-individual "recognition" without which it is not even conceivable. It is the relationship in which, as in the famous expression of Friedrich Hegel, "Ich, das Wir, und Wir, das Ich ist" (Hegel, 1807/1979, S. 11, 144) echoed in Buber (1923). The derailment due to the cessation of mutual recognition very often transforms collective action into its opposite, a "fight to the death" (Vinci, 2009, p. 105). This is demonstrated by the history of parties and movements, especially on the left, and that of churches, studded with schisms and violent and bloody fratricidal struggles. When collective action must take on a strong responsibility, every deviance tends to acquire the significance of an attack on the integrity of the social group and to trigger a perverse circuit that leads to schism.

> The first step toward a schism is the belief that the group identity has been subverted. This belief will prompt negative emotions (i.e., dejection and agitation) and decrease both group identification and perceived group entitativity (i.e., cohesion, oneness). In turn, low group entitativity will reduce the level of group identification. Finally, low group identification and high negative emotions will increase schismatic intentions. It is also demonstrated that the impact [...] on schismatic intentions is moderated by the perceived ability to voice dissent (i.e., the greater the perceived voice, the weaker the impact). (Sani, 2005, p. 1074)

The concepts of cohesion and perceived possibility of expressing dissent emerge in this reasoning based on the observation of repeated concrete experiences from which it is deduced that admitted dissent supports cohesion. Cohesion implies order and integration, or predictability of individual behaviors within the active group (order) and mutual adaptation of individual interests, values, knowledge (integration). It is generally believed that integration (going to some extent against "one's own" in favor of the "common") is supported by order (justified expectation that others will do the same). The literature has never stopped returning to this, as can be read in the essay written together by eleven specialists (Jagers et al., 2020). The addition about the possibility of expressing dissent is, however, decisive. This possibility constitutes the most effective way of making order credible since its cracks are not hidden and can therefore be repaired. It is also a convincing argument in the face of the "paradox of size", that is, in the face of the fact that collective action is all the more necessary the larger the size of the "public good" to be done, and at the same time it would be all the more feasible the smaller the size of the active group. The paradox, which dates to Mancur Olson (1965),[6] is today often referred to the

[6] According to Olson, the reason for the paradox is that the larger the size of the group, the smaller the relative contribution of the individual member. Each member may then believe that the collective

narrow perimeter of reputation at the basis of reciprocity, as in Ostrom and Walker (2003). But this mechanism is actually compatible even with large dimensions of the active group if there is the perceived possibility of expressing dissent. If the degree of this possibility is sufficiently consistent and the expression of dissent is actually practiced within the limits beyond which it would be destructive, this implies a lively process of continuous information exchange that can contribute to the conditions required by reciprocity even in a relatively large active group (McGarty et al., 2009). To this end, the variables linked to uncertainty have an impact. Uncertainty about the means and ends increases and accentuates the reasons for dissent, which could go beyond the limits, transforming from a factor of cohesion to a factor of rupture. In this sense, what matters is not so much the size of the group but the fact that collective action has or does not have precisely defined boundaries in terms of individuality, objects, objectives. Collective action that is certainly capable of sustaining itself will therefore be characterized by the operation that consists in removing from the list of influencing factors (Seravalli, 2022) those that can constitute causes of uncertainty. The result is this.

> Collective action that is certainly capable of sustaining itself is carried out by a precisely circumscribed social group, with an identity, homogeneous in terms of interests and values, poorly integrated with external institutions and markets, which works on a limited set of resources, using technologies that change little, to satisfy stationary and not too urgent needs, with an easy balance between costs and results, which are fairly predictable and fairly distributed. (Seravalli, 2022, p. 173)

The mechanism supporting collective action, sufficient to guarantee its success and duration, would be given in this case by cohesion as order and integration emerging spontaneously from the cost/benefit balance and the superiority of collective results compared to the sum of individual efforts. But this is a trap, because this mechanism is a cumulative process that tends to preserve itself and that pays in terms of poor inclusion and innovation, which are generally abolished to abolish any reason for uncertainty.

People escape from the trap because this limited collective action contradicts the reasons for which it is evoked, which require inclusion and innovation. To put it simply, limited collective action would be of little use. It is therefore a question of obtaining cohesion without exclusion and conservation: collective action as gathering individuals to pursue common goals, but not through the exclusion of potential actors and not through the abolition of uncertainties about the definition of means and objectives. In this way collective action and cohesion propose a difficult perspective: because they are two coessential yet contrasting processes, selection on the one hand, conciliation on the other; because they imply the simultaneous presence of three types of conflict, for recognition, distributive, ideological (Pizzorno, 1993, pp. 196–197);

---

action will be carried out even without his or her contribution. But if everyone thinks this way, the collective action fails. This theory that considers the relationship between contribution and result has been criticized in various ways, in particular finding empirical confirmation of the idea that it is not so much the impact of the individual contribution on the general result that counts but the awareness of what is at stake. If everyone knows that the stakes are high, the incentives to collaborate are significant even in large groups (Weimann et al., 2019).

because they imply seeking what unites in what divides by dealing with what divides in what unites.

Collective action must deal with difficulties that present themselves as specific dilemmas between common good and individual good that are relevant when it must be innovative and inclusive. But it is true that, based on experience and decades of reflection, the commitment to collective action is renewed provided that there are adequate resources, valorization of all contributions to the design and implementation of collective action, good results. The three conditions are essential: adequate resources, valorization of contributions, results. External institutional and network resources, tools for promoting solidarity, monitoring and sanctions, broad and dense interaction between actors, problematic integration between direction and valorization of individual contributions to co-design, benefits that "pay" for cohesion therefore appear indispensable (Seravalli, 2022, pp. 175–195) (Fig. 3.3).

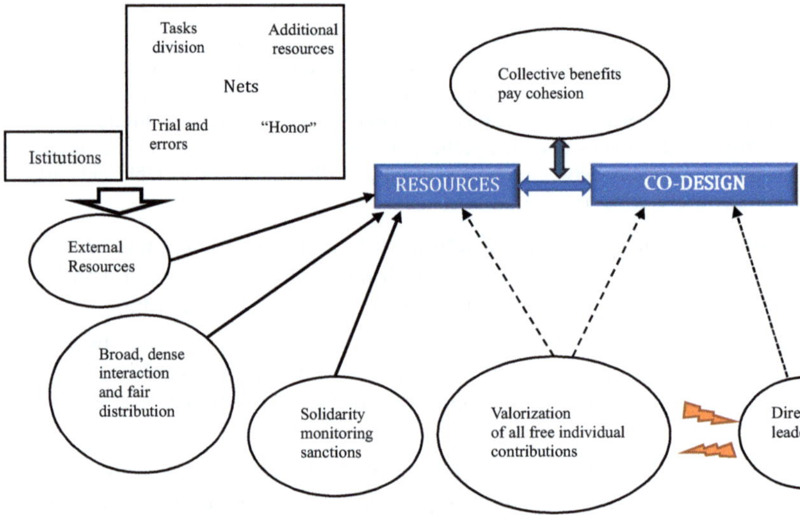

Fig. 3.3 Collective action outline: factors that positively influence coordination from the perspective of resource side and design side of innovative and inclusive collective action. Resources and Co-Design interact as means of solving problems of to do and how to do in order to get results in terms of collective benefits that pay cohesion. *Note* the difficult relationship indicated with "lightning" between direction-leadership and valorization of all free individual contributions can weaken their mutual contribution, therefore indicated with dotted lines; participation in collective action networks brings four types of utility: additional resources of various kinds; the possibility of implementing a division of tasks and exchanges between different collective actions thus more concentrated on their distinctive capabilities; the possibility of learning from the trials and errors of others; and the nourishment of one's reputation within the network as "honorable" presence and action

3.4.2 The Arduous Evaluation of Outcomes

However, the set of levers favorable to collective action represented in this outline cannot be read as a recipe, even if obtained from a lot of investigations, research and reflections. For example, external resources aimed at increasing the benefit/cost ratio can lead to attacks on autonomy. Networked resources help. However, the network is made up of collective actions each grappling with its own dilemmas that make up a collective action in the network. In this way, to resolve problems internal to the "node" one often runs into the importation of external "network" problems. In the left part of the diagram, that of the resources, the evaluation of the results therefore acquires strong and decisive importance: the results, that is, must be there and must be verified. Results, not simply activities carried out, resources used, people involved, as in the "balance sheets" that all social action organizations present. There must be effects in order to demonstrate the objectives: outcomes not just outputs. The assessment of effects must be done in the sense of demonstrating that they have occurred during the work, avoiding the widespread idea according to which if everything proceeds it means that the results will come. The importance of the assessment of results derives from the fact that the effects of collective action must "pay for cohesion" and must also demonstrate to what extent and to what degree, in order to achieve them, reductions in autonomy and importation of external problems can be tolerated. Therefore, the so-called "impact" evaluation is needed. Many studies on the assessment of results defined in this sense in the context of collective action demonstrate the practical impossibility of arriving at exhaustive and "objective" indications. The so-called independent assessment is unlikely: uninformed if independent and not independent if informed. The most realistically conceived one requires new collective action to determine its modalities, and again collective action to determine the modalities of such determination, with a regression that excludes any certain and indisputable landing. As underlined by several studies on the evaluations of a now significant season of social innovations through collective action, they "require holistic measurement approaches, including qualitative methods, [...] of an exploratory nature" (Krlev et al., 2020, p. 538). For example, in the specific field of participatory development initiatives based on places, the "United States Agency for International Development" (USAID) published in 2020 a research report on the evaluation of impact assessments (required by Congress to authorize spending) of over 100 foreign assistance projects funded by various federal agencies between 2012 and 2019 for the participatory promotion in the field of human rights, security, health, food and satisfaction of primary needs, education, environmental protection, fight against poverty, food and health for mothers and children. The most relevant conclusion is that only four of these evaluations out of the total 133 analyzed could be judged absolutely satisfactory as they were capable of answering both fundamental questions convincingly: (1) whether the actions had significant effects, (2) if so, through which mechanisms, if not for what reasons (Velez, 2020).

These difficulties do not lead, however, to judging the evaluation impossible, and as useless if feasible. On the contrary, it remains indispensable and possible, but not with the aim of eliminating doubts, but rather to fuel and guide experiments and learn from their results, however debatable they may always be. In the international panorama, there are now numerous action-research centers with enough experience to allow proposals for "guides" and "manuals" for the evaluation of collective actions, such as the one in Stanford which publishes the magazine "Stanford Social Innovation Review" or the "Centre on Labor, Human Services and Population", which in 2021 released the Report "Assessing the Impact of Community-Level Initiatives—A Literature Review", containing an application proposal, after having underlined that

> credibly assessing the causal impact of initiatives on outcomes of interest is a long-standing challenge in the evaluation literature. [...]. Evaluation designs must account for these challenges, including the difficulty of defining the "treatment," the importance of spillover effects within communities, the interactions between different initiative programs and services, and the difficulties of detecting effects in community-level outcomes. New methods are strengthening our ability to measure the effects of community-level initiatives. Recent advances in quasi-experimental methods suitable for community-level evaluation are promising. In addition, theory-based or mechanism evaluations—i.e., evaluations focused on uncovering the casual links between an initiative's activities and its outcomes—can be especially helpful for learning about an initiative's impacts. Moreover, mixing methods to include qualitative and quantitative approaches can strengthen causal claims. (Congdon et al., 2021, p. VI)

These "special challenges" depend on the fact that the evaluation is useless if it is postponed in time until the achievement of final results can be considered and that it cannot take advantage of a reversible time that would be had if the final results were predictable. The actual realization of the collective action requires an evaluation "in itinere" along the flow of historical time. But this could turn out to be a trap because, as already seen, the ascertainment of the results is difficult and therefore can lead to repeating the practice which is as inconclusive as it is tiring.

3.4.3 Rhetoric

So, faced with this purgatory of the hypothetical, which does not allow arrival at the paradise of certainties, the temptation to compensate with rhetoric must be considered strong, as it is in many experiences which are alive only in words, but are in reality dead. This observation cannot be considered unfounded or exaggerated. There could be many references in this regard. The same story of the "Tennessee Valley Authority", a great experiment in innovative and inclusive collective action inaugurated in the New Deal, foundered in rhetoric despite the important results achieved (Seravalli, 2022, pp. 91–154); and hence, the history of cooperation in Italy (Seravalli, 2022, pp. 71–90). On the other hand, already over a decade ago one could read in a book edited by two experts in participatory policies that a serious and ascertained limitation of an entire season of such bottom-up policies for developing countries, after the failures of the previous top-down season, was "the accompaniment of practices with an almost religious participatory rhetoric" (Cooke & Kothari, 2001, p. 14). This also happened in interventions based in places and organized in such a way as to "put people, their knowledge, their priorities at the centre". Many failures have been attributed to this "religious" excess of rhetoric, more than to other limitations. Finally, 20 years after that book, and 10 years after the launch of the new United Nations initiative for participatory development GPEDC "Global Partnership for Effective Development Cooperation", Jack Taggart, having compiled a report on it, could not help but recommend the "strengthening of tools to ascertain results" to avoid, despite everything, the "tyranny of rhetorical participation" (Taggart, 2022, pp. 1459–1477). Ultimately, the demand for autonomy and the question of resources will inevitably lead to placing fundamental importance on the sense of internal sharing that opens the way to slides toward the rhetoric of participation. This can have particularly negative consequences such as obscuring the reality of the results themselves and as an attack on the value of individualities that, when in circulation, feed the need for rhetoric of participation and sharing.

3.4.4 Fundamental Contradiction

It is necessary to find a way out of this dead end in which collective action seems destined to end up again: as a practice in search of current outcomes of arduous ascertainment destined to die of "religious rhetoric" that mystifies the results. A way out is found by recognizing the usefulness and feasibility of an evaluation of the results "at the margin". However, this way out implies the determination of the "concrete delimited space of possible questions and answers", which can appear and often really be a move of conservation and exclusion. One would therefore arrive at a "fundamental contradiction" which would be inevitable, no matter how much is done, hence, the irremediable denial of any realism of inclusive and innovative collective action. This is the fourth trap. It will be examined point by point.

3.4.4.1 The Evaluation of Outcomes at the Margin

The aforementioned report (Congdon et al., 2021) describes collective action experiences for which it was not possible to apply comprehensive and rigorous impact assessments, but very useful evaluation procedures were nonetheless created according to an approach that could be defined as "at the margin". By renouncing experimental designs (construction of control realities with random assignment), quasi-experimental designs with comparison realities by correspondence, non-experimental designs with coherence analyses on broad empirical evidence, instead repeated longitudinal surveys were used on the relevant changes that gradually occurred. In this way it was possible to observe and interpret the sign and nature of the relationships between changes and outcomes. The same principle of marginal evaluation is also reflected in the techniques increasingly used in the evaluation of social policies, which offer further practical suggestions (Congdon et al., 2017; Díaz-Martin et al., 2023; Fiester, 2011; Ludwig et al., 2011). This is the case of the "mechanism experiments" with which, instead of wanting to ascertain the effects Y of interventions P, which are already known or reliably conjectured, are obtained by levers L that intervene on mediators M ($P \overset{entails}{\rightarrow} L \overset{entails}{\rightarrow} M \overset{entails}{\rightarrow} Y$), this limits the experiment to ascertaining whether and how $L \overset{entails}{\rightarrow} M$. In this way, three concrete advantages are achieved compared to the risk of attempting complete impact assessments and failing to do so: (1) lower costs and greater feasibility of the assessments, (2) more certain and precise identification of the mechanisms underlying the results, (3) more convincing evaluations.

For collective action, several mechanisms are well identified. For example, in order to increase cohesion in a dynamic sense, an egalitarian valorization of all individual contributions is needed, even those that are at first sight eccentric, but also—to some extent contradictorily—a strong leadership. The technique of experiments on mechanisms with ascertainment of results at the margin suggests expanding the active social group to have greater heterogeneity and observe whether the existing leadership holds up or not in the task of ensuring complete valorization of individual contributions without falling into authoritarianism. Another example is that of the connection between intersubjective relationship and results that improve if this interrelation is made denser within the group, which however, tends to make the differences in the distribution of results less tolerable in the sense of individual advantages obtained from the public and the common good at which collective action is aimed. Here the experiment will consist in trying to increase the occasions and improve the opportunities for interaction to see whether the current distribution of results holds up or not. And it would be possible to continue in a similar way: on internal and external resources, on relationships with institutions and with networks, on solidarity, monitoring, and sanctions.

3.4.4.2 Circumscribed Narrative

With the evaluation of results at the margin, the space of rhetoric is also circumscribed, which, no longer overflowing and misleading, can be useful and indeed necessary for the purpose of convincing oneself and others of the goodness and effectiveness of the action despite the partial verification of results. One could say that rhetoric is entrusted with the task of completing what the evaluation of results cannot do, that is, ultimately revoking historical time which is, as such, irreversible, divining the truly unpredictable future. In fact, just as there is evidence of fact that condemns rhetoric, there is other evidence that approves it. And at this point it is possible to understand the reasons but specifying: provided that rhetoric is contained through even marginal verification of results.

> Rather than the limited view of what rhetoric is and does, we return to its roots from which grew 2500 years of thoughtful discussion justifying that rhetoric is the essence of self-governance. [...]. It is important [...] to note the conceptual relationships among common sense, narrative communication, endoxa, and social constructionism. Endoxa is a measure of cultural assumptions and denotes collective identity and social collaboration. These are notions without which the study of organizations would be moot. By addressing endoxa from

> a rhetorical standpoint, we identify its continued centrality to human interactions, including those that take place in an organizational context. Every organization has its own endoxa. It comprises each organization's history, interpersonal dynamics, hierarchies, goals, successes, and failures. (Browning & Hartelius, 2018, pp. 81, 90)

The references could continue, but the best thing to do is to read Peter Brooks' latest book and then the one from almost 40 years earlier in order to retrace his path in reverse: from the celebration of the power of narratives in the 1984 book ("we understand ourselves through stories" Brooks, 1984), to the exploration of its grave dangers in the 2022 book: "It was as if a fledgling I had nourished had become a predator devouring reality in the name of story" (Brooks, 2022, pp. 4–5, 98). Even if in recent years narratives and rhetoric have become increasingly pervasive and oppressive, both in public discourse and in everyday life, following the narrative turn that occurred in the 1970s in psychology, philosophy, and subsequently also in medicine and economics, there remains a fundamental difference between widespread lies and fiction that, modestly, strives to be credible.

3.4.4.3 Going Back to Conservation and Exclusion?

However, in both directions, both in that of the marginal assessment of results and in that of the sensible story and controlled rhetoric, it is essential that the concrete space of the possible questions and answers of collective action be delimited. The effects on the life of collective action of defined, desired, or intervening changes cannot be assessed if at the same time everything else changes. Sensible and plausible stories about the life of collective action cannot be conceived if its basic data are constantly changing in such a way that in practice there is no defined context. Thus, the question arises as to whether one in this way returns to the conservation and exclusion that one has come this far to avoid. Whether this fourth trap is really the most dramatic and definitive, from which it seems impossible to escape since it brings one back to the starting point.

In fact, this is not necessarily true. Indeed, as strange as it may seem, the assistance of a theologian is useful in this context. Alberto Schena and I stumbled upon a way out by working on the thought articulated between philosophy, theology and economics of the great Canadian Jesuit thinker Bernard Lonergan (Seravalli & Schena, 2019). What Lonergan proposes is to obtain innovation and inclusion by controlling the tendencies toward the exclusion of innovation and the dominating and, ultimately, conservative tendencies toward inclusion. The formula descends firstly from the identification of tendencies toward the exclusion of creation/innovation. The reason for these tendencies is in the very nature of creation/innovation which is "a question of understandings [...] that come together, that complement and correct each other, [...], that reveal their defects in their concrete results, that give rise to further corrective understandings" (Lonergan, 1992, p. 100). For this necessary interactivity of understandings, the activation of the process requires a selection of participants. This statement corresponds to the findings of considerable literature on innovation and "learning" organizations, as shown in Seravalli (2011). Lonergan attributes to this

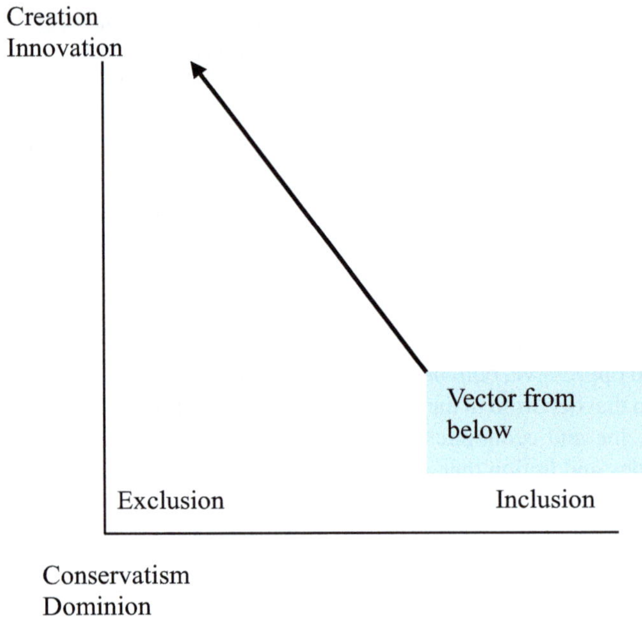

Fig. 3.4 Lonergan's model (a)

process the characterization of "bottom-up human development vector" (Lonergan, 1992, p. 105) (Fig. 3.4).

But there is also a second vector, "from above", identified as the "spirit of the collective that heals" if it does not transform into "domination" and therefore conservative. Lonergan indicates it as "the love that orients man in his cosmos" (Lonergan, 1992, p. 103). A second relationship is established. In this way the tendency from below toward innovation with exclusion is controlled by the tendency from above toward inclusion. Therefore, an "equilibrium point" innovation-inclusion is obtained (E) (Fig. 3.5).

It can be noted that the "spirit of the collective" includes the levers of collective action that in the outline of Fig. 3.3 are indicated as "broad, dense interaction and fair distribution" and "solidarity, monitoring, sanctions", while the "vector from below" includes those indicated as "valorisation of all free individual contributions" and "direction-leadership". Now ordered synergies are established between these levers. So that the examples already indicated regarding marginal evaluation in experiments on mechanisms take on the rank of real strategies. It was said to try to enlarge the active social group (inclusion) and observe whether or not leadership holds up in the task of ensuring complete valorization of individual contributions (innovation) without falling into authoritarianism; and to try to increase the opportunities for interaction (spirit of the collective) to see whether or not the distribution of results holds up (inclusion).

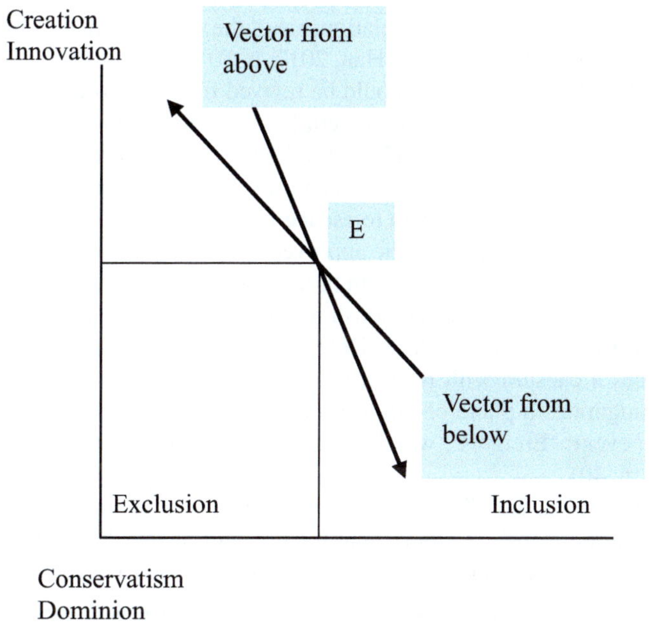

Fig. 3.5 Lonergan's model (b)

3.4.5 Unpopularity Due to "Combative Cynicism"

Unfortunately, the reasoning on the realism of collective action cannot end happily enough in this way. The conclusion which has been reached does not "close the circle". By implying experiments, it defines the authenticity of inclusive and innovative collective action as a research process open to possibilities and risks: meritorious character, but also fragile. Now, faced with the demanding prospect of such research, there is the sad cultural reality of the modern world which dictates its unpopularity in the face of "combative cynicism". The widespread simplifications, the impatience toward complicated discourses and practices, the false and vain verbalizations in all areas, of information, politics, civil society, lead to questioning the way out of the contradiction for which that same reality in crisis, which would require difficult remedies, prevents them by favoring conclusions that combine anarchy and the dictatorship of "combative" cynicism and its "imbecilities" (Scheu, 2019, p. 3). Combative cynicism because, believing one knows everything, one violently opposes those who laboriously seek other conclusions.

One might be suspicious of apocalyptic diagnoses that consider widespread ways of thinking and acting well represented and, at the same time, shaped by communicative digitalization as imbecility that leaves no escape. But it is certainly impressive to note how, according to Byung-Chul Han, all the important figures that have emerged in this journey of critical understanding for collective action have now become empty.

Praxis, which is no longer a double relationship of the subject with the object and with other subjects, should be relearned (Han, 2017, p. 50). The authentic intersubjective relationship has disappeared and should be revived from the ground up (Han, 2017, p. 84). The sensible story has become literally impossible in the sea of futile chatter and artfully invented lies (Han, 2017, p. 97). It is no coincidence that in Han's essay, if the reader looks very carefully, they can only find a short constructive passage, which significantly indicates a path to escape from all this through "idiocy": acting incapable and inexperienced with the approved ways of being and thinking. "Today, an ontological indifference reigns. Both thought and life become blind to their plane of immanence. [...]. Only the relationship with that plane would allow something completely different to begin. Gilles Deleuze says: Faire l'idiot.[7] [...]. Playing the idiot produces a caesura with respect to what is predominant, with respect to the Same. It inaugurates a plane of virgin immanence and makes thought open to the truth, to the event, 'Ereignis', which gives rise to a new relationship with reality" (Han, 2017, p. 40).

According to Han, the idiot is a genius: "the history of philosophy is a history of idiocies, of idiotic leaps". Artificial intelligence will always be beaten by the idiot because "AI is too intelligent to think". But the idiot is also a hero.

> That makes the idiot instantly subversive in our time, where communication counts among the highest goods. Not so much because we value the exchange of information or because we can learn from each other. But rather, because the ever-accelerating communication cycle is what keeps surveillance capitalism going. It feeds the database and helps train algorithms. If everyone were to quit Facebook and Instagram right now, would stop emailing and messaging and throw their smartphones in the ditch – in other words, if all communicative data flows would rigorously come to a halt – then capital would stop flowing too. Capital that is entangled with the interests of those who want to keep an eye on us, whether it's governments, security services, or companies like Cambridge Analytica, who sell the dream of propaganda with guaranteed return on investments to whatever political ideology that is willing to pay for it. The means: data profiles. The source: 'total communication'. The goal: 'total surveillance', as Han calls it (Miriam Rasch – "Eurozine" 19 August 2020).

Fyodor Dostoevsky's Idiot, finally, is the absolutely good man, represented by realizing the ambitious project indicated in a letter to his niece Sofia Alexandrovna.

> I attacked another novel and am now working day and night. The idea of the book is the old one which I always have so greatly liked; but it is so difficult that hitherto I never have had the courage to carry it out; and if I'm setting to work at it now, it's only because I'm in a desperate plight. The basic idea is the representation of a truly perfect and noble man. And this is more difficult than anything else in the world, particularly nowadays. All writers, not ours alone but foreigners also, who have sought to represent Absolute Beauty, were unequal to the task, for it is an infinitely difficult one. The beautiful is the ideal; but ideals, with us as in civilized Europe, have long been wavering. (Dostoevsky, 1868, p. 135)

[7] "The old idiot, closer to Job than to Socrates, wants account to be taken of 'every victim of History' [...]. The new idiot will never accept the truths of History. The old idiot wanted, by himself, to account for what was or was not comprehensible, what was or was not rational, what was lost or saved; but the new idiot wants the lost, the incomprehensible, and the absurd to be restored to him. This is most certainly not the same persona; a mutation has taken place. And yet a slender thread links the two idiots, as if the first had to lose reason so that the second rediscovers what the other, in winning it, had lost an advance" (Deleuze & Guattari, 1994, p. 63).

The conclusion of the journey of how to do collective action is therefore very demanding: it poses the question of from whom one can expect the brilliant, heroic, perfectly good idiocy.

3.5 A Transindividual Remedy

The serious deterioration of the system leaves a painful contradiction. While individualism predominates, individuals are powerless.

> The current historical moment can be described as the predominance of the individual over the collective. The individual reigns supreme in politics, as an ethic of individual rights and freedoms displaces any project of collective liberation. In economics this is even more the case, as the utility maximising individual of neoliberal economics trumps not only any other idea of economic relations but subsumes all social relations. [...]. The individual has become not only the basis of political, cultural, and economic understanding but also the extend of all our aspirations; the individual is both mythologically and prescriptively dominant; it is simultaneously all one needs to make sense of the world and the best that one could hope from it. This complete and utter assertion of the dominance of the individual [...] is haunted by the spectre of its own impotence. Forces beyond its control constantly risk dwarfing it [...] the impersonal forces of finance, [...] technology, or the sheer brutal assertion of the world. (Read, 2016, pp. 1–2)

It is ultimately this contradiction that leads many to hope for collective action from below. But it is inevitable to ask whether this hope does not remain such in the swamp of difficulties in its implementation. It has been demonstrated that there is a path capable of overcoming one by one the traps in which collective action risks getting bogged down. However, this path requires sophisticated thought and action, patience, openness to discussion, research, all attitudes that are foreign and indeed opposed by current verbalism, by overbearing individualism as incapable as it is incompetent, by the poisoning of all the wells of authentic social relations, in a word, as has been said, by combative cynicism. The only recommendation that remains, with which the preceding paragraph ended, is “idiocy against imbecility”. But the idiocy that is claimed is no less arduous, having to be ingenious, heroic, perfectly good. The question arises as to whether there is any help: whether another life is perhaps hidden in the horrible emerging world.

Transindividualist thought seems able to answer this question affirmatively by maintaining that in deep human reality the collective and the individual are determined together and not in opposition. In deep human reality, that is, there would not be the dilemmas of collective action as a systematic contrast between individual good and common good to overcome which one must overcome the traps that have been described, thus arriving at the sophisticated path that clashes with combative cynicism. But not only that. Transindividualist thought maintains that this deep human reality has come to the surface precisely because of neoliberal degeneration, thus being able to imagine an interaction between the intersubjective, which obviously remains, and the transindividual not only because it is “always true” in the depths, but also because it has emerged to the surface. In this way the collective action that this degeneration leads to invoke would be facilitated by the degeneration itself, barring clarifications as will now be seen. The reasoning that will follow can be anticipated in five points.

1. Intersubjective-transindividual. In the "intersubjective" relationship typical of Western civilization, where the dilemmas of collective action are located, it has always been understood that the subject constituted by their interior space relates to themselves, to others, to the world, thus individuating themselves: becoming the concrete singular individual, distinct, determined in time and space. The subject *precedes* individuation. According to transindividual thought, however, intersubjectivity is not the constitutive place of the social bond, but an imaginary, ideological effect of it. The intersubjective is the historical Western warp woven on the original plot of the human which is the transindividual where *singular and collective individuation precedes the individual-subject.*
2. Preindividual. To see how such facilitations of the transindividual can overcome the difficulties of the intersubjective for collective action, it is necessary to clarify the nature of the individuation process that starts from the "preindividual", preceding not only the individual but also individuation. The preindividual is the potential that one has, which pushes toward singular and common individuation, thus facilitating collective action since the emotions, memories, imagination, knowledge, practices that characterize it do not co-determine each other, always leaving unrealized possibilities. However, in the condition of absolute transindividuality without anything else, therefore only the relationship being valid, the result would be senseless, never being able to know who one is and who the others are.
3. Structures, polycrisis, restructuring. Individual and collective individuation takes on meaning through contingent historical "structures" subject to tensions, exhaustion, changes. When, as in contemporary times, there is exhaustion, the condition of polycrisis is disturbing, such as to generate anguish and fear but also push for innovation, for restructuring. But restructuring today is held back by neoliberalism which thrives despite its failures by using the transindividual relations that have come to the surface. It follows that the transindividual relations that have come to light in the crisis of neoliberalism facilitate collective action (individual and collective individuation occur together and not in opposition), but at the same time they hinder it by slowing down the progressive restructuring necessary to give meaning to relations because neoliberalism survives its failures by using the relations that have emerged from the absolute transindividual.
4. An intuition. The way out is found by recognizing that the current institutionalization of impotence due to excess of power is characterized by the use of science as a "humanism of constructive action devoid of emotion", and of faith as an "emotion devoid of action". Therefore, the way out could consist in using faith against science and science against faith, which appears to be the way to realize "the transductive relationship between action and emotion" as "wisdom". Where faith is understood as "substance of things hoped for and argument of the non-apparent" as Dante taught us in the twenty-fourth canto of Paradiso.

5. A formula. This "formula", identified for the purpose of supporting the facilitations of collective action at the transindividual level in the presence of exhausted historical structures, appears singularly connected to the other formula found to resolve the dilemmas of collective action in the intersubjective. Using faith against science and science against faith is in principle, and factually in concrete cases, the way to use inclusion against conservation and innovation against exclusion. One way reinforces the other, authorizing some optimism for a constructive response to the demand for collective action. The formula must be well understood, however. The emphasis must be placed on "use" and on "against". It is not resolved in some dialectical synthesis but must be framed within the scope of negative dialectics; without however reducing it to the pleonastic reiteration of "science against faith or vice versa". One could say this: in the progress of concrete processes, the action dictated by faith in contrast with science (inclusion against conservation) will modify the reality on which the dictate of science against faith will act (innovation against exclusion), as in the performance of a piece of music, where "the irruption of a single note is capable of redrawing the entire harmonic course of the others".

3.5.1 *Intersubjective and Transindividual*

It is natural to think that social relations are intersubjective. The subject appears to exist as a space of interiority that relates to itself and to the world in this way, individuating itself: the individual precedes individuation. This, which seems obvious, is so because it has "deeply marked the entire modern philosophical canon from Descartes to Leibniz, from Kant to German idealism, from Feuerbach to logical empiricism, reaching up to contemporary philosophy and colonizing most of the spontaneous philosophy of the social sciences" (Morfino, 2022, p. 18).

The transindividual is not "a simple alternative to intersubjectivity, but the category capable of explaining the material fabric from which [...] intersubjectivity emerges and in which it is affirmed. In other words: intersubjectivity not as a constitutive place of the social bond, but as its imaginary or ideological effect" (Morfino, 2022, pp. 20–21). The intersubjective is typical of Western civilization. In other civilizations it is not so. Léon Vandermeersch, considered one of the most authoritative contemporary sinologists, wrote for example:

> In the East, especially in China, humanism sees man as a part of the universe like nature. Therefore, traditional Chinese culture conceives of a "unity of man and universe." This is a fundamental difference between the Eastern and the Western cultures, which have different values and different understandings of human beings. [...]. Western democratic thought is somewhat antithetical to the Chinese thought that focuses on harmony, where collective interests take precedence over individual interests. The Chinese believe this is the only way to achieve general social harmony whereas in the Western democratic process, we see the protection of individual interests, where everyone has to protect his or her own interests, which is the norm in Western democratic societies, and this of course gives rise to the supremacy of individual interests. (Vandermeersch, 2023, pp. 5, 6)

Western individualism and the antithetical Chinese collectivism are both ideological or imaginary constructions woven over the underlying fabric of an original humanism, which is neither individualist nor collectivist. Starting above all from the writings of Gilbert Simondon (1924–1989), complex works rediscovered a few years ago, but with notable precedents in Spinoza, Marx, Freud (Morfino, 2022, pp. 56–77), "it is a question of knowing the individual through individuation rather than individuation starting from the individual" (Simondon, 1958/2020, p. 33). The transindividual therefore proposes a paradigm shift, paradigm as a conceptual framework proper to "normal science [...as] research firmly based upon one or more past scientific achievements, achievements that some particular scientific community acknowledges for a time as supplying the foundation for its further practice" (Kuhn, 1962, p. 10).

To facilitate understanding, analogical discourse is useful, analogy as a concept obtained from the experience of something different from that of which it is a concept.[8] In the first chapter of the first part of "L'Individuation", Gilbert Simondon suggests considering the artisanal manufacture of bricks, the same example evoked on pages 243–244 of his other book "Du mode d'existence des objets techniques". If one were to say that a brick is the clay to which the mold has given shape, one would be saying something analogous to what one says about the individual in Western tradition: it would be the subject that has taken shape, individuation, entering into a relationship with the other from itself. In reality, Simondon observes, expert bricklayers and brick makers know that:

> the principle of individuation of the brick is neither the clay nor the mold [...] but consists, on the contrary, in the operation through which the clay has taken shape [...] in a system [...] which also includes the smallest details of the mold and the most irrelevant pressures of this humid soil. [...]. The principle of individuation is the operation that realizes an energetic exchange between the matter and the form [...]. It could be said that [...] it is the allagmatic operation common to both matter and form by means of the actualization of potential energy. (Simondon, 1958/2022, p. 66)

The example of brickmaking can illustrate the profound human process, eminently interactive, individual and collective at the same time, from a "pre-individual" state to the current individuation. The system of brickmaking belongs to the "manufacturing intention", that is, "to the human gestures that have allowed the two half-chains to reunite in a system in view of the operation of taking shape" (Simondon, 1958/2022, p. 68). Gestures, which are aimed at the use of bricks, not just one, for the construction of a wall, a house: a process of collective individuation in a double sense. Not only because clay and mold co-identify but also because many bricks further identify, giving rise to the wall and the house. Thus, the transindividual conceives not only the interactive individuation of individuals but also of society, without any opposition between individual and collective dimensions.

Another analogy is that of "routines". In the pioneering texts of Joseph Alois Schumpeter (1934, pp. 91 and following) and Herbert Alexander Simon (1947, pp. 90

[8] For Enzo Melandri, while the effort to define analogy is arduous and essentially useless, one can say the same about its function, which appears essential in mediating between logic and experience: "The mediation of logic and experience can only occur through analogy" (Melandri, 1968, p. 594).

and following), in the operations of a production process a routine is repeated, but with continuous refinement and adaptation, at the limit of the paradox between permanence and change. It is no coincidence that organizational literature has continued to explore this topic. In a notable essay by Peter Kesting (2023), one can find the microfoundation in the theory of action of "dynamic routines", understood as defined but also changing conduct (Kesting, 2023, p. 183). The analogy of dynamic routines can well illustrate the collective as well as individual character of individuation. Again, they consist in the co-determination of many operational components and are also relevant for "production" and not for a single product. And so, just as routines can decay and lose effectiveness (aging due to a detachment of gestures from intentions) if they are not continually renewed, in the same way:

> if the successive individuations become rarefied and distant, the collective body and soul gradually separate, despite the production of myths and opinions that keep them relatively coupled: from this comes the aging and decadence of groups, which consists in a detachment of the group soul in relation to the group body. (Simondon, 1958/2022, p. 411)

The dynamic nature of routines also allows one to grasp the levers that support the processes of individuation. The dynamics of routines is guided by "coherence indicators" of actions and is confirmed and encouraged to continue in the same direction when the indicators improve, while it is modified and changes course when they worsen. Something similar happens in the adjustment from the preindividual to individuation on the basis of "sensations-perceptions" that induce "impacts-emotions", that is, "pleasure or pain, sadness or joy [...]. Positive emotional states indicate the synergy of the constituted individuality and the current individuation movement of the pre-individual. Negative states consist of conflicting states between the two domains [...]. Affective-emotional [...] modifies the action according to this relationship between the two areas of being a subject, harmonizing them" (Simondon, 1958/2020, p. 340).

In short, the intersubjective is the Western historical warp woven on the original weft of the human, which is the transindividual, where singular and collective individuation precede the individual-subject and where such individuation goes forward on the thrust of synergies of constituted individualities and of the movement of individuation.

3.5.2 *Preindividual*

But one may ask what the preindividual that precedes individuation is. The concept is found immediately in the first pages of "L'Individuation": "The individual will be understood as a relative reality, a certain phase of being that presupposes a preindividual reality before it, and that, even after individuation [...] does not exhaust in one fell swoop the potentials of the pre-individual reality" (Simondon, 1958/2022, p. 33). However, to Andrea Bardin the concept appears as an expedient rather than the solution to the problem posed by individuation, so much so—Bardin observes—that

Simondon at a certain point no longer spoke of it. "We believe that the concept of preindividual in Simondon remains the index of a problem, not a solution [...]. In Simondon in the 1960s the term 'preindividual' no longer appears" (Bardin, 2010, p. 50). A sort of doubt is found in the Conclusions of "L'Individuation": "Such a conception [preindividual state] could be considered exquisitely gratuitous [...] if one knows this state only from what follows it [... as when] one presupposes a creator to account for creation. [...]. [But] the hypothesis of a preindividual state of being is not entirely gratuitous [...] since it is derived from a certain number of thought patterns drawn from the fields of physics, biology and technology" (Simondon, 1958/2022, pp. 443–444). Yet, the "preindividual state of being" is never actually defined by Simondon. Interpreters always cite this passage in which its fundamental characteristic is indicated as "system above unity" without however saying what system it is.

> In order to think about individuation, it is necessary to think about being not in terms of substance or matter or form, but rather as a tense, supersaturated system, above the level of unity, which does not consist only in itself and which cannot be adequately thinkable by means of the principle of the excluded third: concrete being, or complete being, or the preindividual, consists in a being that is more than unity. (Simondon, 1958/2022, p. 35)

This is certainly why Vittorio Morfino makes it disappear by defining the transindividual itself as a "metastable system", that is, a state of equilibrium stable to small perturbations, but unstable to larger perturbations, a system on the one hand not elusive (as it would be if unstable), but on the other always on the verge of changing. The same expression "metastable system" is used by Simondon for the preindividual: a concept, therefore, that would lose its raison d'être if it coincided with the transindividual. "Transindividual is therefore the name of the metastable system that gives rise to psychic and collective individuations, a web of relations that crosses and constitutes individuals and society, methodologically prohibiting the substantialization of one or the other" (Morfino, 2022, p. 154). But the preindividual remains central in "L'Individuation", so much so that other interpreters have sought a definition of it even if this meant moving away to some extent from Simondon's oscillations. According to Read, authors such as Étienne Balibar, Gilles Deleuze, Jacques Derrida, Bernard Stiegler, Yves Citton, and Muriel Combes, but, significantly, also ancient thinkers considered to be at the origins of transindividual philosophy (Baruch Spinoza, Karl Marx, and Sigmund Freud) converge on the fact that its conditions are given by emotions, memories, imagination, knowledge, and practices, so much so that these can be considered the preindividual conditions of subjectivity: "as we have seen, affect [emotions and memories], imagination, knowledge and habits can all be considered preindividual conditions of subjectivity and a basis of transindividual relations" (Read, 2016, p. 248). It can then be considered that these conditions "they do not necessarily affect or determine each other, and necessarily have radically different conditions of dissemination and communication" (Read, 2016, p. 248). In this way, the current individuations according to each of these preindividual conditions do not coincide. And it is from this inconsistency that the process of individuation finds its impetus according to "a new way of conceiving the relation between determination and liberation" (Read, 2016, p. 249). What one is, shown by what one is doing, does not coincide with what one knows, imagines, remembers, or with what makes one feel good. Thus, there is always space for one to fill in being what one is not yet and, at the same time, there is always an incentive to fill it. However, the difficulty that Simondon was unable to overcome, in reality, remains even after this synthesis reported by Jason Read. It is difficult to think that the being that one is not yet is in turn not already, at least as long as the preindividual remains conceived as a state of being.

It would be different if the indicated emotions, memories, imagination, knowledge, practices were read not as *conditions of being* but as its *faculties*, its "possessions". But to grasp the difference, it is necessary to move on to Paolo Virno's proposal, which comes from a move as acute as it is simple: to say the preindividual not as something that one is but as something that one has. One can observe the experience of self-reflection, "from the dialogue of the soul with itself to Descartes' cogito me cogitare", and one discovers that it "presupposes a doubling, or rather a split. The spectator I, who observes with satisfaction or repugnance or amazement the undertakings of the actor I, does not coincide with the latter, but keeps its distance" (Virno, 2017, p. 104). By observing the use one makes of the most varied things, and of one's very existence, "the root and architrave of all other uses", one sees that "the use of oneself is based on detachment from oneself" (Virno, 2017, p. 105). Well, in both cases, both in self-reflection and in the use of one's own life, the reason why there is that split and that detachment exists.

> only because we are not our consciousness, but we have it [...]: if the human animal adhered without any margins whatsoever to its salient characteristics, or if these characteristics had the value of synonyms or analytical predicates [...], the split and distance on which the reference to its own way of being rests would not even be conceivable. [...]. To affirm that the human animal maintains a detachment from its own existence, from the impulses that move it, from the language in which it dwells, is equivalent to affirming that the human animal is not this existence, these impulses, this language, but has them [...] Ultimately: the verb to have, unlike the verb to be, expresses a relationship of belonging that, however, resolutely excludes the identity between the terms involved in it. And it is precisely the deficit of identification with the qualities at one's disposal that opens up the possibility of using them [...]. We only use what we have, never what is consubstantial with us to the point of not being able to distinguish ourselves from it. (Virno, 2017, p. 105.)

It follows that the preindividual that one has is the potentiality of individuation which, never coinciding entirely with its actualization, is always preserved as a further potentiality.

All this allows a step forward. Since the transindividual exists on the basis of the preindividual that one has, it can be seen that it—without anything else—presents an insenseless condition. If only the relation is valid, no one can ever know who they are and who others are and no one can ever have any idea about what to expect from themselves and from others. While each is caught in the reciprocal influence with another, this in turn is caught in the influence with yet another, who, on the other hand, also influences the first. The result is a system in continuous movement without any stability and without recognizable states that would disappear as soon as they were identified. In this way one could say that the transindividual exists, but—as such—cannot have a history because the subjects do not find their meaning in it: "the power of individuation [...] cannot pursue anything because [...] of a lack of overall systematics. [...]. The only possibility of survival for the individual, or rather for the subject, consists [...] in becoming meaning" (Simondon, 1958/2022, pp. 421–422).

In conclusion, the preindividual as a potential that one has, pushes toward individuation at the same time individual and collective (thus facilitating collective action) since the emotions, memories, imagination, knowledge, practices that constitute it do not co-determine each other, always leaving unrealized possibilities. However, in the condition of absolute transindividuality without anything else, therefore only the relationship being valid, the result would be senseless, never being able to know who one is and who others are.

3.5.3 Polycrisis Structures Restructuring

This happens today largely because the "structures" in society are exhausted, those structures that for Simondon provide individuals with their own meaning and satisfy their need for history.

> The individual finds in society a definite need for the future and a preservation of the past, and the future of the individual in society consists of a networked future [...]. The involvement of the individual in society leads him to be this or that [...]. The individual sees himself [...] proposed goals and roles [...] towards types and images, or being directed by structures that he strives to realize by agreeing with them and fulfilling them. Thus society, in the face of the individual, elaborates a network of states and roles through which individual conduct must necessarily pass. [...]. The collective personality of the individual consists of what can acquire meaning in relation to other collective personalities that have arisen at the same time from a play of reciprocal causality. (Simondon, 1958/2022, pp. 397 and 421)

This structuring is what solves the problem posed by the "and so on to infinity" that characterizes the relations in the absolute transindividual. "And so on to infinity" is the title of another book by Paolo Virno (2010), which states:

> The interruption of the infinite regress goes hand in hand with a crystallization of thought and practice. I call crystallization the moment in which a form is fixed, a structure emerges [...]. The crystallization of thought and practice is one with the projection of the infinite regress into a finite order or, if you prefer, into a set of forms and structures not subject to recursive iteration. (Virno, 2010, pp. 105, 106)

Such structures can be emptied with the crisis of a determination not yet replaced by another. Each one then loses their real role and meaning even if perhaps they retain its appearance and are exposed to any senseless drift. In fact, only the "absolute" transindividual plot remains, and it is in these moments that one can see what the human condition is in such a context. Discovering that is disturbing. Vittorio Morfino reports the reflection of Laurent Bove (1996), on chapter XVII of the "Theological-Political Treatise" by Baruch Spinoza regarding the Jewish people. This story-interpretation has at its core the "terror" that takes hold of the people when the old structures are exhausted and the new ones are not yet there, evoked by the voice of God that cannot be understood and therefore instills so much fear that they believe their last hour has come.

> When the Jews decide to transfer, on the advice of Moses, their natural right to God [...], this demands from God – in reality from the imagination of the Jews themselves - [...] answers to problems that until then this imagination was not accustomed to either posing or even solving. [...]. However [...] when they heard the word of God, terrified, they believed their last hour had come [...]. From here comes the panic, which is the effect of this authentic trauma experienced by the Jews, since the situation in which they find themselves exceeds the limits of their tradition, of their memory, of the concatenations woven by habit, that is, the field of possibility of their experience. (Morfino, 2022, p. 121, with passages taken from Bove, 1996, pp. 226–227)

As stated at the beginning, according to Jason Read the West is today in a similar condition. But it is still Paolo Virno who associates the current uneasiness with the unveiling "of what has always been true of the ontological condition of the human animal. It is as if the root had risen to the surface, revealing itself to the naked eye".

> In order to use a unifying term to name the forms of life and linguistic games that characterize our era, I have used the notion of "multitude". This notion, the antipodes of that of "people", is defined by a complex of ruptures, landslides and innovations [...]. We should find a new term here, different from "fear" or "anguish" [...]. What comes to mind is the term disturbing. [...] The concept of "people" [...] is closely linked to the clear separation between a habitual "inside" and an unknown and hostile "outside". The concept of "multitude", on the other hand, hinges on the end of this separation. [...]. In the multitude there is the entire historical, phenomenological, empirical manifestation of the ontological condition of the human animal [...]. It is as if the root had risen to the surface, finally revealing itself to the naked eye. What has always been true is only now being revealed [...]. One could even say that the post-Fordist multitude manifests [...] the very genesis of the human animal, its distinctive characteristics. The multitude synthesizes this genesis, summarizes it. (Virno, 2014, § 3.1)

Paolo Virno shifts the terms fear and anguish toward the term "restlessness" to connect it to the passage from "people" to "multitude", and to the re-emergence of "what has always been true", the absolute transindividual. This shift recalls the one operated by Simondon from anguish as "inner experience of catastrophe" to its active character. Only that, according to Simondon, every individual "performs the test of solitude to discover transindividuality":

> The transindividual relationship consists in the one that Zarathustra establishes [...] with the tightrope walker who, having fallen to the ground, was injured and was abandoned by the crowd. The crowd, in fact, considered him merely for his function and therefore abandoned him after his death, because he had ceased to exercise his function. On the contrary, Zarathustra feels himself to be the brother of this man and drags this corpse with him to give it a worthy burial: for Zarathustra, in fact, the test of transindividuality begins with solitude, in the presence of this dead friend of his. What Nietzsche describes as «wanting to climb on one's own shoulders» consists in the act of every man who carries out the test of solitude to discover transindividuality. (Simondon, 1958/2022, p. 379)

The disturbing decline of collective structures and the emergence of the absolute transindividual would constitute the push for a progressive restructuring of which "every individual" is capable. But it must pass through solitude. One could say this: as the structured social body constitutes and is constituted by roles, when it fails and the multitude takes its place, it can be understood as constituted and constituting solitudes. In this sense, the solitude of Zarathustra, freed from the role he had, is the necessary condition for him to invent and begin to live new rules and new roles starting from the plot of the absolute transindividual: recognizing a stranger in need as a friend, even when he is already dead and can no longer perform the tightrope show or even that of his presence in life. Solitude is of the same nature as restlessness, the feeling due to the decline of habitual collective structures, and it is a condition conducive to innovation. It is the drive to action that meshes with that already seen as preindividual that pushes to translate into individuation.

At the same time, however, solitude slows down progressive restructuring. In the tale of the tightrope walker, solitude also indicates distancing, divergence, dualism between Zarathustra, the one, and the crowd, all the others. Solitude is a condition for new rules and new roles, but also the cause of their remaining sterile. In the current condition, such sterility comes from the fact that "the primary productive resource of contemporary capitalism lies in the linguistic-relational capacities of the human race, in the complex of communicative and cognitive faculties […] that distinguish man" (Virno, 2014, § 6.1). Thus, the obstacle placed in the way of progressive restructuring is neoliberalism that is supported despite its failures even on the re-emerged absolute transindividual. In this way, contemporary forms of life are marked by impotence due to the inarticulate excess of power.

> Oppressive and nagging crowding of capacities, skills, abilities […], the overabundance of a dynamis [power to do] which, failing […] to convert itself into a complex of carefully crafted acts, does nothing but stagnate and macerate […in] uninterrupted training: internships and trial contracts and updates on the most appropriate ways to keep up to date […], a compulsive training […], interminable preliminary training sessions [… which] grow wildly when it is certain that the competition will not take place. […]. Far from counteracting the paralysis that hinders the passage from dynamis to energheia [translation into action of the power to do], training ratifies it and, so to speak, stages it […]. The intellectual proletariat, which values its own loquacity as a dynamis radically separated from energheia, oscillates incessantly between two antithetical and complementary poles […]: telegraphic phrases, sparse labels placed on events and states of things, and vice versa a crowd of stereotyped expressions […] speeches that allude to everything without saying anything, verbal mush. (Virno, 2021, pp. 9–10, 77–80)

One may wonder whether these alarmed considerations of the philosopher are supported by any measurement. The question is fully justified if one considers the number of empirical studies on social media that have become an avalanche in recent years. The interests at stake are enormous and, one can imagine, the direct and indirect influence of large technological companies on researchers is also enormous in the hope (far from disappointed) of demonstrating "scientifically" that they do good. This is probably true. But it is also true that the attention of researchers is obvious due to the enormity of the facts. For example, in the United States.

> In 2014, 89.42% […] of young adults reported regular use of at least one social media site. This increased to 97.5% […] of young adults in 2016. Among regular users of social media sites in 2016, the top five sites were Tumblr (85.5%), Vine (84.7%), Snapchat (81.7%), Instagram (80.7%), and LinkedIn (78.9%). Respondents reported regularly using an average of 7.6 social media sites, with 85% using 6 or more sites regularly. Overall, 87% of young

> adults reported access or use of a smartphone with Internet access, 74% a desktop or laptop computer with Internet access, 41% a tablet with Internet access, 29% a smart TV or video game console with Internet access, 11% a cell phone without Internet access, and 3% none of these. (Villanti et al., 2017)

"Social media may have become an indispensable part of people's routine lives. According to a 2019 Pew ResearchCenter survey, young adults aged 18–29 are the most important force behind the surge in social media growth, accounting for a vast majority of online activity nowadays" (Bouffard et al., 2022, p. 1524). According to a 2023 survey conducted in the United States, "adolescents spend an average of 4.8 h each day on social media platforms. Girls spend 5.3 h daily on social networks, compared to 4.4 h for boys" (Statista).

Some research conducted with the aim of investigating the compulsive use of social media (especially Instagram) has led to the claim that "social media offers a virtual platform in which one may achieve a feeling of being together with others or a sense of belonging [...]. The pleasure and arousal created by the perceived feeling of connection with others reinforces the behavior of excessive social media use" (Bouffard et al., 2022, p. 1533). Furthermore, the most avid Instagram users believe that they are considered by others as not very "pleasant" and criticized in their social environment, while from the answers obtained to appropriate questions they were found to be conscientious (committed, hardworking, punctual), not very self-satisfied (Kircaburun & Griffiths, 2018, p. 165). One could deduce something opposite to the diagnosis of a brake on progressive restructuring given by the "impotence due to excess of power" due to the neoliberal exploitation of linguistic-relational capacities in the re-emerged absolute transindividual. Social media would not slow down but would help to find meaning and role. And they would help precisely those most affected by the discomfort they suffer from in society.

However, almost all these studies have a serious limitation in having measured the use of social media through the responses of the people interviewed. As the few studies that have used and compared both those measures and "objective" measures of time spent on social media seem to demonstrate, the results have been very distorted. Bouffard, Giglio, and Zheng have objectively measured the use of Instagram and the results are not very reassuring. Assuming that the romantic relationship between two people is the case of a collective-individual relationship par excellence, they conducted an experiment on a sample of 234 university students. And they wrote: "We believe that these findings add to our understanding of the processes by which social media influences romantic relationships and highlight the interactive effects of social media and relationship on causing unexpected, adverse consequences" (Bouffard et al., 2022, p. 1522). In fact, it is true that: (1) the use of social media reduces the satisfaction of a relationship, (2) by reducing satisfaction it becomes compulsive and accentuates conflicts and negative outcomes, (3) unless the partners are willing to make sacrifices for each other's benefit.

The question arises as to whether similar results obtained from a single study can be considered representative of a wider range. A study conducted by Nguyen Tien for his master's thesis at the Dutch University of Twente examined 14 studies on the specific topic of the consequences of the use of Instagram (and Facebook) on romantic relationships; and his conclusion is that the available research does not lead to the answer no, but not even to a certain yes.

> The findings highlight that whether relational outcomes are positive or negative depends on how individuals use these platforms, and the mediating and moderating factors involved. However, the results for relational outcomes, as well as for mediators and moderators, were fragmented, making it challenging to draw specific, consistent conclusions. Given the continuous evolution of social media, ongoing research is essential to address its dynamic influence on romantic relationships and relational well-being. (Tien, 2025, p. 35)

But a review of studies on the link between "problematic" media use (which becomes compulsive and does not solve problems) and social anxiety—loneliness concludes in a less uncertain way.

> This review solidifies our understanding of why more socially anxious and lonely individuals engage problematically online [...]. From the cross-sectional studies to date, we see that social anxiety and loneliness are associated with problematic SMU. From the experimental and longitudinal studies to date, we can conclude that loneliness is a risk factor for problematic SMU. It is likely that social anxiety and loneliness may be potential risk *factors and consequences* of one's SMU [...]. It may be important for clinicians to better understand what behaviours on social media are most common among more socially anxious and lonely individuals and attempt to limit the SMU behaviours that exacerbate one's problems. (O'Day & Heimberg, 2021, pp. 9–10)

Some Chinese research on the link between insomnia and compulsive use of social media among university students is also significant: "The results suggest that university students commonly experience sleep disturbance and insufficient sleep. Individuals with SMF [social media fatigue] and SMA [social media addiction] are likely to experience poor sleep quality. [...]. In addition, SMA, FoMO [fear of missing out], and sleep quality affected SMF" (Xinhong et al., 2023). The common feature that emerges from these results of empirical research is a typical vicious circle: when the use of social media is motivated or supported by social discomfort that seeks a remedy, the most frequent result is not relief but the worsening of such discomfort which in turn makes the use of media compulsive. It would therefore be this illusorily reduced but actually increased cost of authentic relationships that is holding back the progressive restructuring toward a new network of roles and meanings in the void left by the failures of neoliberalism. In fact, this restructuring is either done together, especially through face-to-face relationships, or it is not done at all.

In conclusion, individual and collective individuation takes on meaning through contingent historical "structures" subject to tensions, exhaustions, changes. When, as in contemporary times, there is exhaustion, the condition of polycrisis is disturbing, such as to generate anguish and fear but also push toward innovation and restructuring. The facilitations of collective action at the level of the transindividual plot depend on and contribute to such innovation of structures, innovation hindered, however, by the intentional use of transindividual relations by powerful forces interested in preventing it. Restructuring is today held back by neoliberalism that thrives despite its failures by using the transindividual relations that have come to light.

3.5.4 An Intuition

From what has been seen so far, it follows that the transindividual relations that have "come to light" in the crisis of neoliberalism bring, as such, facilitations to collective action (individual and collective individuation occur together and not in opposition), but, at the same time, they hinder it by slowing down the progressive restructuring necessary to give meaning to relations because neoliberalism survives its failures by using the relations of the absolute transindividual. This poses the question of whether there is a remedy.

Perhaps there is. One can look for a trace of it by trying to dissect the resistances to progressive restructuring supported by "interpretations" constructed by the dominant forces that prevent it. This is what Jason Read did, also using the contribution of Yves Citton.

> The neoliberal world [...] aspires to stability [...] overcoming the tensions between worker and capitalist, citizen and worker, in one singular image of the subject as entrepreneur of themselves. This flattening of the very dimensions of individuation [...] produced at the level of myth, of economic relations and of affective composition, constituted as much a particular structure of feeling, of cynism and opportunism, as it is a spontaneous philosophy of homo economicus. [...But] tensions and remnants necessary exist. Even cynism and opportunism are not without their ambivalence. [...] Individuation of the worker as entrepreneur of the self [...] is only possible if the conditions of its production, the narrowing of options through the wage relation and the canalization of desire [...], remain both hidden and naturalised. (Read, 2016, p. 281, with reference to Citton, 2010, pp. 16, 118)

Failed neoliberalism elaborates "myths, economic relations, and affective composition", to maintain itself through the homologation of those included "in one singular image of the subject as entrepreneur of themselves" and "the particular structure of feeling, of cynism and opportunism, as it is a spontaneous philosophy of homo economicus". This allows the system to use technical innovation as the primary task of the entrepreneur of themselves, but excluding: "narrowing of options [...] and the canalization of desire". This is possible only because everything is "naturalised", that is, "attributed to the superior reasons of technology" (Citton, 2010, p. 278); and at the same time everything is "hidden", that is, a matter of "faith". Thus, it is clear that the formula of persistent neoliberalism capable of slowing down progressive restructuring is "science and faith" which, in fact, is at the basis of "dissemination by the media, not only as opinion but as the actual meaning of things" (Citton, 2010, p. 278). In other words, the persistent ideology based on science and faith is functional and necessary for conservative inclusion and exclusionary innovation. Science together with the faith of technofeudalism is evident. Everything is science and there is no doubt about it. But everything is also faith. For the new system it is essential that people believe the machines are at their service, and there is no doubt that those who control them will continually take care to make people believe it. One knows that they are watching and know one better than one knows oneself, but as in the Panopticon, one believes that it is for one's own good.

> We pretend that the apparatus is a person because we are not used to talking to machines [...]. But knowing that it is not a person is our way of coming to terms with its deep knowledge

> of us, which would otherwise be unsettling or frightening. At that precise moment, when we relate to the apparatus as if it were a person when we know it is not, we are at our most vulnerable – ready to fall into the trap of thinking [believing] in Alexa as our Pandora-like mechanical servant.[9] Alas, Alexa is not a servant. Rather, she is an element of cloud-based command capital that is turning you into a servant, with your help and through your own unpaid labor, in order to further enrich her owners. (Varoufakis, 2023, p. 95)

Simondon warned that science and faith are the opposite of "wisdom".

> Science and faith are equivalent to the debris of a stranded spirituality that divides the subject, opposing him to himself rather than leading him to discover a meaning according to the collective. Spiritual unity consists in this transductive relationship between action and emotion, and one could perhaps define this relationship as wisdom. (Simondon, 1958/2022, p. 343)

An intuition follows. It could be that a way out consists in reversing the logic of science and faith. It could perhaps be found by using faith *against* science and science *against* faith in order to construct the "transductive relationship between action and emotion" and preserving the unity of the subject "leading him to discover a meaning (of himself) according to collective". Indeed, it is intuited that the transindividual root that has come to light can bring the lymph of individuation to the subject, both individual and collective without opposition, only if it does not become sterile due to the lack of the ground that nourishes and sustains it. The ground is missing when one is led, as Paolo Virno said, to "loquacity as a dynamis radically separated from energheia, oscillates incessantly between two antithetical and complementary poles: telegraphic phrases, sparse labels placed on events and states of things, and vice versa a crowd of stereotyped expressions, speeches that allude to everything without saying anything, verbal mush". This is precisely what Simondon seems to allude to when he attributes to science and faith "the debris of a stranded spirituality that divides the subject, opposing him to himself". Science and faith imply believing in science and making a science of faith. Believing that every determination is necessarily what it is, that the brick is given by the clay and the mold, that every process is established by its routine, that this belief is incontestable. In this way, the relationship with the other, in itself tendentially generative or at least destabilizing, puts the subject against themselves in a sterile opposition between what they firmly believe and what they glimpse in contradiction. For this reason, using faith against science and science against faith implies breaking the cage that forces the subject against themselves. As will be seen in the examples, this formula effectively leads to accepting the risk of change by opening to the generative comparison, and also to the clash with others, from which derives the inherently provisional individuation, the continuous reciprocal adaptation of the clay and the mold, the dynamic routine, in which everything

[9] In the mythical tale, Pandora was a girl created by the god of fire Hephaestus by order of Jupiter and endowed with the tribute of all the gods with every beauty, virtue, skill, grace, cunning, and ingenuity. Having a servant like Pandora would be the best. As long as she obeyed Jupiter's order not to open the jar he had given her. When she disobeyed and opened it, all the evils contained within rushed furiously upon the world and closed it before the hope that was left at the bottom could emerge.

is always in question. This does not block the action but is instead the only condition that supports it as an effective conjunction between energheia and dynamis.

Preserving the unity of the subject "leading them to discover a meaning (of themselves) according to collective" implies inclusion. Between action and emotion implies innovation. So, using faith against science and science against faith is not in contradiction but rather it is functional to use inclusion against conservation and innovation against exclusion. The latter being, as seen, the recommendation for collective action in the intersubjective. In this way there would be a real meshing between the levers for collective action in the intersubjective and the levers for collective action in the transindividual which, by interacting, could mutually strengthen each other.

3.5.5 A Formula

The formula "use faith against science and science against faith" to "use inclusion against conservation and innovation against exclusion" has the accent on *using* and on *against*. It cannot be resolved in some synthesis but must be framed within the context of negative dialectics. Theodor Adorno proposes the image of the constellation opposed to the system: "The constellation is not the system. It is not the place where everything returns, where everything is smoothed out, but one moment sheds light on the other" (Adorno, 1963/2014, p. 132). Conciliation does not occur on the conceptual ground in which the identical and the opposite support each other and fall together. Conciliation occurs on the ground of praxis, action, experience. "Adorno's gamble lies [...] entirely in this possibility [...] of going beyond its mere formal recognition [of the non-identical], to show in it a protrusion towards the qualitative, irreducible, unregulated element of our experience" (Cicatello, 2016–2017, p. 56). Here one also sees the importance of the term "to use" with which the formula begins. It is in the concrete experience of using faith against science and science against faith (using inclusion against conservation and innovation against exclusion) that "one moment sheds light on the other". It could be said that, in the course of concrete processes, the action dictated by faith in contrast with science will modify the reality on which the dictate of science against faith will act, just as Cicatello observes: "Against every systematic form of knowledge, which Adorno exemplifies in the logic of everything comes back, a knowledge worthy of this name must remain open to the unexpected [...] must resemble the performance of a piece of music, where the irruption of a single note is able to redraw the entire harmonic course of the others" (Cicatello, 2016–2017, p. 57).

This is in theory, but the theory is more convincing if one is able to give examples, if one can present concrete cases that demonstrate its application. In moral philosophy, casuistry was widely used by Greek and Roman philosophers, Jewish rabbis, preachers, Christian teachers, and Islamic jurists when faced with problems of conscience. Which could only be solved by combining the knowledge of moral science with the demonstration of its concrete implementation.[10] The formula obtained does not present a “case of conscience”. But its precise understanding is not simple and immediate. Furthermore, it is necessary to see its operational implications. So, just as in casuistry, case histories that allow people to understand its practical application can be very useful.

3.5.6 From Theory to Practice

The question arises as to where one can look and what one can trace back to see if the formula has actually been applied, if the formula works, and in what ways. What the suggestions are that practice offers to better specify it. The answer can be found at the very origin of Western thought. The formula can be seen at work in ancient examples: the history of the Jewish people told by Spinoza, Nietzsche’s Zarathustra, the myth of Ulysses and the Sirens, the trial of Socrates.

3.5.6.1 Moses

Continuing the reading of the history of the Jewish people:

> Thus arose the need for a second pact in which the Jews relied on the mediation of Moses to self-organize. And the intuition (génie) of Moses - who was in almost total harmony (osmose) with the spirit of his people whose prejudices he shared - was to prescribe to the Jews, in those conditions, something that could not contradict their habits, but which, on the contrary, would make them fully efficient, on a political level, for the well-being of the people. Moses therefore imagines what the Jewish people (the complex of acquired customs and habits) had not been able to imagine without him, that is, stable institutions for the new State. Moses is the productive imagination of the body of the Jewish people which rises, through him, to a higher degree of complexity. Not the spirit of this body, which would guide it as if from the outside, but this body itself to a higher stage of perfection. (Morfino, 2022, p. 121, with passages taken from Bove, 1996, pp. 226–227)

It emerges here that what sterilizes the second meaning of solitude (foreignness), avoided by Moses, is his almost total “osmosis” with “the spirit of his people whose

---

[10] In the long and multifaceted history of casuistry in the Christian era, from the first to the twelfth century, the practical applications are common in the works of the Fathers of the Church, in the determinations of the bishops, in the commentaries on the Scriptures and in the penitential books. After the Fourth Lateran Council (1215), casuistry became a true doctrine in its own right within the context of a reawakened interest in theological studies and in the apostolic activity of the mendicant orders. The work of the Dominican Raymond of Pennafort, entitled “Summa de Poenitentia et Matrimonio”, published around 1235, opened an era in the scientific study of casuistry and established its canons for over 200 years. The sixteenth century was characterized by a great development of theological sciences, due to the Counter-Reformation, in which the Society of Jesus stood out, whose theologians committed themselves to the commentary of the second part of the “Summa Theologica” of Thomas Aquinas, dealing with casuistic questions regarding personal, social, political, and religious duties.

prejudices he shared". In this way he was able to mediate (in the sense of being in the middle) for the self-organization of the people with new institutions: the name that one can understand as referring to the new collective structures made of rules and roles. The new institutions-structures would indeed come from an innovative act, but only if designed in such a way as not to enter into too accentuated contradiction with the habits that should be conducted to greater efficiency, that is, not to exclude. One may question what Moses could have done that he did not do for the "good of the people". He could have used science and faith. Washing his hands of it, he could have left the people the choice: either with science, all stay together (inclusion), reaffirming tradition (conservation) and distancing themselves from God, or with faith, banish (exclusion) anyone who resisted the word of God (innovation). He could have done this to avoid the responsibility of living the conflict, if he had not trusted the people or even God, if he had been cynical to the point of not having any hope for a better future. Since he believed in the progress of the "well-being of the people", Moses took on the responsibility of offering the solution he had devised using faith against science and science against faith: trust in God even against tradition (innovation), but not moving too far away from it—science against faith—avoiding having to exclude someone (inclusion). From here came the progressive restructuring.

3.5.6.2 Zarathustra

The second example is that of Zarathustra, who could have used science by leaving the dead tightrope walker to the dogs (conservation) to stay with the crowd and not separate from it (inclusion). Or he could have used faith by loudly proclaiming his condemnation against the insensitive and ignorant crowd (innovation-exclusion). The feeling that could have driven him would have been, in this case too, the cynicism of believing that no one could be interested in a dignified burial of the dead until proven otherwise, proof that would eventually come only by shaking the crowd, attacking it and publicly condemning its indifference. Instead, moved by empathy for the dead and for the crowd, using faith against science and science against faith, he did not make speeches. He made a gesture, a counter-current gesture (innovation) full of meaning, which however did not blame anyone, thus offering itself to a possible imitation (inclusion).

3.5.6.3 Ulysses and the Sirens

A third example can come from a reworking of the much-repeated myth of Ulysses and the Sirens (Book XII of the Odyssey), starting from the well-known interpretation by Max Horkheimer and Theodor Adorno in "Dialectic of Enlightenment". It is an example a contrariis; a case of non-application of the formula that clarifies its reasons and consequences. Ulysses does not apply the formula and in this way proposes the archetype of instrumental rationality typical of technology; which, however, is only one of the two components of Western thought. The other, which could be called critical rationality, will be at work in the trial of Socrates (next example) in which the formula is applied even at the cost of life. In this way the two examples show that from the beginning the formula faith against science and procedurally science against faith to innovate and include is opposed to science and faith that preserves and excludes.

> Odysseus's thought, equally hostile to his own death and his own happiness [...] knows only two possibilities [...]. One [...] he prescribes to his companions. He plugs their ears with wax and orders them to row with all their might. He who wishes to endure and subsist must not listen to the call of the irrevocable, and can do so only because he is unable to listen. This is what society has always provided for. Fresh and concentrated, the workers must look forward, and leave everything aside. The impulse that would induce them to deviate must be sublimated - with angry bitterness - into further effort. They become practical. The other possibility is the one chosen by Odysseus, the landowner, who makes others work for him. He hears, but he is helplessly tied to the mast of the ship, and the stronger the temptation becomes, the more tightly he is tied, just as, later, the bourgeois will deny themselves happiness more tenaciously the closer they get to it, as their power grows. What he has heard remains for him without consequence: he can only nod with his head to untie it, but it is already too late. His companions, who hear nothing, know only of the danger of the song, and not of its beauty, and they leave him tied to the mast, to save him and to save themselves with him. They reproduce, with their own, the life of the oppressor, who can no longer escape from his social role. [...] Through the subordination of all life to the demands of its preservation, the minority that commands guarantees, with its own security, also the survival of the whole. Between the Scylla of relapse into simple reproduction and the Charybdis of free and uncontrolled satisfaction, the dominant spirit [which] has always distrusted any compass other than that of the lesser evil, has tried to pass, from Homer to modern times. (Adorno & Horkheimer, 1944/1969, pp. 39, 41–42)

One may wonder whether there was another possibility. Whether one could innovate (listen to the song of the sirens from whom tradition dictated to stay away) by including, instead of excluding everyone except himself, as Ulysses did, ending up doing nothing. There was, and one could imagine considering the equally famous speech of Sarpedon reported in the middle of the Iliad. After almost a decade, besieged and surrounded in their citadel, the Trojans have launched a counterattack and pushed the Achaeans back to the coast. The latter have built a wall around the port to protect their fleet, but Hector is leading an attack that, if he manages to break through the wall, will destroy the Greek ships. Sarpedon, king of Lycia and ally of the Trojans, participates in the assault, and before the wall is broken through, he delivers a speech addressing his companion Glaucus. We, says Sarpedon, are noble, privileged, we live above the common herd, and for that we must be braver, more heroic. So let us go. This "let us go", in Emily Wilson's translation reads: "So let us go. Perhaps we shall succeed and gain a triumph by another's death, or someone may triumph over us", in Alexander Pope's translation: "the life that others pay, let us give, and give to fame what we owe", in Robert Fagles': "so let us attack! Give glory to our enemy, or win it for ourselves!", in Richmond Lattimore's: "let us go forth and gain glory for ourselves, or yield it to others". Thus, "responsibility to the people is [...] part of the essential background of the political drama of the epics" (Sutherland, 1979, p. 512), and this responsibility is not circumscribed, but extends to accepting the risk of defeat and death. Ulysses therefore gave a reductive answer

> in the evaluation of power relations, which makes survival [...] depend on the early admission of one's own defeat, so that the cunning man survives only at the cost of his own dream, he pays by disenchanting himself [...]. He can never have everything, he must always know how to wait, be patient, give up [...]. He slips and slinks, this is his way of surviving, and every fame granted to him by himself and others only serves to reiterate that the dignity of a hero is acquired only with the humiliation of the impulse to complete, universal, undivided happiness. (Adorno & Horkheimer, 1944/1969, pp. 64-65)

No, in Sarpedon's speech, Ulysses, to truly be the hero obliged to be like a king, should not have sneaked away. He should have used faith against science and science against faith. He should have plugged his ears with wax, sat at the helm and raised the sail, tied his companions to the oar benches and let them listen to the sirens' song. If fate had allowed it, the ship could have proceeded even with just a breath of wind even if the sailors had stopped rowing. He would have sacrificed himself to allow his companions to hear the sublime song, bringing them home, nevertheless, having in exchange the "enchantment" of true glory to offset the loss of not having heard the sirens' song.

In this example, the change of structures is no longer desired by God, as in the case of Moses, or triggered by an accident, as in the case of Zarthustra, it is sought and nevertheless entering into it is in things. Ulysses and his companions do not want to follow the tradition that recommends staying away from the island of the sirens, but they want to pass close to it and find a way for someone to hear them. The temptation was there, very clear, and the stakes were high: trying to survive without giving up the sublime experience. The action that Ulysses would have had to organize and carry out would then have required a great sacrifice, which would have been repaid by a great prize. Instead, the entry into the change of structures occurred, but not the inclusive innovation. There was excluding innovation, with the result that there was not even innovation but conservation.

3.5.6.4 The Trial and Death of Socrates

Civilization has not been based only on instrumental rationality, as represented in the myth of Ulysses. If the only compass had been that of the "lesser evil", the West would not have been capable of great innovations: unlikely events that were rationalized only in hindsight. The lesser evil implies prediction and calculation that have very little to do with the risk of radical innovations. If it is true that today "the West is a sinking ship", this ship has sailed the seas for a long time, has gone far, has had serious faults but also undeniable successes. At its origins another myth must also be recognized, equally and perhaps more famous and revived than the myth of Ulysses and the Sirens, that of Socrates and his condemnation to death,[11] as a free

[11] The term myth indicates a story that is not very close to the truth, while it exposes the origins of a civilization in the time of heroes, presenting them as intuitively real, thus justifying the forms of existence of the community and providing its models. This term might seem inappropriate here since the life and death of the "greatest philosopher" are historically documented. But the documentation has left wide margins of uncertainty. Eugène Dupréel's critical analysis of the reliability of the

exercise of rationality and indispensable faith in the established order, without the latter being naturally and peacefully reducible to the former. "The trial of Socrates is one of those rare events that have indelibly marked our history [...]. It could not be otherwise, after all, if one thinks of what is at stake: the clash between Socrates and Athens is the clash between philosophy and democracy. Two fundamental values, freedom and participation, that should go together and that instead have led to an irreconcilable, deadly opposition" (Bonazzi, 2018, p. 3). This is precisely what the myth of Socrates warns about: that the essential values of freedom and participation do not go together peacefully, indeed they are, if anything, naturally in conflict and may not find a solution at all.

This is the ever-repeated interpretation of the myth. One could argue, however, that that story says something more. Unraveling its complexity, one sees that it is not only about the opposition between the freedom of rational inquiry and faith in the established order (science versus faith), but presents the entire formula: using science against faith and using faith against science to innovate without excluding in collective action under conditions of structural change. The myth of Socrates warns, however, that the formula can fail, and that to succeed it may require extreme sacrifice.

It is not the case here to recall the whole history of the trial and its interpretations. It is enough to start from that part of the reconstructions, a minority but significant, according to which it was a political trial[12]: nothing to do with the issues just mentioned. As a minority, this thesis did not go that far, only managing to complicate its deciphering. However, it has opened an interesting window if the reason why it was formulated is asked. The crimes for which Socrates was called to answer were

sources, after over 400 pages demonstrating a real "mythical construction" of the character Socrates, concluded a century ago in this way: "Perhaps we will be criticized for having proposed only disputes of the historical truth in the portraits dedicated to Socrates. After having censored them so much, did we not have the duty [...] to also gather together everything that can be presumed true about him? This work must undoubtedly be done, but the preparatory criticism is far from being completed" (Dupréel, 1922, p. 414). A century has passed since 1922, during which a huge mass of studies has been dedicated (also) to doing the work hoped for by Dupréel. But the complete historical truth about Socrates remains inexorably unattainable. The expression "the Socrates problem" has been coined and is considered in some respects insoluble (Ferrari, 2007; Prior, 2006).

[12] The thesis of the political trial for having collaborated in one way or another with the regime of the thirty was supported in ancient times in a lost work by Polycrates, of which there are several testimonies. In modern times, among others, by Isidor Feinstein Stone. His book remains the most cited even today. Stone was not a professional philosopher, but highly esteemed by the specialist of ancient philosophy, Malcolm Schofield (2000) even in contrast to some positions of Gregory Vlastos (1994), author of important studies on Socrates that overshadow his criticism of traditional democracy. Stone's book states: "It was Socrates' political positions [...] that ultimately got him into trouble" (Stone, 1988, p. 138). Mogens Herman Hansen, placing himself in continuity with Stone ("my approach is not far from that of I.F. Stone" [Hansen, 1995, p. 3]) but with the aim of correcting "a series of incorrect interpretations of the sources, and the omission of some important information on the trial" (Hansen, 1995 p. 3.), nevertheless arrives at the same conclusion as Stone. Finally, one can cite Josiah Ober (2006), who 10 years after Hansen recomposed the review of the contributions and sources and arrived again at the same statement. The most relevant mass of literature has responded to all of them.

not respecting the gods of the State and corrupting the youth. But according to the thesis of the political trial, in the absence of the complete text of the indictment, this charge was specious while the real one, such as to justify the condemnation, was in reality that of having been stained by collaboration with the antidemocratic regime of the Thirty Tyrants (404–401 BC[13]), a crime for which he could not be explicitly prosecuted because he was protected by amnesty. The thesis of the political trial was developed to explain two "mysteries": (1) why the trial took place only in 399 BC (when Socrates was already 70 years old, after at least 30 years dedicated to the relentless criticism, for many annoying and antidemocratic, of the poverty on the rational level of the Athenian government and society); (2) why the line of defense chosen by Socrates was so counterproductive as to induce several contemporaries and modern exegetes to think that "he wanted to die" (Bonazzi, 2018, p. 1). An answer to both questions could be given if Socrates' crime had been collaborationism: having been the teacher of several oligarchs, therefore compromised with tyranny, a crime that could and should have been judged as soon as the democratic regime was re-established. It would then have been clear that the sentence had already been decided before the trial, and any defense was perfectly useless: better for Socrates to use the last opportunity to claim his "superiority". However, the thesis of the political trial does not hold up in light of the sources that are able to demonstrate how Socrates, although he had been Critias' teacher, had harshly criticized him in public, had not collaborated with the government of the Thirty, so much so that they had persecuted him and would have had him assassinated if they had not been expelled.[14] But if

[13] In 404 BC Athens had surrendered to Sparta, ending the Peloponnesian War. The Spartans had installed a friendly government led by Critias, Charmides, and 28 other anti-democrats, several of whom, especially Critias, had been students of Socrates. The reign of the "Thirty Tyrants" was short and brutal: arbitrary arrests, judicial murders, confiscation of property, and widespread exile. Plato, no democrat, wrote in the Seventh Letter that the previous democratic age had been a golden age by comparison. Some Athenians fled the city in an army initially based in the Athenian village of Phyle, and a democratic revolt overthrew the Thirty in 403 BC. Critias was killed in battle and others fled. The ensuing peace re-established democratic government, while a new oligarchic polis was established in the city of Eleusis with the survivors of the Thirty regime. An amnesty was issued in Athens, protecting all but the Thirty and some of their closest associates from legal action. Two years later, in 401 BC, following another battle, the polis was finally reunited under a single democratic government. The exact date of Socrates' trial has never been established, but it is placed between the autumn of 400 BC and the winter of 399 BC. In any case, it occurred after the restoration of democratic government, but in the midst of a deep and multifaceted crisis in the Athenian polis.

[14] The reconstructions of the trial have encountered a specific difficulty. It was a question of evaluating the reliability and relevance of the sources to establish which side to tip the scales between Socrates' guilt as an ancient teacher of some of the tyrants and his merits for not having agreed to collaborate with the regime. It could be said that the thesis of the political trial gave more weight to the guilt (incomprehensible today if it was not, as it was not, "incitement to crime") for the effort to place the trial in the time in which the Athenians recognized everyone's right to say anything, but held them responsible for the consequences, even unintended, of their words. Furthermore, the thesis of the political trial neglected to note that in Athens there was not in reality "a compact democratic bloc intent on punishing Socrates" (Bonazzi, 2018, p. 52). Finally, it can be noted that in the entry "Socrates' Trial" of the Encyclopedia Britannica (entry updated in May 2024) the reconstruction coincides with that of Bonazzi who excludes the political trial.

the process was correct,[15] and not a "show trial" like several others of the same period set up with accusations of impiety but for political reasons, if Socrates was really prosecuted for violations against the traditional faith, the two mysteries remain unanswered: why it was only in 399 BC and why he wanted to die?

It is at this point that an explanation can be suggested starting from the crisis of the structures of Athenian democracy, which had not prevented the defeat and then the tyranny. Their simple restoration, which took place, could not solve the problems that had put them in crisis, so much so that Athens was in very serious conditions after 401 BC on all levels (economic, social, cultural, political) and would remain so for over a decade.[16] It was in those conditions that a very strong tension arose between those who desperately clung to tradition and those, like Socrates and his students, who worked for a progressive restructuring[17] starting from the criticism of previous structures. Socrates went to trial and died because in a moment of serious structural crisis he wanted to affirm the reasons of philosophy, using science against traditional faith, a faith that, however, he did not reject at all.[18] And he would have been saved if the people of Athens had succeeded in responding to his provocation

[15] "Deplored everywhere and at every time for its manifest injustice, the story of Socrates is actually part of a well-organized system, much less arbitrary or thoughtless than is normally believed. [...]. The Socratic story was marked by a series of formal steps, aimed at verifying the legitimacy of the accusation, but also at guaranteeing the rights of the accused" (Bonazzi, 2018, p. 16).

[16] "Our account of the collapse and recovery of democracy in Athens highlights a number of factors. Military defeat and the presence of an organized opposition played a major role in the collapse of democracy. However, we identify the deeper cause as a crisis of legitimacy precipitated by performance failures ultimately attributable to a fundamental flaw in the institutional framework. So much so that the restoration of democracy was unable to remedy it. Instead, there was a decade of political turmoil during which democracy remained in question, [...] and it was finally restored but in significantly revised forms" (Carugati & Ober, 2023, p. 26).

[17] It is also possible to specify what the point or one of the main points of this restructuring was. Given the concrete unfolding of events, there was undoubtedly a fragility of the Athenian organization exposed to the moods and errors of a grassroots democracy that would have needed a more professional management. This was precisely one of the central arguments of the Socratic critique. In Xenophon one can read: "The accuser claimed that Socrates was inducing his friends to disregard the laws in force and he did so by saying that it was senseless to elect the governors of the city by drawing lots, when no one would want to employ a pilot by drawing lots, nor a builder nor a flautist, nor anyone else chosen for another activity of this type in which mistakes produce much less damage than those committed in leading the State" (Bonazzi, 2018, p. 46).

[18] This is a crucial point. Socrates was not accused of atheism but of "asebeia", that is, irreverence towards the gods of the State. Socrates firmly believed that "the gods possess a perfect knowledge of things, of good and evil [...] and all that remained was [...] to decipher the message that the divine sign transmits. There is therefore no conflict between reason, philosophy and faith, but an attempt to integrate one's own human wisdom with the perfect wisdom of the gods" (Bonazzi, 2018, p. 89). What was contested to Socrates was essentially a conception of faith in the gods in contrast with the common feeling of that time in those conditions. "On this Socrates, as Plato later, is clear: the numerous prayers that can be read in the dialogues are no longer addressed to the gods to ask for something, but to oneself, as exhortations to assimilate oneself as much as possible to the perfect world of the gods. Piety is therefore redefined: truly pious is he who contributes to the order and beauty of the universe. On this point Xenophon's testimony is not too distant from Plato's, [...except] in insisting on the great respect that Socrates always showed for the rites and all the religious practices of the city, observing them punctually" (Bonazzi, 2018, p. 90).

not by destroying it, but by working on it, using faith against science together with him, a faith rediscovered and transformed by that provocation. Having, moreover, come quite close to succeeding, if it is true that the first vote of the popular jury condemned him with a not sensational majority of 280 against 221.[19] And this being in fact the intention: to die as a last resort to carry his provocation to the end so that a constructive response could come, possibly immediately, otherwise at least after his death.

If this interpretation is as plausible as it seems, then Socrates was really the hero (in fact in the long run he won by making history while his executioners remained only because he remained) who accepted in all respects the challenge that Ulysses refused: to risk his life on the bet that it was possible to create new institutions for Athens by playing science against faith, which he had personally taken charge of; and then—together with the people—faith against science. That is, to innovate and include. All this if the interpretation is plausible. It might not be according to what is written about the torment (or for others the betrayal) of Plato, Socrates' greatest student and witness of the trial, according to which the Master and his philosophy failed. Unlike Moses, who "was in almost total harmony with the spirit of his people and shared their prejudices" so as to "prescribe to the Jews something that could not contradict their habits", according to Plato, Socrates prescribed something in total contradiction with the habits of the people and for this reason he failed. It can be noted, however, that it is not very important to decide whether Socrates failed or whether he was successful in the long run, whether his death was a defeat or the only means left to win even post mortem. Here it is important to note that even in the myth of Socrates the formula using science against faith and faith against science is central: in the first case of failure, because it was not well applied by Socrates unlike what Moses succeeded in doing, in the second of success after death, because the people were missing, who would have applied it only after having killed him.

---

[19] It was a jury of 501 chosen by lot from the 6,000 ordinary citizens who were in turn chosen by lot every year to form the popular juries. They were therefore not jurists, but neither were they unfamiliar with the law and politics since in Athens trials were the order of the day and participation in political life was a very intense activity. There were two votes, as prescribed by law: the first to establish guilt and the second to decide the penalty between that proposed by the prosecution and that proposed by the accused. Socrates opposed the death penalty proposed by Meletus by saying that "he would have deserved the hospitality of the Prytaneum for the rest of his life" (a public building where the sacred fire was kept and common sacrifices were made; ambassadors were welcomed there and it was also the lifelong residence of citizens considered particularly deserving). "Then he proposed a fine that he could afford, that is, half a mina; finally, when some of his friends, including Plato, promised to contribute, he proposed a fine of 30 minas" (Hansen, 1995, p. 18), half a talent, or 10,000 euros today, while half a mina was 167 euros. Despite this last provocation, the votes against him in the second ballot increased by only 80 compared to the first, that is, they were 360 out of 501.

3.5.6.5 Conclusion

In ancient examples, the formula is found precisely in the circumstances in which collective action is involved in the change of structures when the transindividual plot resurfaces. But these are examples far from modern civilization. However, despite the common idea that considers technical-scientific knowledge self-sufficient, in many modern cases this has not been the case. In order to achieve results in conditions of structural crisis, this knowledge had to be openly defeated by the deployment of less scientific, much more emotional-imaginative resources, those summarized by the term "faith". Which, in the process, then had to give way again to science. In the next chapters, two examples are presented. The first concerns a pioneering company in Silicon Valley, at the origin of the greatest leap forward of contemporary capitalism, even if it then degenerated into exploitation, financial speculation, perhaps even into a new post-capitalist system as Varoufakis claims. That enterprise (ROLM) created advanced forms of participation close to those that today Varoufakis and others imagine necessary to fight against this new system. The second example, at the opposite pole, concerns the "people's houses" at the time of the second industrial revolution in Europe, a useful example 1 for discovering the complicated and long processes underlying the progress of the proletarian camp, a discovery that today could be interesting and instructive.

References

Adorno, T., & Horkheimer, M. (1944/1969). *Dialettica dell'Illuminismo.* Einaudi. First edition: *Dialektik der Aufklärung.* Querido, 1944.

Adorno T. (1963/2014). *Drei Studien zu Hegel.* Suhrkamp 1963. Italian edition: Tre studi su Hegel. Il Mulino, 2014.

Arendt, H. (1958). *The Origins of Totalitarianism* - (2nd ed.). Meridian Books.

Bardin, A. (2010). *Epistemologia e politica in Gilbert Simondon - Individuazione, tecnica e sistemi sociali.* Edizioni Fuoriregistro.

Barker, E. (1952). *Principles of social and political theory.* Oxford University Press.

Bonazzi, M. (2018). *Processo a socrate.* Laterza.

Bouffard, S., Giglio, D., & Zheng, Z. (2022). Social media and romantic relationship: Excessive social media use leads to relationship conflicts, negative outcomes, and addiction via mediated pathway. *Social Science Computer Review, 40*(6), 1523–1541.

Bove, L. (1996). *La stratégie du conatus: Affirmation et résistance chez Spinoza.* J. Vrin.

Brooks, P. (1984). *Reading for the plot: Design and intention in narrative.* Harvard University Press.

Brooks, P. (2022). *Seduced by story: The use and abuse of narrative.* New York Review Books.

Browning, L. D., & Hartelius, E. J. (2018). Rhetorical analysis in management and organizational research 2007–2017. In Ø. Ihlen & R. L. Heath (Eds.), *The handbook of organizational rhetoric and communication.* John Wiley & Sons.

Buber, M. (1923). *Ich und Du.* Insel-Verlag.

Carugati, F., & Ober, J. (2023). Chapter 2—Democratic collapse and recovery in ancient Athens. In A. Fung, D. Moss & O. A. Westad (Eds.), *When democracy breaks: Studies in democratic erosion and collapse, from ancient Athens to the present day* (pp. 25–42). Oxford University Press.

Cicatello, A. (2016/2017). Il negativo in questione - Una lettura di Adorno. *Consecutio Rerum* I(2), 49–63.
Citton, Y. (2010). *L'Avenir des Humanités – Économie de la conaissance ou cultures de l'interpretation*. La Découverte.
Collier, P., & Kay, J. (2020). *Greed is dead—Politics after individualism*. Allen Lane.
Congdon, W. J., Kling, J. R., Ludwig, J., & Mullainathan, S. (2017). Chapter 4—Social policy: Mechanism experiments and policy evaluations. In E. Duflo & A. Banerjee (Eds.), *Handbook of economic field experiments* (Vol. 2, pp. 389–426). Elsevier.
Congdon, W. J., Simms, M., & De Vita, C. (2021). *Assessing the impact of community-level initiative—A literature review*. OPRE Report #2021-4.
Connolly, W. E. (2013). *The fragility of things: Self-Organizing processes, neoliberal fantasies, and democratic activism*. Duke University Press.
Cooke, B., & Kothari, U. (2001). *Participation—The new tyranny*. Zed Books.
Crouch, C. (2020). *Post-Democracy after the crises*. Polity Press.
Curcio, G. G., & Papini, R. (2016). *Jacques Maritain e il Concilio Vaticano II*. Studium.
De Benoist, A. (2014). *Quatre figures de la révolution conservatrice allemande: Werner Sombart, Arthur Moeller van den Bruck, Ernst Niekisch, Oswald Spengler*. Les Amis d'Alain de Benoist.
Deleuse, G., & Guattari, F. (1994). *What is philosophy?* Columbia University Press.
Díaz-Martin, L., Gopalan, A., Guarnieri, E., & Jayachandran, S. (2023). Greater than the sum of the parts? Evidence on mechanisms operating in women's groups. *The World Bank Research Observer, 38*(1), 1–35.
Dostoevsky, F. F. (1868). Fyodor Dostoevsky to Sofia Alexandrovna, Geneva January 1, 1868. In *Letters of Fyodor Michailovitch Dostoyevsky to his family and friends* (p. 135), trans. Ethel Golburn Mayne. Chatto and Windus, 1914.
Dupréel E. (1922). *Légende socratique et les sources de Platon*. Les Edition Robert Sand.
Dyson, K. (2021). *Conservative liberalism, ordo-liberalism, and the state—Disciplining democracy and the market*. Oxford University Press.
Ferrari, F. (Ed.). (2007). *Socrate tra personaggio e mito*. Rizzoli.
Fiester, L. (2011). *Measuring change while changing measures: Learning in, and from, the evaluation of making connections*. The Annie E. Casey Foundation.
Hale, S. (2004). The communitarian 'philosophy' of new labour. In S. Hale, W. Leggett, & L. Martell (Eds.), *The third way and beyond—Criticisms, futures, alternatives* (pp. 87–107). Manchester University Press.
Han, B-C. (2017). *L'espulsione dell'Altro – Società, percezione e comunicazione oggi*. Nottetempo Edizioni.
Hansen, M. H. (1995). The trial of Sokrates from the Athenian point of view. *Historisk-Filosofiske Meddelelser, 71*, 1–36.
Harris, A. L. (1942). Sombart and German (National) socialism. *Journal of Political Economy, 50*(6), 805–835.
Hegel, G. W. F. (1807/1979). *System der Wissenschaft. Erster Theil, die Phänomenologie des Geistes*. Georg Wilhelm Friedrich Hegel Werke Band 3. Frankfurt: Holzinger, 1979. First edition Bamberg und Würzburg: Joseph Anton Goebhardt, 1807.
Hesse, J.-O. (2014). New 'fundamental laws of capitalism'—Thomas Piketty and economic history. *VSWG Vierteljahrschrift Für Sozial- und Wirtschaftsgeschichte, 101*(4), 5000–5005.
Honneth, A. (2024). *The working sovereign: Labour and democratic citizenship*. Polity Press.
Jagers, S. C., Harring, N., Löfgren, Å., Sjöstedt, M., Alpizar, F., Brülde, B., Langlet, D., Nilsson, A., Almroth, B. C., Dupont, S., & Steffen, W. (2020). On the preconditions for large-scale collective action. *Ambio, 49*, 1282–1296.
Kesting, P. (2023). (Ex)Change of routines: An action-based microfoundation. *Schmalenbachs Zeitschrift Für Betriebswirtschaftliche Forschung, 75*, 173–194.
Kircaburun, K., & Griffiths, M. D. (2018). Instagram addiction and the Big Five of personality: The mediating role of self-liking. *Journal of Behavioral Addictions, 7*(1), 158–170.

Krlev, G., Mildenberger, G., & Anheier, H. K. (2020). Innovation and societal transformation—What changes when the 'social' comes in? *International Review of Applied Economics, 34*(5), 529–540.

Kuhn, T. S. (1962). *The structure of scientific revolutions*. The University of Chicago Press.

Lonergan, B. (1992). Insight—A study of human understanding. In F. E Crowe & R. M. Doran (Eds.), *Collected works of Bernard Lonergan, vol. 3*. Lonergan Research Institute and Regis College.

Ludwig, J., Kling, J. R., & Mullainathan, S. (2011). Mechanism Experiments and Policy Evaluations. *Journal of Economic Perspectives, 25*(3), 17–38.

Lukács, G. (1973/1981). *Per l'ontologia dell'essere sociale II*, a cura di A. Scarponi. Editori Riuniti, 1981. Tr. it. di Zur Ontologie des gesellschaftlichen Seins. Die Arbeit (Ontologie-Arbeit). Darmstadt/Neuwied: Luchterhand, 1973.

Maritain, J. (1936). *Humanisme intégral*. Editions Montaigne.

McGarty, C., Bliuc, A., Thomas, E. F., & Bongiorno, R. (2009). Collective action as the material expression of opinion-based group membership. *Journal of Social Issues, 65*(4), 645–879.

Melandri, E. (1968). *La linea e il circolo - Studio logico-filosofico sull'analogia*. Il Mulino.

Morfino, V. (2022). *Intersoggettività e transindividualità*. Manifesto Libri.

Mounier, E. (1932). Refaire la renaissance. *Esprit, 1*(1), 5–51.

Musté, M. (2018). *Marxismo e filosofia della praxis – Da Labriola a Gramsci*. Viella.

O'Day, E. B., & Heimberg, R. G. (2021). Social media use, social anxiety, and loneliness: A systematic review. *Computers in Human Behavior Reports, 3*, 1–13.

Ober, J. (2006). *Socrates and democratic Athens: The story of the trial in its historical and legal contexts*. Princeton/Stanford Working Papers in Classics.

Olivetti, A. (1945). *L'ordine politico delle comunità*. Ivrea: Nuove edizioni Ivrea.

Olson, M. (1965). *The logic of collective action: Public goods and the theory of groups*. Harvard University Press.

Ostrom, E., & Walker, J. (2003). *Trust and reciprocity: Interdisciplinary lessons for experimental research*. Russell Sage Foundation.

Owen, R. A. (1827). *New view of society and other writings*. J.M. Dent & Sons Ltd.

Papini, R. (1981). *L'apporto del personalismo alla costruzione dell'Europa*. Massimo.

Piketty, T. (2014). *Capital in the twenty-first century*. Cambridge MA.

Piketty, T., & Saez, E. (2007). How progressive is the U.S. Federal tax system? A historical and international perspective. *Journal of Economic Perspectives, 21*(1), 3–24.

Pizzorno, A. (1993). Come pensare il conflitto. In *Le radici della politica assoluta*. Feltrinelli.

Prior, W. J. (2006). The Socratic problem. In H. H. Benson (Ed.), *A companion to Plato* (pp. 25–35). Blackwell Publishing.

Putnam, R. D., & Romney, G. S. (2020). *The upswing: How we came together a century ago and how we can do it again*. Simon & Schuster.

Rajan, R. (2019). *The third pillar—How markets and the state leave the community behind*. Penguin Press.

Read, J. (2016). *The politics of Transindividuality (Historical Materialism)*. Brill.

Ricœur, P. (1983). Meurt le personnalisme, revient la personne. *Esprit, 73*(1), 113–119.

Rosanvallon, P. (2006). *La contre-démocratie – La politique à l'âge de la défiance*. Éditions du Seuil.

Sani, F. (2005). When subgroups secede: Extending and refining the social psychological model of schism in groups. *Personality and Social Psychology Bulletin, 31*(8), 1074–1086.

Scheu, R. (2019). Prefazione. In P. Sloterdijk (Ed.), *Falsa coscienza*. Mimesis Edizioni.

Schofield, M. (2000). I.F. Stone and Gregory Vlastos on socrates and democracy. *Apeiron. 33*(4), 281–302.

Schumpeter, J. A. (1934). *The theory of economic development; an inquiry into profits, capital, credit, interest, and the business cycle*. Harvard University Press.

Seravalli, G., & Schena, A. (2019). *Un'utopia "intelligente": l'economia di Bernard Lonergan SJ*. Accademia University Press.

Seravalli, G. (2011). *Conflitto e innovazione: le capacità innovative delle imprese tra organizzazione e intenzionalità.* Egea.

Seravalli, G. (2022). *Dilemmi dell'azione collettiva.* Europa Edizioni.

Simon, H. A. (1947). *Administrative behavior*. Macmillan.

Simondon, G. (1958/2020). *L'individuazione alla luce delle nozioni di forma e d'informazione.* Milano e Udine: Mimesis. Edizione in francese *L'individuation à la lumièere des notions de forme e d'information.* Grenoble: Editions Jérôme Millon. This edition is the complete version of the 1958 doctoral thesis, parts of which had appeared in several publications, including the main ones in 1964: Introduction, first two chapters of the first part, second part and conclusions (Presses Universitaires de France); in 1989: hird and fourth part (Aubier Éditeur); and in 1995: (parts already published and in addition the third chapter of the first part, some paragraphs previously omitted and three supplements (Editions Jérôme Millon).

Stone, I. F. (1988). *The trial of Socrates.* Little Brown.

Sutherland, R. W., Jr. (1979). Popular accountability in the Iliad and the Odyssey. *The Review of Politics, 41*(4), 501–512.

Taggart, J. (2022), A Decade Since Busan: Towards Legitimacy or a 'New Tyranny' of Global Development Partnership? "*Journal of Development Studies,*" 58, 8, 1459-1477.

Tien, N. (2025). *The association between social media use and romantic relationship outcomes: A scoping review* (Master Thesis Faculty of Behavioural Management and Social Sciences Positive Clinical Psychology & Technology, University of Twente).

Tilly, C. (1985). Models and realities of popular collective action. *Social Research, 52*(4), 717–747.

Tönnies, F. (1887). *Gemeinschaft und Gesellschaft - Abhandlung des Communismus und des Socialismus als empirischer Culturformen.* Fues.

Vandermeersch, L. (2023). Western individualism and eastern collectivism from a transcultural perspective. In L. Chen & K.-H. Pohl (Eds.), *East-West Dialogue* (pp. 3–8). Dolphin Books Co.

Varoufakis, Y. (2023). *Technofeudalism: What killed capitalism.* Bodley Head.

Velez, I. (2020). *Assessing the quality of impact evaluations at USAID.* E3 Analytics and Evaluation Project. USAID.

Villanti, A. C., Johnson, A. L., Ilakkuvan, V., Jacobs, M. A., Graham, A. L., & Rath, J. M. (2017). Social media use and access to digital technology in US young adults in 2016. *Journal of Medical Internet Research, 19*(6), Article e196.

Vinci, P. (2009). Sapere assoluto come riconoscimento. *Archivio di Filosofia, 77*(2/3), 105–117.

Virno, P. (2010). *E così via all'infinito – Logica e antropologia.* Bollati Boringhieri.

Virno, P. (2014). *Grammatica della moltitudine - per un'analisi delle forme di vita contemporanee.* DeriveApprodi.

Virno P. (2017). *Riflessioni sul verbo 'avere'* https://api.semanticscholar.org/CorpusID:149241447

Virno, P. (2021). *Dell'impotenza – La vita nell'epoca della sua paralisi frenetica.* Bollati Boringhieri.

Vlastos, G. (1994). *Socratic studies.* Cambridge University Press.

Weimann, J., Brosig-Koch, J., Heinrich, T., Hennig-Schmidt, H., & Keser, C. (2019). Public good provision by large groups—The logic of collective action revisited. *European Economic Review, 118*, 348–363.

Wrenn, M. V. (2022). Corporate mindfulness culture and neoliberalism. *Review of Radical Political Economics, 54*(2), 153–170.

Xinhong, Z., Taoyun, Z., Linlin, D., Xiaona, Z., Zhihan, L., & Hao, J. (2023). Exploring associations between social media addiction, social media fatigue, fear of missing out and sleep quality among university students: A cross-section study. *PLoS ONE, 18*(10), Article e0292429.

Young, M. C. (2020). Conservatism and communitarianism: Two or one? *The Canadian Society for Study of Practical Ethics/Société Canadienne Pour L'étude De L'éthique Appliquée.* SCEEA 4.

Chapter 4
ROLM in Silicon Valley

4.1 Introduction

ROLM was a leading figure in the development of "Silicon Valley",[1] whose history can be reconstructed in detail using the "case study" prepared at Stanford by Adrian Bernard Ryans[2](1988), essays by David Lane and Robert Maxfield[3] (1997, 2005) and Catherine Maxfield's book (2014). The analysis of this example is recommended for its complete documentation that allows the exclusion of arbitrary interpretations, a risk that almost always exists in case studies. However, to illustrate the collective action from below with which to save oneself from neoliberalism and even more from technofeudalism, it may seem incongruous to bring an example located at the center of rampant capitalism that in many ways was one of the bases of neoliberalism and now of Cloud Capital. In this regard, it is recommended to read Malcom Harris' book "Palo Alto A Story of California, Capitalism, and the World", an indispensable counter face of the story that will follow, so as not to forget that what seems "beautiful and heroic" should not obscure the fact that the darkest soul of current neoliberalism also came from it. From there began the model of progress through victory, defeat, and

[1] It was Santa Clara County, named after the Spanish mission, known before the 1960s as "The Valley of Heart's Delight" for its endless orchards, a spectacle of blooms in spring. It was one of the world's leading fruit-producing and packing regions. Silicon Valley arose in these places, uprooting the trees and replacing them with warehouses, which even now stretch as far as the eye can see. And replacing "heart's delight" with money in spades.

[2] He was assistant professor and then associate professor at the Graduate School of Business, Stanford University. Today he is professor emeritus of the IMD (International Institute for Management Development).

[3] Robert R. Maxfield was a co-founder of ROLM Corporation where he played a leading role until its acquisition by IBM in 1984. Since 1988 he has been a consulting professor in the Department of Management and Engineering at Stanford University. He is chairman of the Maxfield Foundation which he created in 1986 to support scientific research and education. He is a director of Echelon Corporation and a trustee of the Santa Fe Institute.

G. Seravalli, *Collective Action in the Age of Polycrisis*, Contributions to Economics,
https://doi.org/10.1007/978-3-032-12653-5_4

the rapid elimination of losers, the rise of a culture of venture capital that transformed every enterprise into a gamble, a highly segregated workforce.

> America imported a bifurcated cohort of immigrants to fit a bifurcating pattern of employment, and for every Silicon Valley investor or board member or founder from the Third World, there was a family of refugees in a local basement performing the low-wage manufacturing labor that animated the computer industry's numbers. Neocolonialism provided more than a market for Silicon Valley's electronics; it provided a labor force as well. (Harris, 2023, p. 620)

It was the ideology of the winner who takes all without mercy, the roughest evolutionism according to which the fit must thrive and the unfit must die; a way of thinking that dominated even the schools of Silicon Valley, pushing the youth to singularly high suicide rates, as the beginning of Harris' book movingly recalls.

> The suicides started in 2002. That year, a Palo Alto High freshman stepped in front of the Caltrain, the same locomotive line on which Leland Stanford built the town. Thirteen months later, one of his classmates ended his life the same way. Both picked the Churchill Avenue crossing, right near the school. In 2009, four more students between the ages of thirteen and seventeen killed themselves at the Meadow Drive crossing near their school, Gunn High. Another string of Palo Alto teenagers died by train in 2014 and 2015. These deaths were well publicized, particularly as a social-scientific example of the rare "double cluster"[4] of suicidality, as if it were an unusual astrological phenomenon. The Atlantic magazine ran a cover story on the "Silicon Valley Suicides," and no investigation of self-destructive teens was complete without a reference to Palo Alto. One thing the coverage missed was that the official tally undercounts the victims by at least half because it excludes young people who killed themselves after graduation, even when they returned to the tracks to do it. The community experienced not two clusters but a constant flow of tragic deaths in the twenty-first century. It continues: a month before I finished this manuscript, a twenty-two-year-old Gunn High graduate ended his life on the tracks. As kids, when we talked about the place where we lived, my brother, sister, and I used to make morbid jokes about Sunnydale, the fictional California setting for the TV show Buffy the Vampire Slayer, where perfect weather conceals the portal to hell under the high school. As I got older, I began to think of the idea earnestly. We have a word for idyllic towns where the youth suicide rate is three times as high as it's supposed to be: haunted. Palo Alto is haunted. (Harris, 2023, pp. 13–14)[5]

But bringing an example placed in a context of this kind is not so incongruous, remembering that the birth of the technological district occurred at the exhaustion of the Keynesian-Fordist-Taylorist paradigm. The same problem seen in the ancient examples arose for American capitalism: inventing the elements of a new structure. And this realization took place in Northern California, in the San Francisco Bay area, where the absolute center of post-modern capitalist intelligence was located.

---

[4] "Suicide cluster is defined as three or more united suicide events in a series in a common space, such as a school or community, and/or in a limited and contiguous time frame, usually 7 to 10 days. It has been estimated that 5% of adolescent suicides occur in clusters" (Walling, 2023, p. 104).

[5] Harris also offers a counter-current profile of Steve Jobs. He describes Xerox's contract with Apple in the late 1970s as motivated by the opportunity to build a personal computer without high labor costs. Jobs was valuable to Xerox because Apple combined a great brand with the worst labor practices in Silicon Valley, outsourcing piecework to a non-union workforce composed largely of women from Southeast Asia.

The example can then be considered pertinent for the purpose of seeing how capitalism managed to get out of the impasse, as should be done. On the other hand, in Italy, before ROLM, there was, Adriano Olivetti and his "utopia" realized in a highly successful enterprise, on a human and community frame, which was then intentionally destroyed by Italian capitalism, which, vulgar and arrogant, had deeply hated the overly enlightened entrepreneur. There is no space here to explain in detail how the path indicated by Olivetti and ROLM was first distorted and then lost. It can be said, however, that in that story no inevitable reasons emerge. That model was perfectly efficient from every point of view. Adriano was "wrong" to die too soon, ROLM was wrong to accept the IBM offer, "an offer that could not be refused", as Loewestern (one of the founders) said in an interview, the proceeds of which radically changed the standard of living of thousands of employees who owned ROLM shares. After 16 years of activity, the end came due to too much success. The adventure had begun in an abandoned agricultural shed,[6] and 16 years later, when it was bought by IBM, ROLM had a turnover of one billion dollars and 10,000 employees.

4.2 The Origins

Founded in 1969 in Cupertino by four engineers who came from Rice University in Houston, the firm took its name from the initials of the founders' surnames Richeson (Gene), Oshman (Ken), Loewestern (Walter), Maxfield (Robert): ROLM. Rice's engineering school was one of the toughest and most renowned in the United States, and its graduates came to Stanford by the hundreds in those years, attracted by the intelligent program[7] in an agreement with local businesses which allowed engineers to be paid full time to work 30 h a week and study for their doctorate the other 10. ROLM purchased the license for a minicomputer (as a device that weighed 50 kilos and cost $8,000, $60,000 today, was called back then) from "Data General", the 16-bit "Nova" model, in exchange for a commitment not to sell competing products. This was the versatile basis for the transformations they had in mind: to build a small, light but robust computer to be installed on military vehicles, helicopters, fighter planes, vibration-proof, capable of operating in the rain, snow, or the hottest sun, easy to fix, easy to reprogram (in 30 days and no longer in a year as was the rule

[6] Since renting buildings in the development areas made available to start-ups near Stanford University was quite expensive, the four founders looked for another solution and found it in the area where several industrial buildings were being built called Vallco Park in the Cupertino area, in the triangle between Interstate 280 to the north, Wolfe Rd to the west, and Steven Creek Blv to the south. However, since the work was dragging on, an owner suggested that the young engineers move into the old plum warehouse he had abandoned. Until a few years earlier, plums had been the most important product in Santa Clara County, with exports of 100,000 tons a year.

[7] The program, which was to become one of the cornerstones of the development of Silicon Valley, was invented by Burt McMurtry, the legendary chairman of the Board of Trustees of Stanford University, to whom the beautiful pavilion that houses the Department of Art History, designed by Diller Scofidio & Renfro, inaugurated in 2005 and costing 87 million dollars, is dedicated.

when computer companies responded to demand for new applications by redesigning the entire device). In the first fiscal year ending in June 1970, ROLM recorded a loss of $350,000. But from the following year things went much better. The fiscal year 1971 closed with a net profit of 150,000 dollars on a turnover of 1.5 million. In 1972, the profit was 338,000 and the turnover 2.3 million, while the employees had reached 58. In the autumn of the same year, the business moved to a new 2,800-square-meter building expanded to 4,000 the following year.

ROLM was the model of a new entrepreneurial style: non-bureaucratic, oriented toward problem solving rather than compliance with procedures, attentive to the well-being of employees with flexible working hours, personal and family services in the workplace, guarantee of real appreciation of merit, profit sharing.

> Beneath the enduring success of familiar technology companies [...] lies the bedrock of a pioneering company whose name is seldom heard around Silicon Valley these days. Thanks to its technological breakthroughs, stellar financial performance, and unique corporate lifestyle, ROLM regularly made headlines in the New York Times, the Wall Street Journal, and BusinessWeek. Known as a Great Place to Work, ROLM blurred the line between work and play [...]. I embarked on this journey—writing the story of ROLM Corporation—because the company played such a vital role in the creation of Silicon Valley that its history deserved to be recorded. (Maxfield, 2014, p. 8)

In 1973, sales were $3.6 million, profits $321,000, and employees were 114, of whom 27 were engineers, a third with a doctorate. This small reduction in profits in 1973 added a warning sign to a situation that, despite the good results, had two rather serious problems, one internal and one external. In Maxfield's testimony, the internal problem was that "we had no capacity to do anything but nourish the 1601 and 1602" (Maxfield, 2014, p. 69). In President Oshman's testimony, it was that the young company could not consider itself safe. The country's economic situation was rapidly worsening, so the risks would increase because ROLM had not diversified. It remained almost totally dependent on a single customer, the Pentagon, having not been able to penetrate the industrial user market enough, while it could not enter other segments because of the agreement with "Data General". This was the situation, even though Richeson had already left. Loewestern had realized that Richeson was only capable of selling to those with technical knowledge like his. Thus, he had been replaced with people competent in commercial practices, but there were no adequate resources to invest, as Maxfield said. The external problem was that a new federal regulation would soon require suppliers to essentially hand over process protocols to the Government, which was reasonable in many cases where Defense had paid for the research and development of technologies. However, it was not reasonable in the ROLM case, which had conceived and developed its products with its own resources and now risked unfair competition since it could no longer keep its experiences and procedures confidential. So, it was decided to rely on this interpretation to deny such a transfer despite fears for the orders if it were not accepted. It did not go that way, but this was only known in hindsight.

4.3 Faith Against Science

It was between 1973 and 1974 that ROLM changed its nature by entering a new sector with an act of faith against rational reasoning.

In 1956 a court had established (Hush-A-Phone case) that in the United States private devices could mechanically connect to the telephone system controlled 90% by AT&T without its permission. It was the first crack in a regulatory framework and conduct that since 1913 had allowed a monopoly[8] to that telephone company which, in the 1970s, reached one million employees and an invested capital that exceeded that of "General Motors", "Exxon", and "Mobil" together. In 1968, the "Federal Communications Commission" extended this permission by allowing electrical connections, such as the then pioneering "Carterphone" (a device invented by Thomas Carter and produced by "Carter Electronics" that made radio and telephone talk) for which the rule was called "The Carterphone decision". This decision had great consequences on private telephone networks (PBX—Private Branch Exchange) within companies and organizations connected to the national network, internal networks which were also provided by AT&T but remained very backward as the monopolist had no interest in innovating this part of its paid service anyway. AT&T tried to take cover. However, having never paid attention to PBX systems, it started a program that would have led to new models only after five years and it got the setting wrong, which remained electromechanical. In the early 1970s, the number of these systems in the United States was 125,000, for a value of 3 billion dollars at the time. A significant market was opening up. A new role was also born: the "interconnection providers", who configured, installed and maintained corporate communication systems in competition with AT&T. Their size and operating methods were diversified. Local providers for small companies dealt with systems with fewer than 50 internal telephones. For large systems, there were national providers, some of which, such as "ITT" and "Stromberg Carlson", also produced PBX equipment. But the equipment sold was quite similar to that already present and the competition was mainly focused on price. In 1973, some manufacturers of electronic equipment produced PBXs with superior technology, but the major innovations that had already affected the means of calculation were considered far away. It was thought that it would take at least eight or nine years to have digital switching and computerized control.

ROLM was the first company to propose a computer-assisted electronic system. Already in a 1972 memo, President Oshman had mentioned the opportunities that had opened up in telephone interconnection. Discussions among managers and executives began at the end of 1972 and lasted a year. The positions were articulated. Many thought that this perspective was wrong in itself: "No, we've got enough on our plate as it is—let's just keep doing what we're doing" (Maxfield, 2014, p. 71). Others thought that it could even be theoretically correct but certainly not realistic. Using

[8] In 1974, AT&T was again taken to court in an antitrust case and this time lost its monopoly that had been in place since 1913. The case was settled in 1984, having lasted 10 years, and ruled that AT&T had to divest itself of the two dozen companies it had acquired over time, so that these smaller companies could operate their own local telephone networks.

their knowledge, they knew all the means that AT&T was able to use to embarrass those who seriously threatened its market power by competing where it had fewer defenses, that is, on the quality of its products, while tolerating the competition on prices that it easily countered. As "Electronic News" wrote: "Snatching crumbs from the lion's plate can be very dangerous", and then added, but it was already 1979: "but that's just how ROLM became great" (Maxfield, 2014, p. 157). Robert Maxfield recalled those phases in his commemorative speech on Osman's death on August 6, 2011: "Needless to say, many people, including some of ROLM's venture capital backers, believed the management team had gone mad to challenge AT&T" (Maxfield, 2013, p. 235). The predictions were all correct. AT&T implemented an impressive series of countermeasures after the commercialization of the ROLM system: selling its traditional PBX systems below cost; artificially but apparently justifiably extending the connection times of these systems with its network; slowing down any response from the customer service which was indispensable especially in the first few months; completely unfounded but uncontestable invention of damage to the network caused by such connections; and up to the obligation imposed on each user to pay the rental of a "security device"—a small box with a couple of transistors that cost a few dollars, charged from 5 to 50 dollars a month depending on the user. "AT&T cheated every customer for years. The phone company charged whatever rental fee each state's PUC could be talked into permitting. It was basically the customer's fine for choosing to install non-AT&T equipment" (Maxfield, 2014, p. 124). In the end, the conviction prevailed that the gamble had to be accepted, and not so much for rational considerations (in practice all against it), but for the confidence that if there were alternatives, many users would stop putting up with AT&T's arrogance. The telephone company not only imposed the "atrocious monstrosity" of the PBX that ROLM itself had acquired, weighing four quintals for 100 telephones. Furthermore, faced with any request for improvement, their philosophy was "Sir, we're the phone company. We don't care. We don't have to" (Maxfield, 2014, p. 124).

When ROLM completed its CBX (Computerized Branch Exchange), it was an exceptional piece of equipment: no more cumbersome or heavier than a portable typewriter. Sales had begun to rise in 1975 and 1976, but they were far from those expected on the basis of the faith that had triggered the entry into the telecommunications sector. A feeling of disappointment was felt in the departments and offices. Even at the end of 1977, the sales of the Telecom division had failed to match those of the computer division. Fears of losing defense contracts had proved excessive, and ROLM had produced, with the 1666, a computer that was very advanced for its time and had been very successful. In reality, the computer/Telecom comparison was too severe. But expectations had been high and the results had not met them. The return on sales continued to decline, after the reduction in 1973 from the exceptional level of a year earlier. Why a product "that was supposed to sell itself" did not sell well enough was the question everyone was asking inside ROLM (Fig. 4.1).

A graphical representation can be useful for the purpose of following the story and the interpretation. A "result index" can be the geometric mean of complementary components: turnover, employees, profit on turnover, and profit on employees. With

Fig. 4.1 ROLM: Sales, employees, and net profit in the first 10 years. *Source* Figure obtained by processing data from Maxfield (2014)

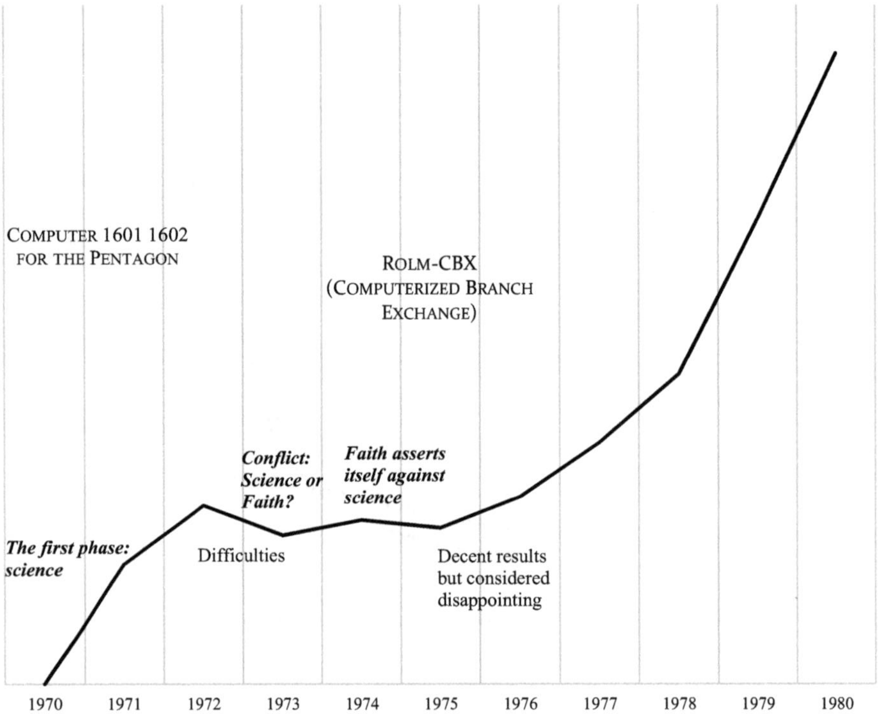

Fig. 4.2 ROLM: trend of the result index, phases, results, products, process (first part). *Source* Figure obtained by processing data from Maxfield (2014)

this index represented as a function of time, the following figure is obtained that allows one to associate the trend of the index values with the phases of ROLM's life (Fig. 4.2).

The question to ask was why a product that was supposed to sell itself did not sell enough. The answer came from faith when it translated into inclusion, thus applying the formula.

Given the technology to be used and the structure of the market, ROLM had decided to build a medium-sized CBX, capable of managing from 100 to 800 internal telephones. The computer would have been too expensive for smaller devices, while in systems with thousands of extensions the sales cycles would have been too long and AT&T's war would have been more ferocious. Then there was the crucial problem of marketing. After careful evaluation, it was understood that setting up its own sales/installation/assistance network would have required too much time and too many resources, which were not there. It was therefore a question of deciding which connection providers to turn to. The most "scientifically" obvious choice was that of one or two large national providers who would be able to appreciate and use the technical innovations well and contribute to them. But there were strong objections from those who feared that one or two national providers could undermine ROLM's autonomy. After much back and forth, autonomy and its own identity, important values since the company's birth, combined with confidence in its own distinctive capabilities, made a "not rational" line prevail. It was decided to go toward small independent local providers, despite the fact that it was well known that they only sold modest equipment and had no experience with potential CBX customers: medium-sized companies and organizations. The choice was truly risky. But it was this choice that led far.

It was clear that it was necessary to set up a vast program of mutual information and training between ROLM and providers. The local providers literally had to learn a new paradigm while ROLM had to understand who they were, what mentality they had, who they worked with. And that was exactly how "the TM issue" emerged, completely unsuspected, completely unexpected, surprising. The TMs, Telecom Managers, were those in charge of managing the internal communications of companies and organizations that became ROLM customers by purchasing a CBX. The TMs were the terminal of the system, considered as such of little importance, the easily replaceable last link in the chain. However, since the local supervisors had very different opinions on the TMs, in ROLM it was decided that the "question" had to be clarified. In this way some things were understood that had great importance. Although their role seemed modest, in reality the TMs could influence the purchase or not of new equipment, which in essence nobody really took care of. But it was not possible to understand why after having seen the new CBX systems, in general, the TMs were not in favor of purchasing them. The new computerized systems would help them in their everyday work, this was clear to them too. Which makes one ask why there was all this resistance. The reason was understood only after the ROLM officials in charge of following the TMs were inspired to dig into the personal and professional history of these internal communications managers and discovered that it was modest, and in contrast with their not insignificant responsibilities: the telephone costs of their companies reached up to 5% of the turnover. The reason for this contrast became clear little by little by recording the stories that the TMs told after many of them had been "included" with effort and attention. In their professional history there was not much they could do. They knew it and their bosses knew it. They were the interface with AT&T, and a powerless interface, since, in every circumstance, they only had to report and report the response. Every contribution on their part, every request, was not expected, was not allowed, was of no use. The Carterphone decision had put an end to the dependence on AT&T, but it could not change patterns of behavior and thought formed over the course of decades. What the TMs were dealing with was still simply a switchboard connected to the telephones on one side and to the outside line on the other; managing it only meant making sure that the phones were where they were needed, that they were connected and working, that the switchboard operators connected them when there were calls.

After months of understanding all this, ROLM officials also understood that there was a great opportunity if there was a way to overcome this considerable difficulty. A device had to be put in the hands of TMs that could significantly, clearly, and documentably reduce telephone costs so that they could become "heroes" while up to that point they had been "the last wheel of the wagon". It was at this point that someone remembered the provocation of a TM during a refresher seminar, who had asked whether a CBX was capable of performing ACD functions, such as those used by airlines to manage reservations. Automatic call distribution (ACD) consists of freely programmable routing of a large number of calls to service operators, competent for problems, allowing monitoring, supervision, collection, and analysis of traffic patterns. The ACD systems existing at the time were very large and very expensive. For this reason, the TM had asked that clearly provocative question. The meaning was: if the small ROLM apparatus had been capable of having ACD then yes it would have deserved the attention that the ROLM salesmen demanded, but this was impossible. No one could seriously believe that it was possible to put in a small apparatus the capacity to apply complex procedures used only by the big airlines or the big credit card companies or the big suppliers of electricity and gas, in addition to the Pentagon and the CIA. Faith translated into inclusion had given its result which was a provocation. At that point the question was what the path to follow while remaining in faith could be. As confidence in one's own resources, abilities, reputation and as a general and convinced belief that the small ROLM apparatus could not have the ACD, faith would have advised to wait, not to respond to the provocation, because the provocative TM would have gradually convinced himself.

4.4 Science Against Faith

Instead, science entered the field against faith and the improbable was made possible. This was demonstrated by the engineers thus called back to the fore, who accepted the challenge and developed the model that finally gave the long-awaited success. The ACD allows for strong reductions in telephone costs and certifies them in an indisputable way. It reduces incorrect or useless call routing, allows for the accumulation and processing of data on frequent callers, preparing responses and reducing the number of calls, allows for traffic to be routed to free lines, avoiding waiting and callbacks, and allows for the easy avoidance of unauthorized uses of the internal network. As soon as the TMs realized that they could demonstrate reductions of even 30–40% in telephone costs, the success of the ROLM device was not long in coming. The Telecom division's turnover doubled in 1978, tripled in 1979, and doubled again in 1980. Net profit on turnover had this trend from 1976 to 1980: 5.7% 6.4% 7.2% 8.8% 9% (Fig. 4.3).

This was the outcome of an innovative process because it was inclusive. The choice to turn to local independent providers and TMs was decisive, while a national provider would have been the ideal partner to enhance and develop the innovation of the CBX in the natural selective logic. But to achieve these results it was also important to use innovation to defeat the conservative tendencies of inclusion. The included TMs brought a conservative mentality and practice and it was necessary to move them from these positions with a significant innovative effort on a technical-scientific level.

The example thus demonstrates the close connection between inclusion-innovation with faith against science and science against faith. And it also shows the

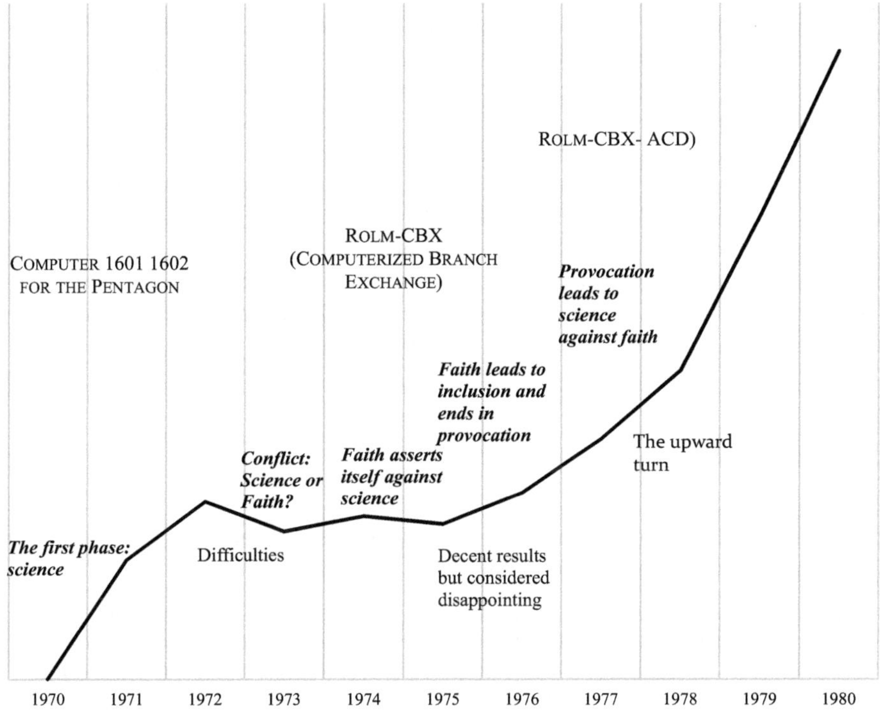

Fig. 4.3 ROLM: trend of the result index, phases, results, products, process 1970–1980. *Source* Figure obtained by processing data from Maxfield (2014)

reason for this connection. Including to innovate required trust in one's own values and intuitions against the rational logic that would have led to exclusion in order to work with those who were a priori capable of innovation (the national provider). Innovating to overcome the conservative tendencies of inclusion then required science versus faith, that is, using the knowledge of engineers and not simply hoping that the included partners (the TMs) would convince themselves by relying on the strength of the faith that had involved them.

The ROLM process was therefore

$$\text{Science} - \textit{Innovation}\ (\textit{CBX})\ \underrightarrow{\textit{would lead}}\ \textit{Selection Exclusion}\ (\textit{nationalprovider});$$

$$\textit{Faith against Science}\ \underrightarrow{\textit{lead}}\ \textit{Inclusion}\ (\textit{TM})\ \underrightarrow{\textit{would lead}}\ \textit{Conservation provocation};$$

$$\textit{Science against Faith}\ \underrightarrow{\textit{lead}}\ \textit{Innovation}\ (\textit{CBX} - \textit{ACD})$$

Such a process is far from a "linear" model in which, once the mechanism has been set up, certain inputs are transformed into certain outputs without any interventions other than maintenance. Since contrasting logics must be systematically applied (faith against science and science against faith), at each step each logic will tend to deviate from the effective process by pushing to assert its own truth (this tendency is indicated above as "would lead"). Following a logic of instrumental rationality, a national provider should have been used. Following a fideistic logic, the TMs should have been convinced by themselves. But in the meantime, the sector and the market were moving forward and the spaces for ROLM would have shrunk. If a non-linear process was therefore decisive, a constant push was also necessary as it was not possible to count on any peaceful automatism. And the push could only come from a great stake. The results achieved must be compared to the aspirations, which were not limited to the significant prospect of rapid growth.

4.5 Great Aspirations

It was not just about finding the way to Ithaca. There was something more at stake: realizing a dream, living the experience of hearing the song of the sirens.

> All four founders had worked for large companies before breaking out on their own. In the early days of ROLM, they often discussed what they had liked and not liked about their former employers. They particularly disliked the regimented approach to advancement opportunities and the lack of attention to individual contribution. All employees were reviewed at the same time and typically received the same annual raise at the same time with little regard to contribution. Promotions too could occur only at specific times of the year. Seniority was protected—some positions could be applied for only after the employee had a certain number of years of experience in the existing job. ROLM's founders believed that rigidity not only dampened individual creativity and commitment, it seemed to thwart success of the company. «We knew we needed to hire a lot of people», said Maxfield in an interview, «and we wanted them to have values similar to ours. So even when we were on Forge Drive we talked about what it would take to hire people like that and keep them happy and productive». (Maxfield, 2014, pp. 165–166)

The dream of the founders of ROLM was truly progressive, although it did not prevent, once captured, that it turned into the nightmare of a "haunted" Silicon Valley. The realization of this new corporate style required an impressive set of inclusive innovations, outward as seen, but also inward, for employees. The following is a non-exhaustive list.

Rules and practices. No directives, guides, perorations, proclamations were issued, so frequent in the shoddy imitations that would follow, often only formalistic and hypocritical to hide the reality of traditional exploitation. Instead, gestures were made aimed at orienting attitudes: "We treat each person equally, respect personal privacy, provide encouragement for success and opportunities for creativity and value merit (focus on substance not form, do not blame others, do not point fingers, but find the solution). [...]. We evaluate the results, we record the reactions, we modify the behaviours accordingly" (Maxfield, 2014, p. 175–176).

Working hours. Flexible hours became the rule and not the exception. It was important that the work was done, not that the hours were respected. Entry and exit were flexible. "Employees could arrive and leave [...] at any time. The early risers arrived before dawn; the night owls could be found in their offices after midnight" (Maxfield, 2014, p. 182). During the day, if someone wanted to take a coffee break or to have a chat, they could do so at their discretion. There were self-service refreshment points almost everywhere. One day a sign signed by Ken (the President) appeared: "If you take the last cup, make another pot. If you are too busy, call me and I will come and do it. Needless to say, there was always a full pot" (Maxfield, 2014, p. 180). During the year, holidays were planned based on the needs expressed by employees. Later, the sabbatical period was introduced.

> Ken Oshman proposed a sabbatical policy to the board of directors: three months of continuous, fully paid vacation after each six years of service. According to Maxfield, one director asked, «This applies only to key management, right?» Oshman answered, «Nope. Everyone». «Even the assembly line workers?» «Absolutely». That egalitarian approach was revolutionary among U.S. companies. The employee was guaranteed his or her job upon return; someone would be trained to do the job in the interim. The first person to take a sabbatical was Vineta Alvarez, the first assembler of the Rugged Nova 1601. Some ROLMans used time off to remodel a home, travel with families, or pursue passions such as antinuclear activism or painting. Most employees returned refreshed, ready to adopt new approaches. (Maxfield, 2014, p. 176)

A sports complex was built on the company's "campus" which.

> turned into far more than a fitness trail or a couple of basketball hoops. It included a twenty-five-yard, six-lane lap pool and a second "fun" pool, plus saunas, steam rooms, tennis courts, racquetball courts, a jogging track, and a weight room. Aerobics, kickboxing, and yoga classes were offered before, during, and after normal work hours. Employees were free to attend at any time, provided their work got done, and could bring their families on weekends. In fact, management encouraged sports. The employee handbook said, «If a sufficient number of employees express an interest in an approved activity, and are willing to organize and maintain the program, ROLM will back the group and provide the necessary equipment». Employees were quick to take advantage of this opportunity: A ski club, a chess club, a running club, a basketball league, a volleyball league, and a flag football league all sprang up. (Maxfield, 2014, p. 178)

Robert Maxfield, in a speech to new hires in 1979, said:

> You're coming into ROLM at an amazing time. We're growing very fast, grabbing market share, doubling manufacturing capacity. We have lots of exciting products in the wings. There's far more work that needs to be done than can possibly be done. If you see something you can do, jump in and do it even if it's not "your job." Work as hard and as long as you want. Be as innovative as you can possibly be. Do the best you can. This experience can really make a difference to your career. But if you just want to work eight to five, that's fine too. (Maxfield, 2014, p. 187)

Treatment and employment regime. Egalitarianism was taken care of.

> The egalitarian atmosphere extended to many facets of the workplace. In the parking lot, for example, even Oshman had no reserved space. From his perspective, if you wanted a good parking spot, you should arrive early. Casual Fridays was a no-brainer in this company's culture: jeans, polos, and sandals. And executive breakfasts, where small groups of ROLM employees from all levels could meet with top executives in an intimate setting—with no questions off limits—were common. This egalitarian, open approach stood in stark contrast

> to traditional U.S. companies, which maintained an invisible but firm barrier between the ranks of employees. (Maxfield, 2014, p. 177)

Everyone, not just executives and managers, were given options to purchase ROLM shares in a graduated quantity to reward merit. Furthermore, they were given with permission to exercise them over the course of four years to encourage loyalty to the company and reduce turnover. The system adopted was very favorable.

> Stock options gave the employee the right to purchase stock in the future at the "strike price"—the fair market price of the stock on the day the options were granted, regardless of what the stock was selling for on the day the option was exercised. For example, say a four-year option on 1,000 shares of stock was given to an engineer on April 15, 1978, when the price on Wall Street was $20 per share. On each anniversary of that date for four years, that employee could exercise 25 percent of the option. That is, he or she had the option to buy 250 shares at $20, even if the stock was trading for $70 a share on Wall Street. Those shares could be sold for immediate gain or held in hopes the stock price would further increase. Of course, if the strike price was underwater—that is, if the market price was lower than $20—the employee would not exercise the option at that time. (Maxfield, 2014, p. 185)

One of the most important innovations introduced in the organization of work compared to the dominant standards was the abolition of minute control over performance with the advantage of reducing monitoring costs and supporting innovation. Indeed, this was the organizational form that, made central in the neoliberal ideology of the "self-entrepreneur", was thus distorted and transformed into self-exploitation in contexts where all the rest of the ROLM environment and philosophy was missing. It should be remembered that, as has been said, the ideology of the self-entrepreneur typical of neoliberalism is alienating "only as long as the channeling of desires in meritocracy remains at the same time naturalized and hidden". In ROLM it was quite the opposite: not at all naturalized and hidden, but rather explicitly artificial and flaunted every day.

> ROLM was among the companies cited in the 1984 book The 100 Best Companies to Work for in America, with special attention paid to the company's athletic facilities, flex-flex time, and lack of hierarchy. The downside of the increased publicity these facets attained was the superficial appearance that ROLM was a cool, laid-back company, as if employees could sit in the hot tub or work—their choice. But as Gibson Anderson noted in the book, ROLM had a very competitive atmosphere: «This is no loosey-goosey, hip California place … We fire people. We do not guarantee lifetime employment. We believe it's bad for morale to have deadwood around». Time magazine's cover article on the «new breed of risk takers» in Silicon Valley acknowledged that ROLM was one of the earliest companies to rise above the inevitable problems of fast-paced growth and technological change: Executives in the valley face a few acute problems because of their highly competitive environment: keeping workers satisfied in order to reduce job hopping, and maintaining the small-company entrepreneurial spirit as firms grow larger. ROLM has been a pioneer in developing a new corporate life-style that encourages worker loyalty and innovation. The ROLM Philosophy was built on a fundamental belief that any individual, when properly prepared, would be able to assume responsibility for his or her work with as few controls as possible. Broad goals were established: have the competitive analysis done by September, for example, or the new finance system online by the first of the year. But there was leeway in how those goals were accomplished, as long as they were accomplished within the set budget. This lack of micromanagement meant that individuality was given room for expression. As Oshman told the San Jose Mercury News,

> «If we had all our people marching to the same drumbeat, we couldn't get much innovation». (Maxfield, 2014, p. 191)

Work environment. Workplaces were built to be pleasant, welcoming, inclusive.

> In late 1975, the company signed a forty-year lease on twenty-one acres near Great America Parkway in Santa Clara [...]. Among fifteen competing architects who submitted design proposals [...], Oshman selected the only one who had no previous industrial experience—Goodwin (Goody) Steinberg, who had been a student of Bauhaus architect Ludwig Mies van der Rohe. Steinberg described his approach to designing the ROLM headquarters in his book about architecture in Silicon Valley: «I applied the residential model to the workplace as I painted a picture of integrating indoor and outdoor space for maximum enjoyment and utilization. I addressed security issues not with locks and alarms but with pools of water and landscaping that limited authorized access. My sketches reflected the innovative philosophy and principles of the ROLM business plan itself». [...]. In August 1977, ROLM's two newly formed divisions moved into 4900 Old Ironsides Drive in the city of Santa Clara. [...]. By 1979 the stunning campus had been fully built and encompassed six single-story buildings. Gingko, decorative plum, and almond trees shaded paths that wound around grassy lawns. A brook spanned by arched wooden footbridges meandered through the property. Boulders were added to the stream to create the pleasing effect of a babbling brook. Koi, water lilies, and papyrus plants thrived in a pond that later became home to a beloved bronze alligator. The stream was stocked with young trout in the spring. Just walking between meetings from one building to another amid the lush landscape provided a respite of serenity in an otherwise intense workday. Inside, expansive windows provided a light, airy work environment. Managers' offices were located in each building's interior space, with no windows—instead they were surrounded by wood-and-fabric cubicles where staff benefited from abundant sunshine and a view of the outdoors. A recreation facility and a cafeteria that opened to allow outside dining were remarkable perks. External gathering spaces encouraged an ambience conducive to interaction, interdependence, and integration. Plenty of parking spots ringed the outside perimeter. As visitors walked from the parking lot to Building 1, they passed a pond with a tall fountain and billowing, blooming shrubs, but motorists driving by glimpsed little of the unique, park-like serenity that employees experienced daily. (Maxfield, 2014, pp. 172–174)

4.6 A Singular but Imitable Experience

In light of all this, two questions must now be answered in order to attribute exemplary value to the ROLM case: whether it was a remarkable experience, or, given the conditions, nothing special. And if remarkable, whether it was perhaps exceptional and essentially unrepeatable.

4.6.1 *The IBM Mistake*

The first question can be answered that it was special as demonstrated by what happened after the acquisition by IBM ("International Business Machine") which already had a stake in ROLM. At the end of 1987 IBM decided to acquire it "causing enormous clamour, driven by the prospect of combining computer and telephone technology".[9] The acquisition, however, proved to be a bad deal. The highly hierarchical IBM corporate style was unable to include and valorize the alternative ROLM style: different production and commercial strategies, different abilities to combine and alternate technical-scientific and "visionary" resources, different ability to valorize merit, different ideas around bureaucratic-disciplinary functions. All these differences proved to be irreconcilable.

> There wasn't anything in Rolm's pool of resources that IBM didn't already have. Rather, it was Rolm's processes for developing and finding new markets for PBX products that mattered. Initially, IBM recognized the value in preserving the informal and unconventional culture of the Rolm organization, which stood in stark contrast to IBM's methodical style. However, in 1987 IBM terminated Rolm's subsidiary status and decided to fully integrate the company into its own corporate structure. IBM's managers soon learned the folly of that decision. When they tried to push Rolm's resources—its products and its customers—through the processes that had been honed in the large-computer business, the Rolm business stumbled badly. And it was impossible for a computer company whose values had been whetted on profit margins of 18% to get excited about products with much lower profit margins. IBM's integration of Rolm destroyed the very source of the deal's original worth. (Clayton & Overdorf, 2000)

The analysis, presented in these terms in the Harvard Business School case study, is so at odds with the story that IBM executives tried to accredit, that it highlights their shock at the mistake they made. Which cost them $500 million in losses when IBM decided, at the end of 1988, to sell the ROLM business to "Siemens".[10] IBM executives repeatedly stated that the decision to sell was due to the difficulty of combining telephone and computer technologies: "the convergence of computers and communications has proven to be much more difficult than anyone imagined".[11] But ROLM had already done it, and with great success. The truth is, as Harvard analysts wrote, that IBM was unable to integrate and valorize an entrepreneurial style incompatible with its own. It could be said that its managers applied the formula in reverse: conservation and exclusion.

4.6.2 Echelon

The proof that the experience was imitable can be found in the corporate history of "Echelon", founded in 1988 with headquarters in Santa Clara, North-West of Cupertino, by the same Ken Oshman, who had left ROLM-IBM, and by Armas Clifford

---

[9] Carla Lazzareschi: *IBM: Hanging Up on Phone Business, to Spin Off Rolm*, "Los Angeles Times"14 December 1988. In 1987, IBM launched the third generation of personal computers (PS/2) when it had just concluded a downsizing of its staff (from 410,000 employees four years earlier to 390,000) due to the deep crisis caused by the exhaustion of the enormous success achieved with the mainframe "System 360". The largest information technology company in the world was in the midst of a shift toward greater production diversification, toward distributed computing.

[10] IBM's profits were then 1180 million dollars (1987) and so the loss was a substantial 42%, serious even in relation to the large size of the multinational.

[11] Carla Lazzareschi, cit.

Markkula Jr. (Mike). Echelon produced control systems used in the late 1980s in large buildings (air conditioning, lighting, elevators, security), in electromechanical plants, in the handling of liquids and granular solids (chemicals, breweries), in the new home automation sector. The systems were different, but all responded to the classic cybernetic paradigm: peripheral sensors and actuators connected to a central computer that processed incoming data and sent operating commands back to peripheral terminals. The idea of Echelon arose from the observation that in principle the different control problems had a common core and therefore, with the appropriate technology, it was possible to move to distributed control, or a system in which information is processed peripherally in a network of intelligent nodes.

The fields of application were potentially vast, and Echelon took seriously the engineers' idea that such a technology would almost impose itself, as personal computers had imposed themselves by supplanting the system of large calculators connected to "dumb" terminals. This was the structural change in which Echelon was inserted: the transition from mainframe to distributed computing that was already underway. It took two years of work, but in 1990 Echelon created the new universal control technology: LonWorks®. Its market success now depended on solving a problem: how to facilitate the transition from the centralized to the distributed control paradigm by a small company faced with a system with many companies, some large, dominated by the traditional paradigm. Echelon's strategy was oriented in two directions: (1) convince the largest companies, especially in the large building automation sector, to use LonWorks® in traditional control systems by leveraging its lower cost; (2) promote the new distributed control system to small installers by leveraging its greater efficiency (Lane & Maxfield, 2005, p. 19).

After the start-up phase, from 1992 to 1995 there was considerable success in the first direction, less so in the second. But above all, in 1995 and 1996 growth stopped. Compared to the forecasts made five years earlier, there was clearly an impasse. This is demonstrated by the data covering the entire life of Echelon from its foundation to the year of its acquisition by "Adesto Technologies" (Fig. 4.4).

Four phases can be noted. Starting from the last two, one notes the collapse of profits and turnover since 2004 followed by strong instability due to the slow and fluctuating developments of home automation. Contrary to widespread predictions, the development of home automation was held back for cultural reasons (habits that were difficult to dislodge), for regulatory reasons (adjustments to the regulation were required that did not happen or took a long time to come), but also for technical–economic reasons. The cost and rigidity of the systems, however modernized, were at that time rather discouraging for consumer users, while industrial users required something more than the control apparatus. They required a fully equipped network, as Echelon began to build (among other things, one of the first large orders came in 2006 from ENEL). But in this sector, where it was forced to enter, the competition was very strong since several large companies were already active (ABB Ltd., General Electric, Holley Technology Ltd., Elster Group SE, Iskraemeco D.D., Itron, Inc., Landis, Schneider Electric SE, and Siemens AG). Thus, in the last phase from 2014, profits recovered but at the price of a radical downsizing of the company and then, from 2018, with the renunciation of autonomy with the acquisition by Adesto.

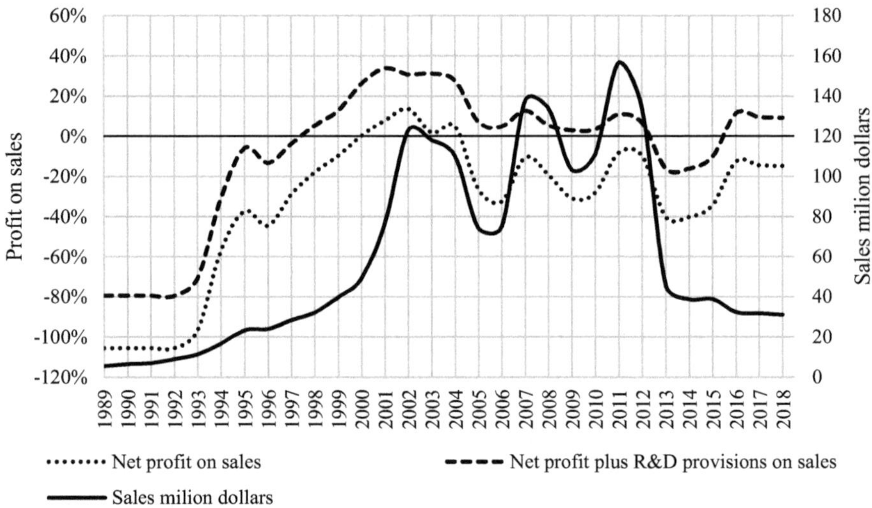

Fig. 4.4 Echelon: Sales, employees, net profit, and net profit plus provisions for research and development. *Source:* Figure obtained by processing data from Maxfield (2014), Lane and Maxfield (2005). *Note* Echelon always adopted a practice of high provisions for research and development even at the cost of almost always exposing net losses. It was a strategy aimed at completely self-financing innovation expenses that the stock market valued positively

But the two phases that are most interesting are the first and the second. The second phase, which began in 1997 and continued until 2004, saw six or seven years of success that led to a tripling of employees (from less than 100 to more than 300) and turnover (from 4 to 12 million dollars). However, this phase followed another more contrasting one. As already mentioned, after the launch of the innovative LonWorks® device in 1990, and two years of start-up, growth was notable but stopped in 1995. Then four years were needed for the real take-off, which instead, according to the engineers, should have come almost immediately. The obstacle was constituted by the lack of system integrator companies that could interface with the installation companies to counter, on the basis of evident convenience, their practice of using their own (inferior) control technologies. It was therefore necessary to promote this network of LonWorks® system integrators. It was at this point (it was mid-1995) that two conflicting strategic lines emerged (Lane & Maxfield, 2005, pp. 18–21) supported by two different visions. The engineers had created a new product, LonPoint®, adding a programmable control algorithm to the LonWorks® integrated circuit, a more flexible and customizable technology. On this basis, a line was suggested by the experience that had been started which, reasonably, wanted to build on the results achieved. It was aimed at large companies, such as "Olivetti America" and "Ameritech", which supplied systems to large office complexes, in the first case, and to large residential complexes in the second, offering a technology capable of significantly improving their functionality. It was the "science" line. The other line was that of "faith", which wanted to focus instead on the perspective, which had been a losing one until then, of involving small independent suppliers in competition with large companies in the medium-sized plant segment, using equipment that was adapted to customer specifications. This was exactly what ROLM had done with the involvement of local suppliers and TMs for the CBX, that is, to innovate by including.

An episode of a clash between these two lines, which called into question the very identity of Echelon, took place in mid-December 1996 (Lane & Maxfield, 2005, p. 22). The argument of the "scientific" line was that one could not turn one's back on the large system integrators otherwise they would develop alternative products, and it would be them who would turn their backs on Echelon. The "faith" line (supported in particular by former ROLM executives) countered that they would not easily accept replacing their technologies with the new one, while the small ones had to buy the control technologies from others anyway and therefore it was possible to convince them to use the new more efficient ones. The line of science, of instrumental rationality, then proposed a compromise: to continue on the path already taken and slow down the development of products on the LonPoint® track to wait for the results of the experiments that would be made.

The Echelon process according to "science" should have been:

$$\begin{gathered} Science - Innovation\ (LonWorks - LongPoint) \\ \underrightarrow{lead}\ Selection\ Exclusion\ (Great\ integrators); \end{gathered}$$

$$Science + Great\ integrators\ \underrightarrow{lead}\ Conservation - await$$

The management did not take this reasonable path, however, and decided instead to move forward quickly to explore the second path, even though doubts remained strong (Lane & Maxfield, 2005, p. 33): even though it was truly a question of faith.

The Echelon process according to the "faith":

Science – Innovation (LonWorks – LongPoint)
***would** lead Selection Exclusion (Great integrators)*;

Faith against Science lead Inclusion

(Small integrators) confident to convince them to Innovate with LongPoint

So, it was decided to visit the IBM office control system in New York City in the fall of 1996, at the invitation of "TEC" who had installed it. It was not a major decision, on the contrary, and it would not have been made normally given that TEC was a small systems integrator, which would not have been very interesting if there had been no faith. Instead, decisive consequences came from that "insignificant" trip. The Echelon guests returned from that visit with the awareness that they did not know much of what the TEC technicians showed them; in particular in two directions. First, the control systems applied in practice were much more complex than they had thought and therefore the programmability of the distributed control had to be much simpler. Second, the installation and programming had to be done in a very short time and "without a security net". On the basis of these findings, the engineers began to modify the apparatus to make it easier to install and use.

The process was not short and, already in sight of the finish line, a crucial episode occurred. In September 1997, a three-day meeting of system integrators, including those from TEC, was held, intended as a refresher course, even though some of the new LonPoint products were not yet fully developed. Echelon officials presented prototypes and described plans for their completion. They also asked for comments and suggestions, as they always did but without much conviction. The small system integrators, however, embraced the opportunity with enthusiasm and bombarded Echelon with suggestions: add I/O capability with 24-V relays; add functionality with variable temperatures and adapted start sequences; increase throughput (too many seconds to wait between dragging and dropping a device before the configuration plug-in loads); add security (more people need access to the system, but not all can change the configuration); improve visualization; add more control data; and add clear error signals to the readout.

Here too, as in the ROLM case, inclusion had given rise to provocation. In this case, however, it did not come from a conservative cynicism as in the case of the TMs for ROLM (if you were capable of doing something new that would be useful to us..., but you won't be capable). The provocation was directly constructive. The small system integrators had said: we will remain as we are, but if you make these innovations, if you are capable of doing so, then everything will change. The Echelon process was ultimately this:

Science – Innovation (LonWorks – LongPoint)
would lead Selection Exclusion (Greatintegrators);

$$\textit{Faith agains Science} \xrightarrow{\textit{lead}} \textit{Inclusion}$$

$$(\textit{Small integrators}) \xrightarrow{\textit{basically}} \textit{Conservative}$$

$$\textit{but constructive provocateurs}$$

$$\textit{Science against Faith} \xrightarrow{\textit{lead}} \textit{Innovation} \ (\textit{Long Point}2.0)$$

Echelon engineers had been pushed to change their interpretative canon. They had understood that the problem with small system integrators, who did not know much about electronic engineering, was not so much the technical superiority of the product, but above all its ease and transparency of use. Hence, the benefit for Echelon was decisive. The products ready for delivery in the spring of 1998 contained the main recommended changes (LongPoint 2.0). The proof of success came in the second visit to IBM when, after installing the new system in one part of the offices, a storm cut the power and when it came back on everything automatically went back to normal, while in the other part "the maintenance people have to scramble around to reset every Sage controller" (Lane & Maxfield, 2005, p. 32). In 2003, 15 years after the birth of Echelon, 4,000 companies had purchased the new technology (Fig. 4.5).

But its further diffusion was not as expected. Much depended on the real sensitivity to the urgent need to reduce energy consumption. In the 2006 Shareholders' Report one could read: "Our products make energy saving affordable. [...] In Sweden, both Vattenfall and E.ON Sweden have connected hundreds of thousands of consumers with Echelon's NES advanced metering infrastructure, improving the stability and

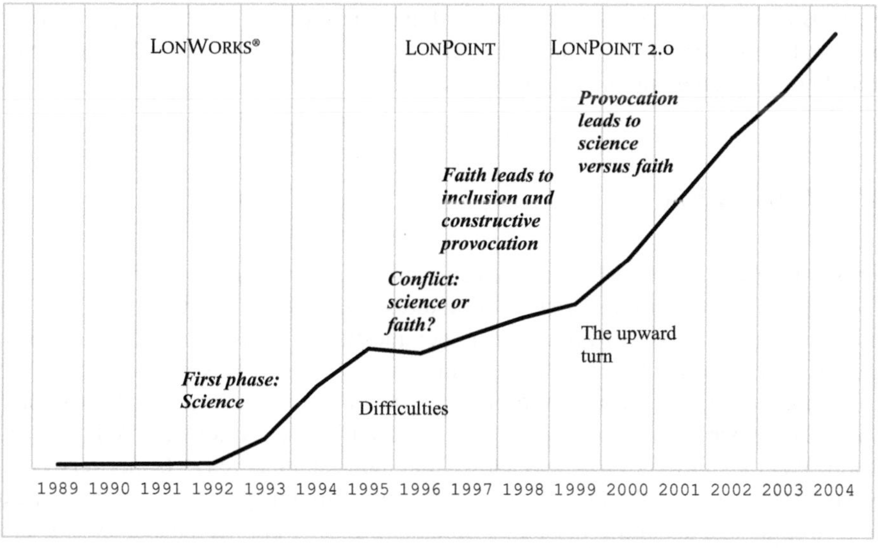

Fig. 4.5 Echelon: trend of the result index, phases, results, products, process (1989–2004). *Source* Figure obtained by processing data from Maxfield (2014), Lane and Maxfield (2005). *Note*: Result index as in the case of ROLM

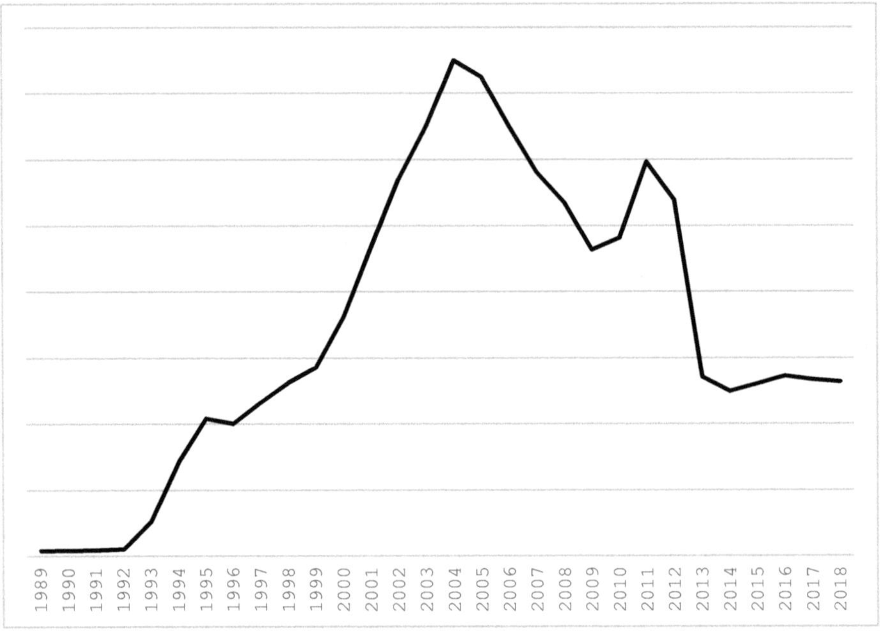

Fig. 4.6 Echelon: trend of the result index (1989–2018). *Source* Figure obtained by processing data from Maxfield (2014), Lane and Maxfield (2005)

quality of electricity supply [...] laying the foundation for consumer reduction strategies". But at that time, it was in the midst of the season of the lowest energy costs that occurred in the United States and Europe. It was therefore the context that prevented Echelon from achieving the results it deserved (Fig. 4.6).

4.7 Conclusion

These modern examples of collective action in private companies that have progressively faced a multifaceted crisis of structures demonstrate that the "formula" has truly and successfully been applied. Another question is whether or not these companies based on forms of participation from below can be proposed as alternatives to contemporary capitalism or to the transition to technofeudalism that has already taken place. These participatory experiences have been historically defeated. What can be said is that they have nevertheless shown that they can be efficient from every point of view. Thus, they could return in a desirable future for business forms in the context of a struggle against authoritarian domination This is what Varoufakis, who sees a struggle for the socialization of Cloud Capital even from below as possible, hopes, as does Bruno Jossa, who, as will be seen, believes a struggle for the self-management of companies and the system is possible.

The next example, that of the people's houses, refers to a completely different world, that of the proletarian condition during the Industrial Revolution between the nineteenth and twentieth centuries. Those were distant times, at the beginning of industrial capitalism that has literally disappeared today, which were also times of transition, as are these times, in which traditional structures are exhausted, and new ones must be built. It will be seen that the subordinates, enslaved and deprived of effective citizenship, like today, faced a dual problem: to build collective practices, "usable things, tools within reach of many hands, double Lilliputians of general cooperation on which, by exercising their use, one cannot stop intervening" while at the same time developing an alternative proletarian culture. Even in the case of the people's houses, it will be seen that the formula faith against science and science against faith was applied.

References

Clayton, M. C., & Overdorf, M. (2000, March–April). Disruptive innovation—Meeting the challenge of disruptive change. *Harvard Business School Magazine*.

Harris, M. (2023). *Palo Alto: A history of California, capitalism, and the world*. Little, Brown & Company.

Lane, D. A., & Maxfield, R. (2005). Ontological uncertainty and innovation. *Journal of Evolutionary Economics, 15*, 3–50.

Lane, D. A., & Maxfield, R. (1997). Foresight, complexity and strategy. In B. Arthur, S. Durlauf, & D. A. Lane (Eds.), *The economy as a complex evolving system 2* (pp. 169–198). Addison-Wesley.

Maxfield, K. (2014). *Starting up Silicon Valley: How Rolm became a cultural icon and fortune 500 company*. Emerald Book Company.

Maxfield, R. (2013). M. Kenneth Oshman. *Memorial tributes* (Vol. 17, pp. 233–237). The National Academies Press.

Ryans, A. B. (1988). M209A *ROLM case study*. Stanford University Publication.

Walling, M. A. (2023). Suicide contagion. *Current Trauma Reports, 7*(4), 103–114.

Chapter 5
The People's Houses

5.1 Introduction

People's houses have had a long history from the end of the nineteenth century to the present day. Many have been closed,[1] but several have been able to survive for a century and a half, sometimes rising from the ashes, figuratively but also literally after being burned by reactionaries and fascists. Sometimes, even today, they are places of collective action. The example of the people's houses is useful in this research. And it could be useful for sick contemporary society. They were, and sometimes remain, as Paolo Virno hoped: "from the beginning and entirely supra-individual, collective practices, usable things, tools within reach of many hands, Lilliputian doubles of cooperation on which, by exercising their use, they never cease to intervene". According to Margaret Kohn, the "careful" analysis of these places "can strengthen a concept of democracy that is useful today" (Khon, 2003, p. 2). This is far from an isolated judgment. For example, in remembering the Maison

[1] A particularly serious loss was that of the famous "Maison du Peuple" in Brussels (1899), a masterpiece by the architect Victor Horta commissioned by the Workers' Party, a magnificent Art Nouveau creation. It was demolished in 1964, despite an international protest movement of over 700 architects, and in its place a 26-storey office block was built: Blaton Tower, named after the builder who, surreally, was the same one who had built most of Horta's works. This demolition was one of many perpetrated between the 1950s and 1960s when the Belgian capital was "Brusselized", a neologism coined to describe the senseless destruction of entire historic districts of a city. But not by bombers, which were said to be "Coventrized", like the English city of Coventry which was razed to the ground by the Germans in 1940. But in peacetime, by building speculation. With the establishment of the European Community bureaucracy in the Belgian capital, the real estate developers, with the complicity of the Community itself, the municipal authority and the Belgian government, made huge deals by purchasing and demolishing entire neighborhoods to build in their place buildings of reinforced concrete without any merit and, in between, the infamous urban highways. And the virtual reconstruction in three dimensions of the Maison du Peuple, produced by "Alice Laboratory and Horta Museum", which can be "visited" online today, is pathetic, although useful.

G. Seravalli, *Collective Action in the Age of Polycrisis*, Contributions to Economics,
https://doi.org/10.1007/978-3-032-12653-5_5

du Peuple in Brussels, Owen Hatherley in "The Architectural Review" (4 September 2018) wrote:

> What [... matters] is that these ideas and these buildings are [...] relevant in an era when the radical left [...] has to rebuild itself from scratch. It doesn't have the infrastructure, the materials, the money [...]. But neither did the Belgian Workers' Party in the 1890s. What workers did have was enthusiasm and the ability to channel it into small-scale cooperatives and grassroots organizations, which then stamped their presence on the city and, in the process, sought to create spaces where life was, in a microcosm, better and fairer. The architecture they chose to express this was attractive, decorative, ultramodern and open. The moment of socialist Art Nouveau could be surprisingly useful for the contemporary left. A left-wing populism needs its Maisons du Peuple. (www.architectural-review.com/essays/socialist-class-the-houses-of-the-people)

There is even an experience studied (by three researchers from the Universities of Linköping and Malmö[2]) of reinventing a people's house to make it an anti-neoliberal tool, just as hoped.

> Departing from a reading of the Stockholm uprising in 2013 as a potential 'window of opportunity', we relate this issue of urban mobilisation to the 'reinvention' of the old working-class common of the 'People's House'. In focus stands the case of the community centre, Folkets Husby (Husby of the People), founded in 2016 in the Stockholm community of Husby, from where the 2013 uprising took off. The new community centre was envisioned as an 'oasis for organisation' in a capital torn apart by socio-spatial polarisation. (Schierup et al., 2021, p. 908)

But there is much more, as will be seen in a quick reconstruction of the different configurations of the people's houses in Europe between the nineteenth and twentieth centuries.

In various experiences, they were the places of an operating collective subjectivity and of the elaboration of an alternative proletarian culture, which was indispensable to find specific methods of collective action capable of actually solving workers' problems.

The people's houses, intertwining the same development of the proletarian movement at the time of the first industrialization, at the end of an old world and at the making of a new world, required long and very painful processes. And yet, they were created against seemingly insurmountable difficulties. It makes one ask how it was possible for them to succeed. How it was possible considering that Rinaldo Rigola, first secretary of the CGIL in 1906, who remained in office until 1918, wrote in his autobiography:

> The workers' struggles and their defeats in the 1860s and 1870s had led the majority of people I lived with to believe that there was an iron law according to which workers would

[2] The essay reporting on this study was published in the journal "Critical Sociology" promoted and supported by the "Association for Critical Sociology". Initially titled "Insurgent Sociologist", the journal was born in the late 1960s from the Sociology Liberation Movement in controversy within the American Sociological Association (ASA). University of Berkeley sociologist and former ASA president Michael Burawoy wrote: "Without criticism, sociology is lost, and 'Critical Sociology' offers it in spades: it is a pillar of our discipline".

> always break their horns whenever they tried to do things differently from what the bosses wanted: the rich are made to command and the poor to serve. The elders advised the young not to get involved in things outside of their profession and their family, since there is nothing to be done about the tribulations of the poor christs. While families help each other in times of misfortune to the point of sharing the last morsel, there is very little sense of solidarity at work. Prostrating oneself, speaking badly of comrades, being overzealous, and informing are things that the poor moral sensitivity of the working class does not shy away from. Meanwhile, the bosses say: What rights? Workers have no rights. Machines increase the risk of injury, crises increase the risk of unemployment, fatigue increases the risk of disability. It's a problem. But what does the boss have to do with it? The worker should think about saving for the days when he will be unable to work. (Rigola, 1939, pp. 27, 32, 69)

This was 40 years after the appeal of Flora Tristan in 1843, an extraordinary worker, activist, writer who toured France and England to document the condition of the proletariat and fight for the "holy cause" of their emancipation (the industrial Piedmont that remained in Rigola's memories was 40 years behind France).

> Workers, men and women, listen to me. Your condition is miserable, painful: in good health you do not have the right to work, sick, infirm, wounded, elderly, you do not have the right to hospital, poor, you do not even have the right to alms because begging is prohibited by law. Such an existence is a real torture. All the eloquent voices of the most intelligent and devoted men to your holy cause have not succeeded in twenty-five years in urging the Government on the danger represented by seven or eight million exasperated workers who in great numbers are forced to choose between suicide and theft. For twenty-five years now everything has been said and repeated and in every form. There is nothing more to say and write because your unhappy condition is known to everyone. There is only one thing to do: act. The day has come when it is up to you and you alone that the task of acting in the interests of your cause belongs. It is a question of life or of poverty and hunger. Experience and facts tell you that the Government cannot or will not concern itself with your fate. But your action is not armed revolt, not street riots, not arson, not looting. No, because destruction, instead of remedying your ills, would only make them worse. The riots in Lyon and Paris have shown you this. There is only one path left for you, legal, legitimate before God and men: it is the UNIVERSAL UNION OF WORKERS, a union that will have the purpose of ESTABLISHING THE WORKING CLASS and of building many buildings (Palaces of the Union) throughout France. In these places children of both sexes from six to eighteen years of age will be cared for, sick workers and the elderly will be hospitalized. You will say to me: but how can we unite for this great work? We are all scattered, often even enemies and at war with each other. Workers, put aside all your petty rivalries and form a compact, solid, indissoluble UNION. Think carefully. The effort is probably the last you will be able to make because if you do not respond to the call if through selfishness or unconsciousness you refuse to unite, there will be nothing left but to pronounce over you the words that are said over the dead. (Tristan, 1843, pp. 4–8)

The following year, the young Karl Marx, who was certainly not naive, but was animated by great "faith", went fishing for hope in singular places and moments:

> When communist workers gather together, their primary aim is doctrine, propaganda, etc. But in doing so they also take on a new need, the need of society, and what seems to be a means has become an end. This practical movement can be observed in its brightest results if one looks at a meeting of French socialist "ouvriers". Smoking, drinking, eating, etc., are no longer mere means of staying together, means of union. [...] union, conversation [...] have in their turn the brotherhood of men as their aim [...]: with them it is not a phrase, but a truth, and the nobility of man radiates towards us from those work-hardened faces. (Marx, 1844/1970, p. 207)

The lesson of that distant experience could be this: in the face of the crisis of the contemporary world one should not despair; it is difficult to think that the present condition is worse than that of the proletariat of that time. They did not despair and, it cannot be forgotten, they succeeded in the laborious construction of an effective counter-power that, after the Second World War, allowed the West a state of well-being and 40 years of economic-social equilibrium. But one must not forget how long and difficult it was to find progressive solutions to the "social question".

In the many phases of their history, in the various national and local worlds, the people's houses have been a complex reality. Some were modest and with few functions, others large with many activities. They had meeting places, often a restaurant, accommodation, a room for meetings and shows. The workers' cooperatives, which had often built them, kept offices and warehouses there, produced and sold good quality bread at reasonable prices, distributed fuel and consumer goods, often had work and housing cooperatives. They were the headquarters of reformist or revolutionary unions, of parties of socialist, social democratic, anarchist, communist inspiration, they gave economic and health support to proletarian families, subsistence to strikers, contributions in work and money for propaganda and political and union militancy. They were an open space in opposition to the exclusive practices of the bourgeois clubs, albeit with regulated admission so as not to offer opportunities for intervention by the police and to avoid provocations. The people's houses took on strong symbolic values: to represent the visibility of the proletarian class and its ethical and technical capacity, its stability, unity, and solidarity, its roots in the territory, the preservation of memory, the model and hope of future society. For this purpose, the buildings were sometimes commissioned to well-known architects and were always challenging in relation to the means available to the proletarian movement.

A typology can be composed on the basis of five classification factors: spaces used as; users-actors; salient features of the purposes; salient features of the results; symbolic value, image of. There are five types that can be ordered according to the increasing commitment required for their construction and management. As can be seen in the Table 5.1, they go from one extreme to the other. At the level of minimum commitment, there are some people's houses that could have been at the beginning (or become over time as the last stage of a long degradation) almost "non-places".[3]

[3] This qualification, as reported by Antonio Fanelli (2014, p. 150), is suggested in an article by Enzo Brogi that appeared in "L'Unità" on 17 February 2012: "The People's Houses – Our History". A regional councillor for the PD and former Mayor of Cavriglia, a journalist and writer, Brogi cannot be suspected of disrespect or underestimation of communist traditions and the People's Houses, as can be seen by reading, for example, his article in "Tirreno" (19 May 2024): "When I went to live in Cavriglia, not even ten thousand inhabitants, there was practically only that Party and a People's House. A stubborn land of miners and anti-fascists where the PCI had brought everyone together. Ten sections and over 1500 members. [...]. That membership card made you feel part of a collective that dreamed of more justice, equality, the Constitution. Kept with pride even when carrying it in your pocket could mean paying a personal price or for your family. Different from today when even the electoral lists are increasingly whitened by the party symbol". Brogi is criticized by Fanelli for "having brought up a concept antithetical to the people's houses", also criticizing the great anthropologist Marc Augé for having proposed a theory, that of non-places, "as compelling

Table 5.1 People houses typology, on the basis of growing commitment

Type	Spaces used as	Users-actors	Salient features of the purposes	Salient features of the results	Symbolic value, image of
1	Almost non-places	Anonymous	Indefinite	Random	Absence
2	Meeting places	Anonymous-regulars	Undesigned recreational	Unspecified user dependent	Temporary sociality
3	Places of congregation	Regulars	Cultural recreational help and self-help	Unspecified dependent on users and management	Eventual-potential community
4	Sociopolitical containers	Members and supporters	Recreational cultural self-help and political specific to individual associative entities	Specified and dependent on the individual entities and partly on the agreed management	Community as sum of collectives
5	Establishment of an agent subjectivity	Activists and recruitables	Everything useful to strategies specific to the people's house itself	Collectively specified, pursued, obtained	Strong unified agent community

At the other extreme, at the level of maximum commitment, there are the people's houses as "agent communities"[4] whose distinctive character is to be subjects of social and political action as such, as well as tools used by the various collective subjects hosted. These are the people's houses that have attracted the most attention, often neglecting the nature of their specific historical conditions.

---

and destined for media success as it is susceptible to profound criticism". It is clear instead, as demonstrated in many parts of Fanelli's book, that one cannot speak of people's houses in general. In Augé's non-places individuals lose their personal prerogatives to exist only as users, and this is what has happened in several cases in which the people's houses still exist in name but in fact have become only bars and dance halls, being at the opposite extreme to the "agent communities".

[4] Fanelli (2014, p. 3) uses the term "proletarian heterotopia" with reference to Foucault. But the reference appears pertinent only for one aspect, that of otherness which in "heterotopic places" is, however, rather passive, as one can see in the examples that Foucault names: barracks, retirement homes, psychiatric clinics, prisons, cemeteries, museums, fairs, brothels. These places "have the curious property of being in relation with all other places, but with a modality that allows them to suspend and neutralize […] the set of relationships that are outlined, reflected and mirrored by them" (Foucault, 1984/2010, p. 12). As will be seen, the people's houses as acting communities were much more.

Despite this extreme heterogeneity, Margaret Kohn has proposed a definition (for types three to five) that contains "four common principles".

> There are four principles that summarize the characteristics of the houses of the people and distinguish them from the bourgeois associationalism, clandestine revolutionary organization, and the paternalistic societies for the betterment of the working class. First, they were complex structures for bringing together diverse organizations. Second, they were financed collectively by their members. Third, they were managed democratically by workers themselves. Finally, participation was not limited by economic status or political or religious membership but was based on shared the commitment to improving the economic and social life of the subaltern classes. (Kohn, 2003, p. 100)

5.2 Alternative Proletarian Culture

To create the people's houses, overcoming serious difficulties and adapting them to different contexts, it was essential to develop an alternative proletarian culture as a development of a vision of the world and life (culture) specific to the class of workers who own only the workforce (proletarian), a culture different from that of the dominant class and in contrast (alternative) to it.

Elaboration does not mean creation from nothing because the subalterns have always had their cultural forms before proletarianization. "The historical character and human significance of the cultural forms of the subaltern popular world", which have always been "the cultural counterpart of a social condition",[5] were part of the definition of alternative proletarian culture proposed in 1935 by Gramsci: «as a conception of the world and of life […] of certain strata […] of society, in opposition […] to the official conceptions of the world or, in a broader sense, of the historically determined cultured parts of society» (Gramsci, 1935/1977, p. 2312).

> In the succession of Gramsci's reflections on folklore, […] a process of growth is evident. […]. In 1929 Gramsci considers folklore simply as a "conception of the world" of certain strata of society, which are not touched by modern currents of thought: compared to the definitions then current, there is already the certainly not negligible novelty of affirming that folklore is a conception of the world; however, the decisive innovation that makes the text of 1935 so important is missing, and that is […] the connection between socio-economic condition (and opposition), and socio-cultural condition (and opposition). In 1929 folklore is only aged and outdated thought; in 1935 it becomes the cultural counterpart of a social condition. (Cirese, 1976, p. 147)

In turn Ernesto De Martino in 1949[6] ("Intorno a una storia del mondo popolare subalternno") cited a passage by Gramsci from "Il materialismo storico e la filosofia di Benedetto Croce" to underline that a bridge between traditional folklore and modern

---

[5] De Martino (1949, p. 427) and Cirese (1976, p. 147).

[6] De Martino had already published "Naturalismo e storicismo nell'etnologia" ("Naturalism and Historicism in Ethnology") (1941) and "Il mondo magico: prolegomeni a una storia del magismo" ("The Magical World: Prolegomena to a History of Magic") (1948). "It is known that de Martino followed with great attention the process of publishing Gramsci's works, which began in 1947, with the Letters from Prison and, from 1948 […], with the Prison Notebooks" (Pizza, 2013, pp. 78–79).

proletarian culture can only be found by understanding the meaning of "primitive cultural institutions"[7] as a mythical articulation of chaos (the drama of being rejected) and a restorative action[8] "naive millenarian faith, [...] mythology, [...] magical attitudes" (De Martino, 1949, p. 420). In this way,

> although [...] it is appropriate, in political action, to continually take into account the cultural traditions of the subaltern popular world, using them [...] in a progressive sense, the task of high culture [...] always remains that of historicizing the «popular» and the «primitive», of using towards the archaic that historical piety which contributes to the prophylaxis against the enduring ideal efficacy of archaisms and benefits the maturation of the vital germ of the «modern popular reform» and the formation of collective lay persuasions. (De Martino, 1949, pp. 420–421, underlining in the text)

The important topic of the ways of grafting into "folklore" will be examined more carefully later. But it is in "high culture" that the determining contents of such a "modern popular reform" must be found. If it were not for the "Manifesto" of Marx and Engels, it will be seen that the development of an alternative proletarian culture between the nineteenth and twentieth centuries could have been without any doubt: *learning, development and practice of the non-oppositional agreement between collective and individual interest against the individualism typical of the capitalist market system.* In the Manifesto it was instead stated that such a culture had to be only the awareness that "their goals can only be achieved with the violent overthrow of every existing social order" (Marx & Engels, 1848/1974, p. 493).[9] In this way, the construction of proletarian culture before the revolution had to be

[7] "It was [...] observed that research was almost exclusively engaged in the collection and classification of material, or in its arrangement according to space, time and causality. This immense amount of work is instead offset by the relative paucity of results concerning the meaning of primitive cultural institutions, all or almost all still shrouded in dense darkness, or the object of explanatory hypotheses that in reality explained nothing at all" (De Martino, 1949, p. 411).

[8] "This existential drama [of the subaltern classes] of the presence that risks not being in the world and that, in order to be there in some way, redeems itself through the mythical articulation of the insurgent chaos and the demiurgic of the compensatory and reparative action, precisely this drama was the object of my 'Magical World': but this drama declared itself to me with ever greater evidence as the drama of beings rejected by 'history', lying in a condition of radical alienation, outcasts in a world that was not 'theirs', and who hour by hour, day by day, and over a long period of years, in the chain of generations, had accumulated the pain of this outcast: hence the anguish was always nested in the soul, and broke out in the critical moments of existence, in the face of death, in the face of the forces of nature, in the face of hunger, in the solitude of the night, etc." (De Martino, 1949., p. 434).

[9] Henri Maler (2024) has presented a "meticulous, indeed fussy, exposition of the conception of the proletariat developed by Marx starting from 1843" in which a caesura that occurred between the writings preceding and those after 1845 is highlighted. "Marx, in 'The German Ideology' and then in the 'Manifesto', clearly introduces a decisive modification. The historical conditions of human emancipation are not on the shoulders of the proletariat, but [...] on the material conditions: the revolutionary vocation of the proletariat and the communist vocation of the revolution are inscribed in the development of the productive forces [...]. The awareness of the necessity of a communist revolution for the proletarians does not arise from [...] the awareness of their social being; it arises from the revolution itself".

considered unnecessary (beyond this awareness), and the subsequent one could only be constructed after the revolution had been accomplished.[10]

5.2.1 "Utopian" Socialists

To consider the thinking of the "utopian socialists" from the early nineteenth century, Saint Simon[11] is the first character who comes to attention. In his work "L'Organisateur", composed between November 1819 and February 1820, Saint Simon foresaw the emergence of a new need for reconciliation between collective interest and individual freedom for modern "industrial capacity" itself. One cannot demand more than a "small degree of command" because "in industrial capacity", to be efficient, individual conduct must spontaneously adhere to the collective enterprise. In this way, the emerging reality itself would have brought with it the push for collective action of the proletariat for their emancipation.

> Temporal power in the ancient system, being military, required by its nature the highest degree of passive obedience on the part of the nation. On the contrary, in industrial capacity [...] arbitrariness does not and cannot enter, since, on the one hand, everything is judged on

[10] Between 1904 and 1920, a clash took place between Aleksandr Aleksandrovič Malinovskij (1873–1928), known as Bogdanov, and Lenin on proletarian culture, a clash that Lenin ended with Bogdanov's defeat: in December 1920, a decree of the Central Committee of the Bolshevik Party condemned the autonomy of the Proletkult "as a petty bourgeois attempt to create an institution alien to Soviet power". Bogdanov's activity (including Proletkult) had long been, important, a serious alternative to the dirigiste degenerations of Bolshevism. "With the [...] 'Vpered' group, born to create and spread a new proletarian culture, Bogdanov had launched the manifesto 'The cultural tasks of our time', which aimed to develop Marx's last thesis on Feuerbach [...]. The program envisaged the implementation of a philosophy of action through the training of workers and peasants, to prepare them to independently lead the revolution on an operational and organizational level, and also ideologically and culturally. The tools envisaged were the foundation of the Proletarian University, which was actually started in Moscow, and of a workers' encyclopaedia on the model of the Enlightenment. On this basis, in 1917, on the threshold of the October Revolution, the Proletkult (Institute for Proletarian Culture) was born which, welcomed with great favour in the factories, came to count up to 500,000 members, more than the Bolsheviks registered in the party. In its first formulation, the programmatic text of the movement presented harsh criticisms of Lenin and the other Bolshevik leaders, bureaucrats whose authoritarian behaviour, personality cult and egoism were emphasized. The antidote to dirigiste degenerations was for Bogdanov the formation of a proletarian culture as an independent expression of civil society, in the belief that cultural revolution was the prerequisite for revolution, and cultural hegemony the prerequisite for political hegemony" (Ghetti & Iacarella, 2021).

[11] Claude-Henri de Rouvroy, Count of Saint-Simon (1760–1825), took part in the American War of Independence at the age of 17. He returned to France with the rank of colonel but retired from military life in 1785 to undertake various enterprises that contributed to increasing his fame as an adventurer and utopian. In 1789, the revolution interrupted the life of a noble, rich philosopher, scientist, and traveler. After being imprisoned and risking the guillotine, he was elected president of the electoral assembly of Falvy (department of the Somme) and, addressing the voters, renounced his title. He lost all his wealth. But he rebuilt it with a transport company with which he made a fortune that he later lost again. From 1797, having left business at the age of 37, he devoted himself to studies and research. He is considered a reference for "utopian" socialism.

> the level [...] of general prosperity, and on the other hand the execution of this plan cannot require more than a very small degree of command of men over one another. (Saint-Simon, 1820/1869, vol. 4–5, Huitième lettre)

Saint Simon's was truly a "utopian" position but in the sense of extremely modern and capable of looking very far ahead. As seen in the second chapter, the question of command in the capitalist system has not been resolved through the practiced hierarchical and competitive ways. So much so that neoliberalism has "had to" invent the way of self-discipline through the myth of the subaltern "entrepreneur of themselves". And today, with its failure, one is led to hope for collective action in which individual interest is reconciled with the common good, as Saint Simon already saw as indispensable for modernity two centuries ago.

From this descriptive-interpretative perspective of Saint Simon, moving on to a normative one, for François Marie Charles Fourier (Besançon 1772–Paris 1837)[12] this agreement between individual and collective interest constituted the third condition for the society of "harmony" (of the nine that he had indicated in 1829, the other eight implying institutions and structures).[13]

> Charles Fourier has been nicknamed the "Father of Socialism". He was certainly one of the first to denounce and condemn the individualism exalted by the Revolution, to proclaim the reality, until then barely suspected, and the superior dignity, universally ignored, of the social body, or, to use his own words, «of the social movement». (Lafontaine, 1911, p. 5)

---

[12] "He was born in Besançon in 1772 and lived through the Revolution without taking any active part in the political maneuvers that were stirring up France and its minds. His father had acquired a certain affluence in the drapery trade [...]. Fourier was employed at a young age as a clerk in Lyon, then in Rouen. He traveled for various firms in Germany and Holland. In 1793, at the age of twenty-one, he founded a large grocery and colonial goods store in Lyon, where he had returned. The time was hardly propitious for business, and Fourier ruined himself. Forced to undertake military service, he was incorporated into the eighth regiment of mounted hunters. After two years, he was able to obtain leave for health reasons and returned to Lyon, where he once again took a commission. [...]. From this time on, Fourier's thinking was awakened: he read, in his free moments, works dealing with fashionable questions, political, military, diplomatic subjects, social and industrial questions, controversies on the problems of political economy. He was particularly interested in the works of Rousseau and the Encyclopedists, in the publications of Claude de Saint-Martin, the 'Unknown Philosopher' [...]. Later he would read the Physiocrats, the English economists and moralists, Bentham, Adam Smith, Richard, Owen, Mackintosh, the brochures and articles of Saint-Simon, but he would never allow himself to be completely dominated by any doctrine. He would always adopt a premeditated coquetry in thinking for himself and even against others" (Lafontaine, 1911, p. 3).

[13] "1) Guarantees against theft [...] due to the impossibility of using stolen goods; 2) satisfactory remuneration of the three industrial faculties [...] capital, labour and talent; 3) harmony between collective interest and individual interest [...] always in opposition in the 'civil' order; 4) [...] guarantee of employment [...] despite [...] a decent minimum wage; 5) valorising competition, instead of devaluing competition (that of economists, which gradually leads people to poverty, lowering wages and degrading work); 6) [certainty] of fortune through the practice of truth, and of [...] ruin through the practice of lies; 7) [...] valorisation of instincts, their application to industry [...]; 8) appropriate use of the sexes and ages [...]; 9) balance and limit of the population, whose indefinite increase would make all the ways of wealth illusory and would disunite social gatherings" (Fourier, 1829, p. 586).

And it was a possible and necessary cultural construction for the emancipation of the proletariat, a process explicitly not postponed until after the overthrow of the system. For Fourier, the overcoming of capitalism was not required if the second condition was "satisfactory remuneration of the three industrial faculties: capital, labour and talent" (Fourier, 1829, p. 586), even if it had to be a capitalism with economic-social balance: «guarantee of employment despite a decent minimum wage, valorising competition, instead of devaluing competition (that of economists, which gradually leads people to poverty, lowering wages and degrading work)» (Fourier, 1829, p. 586).

A similar conception could be found throughout the entire French "romantic socialism" between 1825 and 1848, even in the elaborations, such as those of Pierre Leroux,[14] who wanted to abolish capitalism, albeit progressively and without violence.

> Pierre Leroux was one of the most influential socialist theorists on the French novel between 1830 and 1848. Part of this influence is due to the unique position he occupies in the history of socialist thought: Leroux was the only theorist who was simultaneously a philosopher, a partisan of democracy and, even more important [...] a literary critic. Among those novelists influenced by him were Sainte-Beuve, Eugène Sue, and particularly, George Sand and Victor Hugo. Leroux's thinking began to act upon French novelists as early as 1831, just about the same time his particular brand of socialism received its most complete expression in the articles he wrote for la Revue Encyclopédique. [...]. Leroux [...who], coined the word Socialism [...], [...and considered] the necessity to ally social reform and the change of institutions with communities aiming at a moral regeneration [...]. His optimism became contagious because it placed the potential for perfectibility in man's own hands, and it envisioned the democratic system as the only viable means of transformation. His aim, like that of Fourier, was to achieve a state of social harmony without resorting to violence. [...]. This goal necessitated the emancipation of the proletariat. (Brown, 1986, pp. 74–75)

Pierre Leroux's optimism was actually much more cautious than Fourier's precisely on the conciliation between individual interests and the collective good. He had invented the term "socialism" to deprecate "absolute socialism" that would have annulled individual freedoms[15] warning that the tendencies toward individualism and collectivism were both strong and "horrible".

---

[14] Pierre Henri Leroux (Paris 1797–Paris 1871) was a bricklayer and printer; but he had finished high school in Rennes and had won admission to the Polytechnic, which however he could not attend in order to help his mother and three brothers after the premature death of his father. Among his many works, a particularly important one was the monumental "Encyclopédie nouvelle. Dictionnaire philosophique, scientifique, littéraire et industriel" which he directed together with Jean Reynaud and which Heinrich Heine judged to be the work that, for the socialist and republican thought of the nineteenth century, was what the Encyclopedia of Denis Diderot and Jean-Baptiste Le Rond d'Alembert had been for the previous century.

[15] "I am undoubtedly a socialist, [...] if we want to understand by socialism the Doctrine that does not sacrifice any of the terms of the formula: Liberty Fraternity Equality Unity, but which reconciles them all. [...]. When I invented the term Socialism to contrast it with the term Individualism, I did not expect that, twenty years later, it would be used [...] indiscriminately [...]. I refer the reader to the History of Socialism (which he will find in one of the subsequent volumes of this edition), contenting myself with protesting against those who have taken the opportunity to find me in contradiction with myself" (Leroux, 1834/1850, p. 376).

> Liberty and Society are the two equal poles of social science. Let no one say that society is merely the result, the sum, the aggregation of individuals; because that leads us to what we have today: [...] the misery of the majority. [...]. But let no one say either that society is everything and the individual is nothing, that society comes before individuals, that citizens are nothing more than [...] functionaries of society, who must find, whether they like it or not, their fulfillment in everything that contributes to the social goal [...]. Instead, let society be the result of the free and spontaneous life of all those who compose it. Do not wish that the life of each man be made to serve the social life you have imagined: [...] that road leads only to stupidity and despotism. [...]. Thus, we remain in perplexity and uncertainty, equally attracted to and repelled by two opposing magnets. Yes, the sympathies of our time are equally strong, equally intense — liberty or equality, individuality or association. Faith in society is total, but so is faith in individuality. From this arises an equal drive toward these two desired aims, and an equal distance from the exclusive exaggeration of either one or the other — an equal horror of both individualism and socialism. (Leroux, 1834/1850, pp. 374–377)

In 1842, to indicate the call for collective action from below (fraternité), Étienne Cabet[16] used the term "communism". In the ideal society, "Icaria", the preparation of food and the communal dinner in "superb and elegantly furnished rooms" (just like in the largest and most prestigious people's houses) were particularly important tools for "fraternization" (Cabet, 1842, p. 54). A year later, Flora Tristan (Paris 1803–Bordeaux 1844) proposed the "Palais de l'Union Ouvrière" in the popular booklet Union Ouvrière of 1843 that Lorenz von Stein considered "very lucid" in his "History of the Socialist Movement in France". According to the German historian, Flora Tristan "demonstrated that she was aware, more than any other contemporary author, that the working class is an entity and that in order to improve its conditions it must recognize itself as such and strive to achieve a solidarity that helps it move towards a common goal" (Stein, 1850/1964, p. 308).

A year later, in 1844, the young Marx also evoked brotherhood as a collective learning of the workers in the third of the "Economic and Philosophical Manuscripts". In the summer of 1846, in the "anti-Kriege circular" (in reality anti-Weitling)[17] Marx

---

[16] Étienne Cabet (1788–1856), lawyer, one of the leaders of the 1830 movement in Paris, later elected to the Chamber of Deputies, was one of the most famous French authors of political and social writings: his periodical, "Le Populaire" reached an exceptional circulation for the time of 28,000 copies.

[17] Engels wrote in his "History of the Communist League": «A young student from Westphalia, Hermann Kriege, had gone to America, presented himself as an emissary of the League, and had linked himself with the madman Harro Harring to convulse south America counties by means of the League. He had founded a newspaper in which he preached a communism based on "love", overflowing with love and ultra-sentimental. We violently opposed this in a circular which did not fail to have an effect. Kriege disappeared from the scene of the League» (Engels, 1885, p. 213). Wilhelm Weitling (Magdeburg 1808–New York 1871), the illegitimate son of a seamstress and a soldier, was also a tailor and traveled around Germany for work but was also in Vienna and Paris (in 1837) where he began his self-taught path following the French socialists of the time. In Paris he joined the League of the Outcasts, a German socialist organization founded by Theodor Schuster, which was later called the League of the Just and then the Communist League. His book "Garantien der Harmonie und Freiheit" was highly praised by Marx: «As regards the [...] cultural capacity of the German workers [...], I refer to the brilliant writings of Weitling, which, even in theory, often go further than Proudhon himself [...]. Where could the bourgeoisie - including its philosophers and

went so far as to write a violent and mocking attack against those who had spoken of brotherhood, as he himself had written two years earlier.

> This rural priest transforms the struggle for communist society into the «search for that great community spirit». He lets this «great spirit flow beautiful and full from the cup of communion» and «burn the holy spirit from the eye of his brother». [...]. This metaphysical result is preceded by the confusion of communism with communion: «The spirit that conquers the world, the spirit that commands the storm and the thunderstorm (!), the spirit that controls the blind and heals the lepers, the Spirit that gives all men to drink one wine» (we prefer the multiple varieties) «and to eat one bread» (the French and English communists demand more), «the eternal and omnipresent spirit is the community spirit». If this «spirit» is «eternal and omnipresent», then it is impossible to understand how private property could have existed for so long [...]. But of course it was not «recognized» and was therefore «eternal and omnipresent» only in his imagination. (Marx, 1846/1972, pp. 11–12)

The heated but frequent tones in the verbal violence of the times are striking. In any case, the reasons for the split were different: the evolution of Marx and Engels' thought that would be exposed shortly thereafter in the Manifesto, a problem of direction of the movement which was moving toward the constitution of the Communist League (London June 1847), but those tones were also explained by a serious breakdown in personal relationships. Engels wrote:

> Weitling later [1846] came to Brussels. But he was no longer the naive young tailor who, amazed at his own talent, tried to imagine what a communist society would be like. He was the great man persecuted by the envious because of his superiority, who sensed rivals, secret enemies and snares everywhere; the prophet, hunted from country to country, who carried the recipe for realizing heaven on earth ready in his pocket and imagined that everyone wanted to steal it from him. He had already quarrelled with the men of the League in London, and even in Brussels, where Marx and his wife especially treated him with almost superhuman patience, he could not get along with anyone. So, he soon went to America». (Engels, 1885, p. 214)

5.2.2 Utopians or "Scientific"?

Ultimately, it can be said that, in the years between the end of the nineteenth century and the beginning of the twentieth century, the possible "modern popular reform" was based on the elaboration of an alternative proletarian culture as a discovery of the ways of reconciling individual and collective interests for a wide range of objectives: from the progressive construction of a new social order from below to the awareness of the historical necessity of the dictatorship of the proletariat. Part of the

---

scholars - point to a work similar to Weitling's: Garantien der Harmonie und Freiheit, in relation to the emancipation of the bourgeoisie, to political emancipation? If one compares the dull, sappy mediocrity of German political literature with this enormous and brilliant literary debut of the German workers [...], one must prophesy that the German Cinderella will look like an athlete» (Marx, 1844/1976, pp. 404, 405). This passage, written in August 1844, contrasts most strikingly with the attack launched only two years later against Weitling through Kriege (Weitling was the only one not to sign the circular against Kriege by the group formed by Marx, Engels, Gigot, Heilberg, Seiler, Westphalen, Wolff).

same elaboration process was also the continuous torment given by the clash, which was often violent, between these very different positions where each accused the other or the others of "utopianism": the affirmation of an ideal model of society that is unachievable on the basis of the arguments and considerations that support this affirmation. The accusation of utopianism was explicit by Engels against "romantic" socialism, "unscientific socialism", in the essay "Socialisme utopique et socialisme scientifique".

> The immaturity of capitalist production and the immaturity of the class situation corresponded to the immaturity of theories. The solution to the social problems, which still remained hidden in the social relations of the embryonic economy, had to spring from the brain. Society presented only anomalies; their elimination was the mission of thinking reason. For this purpose, it was a question of inventing a new and more perfect social regime and guaranteeing it from the outside through propaganda and, if possible, through the example of model experiences. These new social systems were condemned in advance to utopia. The more they were elaborated in detail, the more they had to lose themselves in pure fantasy. [...Now] the new productive forces have surpassed the bourgeois form of their employment; and this conflict between the productive forces and the mode of production is not a conflict born in the minds of men like, for example, that of original sin and divine justice: it is there, in fact, objectively, outside us, independently of the will or the very behaviour of those who have provoked it. Modern Socialism is nothing but the reflection in thought of this actual conflict. (Engels, 1880, pp. 30, 41)

The accusation of utopianism aimed instead at "scientific socialism" was implicit on the part of the French socialists: either because they were convinced that the violent revolution would betray its promises or because it would demand the unbearable elimination of individual liberties. And it is noteworthy that a century after the October Revolution, Bruno Jossa published an essay to argue that the "utopian" socialists of the conciliation from below between individual and collective interests were realists while the planning born of Marxism-Leninism was utopian.

> The objective of my investigation is to argue that socialism must be defined as a system of labour managed firms. Centralised planning is not a possible socialism since it envisions a system in which men have not personal interest to produce. A system of producer cooperatives, on the contrary, is devoid of such utopian strain since the members of its firms would produce with the aim of maximising the satisfaction associated with their work. For this reason, it is possible to argue that the socialism is evolving from its utopian stage to the scientific stage of the modern theory of producer cooperatives. (Jossa, 2015, p. 1)

All things considered, the article by the young Gramsci in "Il Grido del Popolo" (29 January 1916) can be considered in conclusion, "which specifies the contours of the development of an alternative proletarian culture justifying it on a philosophical and historical level against the positions, far from negligible, of a certain philosophy of history according to which the destiny of the subalterns would be that of being inevitably either swallowed up by capital or forced to subvert it as subalterns" (Guzzone, 2020, p. 465). Gramsci wrote:

> Culture is [...] organization, discipline of one's inner self, it is taking possession of one's personality, it is the conquest of a higher consciousness, through which one can understand one's historical value, one's function in life, one's rights and one's duties. But all this cannot happen through spontaneous evolution [...] but through intelligent reflection, first by some

and then by an entire class, on the reasons for certain facts and on the best means to convert them from an occasion of vassalage into a sign of rebellion and social reconstruction. [...]. It is through the criticism of capitalist civilization that the unitary consciousness of the proletariat has been formed or is being formed, and criticism means culture, and not spontaneous and naturalistic evolution. [...]. It means having notions of what nature is and its laws in order to know the laws that govern the spirit. And learning everything without losing sight of the ultimate goal, which is to better know oneself through others and others through oneself. (Gramsci, 1916)[18]

5.3 Paternalism's Houses

"It is essential [...] to examine the history in relation to the specificities of individual countries, where the associations and the material headquarters of the associations had different origins and functions, and where the same word [...] people's house had different values and meanings" (Degl'Innocenti, 1984, p. VI). The people's houses of Tsarist Russia were peculiar, starting with the one in Tomsk in southwestern Siberia, opened in 1882 and often mistakenly considered the first in Europe, and followed by 20 more in St. Petersburg by the end of that decade. "In the reality of Russia, the non-political nature of the people's houses is evident: they were cultural and educational institutions also frequented by the petty bourgeoisie" (Alekseeva & Kazakova-Apkarimova, 2020, p. 952). The most important, the "People's House of Emperor Nicholas II" inaugurated in 1902 in St. Petersburg (Aleksandrovsky Park), was built on the initiative of Prince Oldenburgsky, president of the "Committee for the Protection of Popular Sobriety". These public committees with private participation established in many cities had the task of organizing recreational, cultural, and "anti-alcohol" propaganda activities. From 1897 to 1903, 137 "people's houses" were built (Alekseeva and Kazakova, p. 955). It can be said that they were hybrids between the paternalistic initiative for the "improvement of the lower classes" and petty bourgeois associationism. In terms of their paternalistic aspect, they were not even pioneers,

[18] Cesare Bermani demonstrated that Gramsci then enthusiastically adhered to Bogdanov's program. "Gramsci's adherence to the proletkultist theses was almost total in the years 1920–22 [...]. It is therefore not surprising that, at the same time as the resumption of the daily newspaper 'l'Ordine Nuovo', the Institute of Proletarian Culture was founded in Turin - again on Gramsci's initiative [...]. On 3 January 1921 [...] a committee met to study the program and the statute of the Institute [...]. This committee launches an appeal to all proletarian organizations, both political and economic, to participate in the meeting to establish the Institute, which is held on the evening of January 13th [...] and approves [...] the statute and the constitution of the Institute of Proletarian Culture, in whose program [...] drawn up by Zino Zini, [...] typically Gramscian accents shine through, so much so as to make one think that Gramsci was its greatest inspirer: [...]. 'The proletariat will not be able to aspire to its total redemption, and much less ensure in a stable way the fruits of its victorious affirmation in the sphere of political and economic struggle, if it does not first create for itself, for future generations of men, who will descend from it, a new model of education, which is the spontaneous, direct, immediate expression of its needs, its aspirations, its ideal of civilization and humanity'" (Bermani, 1981–1982, pp. 28–29).

having been preceded almost 70 years earlier by British initiatives, such as Robert Owen's "Institute for the Formation of Character" inaugurated in 1816.[19]

This inauguration took place in the third of six phases of Owen's life (1771–1858), the "most splendid" (Harrison, 1969, p. 4) from 1800 to 1824, when industrial success and advanced ideas on social problems earned him first wide notoriety and consensus but then, on the part of supporters, also criticism that accompanied the radicalism of the subsequent phases; the radicalism that would also earn him the title of "father of English socialism", although his profile remains elusive. "An elusive historical figure, Owen's legacy has been constantly reinterpreted since the 1860s, generation after generation, thus informing much of the British socialist tradition" (Siméon, 2012). He was and remains a figure rich in nuances, not only for the very different positions had he assumed in the different seasons of his life, but also for his peculiar paternalism in the 1800–1824 season. It should be noted that the term paternalism should not even be used, so varied were its versions,[20] and Owen and the "Owenist" movement, conceived—as shall be seen—a particular paternalism

[19] Among the many figures who went to New Lanark in that same year of 1816 was the future Tsar Nicholas I when he was 20 years old. He was the great-grandfather of Nicholas II to whom the house in Aleksandrovsky Park was dedicated. Owen's son said: «The young Duke's behaviour appeared to me to be spontaneous, serious and cordial. He listened with considerable attention for two hours or more to an exposition, made by my father, of his peculiar ideas for the betterment of mankind, and showed a lively interest in everything he saw at New Lanark, both at school and in the factory. Count Gurowski, who knew Russia well [...], speaking of him as he was in his youth, admits: 'His first inclination was to be a reformer. He believed that his mission was to lead his people towards light and civilization'» (Owen 1873). In Robert Owen's autobiography these two hours, called "conversation", are confirmed and it is said of the singular proposal of the Duke, warned of the alarm raised in England by Malthus' ideas: «If your country is overpopulated, I can take you and two millions of people with you to Russia and put at your disposal all you want to form manufacturing communities like this. I thanked his Imperial Highness for the generous offer, but being entirely independent as to economic means and being very attached to New Lanark [...] and what I had done there, I declined the offer and had no doubt that I was making an unpleasant impression» (Owen 1857, p. 146). Count Gurowski's observation about the alleged youthful reformist tendencies of the future Nicholas I contrasts sharply with the reputation of a reactionary, pedantic, arrogant despot that he acquired as Tsar, especially after he had bloodily suppressed the revolt of nobles and officers of the guard (strongly reformist-leaning Decembrists, 14 December 1825) who, unaware of Constantine's secret renunciation in 1823, considered his younger brother Nicholas a usurper after the death of Tsar Alexander I. If Nicholas I renounced his youthful reformist aspirations, they were evidently buried in Russia since Nicholas II promoted paternalistic initiatives more backward than those his great-grandfather had admired at New Lanark 70 years earlier.

[20] This refers to English paternalism between the eighteenth and nineteenth centuries, which in turn was very different from the paternalism of the Continent, not to mention that of Tsarist Russia, especially on the typically English aspect of the pluralistic system of rights and obligations. At that time the term paternalism did not exist. People spoke of "patriarchal principles" or "paternal government". "And it did not exist as a system of well-defined axioms [...]. Instead, it formed a variegated set of attitudes and beliefs [...] that combined in different ways in the minds of the different protagonists, very often in ways that were anything but coherent" (Roberts, 1979, p. 1). David Roberts however, recognizing that one cannot avoid using the term due to the weight of its history, manages to formulate the "model" that he sees characterized in England by four "assumptions" on the social order: (1) authoritarian (fathers, judges, parish priests, masters, command and they are owed sacrosanct obedience under penalty of severe punishment), (2) hierarchical (that there is someone above and someone below occurs by natural law and there is no room for any

as a general attitude of government, with the position they assumed on the poor laws. For the houses of paternalism, it is noteworthy to find that the term "The Folk Hall" is used for educational entertainment environments in some workers' villages, which were built thanks to the paternalistic initiative of enlightened industrialists throughout the century inspired by Owen's doctrine and his achievements in New Lanark in Scotland. The (not exhaustive) list includes Edward Akroyd in Copley near Bradford from 1849; Price's Patent Candle Company in Bromborough Pool (Cheshire) from 1853; Titus Salt from 1854 in Saltaire (Bradford); Henry Ripley from 1866 (Ripley Ville), also near Bradford; William Pickles Hartley in Aintree, Liverpool district, from 1888; William Hesketh Lever in Port Sunlight on the outskirts of Liverpool from 1888; George Cadbury in Bournville, six kilometers south-west of Birmingham, from 1895; and Joseph Rowntree from 1901 in Earswick near York.

5.4 English Workers' Club

The most widespread true people's houses, and not the work of industrial paternalism, were called "Working Men's Clubs" in England. Even if they did not have the name, and even if they were initially often born on the initiative of philanthropists, they acquired at a certain point the substance of people's houses respecting the second, third, and fourth criteria of Kohn's definition: collectively supported by the members, governed democratically, with open although regulated participation. However, they only partially respected the first criterion: they were not complex structures, their functions of meeting and entertainment, educational and sporting, included little of the political and trade union ones. Nonetheless, they played an important role in contributing to the formation of a particular proletarian culture which, even if not entirely alternative to the bourgeois one, contained practices and values of democratic participation.

On 14 June 1862, the CIU (Working Men's Club and Institute Union) was established in London, promoted by the Reverend Henry Solly to organize workers' clubs built on the initiative of philanthropists.[21] Solly had written the manifesto:

> This Union is formed for the purpose of helping working men to establish Clubs or Institutes where they can meet for conversation, business and mental improvement, with the means of recreation and refreshment, free from intoxicating drinks; these clubs, at the same time,

---

egalitarian instance), (3) organic (society is a body and each component has its place and its role), (4) pluralistic (the social system is formed in concentric circles so that the essential direct contact between the leader and the led is achieved) (Roberts, 1979, pp. 2–5).

[21] The history of the CIU states that on that day, under the chairmanship of the Lord Chancellor (Lord Brougham), a meeting was held at the Law Amendment Society's Rooms in Waterloo Place, attended by Mr Bainbridge the upholsterer, Mr Bebbington the merchant, secretary of the Westminster Working Men's Club, the Reverend Solly and the Reverend Rylance who were appointed joint honorary secretaries of the new organization. A few months later, Solly became the first general secretary of the Union with a salary of £200 per annum and opened the first offices of the Union at 150 The Strand (https://ciu.org.uk/History).

> constituting societies for mutual helpfulness in various ways. [...]. It will be the aim of the Council of the Union to assist in extending or improving existing Associations which have in view objects of a kindred nature with the above as well as to promote the establishment of Clubs or Institutes where no such Associations may now be found. [...] The Council also recommend that at least half of the managing body should be bona fide Working Men». (https://ciu.org.uk/History)

By the end of the first year, Solly reported that the Union had been instrumental in the formation of 13 clubs; that 14 more had joined the Union, that 10 were in the process of being formed, and that 17 more had received assistance. The philanthropists who helped to establish and run the clubs were driven by the purpose of making them instruments for the homogenization of the working class.

> The ultimate answer to working-class problems was for working men to become as much like the "respectable" classes of society as was possible. It has been demonstrated how the need to mitigate class antagonism was ever present in the minds of social reformers like Solly and Platt. Historians of the nineteenth century tend to forget that, for most of the period, there was little to lessen the apprehension with which the urban proletariat was regarded by the ruling middle and upper classes. They could not know that a reformist Labour Movement would eventually emerge. But they did know that if society was to remain as they believed it should, it was necessary to convince working men of its benefits and rewards; it was necessary to coopt at least some of them. Their fear was not only that of a violent, bloody revolution. It was also, perhaps predominantly, the fear of an uneducated, drunken, unrefined working class coming to dominate, through natural political progress, the centres of power. A working class that was, in their terms, ill-equipped to rule. (Price, 1971, pp. 142–143)

Thus, the various activities were intended to attract workers to meeting and escape places,[22] encouraging them to use other opportunities, especially educational and sporting ones, especially the "noble art" of boxing (education and entertainment together). In a sample of 25 London clubs examined in 1891, Stan Shipley (1984, p. 320) reported that 9 regularly hosted conferences, 15 organized balls, 16 hosted orchestras and bands, 18 boxing, half boasting professional boxers. Football interested only 4 clubs, rowing 6, cycling 7, Cricket 9. The data in Table 5.2 and Figs. 5.1 and 5.2 present a significant reality, progressively widespread as industrialization progressed[23] very present in London and then in the industrial areas of the North (Northumberland, Durham, Yorkshire).

The growth of the clubs accelerated between 1890 and 1900, explained by two regulatory changes that occurred in the mid-1880s, reforms so incisive that they made them proletarian self-managed. The abolition of 50% of managers elected by vote of supporting members was established, with their consequent disappearance from the social structure of the CIU. At the same time, there was the progressive abolition of the bans on selling beer in associated clubs. From there came a new

[22] "James Hole [...] illustrated this new perception when he wrote [...] To raise the working men we must take hold of him where he is, not where he is not. Attract him, get possession of him and you may lead him by degrees to something better" (Price, 1971, p. 118).

[23] The exception of Cumbria, where a high share of non-agricultural employment is not accompanied by a high number of clubs, is explained by the fact that it is traditionally one of the most tourist-intensive regions in England (Lake District National Park), where non-agricultural activities were therefore not predominantly industrial.

Table 5.2 Number of working's men club affiliated to CIU by region in England and Wales

	1863	1874	1889	1899	1909	1912
East of England	1	7	10	16	14	20
Cumbria	0	0	0	3	6	8
Wales	0	1	2	7	42	58
East Midlands	1	12	17	77	98	99
Northumberland	0	0	0	2	46	58
Durham	0	0	0	2	125	157
West Midlands	1	8	11	34	84	97
South West and South	1	9	13	94	92	114
Yorkshire	2	18	26	99	341	400
Lancashire and Cheshire	6	47	68	129	211	232
Greater London	15	126	182	217	248	269
Total	27	227	329	680	1307	1512

Source Table obtained by processing data from Marlow (1984, pp. 340, 354)

impulse regardless of any other circumstance. (This consideration must be kept in mind to avoid unlikely parallels with completely different processes that, in the same years, led to the construction of the people's houses in Germany, Belgium, France, and Italy). The reform had a long gestation and was anything but peaceful. Since August 1880,

> Mr. Fishbourne of St. James's and Soho club, who was to play a very important role in carrying through the reform, asserted the necessity of making «the Union more truly representative of the clubs. To affect that object there should be a reform in the system of representation, and the Union should be maintained by the Clubs rather than by outside subscribers». [...]. The issue was opened for debate, and [...] the Union officials [...] in the first place persistently tried to discredit the movement by stigmatising it as a class move - which indeed it was, but which failed to discredit it in the eyes of the club-men. In the second place, the officials were adamant that members were as yet ill-equipped to assume the responsibilities of governing the movement [...]. In the third place [...] if the clubs no longer wanted their wealthy supporters, then they had to realize that they would have to carry the burden of supporting the Union and he doubted their willingness to do this. [...]. What [they] failed to realize was that the Clubs were demanding to take control of the movement from the middle classes. The argument that the expertise, finance, and moral values of the middle classes were needed to guide the movement was basically irrelevant. Individual clubs had thrown off their patrons, and it followed that the Union, which embodied the purpose, objects, and central direction of movement, should do the same. The idea that middle-class guidance was necessary to accomplish moral and social improvement seemed the club men to be degrading nonsense. [...]. By April, 1884, the changeover had been completed. The Club and Institute Journal which had persistently opposed reform reported a meteoric rise in its readership and claimed that it was now flooded with more articles and reports than it could possibly print. At the Annual Meeting of the Union, in June, there was a noticeable dearth of Lords, and lip service was paid to the «magnificent principle that we have now brought this Working Men's Club and Institute Union to recognize that taxation and representation go together». In spite of the fears of the traditionalists the club members took the movement into their own hands without

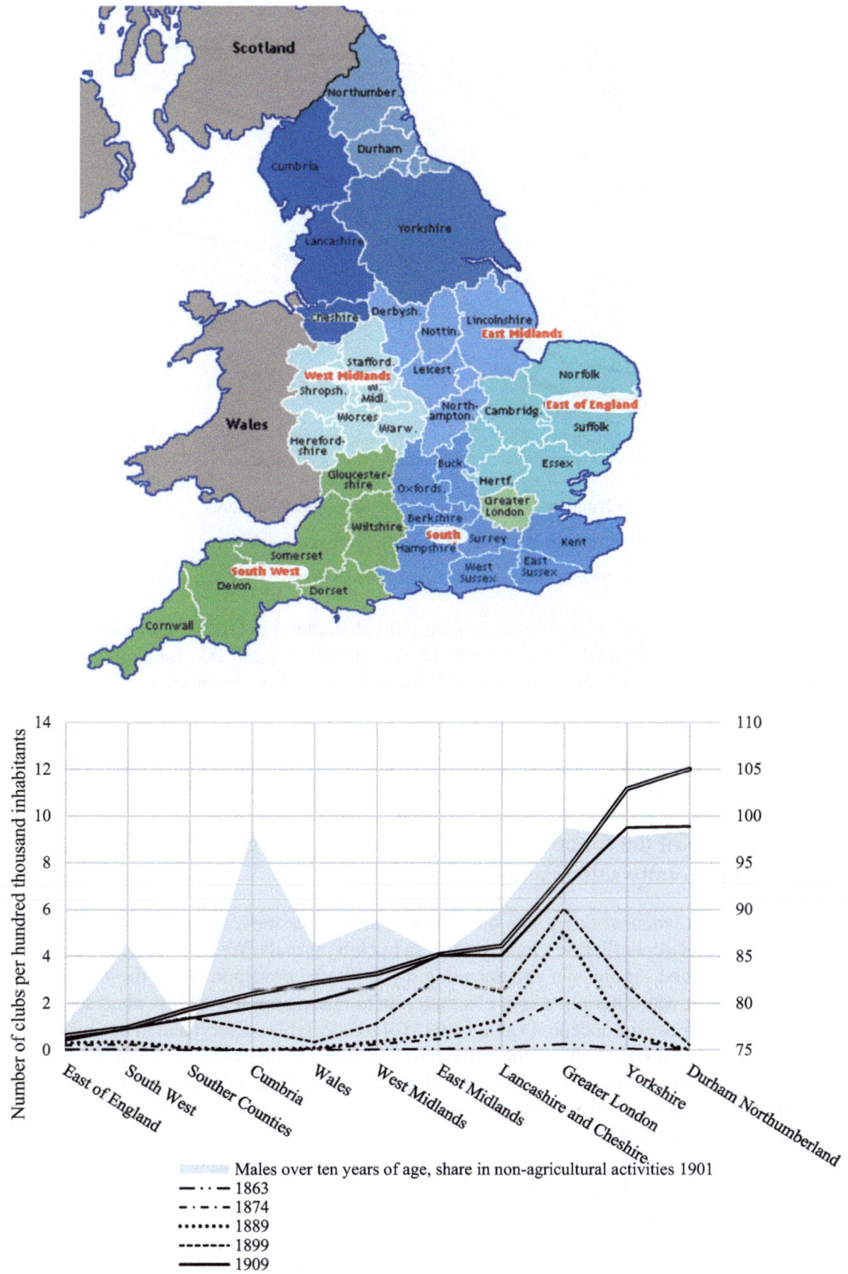

Fig. 5.1 Number of CIU-affiliated workers' clubs per 100,000 inhabitants and share of males employed in non-agricultural activities. *Sources* See Table 5.2 and *Census of England and Wales 1901—General Report with Appendices*. London: Darling & Son 1904

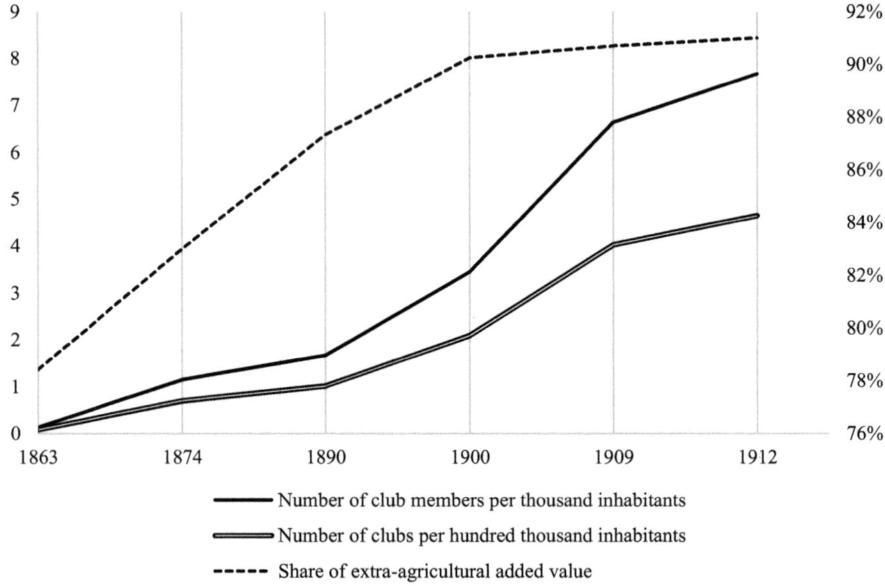

Fig. 5.2 England and Wales: share of non-agricultural value added in GDP, total number of CIU-affiliated clubs per 100,000 inhabitants, number of club members per 1,000 inhabitants. *Sources* See previous table and figure, Allen (2000), and University of Groningen database.

> any disastrous consequences. The subscribers left, and with their exodus the Union became financially solvent and a true working-class organization. (Price, 1971, pp. 135–139)

The original set up of the functions, however, did not undergo radical changes when the clubs became totally self-managed.

> We [...] know that when working men had taken control of the movement the preaching its ideals - such as class conciliation - figured far less in club journals. We do not know the role the movement played - if any - in and encouraging the "safe" development of the working-class movement. It was, after all, a very clear attempt to intrude upon working- class society and culture and impose the accepted value system (of) respectable society; and in this respect it was a clear consequence fear, latent or otherwise, in which the masses were held by the (middle?) and upper classes. For it was no accident that aristocrats, industrialists, clergymen were all jointly involved in propagating the movement in trying to impose its ideology upon the working class. It might be of some significance that the movement emerged in the "breathing space" of nineteenth century capitalism, 1850-1880 - a time when overall rise in living standards provided the opportunity for this (?) of activity to thrive, and also the time when reformism became the (?) of the fledgling Labour Movement. The impact of this kind of control upon these developments within the working-class movement needs to be carefully assessed. Among all the social reforming institutions that can be viewed as agencies of social control the clubs perhaps the most important. They were the largest and most successful of all the efforts through which Victorian England set out to ensure assimilated and acquiescent proletariat. (Price, 1971, p. 147)

The success of the clubs in this sense fits into that process whereby "the traditional popular culture of England was, if not annihilated, at least fragmented and weakened by the dislocations of the Industrial Revolution. What is left, with what in the new conditions has been newly made, is small in quantity and narrow in range. It exacts respect, but it is in no sense an alternative culture" (Williams, 1960, p. 339). This judgment, reiterated several times, is not contradicted by the important practice of democratic rules.

> The working class [...] has not, since the Industrial Revolution, produced a culture in the narrower sense. The culture which it has produced, and which it is important to recognize, is the collective democratic institution, whether in the trade unions, the co-operative movement or a political party. Working-class culture [...] is primarily social (in that it has created institutions) rather than individual (in particular intellectual or imaginative work). When it is considered in context, it can be seen as a very remarkable creative achievement». (Williams, 1960, p. 346)

It was not a small thing. Indeed, it was such that it forced Williams to specify that, insufficient for a "culture in the strict sense", it was more than sufficient for an alternative proletarian culture even if differently specified, as will be shown, with respect to the German, French, Belgian cases; and also, in more articulated ways, the Italian one. The result was in fact notable in the face of the consolidated English institutions of restricted suffrage (Tholfsen, 1961, p. 228) and in general of the oligarchic forms of the exercise of power. The judgments of other analysts must also be understood in this way: the fact is that the English socialists[24] "they never managed to develop an alternative culture" (Waters, 1990, p. 3); "when we looked back at the history of the Labour Party, at the biographies and autobiographies of various prominent members and leaders, we had to strain hard to find even the occasional reference to cultural politics or even any aspect of popular culture" (Mulgan & Worpole, 1986, p. 11).

In the Working Men's Clubs the concrete implementation of democratic practices was accompanied by the development of a proletarian culture that, except for this aspect, was quite homologated to that of the dominant classes. It is necessary to understand what the specific conditions were that led to this result. This is to discover whether between the nineteenth and twentieth centuries in other conditions and in other countries it was instead possible and indispensable to develop a proletarian culture in the strict sense, which was completely alternative to that of the dominant classes. The English conditions to which attention must be paid are three: (1) the legacy of Owenism, (2) the times of industrialization, (3) the failure of the Chartist movement and the bourgeois proposal of culture as a social glue.

5.4.1 *Owenism's Legacy*

Starting from the concrete reality of New Lanark where Robert Owen had implemented his advanced social experiments in the early nineteenth century, Owenism

---

[24] SDF Social Democratic Federation, SL Socialist League, ILP Independent Labour Party, Fabian Society.

developed a specific position on the question of the Poor Laws that deeply influenced the English socialist tradition. It did not accept either of the two opposing orientations—subsidies and free market—both considered to be typical of the "usual system".[25] He elaborated a third position which, for better or worse, gave the English socialist movement a particular long-lasting character.

5.4.1.1 The Question of the Poor

> Under the umbrella of the Poor Laws (a problem inherited from the late eighteenth century[26] and aggravated by the impact of the Napoleonic Wars), was subsumed a complex of socio-economic issues and decisions of social policy. From the 1780s to 1834 no subject was more prolific of pamphlets, books and homilies. Every country parson felt qualified to prescribe his nostrum for the cure of rural pauperism; political economists, social reformers and country gentlemen all held emphatic views on the 'Poor Law question'; while successive governments managed to avoid anything so controversial as a comprehensive reorganization of the system. (Harrison, 1969, p. 13)

The relevance of the problem was very evident to everyone both for the social disorder, always latent and linked to widespread poverty, and for moral reasons.

[25] The "usual" system of authoritarian paternalism was also expressed in the evolution of the poor laws. First, the "Speenhamland" of the guaranteed minimum subsistence was launched (Gilbert law of 1782): the good father of the family guaranteed subsistence to all its members. Then, after decades of ideological opposition (also motivated by the high cost of subsidies and by real and presumed scandals in management), new rules were put in place (especially with the reform of 1834) to provide assistance in such a way as to induce as many people as possible to do without it. Thus, the other side of authoritarian paternalism was applied: the good father of the family punished the idlers. In both cases, the assumption was that the poor were not active subjects capable of strategies, but only "biological machines" as in Malthusian theories, so that with subsidies the population would increase by reducing wages. As Alfred Marshall had already pointed out in 1893, subsidies had actually improved the living conditions of workers who invested in their productivity and increased their bargaining power, resulting in increases and not reductions in wages (Blaug, 1963, p. 153).

[26] The reference here is to the "old laws" on the poor passed in 1601 under the reign of Elizabeth I, which originated with the suppression of monasteries and the closure of lands. Between 1536 and 1541, to finance his military campaigns, Henry VIII had expropriated the assets of 900 houses that housed 12,000 religious men out of a total population of the kingdom that did not reach three million inhabitants. This did not deprive the poor of all support, since the system of expedients they used to obtain subsistence was extraordinarily complex (King & Tomkins, 2003), but it had taken away a significant portion, traditionally provided by the monasteries, whose lack was felt even after 50 years. On the other hand, the enclosure of lands traditionally used as commons, claimed by the ancient owners (real or "created" through the falsification of documents) in the lowland areas of central and southern England, which had begun more than a century earlier, accelerated between the sixteenth and eighteenth centuries (by 1701 70% of the land in the whole country had been privatized). The causes of the enclosure of the lands were first the international increase in the demand for wool which promised large profits on lands converted to sheep pasture, then the increase in the price of cereals which allowed high profits by introducing capitalist methods of cultivation. The enclosure of the lands in the century and a half before 1607 caused 50,000 peasants to lose all sources of income and forced them to abandon their villages, several of which fell into ruin (data calculated on information from Edwin F. Gay, 1903, p. 581).

Moral concerns were partly countered by the condemnation of culpable poverty with regard to the major "scandal" of child labor, due to need as well as a long tradition. But it was above all the fear of disorders, often in fact caused by a mass of indigents including various categories of "criminals" that kept the discussion on the laws against poverty alive and widespread. Disorders that, after the Revolution in France, could also be feared as being able to degenerate in an uncontrolled manner.

> If we are to credit one of the most industrious investigators, Patrick Colquhoun,[27] there were [in London], at the turn of the century, 50,000 harlots, more than 5,000 publicans, and 10,000 thieves in the metropolis alone; his more extended estimates of criminal classes, taking in receivers of stolen property, coiners, gamblers, lottery agents, cheating shopkeepers, riverside scroungers, and colourful characters like Mudlarks, Scufflehunters, Bludgeon Men, Morocco Men, Flash Coachmen, Grubbers, Bear Baiters and Strolling Minstrels totals (with the former groups) 115,000 out of a metropolitan population of less than one million. His estimate of the same classes, for the whole country, – and including one million in receipt of parish relief – totals 1,320,716. [...]. The figures [...] are impressionistic estimates. They reveal as much about the mentality of the propertied classes (who assumed — not without reason — that any person out of steady employment and without property must maintain himself by illicit means) as they do about the actual criminal behaviour of the unpropertied. And the date of Colquhoun's investigations is as relevant as his conclusions; for they were conducted in the atmosphere of panic in the aftermath of the French Revolution. In the two decades before this there was an important access of humanitarian concern amongst the upper classes; we can see this in the work of Howard, Hanway, Clarkson, Sir Frederick Eden, and in the growing concern for civil and religious liberties among the small gentry and the Dissenting tradesmen. But "the awakening of the labouring classes, after the first shock of the French Revolution, made the upper classes tremble», Frances, Lady Shelley, noted in her Diary". (Thompson, 1964, pp. 55, 56)

According to Gregory King's estimates, at the end of the seventeenth century poverty affected half of the entire population of the kingdom: out of just over 5 million inhabitants, the people without the means necessary for mere subsistence would have been 2.5 million. In the absence of a population census, carried out for the first time only in 1801, these estimates were based on the far from reliable surveys obtained for the application of the tax "on hearths". While it has long been demonstrated that King's estimates for the total population were almost correct,[28] after long discussions on the most appropriate methods of estimation, today it is believed that the figure of the poor was exaggerated (Arkell, 2006) being more reliable a figure of 40%, in any case an alarming percentage. This figure corresponds to that of the "casual workers and unemployed" of the social structure reconstructed by Peter Lidert (Figs. 5.3 and 5.4).

With these data, it is possible to clarify the issue that has troubled historiography on the first English industrial revolution, that is, the persistence and for many (Feinstein, 1998) the worsening of proletarian poverty, but on the other hand, the increase in the average real wage of industrial workers, today considered indisputable (Allen, 2009).

[27] Patrick Colquhoun (1745–1820) published in 1796 his "Treatise on the Police" in which he tried to establish the extent of the criminal phenomenon and to propose the solutions he had conceived, especially the reorganization of the London police.

[28] Glass (1950) estimated that there were 5 million, half a million less than King's estimate. Today the figure of 5.2 million th is generally agreed upon.

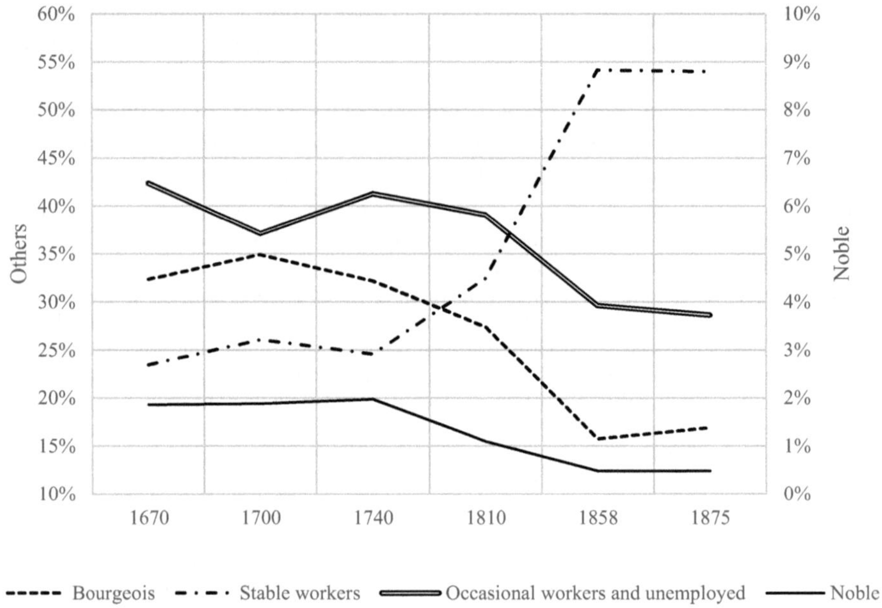

Fig. 5.3 Percentages of household heads by category in England and Wales. *Source* Figure obtained by processing data from Lindert (1986, p. 1137)

The crucial distinction is between "permanent workers" and "casual and unemployed workers". The latter category remained a constant 40% of heads of families until the early nineteenth century, but increased in absolute value from 525,000 in 1670 (out of a total of 1,240,000 inhabitants) to 780,000 in 1810 (out of a total of 2 million). It is also noted that the modest figures of their personal assets at the end of the seventeenth century, corresponding to a year's wages for an industrial worker (Griffin, 2018, p. 85), remained so throughout the century while those of the stable workers increased from 1740 until reaching 300 pounds in 1810, equal to 6 years' wages for a clerk. Ultimately, this confirms what Edward Palmer Thompson wrote:

> We might show that the labourer or carter in regular employment increased his real wages over this period, while the increase in population in the village — casual labour and unemployed — led to an absolute increase in the number of the poor. And while this might be most evident in agriculture, the same hypothesis must be borne in mind when discussing the overall national picture. If, for the sake of argument, we take the hypothesis that 40% of the population (10.5 million) was living below a given "poverty-line" in 1790, but only 30% of the population (1.8 million) in 1841, nevertheless the absolute number of the poor will have increased from about four million to well over five million. More poverty will be "felt" and, moreover, there will in fact be more poor people. (Thompson, 1963, p. 232)

On the moral side, the medieval concern for the needy had long since disappeared and the condemnation of the "guilty poor" was now well established. But the sale of

Fig. 5.4 Personal wealth of heads of families by category England and Wales. Nobles scale on the right, others scale on the left. Values in sterling 1875. *Source* see Fig. 5.1

bread was regulated,[29] then a fundamental subsistence consumption, which testified to the persistent belief in society and government that one could not "let it happen and let it pass" (as a minority liberal current would have wanted) when there was a risk of increasing innocent poverty: one testified that such innocent poverty was widespread and very alarming.

5.4.1.2 Children's Work

Then there was child labor due to various causes, but certainly also to the state of need of poor families. Historiography has today set aside an entire period of studies that seemed to attribute the atrocious exploitation of child labor only to the second

[29] As Thompson (1971, p. 88) explained, as the century progressed and the new nineteenth century approached, the application of the canon of the ultra-regulated market was in fact increasingly "fragmentary". This canon considered any practice illegal, which had even only potential consequences on the increase in the price of bread, regardless of their usefulness in supporting its supply in the medium and long term, including "engrossing" (wholesale trade), "forestandling" (contracts aimed at guaranteeing a certain income to the producer), "regrating" (intermediation). Even applied in a fragmentary way, this was the canon that remained an "ideal" reference, to which one returned in emergency phases when the price of bread increased, endangering livelihoods.

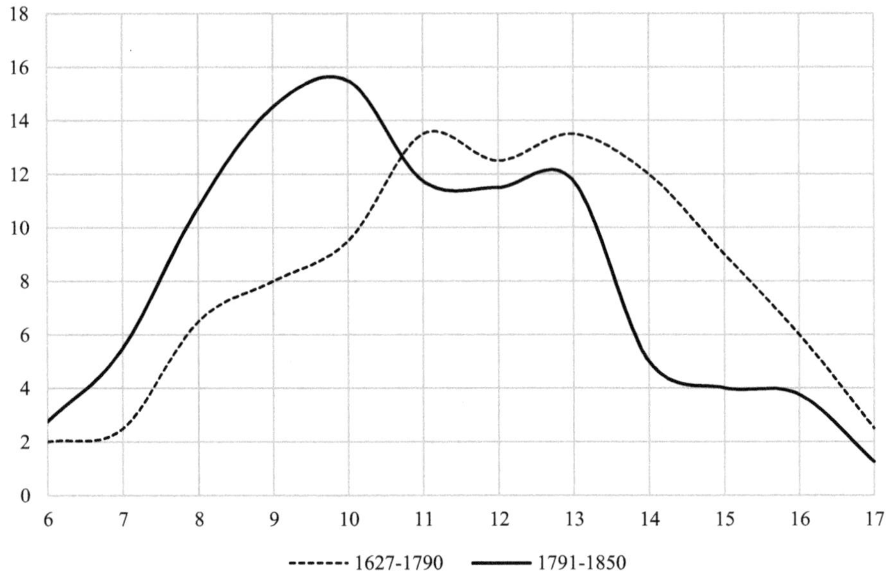

Fig. 5.5 Age of first employment of boys born in the years 1627–1790 and in the years 1791–1850. *Source* Figure obtained by processing data from Humphries (2013, p. 402)

industrial revolution.[30] It was exploitation that had existed, and for a long time, in the fields and pastures and in service in the homes of landowners, activities that were still dominant throughout the eighteenth century, with working hours of no less than 12 h a day. Child labor was considered normal in a very young society: at the beginning of the nineteenth century the share of the population under 15 was double that of a century later, life expectancy at birth did not reach 40 years, a 14-year-old was considered an adult (Lee & Schofield, 1981, p. 23). However, from the mid-eighteenth century it had partly replaced but partly added to the home-based work of the proto-industry and then of the factory. It was this that led to previously unknown conditions that deserved condemnation: the advancement of the age of entry into work even under the age of nine and the unbearable lengthening of the working day to even 16 h. This advance is documented in the best available research on child labor between the eighteenth and nineteenth centuries. The age of first work, traditionally from 11 to 14 years, was brought backward to 9–10 (Fig. 5.5).

[30] As John Belchem explained, this "slip" that needed to be corrected came from another correction rightly made by the historiography itself to free itself from the "obsession of technological determinism" which interpreted the first industrial revolution as capital intensive. "No longer obsessed with technological determinism, economic historians now stress the importance of what Maxine Berg has called 'the other Industrial Revolution' […] which included domestic industry and artisan workshops much more than it did the factory system; an Industrial Revolution which relied on tools, small machines and skilled labour much more than it did on steam engines and automatic processes; an Industrial Revolution which was created by women and children at least as much as it was by male artisans and factory workers" (Belchem, 1991, p. 11; citing Berg, 1990).

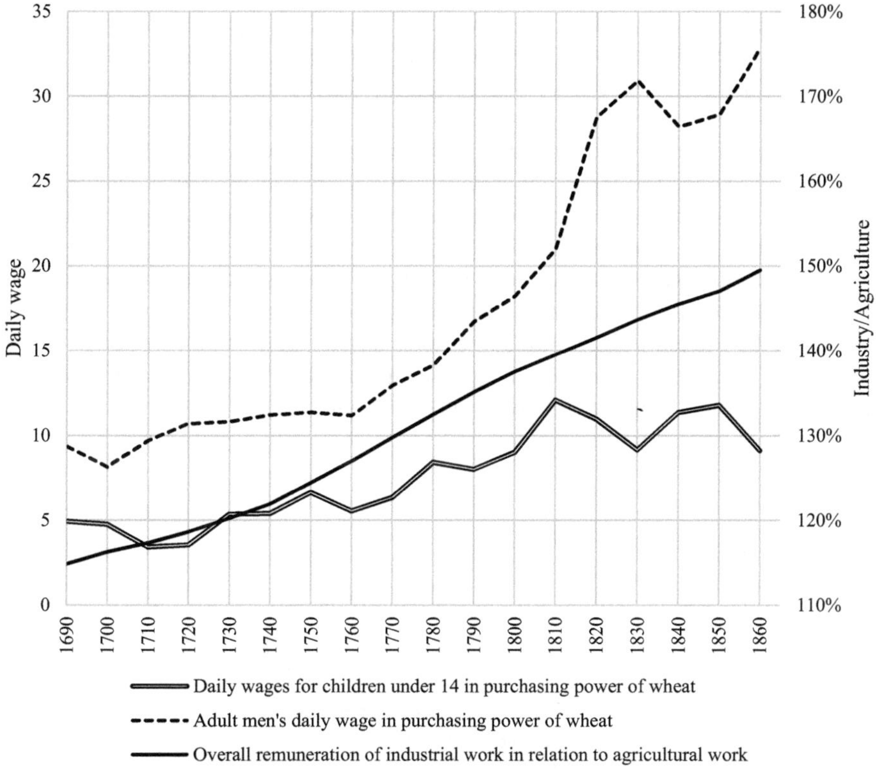

Fig. 5.6 England and Wales: trends in total remuneration of labor in industry in relation to agriculture and in daily wages of boys and adult men expressed in purchasing power of grain. *Source* Figure obtained by processing data from Horrell and Humphries (2019)[31]

There is no such systematic data on working hours. However, historians have found consistent evidence: «For the child and female workforce, fourteen-to-sixteen-hour days with only a forty-minute break were common» (Rule, 2014, p. 310). This increase in the use of child labor was due "to a series of coincident developments, including the increase in the relative productivity of children as a result of early mechanization and the new division of labor" (Humphries (2013, p. 415), that is, the increase in tasks that did not require the strength of an adult. In this regard, data have been reconstructed that allow documentation of this mechanism (Fig. 5.6).

[31] To obtain this data, Sara Horrell and Jane Humphries of the Universities of Oxford and Cambridge have done exceptional work. In the absence of real statistical findings for those times, they constructed "the first long-run wage series for child workers which we can then relate to trends in the cost of living as well as in the wages of adult men and women. While we stand on the shoulders of other economic historians who have assembled data for particular times and places [...], we have uncovered many new primary sources and use 3873 observations spread over nearly 600 years to generate this first long run series. While evidence on occupations and wages cannot compensate for our ignorance about the size of the child labour force, they can provide the basis

The first mechanization can be considered represented by the increase in industrial productivity (increasing continuous line), and the new division of labor by the increase in the daily wage of adult men (dashed line) clearly higher than the more modest increase in the wage of boys (double line). This gap indicates a segmentation of the labor market in which the work of boys paid less was complementary to that of adults and supported their higher wages. But there was obviously also an effect on the supply side: the increase in the employment of boys and children depended on "unstable adult wages and pockets of poverty, family instability and fragility of household heads" (Humphries, 2013, p. 415). For this aspect too, the data of Sara Horrell and Jane Humphries are valuable (Fig. 5.7).

Before the Industrial Revolution, the labor market model that these data suggest was gender-dual. Male workers had significant bargaining power, so much so that to induce them to perform casual work (overtime), the remuneration had to be higher

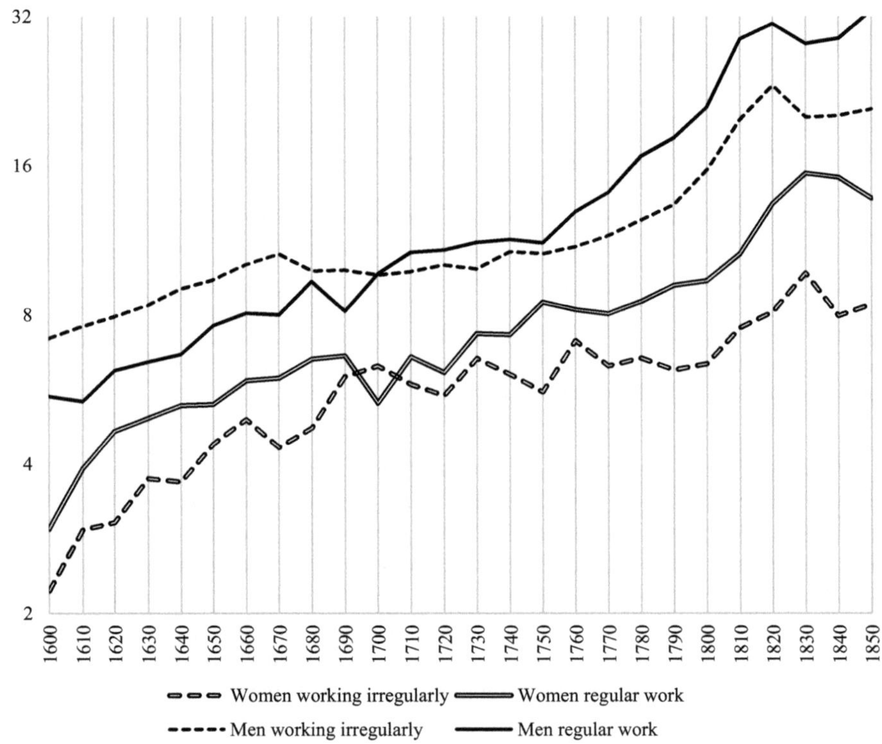

Fig. 5.7 Daily remuneration in real terms of men and women, for regular and irregular (casual) work. Logarithmic scale. *Source* Figure obtained by processing data from Horrell and Humphries (2019)

---

for careful inferences about how child labour related to long run growth and structural change" (Horrell & Humphries, 2019, p. 1).

than that of regular work. For women with less bargaining power, irregular or overtime work was instead paid less than regular work. In other words, women offered casual work driven by necessity, men by opportunity. With the Industrial Revolution, these data indicate that the necessity model became general, for women but also for men. Ultimately, the increase in the work of boys and children was linked to necessity and therefore became morally censurable. But it was also linked to reasons of efficiency. It is no coincidence that the legislation intended to reduce the working hours of children was at the same time very precocious and very impotent.

The first law of 1802 established that no apprentice in textile factories could work more than 12 h a day, and night work was prohibited. But this provision, lacking enforcement tools, had no effect; just like the new law of 1819 that limited the working day of children in cotton mills to 12 h again, also prohibiting the hiring of children under 9 years of age. One must wait until 1833, 31 years after the first law of 1802, for a law finally equipped with an inspection service to enforce it, which established the prohibition of making children from 9 to 13 years of age work more than 48 h a week, prohibiting the hiring of children under 9 years of age. But Clark Nardinelli wrote that

> Most students have praised the Factory Acts for leading to the decline of child labor, thereby improving the welfare of children, the available evidence implies that the Factory Acts only speeded up a movement which was already taking place. Rising real income and technological change were the main causes of the decline of child labor. (Nardinelli, 1980, p. 739)

Children under 13 employed in the cotton industry were 20% of the workforce in 1816 and fell to 13% in 1835, in the linen industry from 23 to 13%. These reductions occurred before the actual application of the 1833 law which was delayed because it was not taken as seriously as the previous ones until the actual outcome of the inspections. Thus, Nardinelli ascertained that: «for the textile industries as a whole much of the decline in child labor before 1835 was caused by the shift from water to steam power. [...]. Technological progress other than the shift from water to steam played the leading role in reducing the demand for children after 1835. The major such change was the adoption of self-acting spinning mules» (Nardinelli, 1980, p. 746). The effect of the rules was added without being decisive.

5.4.1.3 Owen's Position

Having said all this to clarify the nature and extent of the problem of poverty, Owen's position at the beginning of the nineteenth century saw the remedy by raising the level of reflection and the reforms desired to eliminate the "causes of causes".

> I [...] found the population of this place similar to that of other manufacturing districts. It was, with some exceptions, existing in poverty, crime, and misery; and strongly prejudiced [...] against any change that might be proposed. The usual mode of proceeding on the principles which have hitherto governed the conduct of men, would have been to punish those who committed the crimes, and to be highly displeased with every one who opposed the alterations that were intended for his benefit. The principles, however, upon which the

> new system is founded lead to very different conduct. They make it evident, that when men are in poverty, when they commit crimes or actions injurious to themselves and others, and when they are in a state of wretchedness, there must be substantial causes for these lamentable effects; and that, instead of punishing or being angry with our fellow-men because they have been subjected to such a miserable existence, we ought to pity and commiserate them, and patiently to trace the causes whence the evils proceed, and endeavour to discover whether they may be removed. [...]. The immediate causes of them were soon obvious: nor were the remote ones, or the causes of those causes. [...] I found [...] that those might all be traced to ignorance in which our forefathers existed, and in which we ourselves have continued to this day. (Owen, 1857, pp. 339–340)

According to Owen, ignorance was the cause of the causes of poverty that had to be eliminated through education. But this position, which postponed the effects of a possible reform in time, actually translated into the renunciation of influencing the concrete issues of the present. The liberalist turn implemented with the law of 1834 thus also represented a defeat for him, which linked him to the opposed "old system" guilty of not having offered alternatives to the previous law on the poor.

> The Benthamites, unfeeling and rational, the Whig aristocracy, jaunty and indifferent, and the hard and pious Manchester Liberals, all of them argue for an atomized society built on self-interest, laissez faire, and that utilitarianism which Kirk calls «the surly apology of a hideous and rapacious industrialism». Contending against these Benthamites, Whigs, and Liberals are the Tories, alarmed at the cruelty of life in factory towns [...]. Not only do the Tories see the evil, they are also possessed of a vision of an organic, benevolent society, which will remove cruelty and ugliness and neglect. [...]. But in all this discussion, few writers have asked whether the Tories did translate these ideals into practice, whether they did contribute to the wellbeing of the working class. The answer to this question comes up immediately against an imposing difficulty. The principles of Tory paternalism do not lend themselves to effective legislation or improved administration. Coleridge, the most profound and influential of these theorists, looked to the moral regeneration of the individual, not to the reforming state, and he envisaged the Church of England as the head of a paternalistic society. [...]. They offered no alternative to the old poor law, which had pauperized and demoralized the agricultural laborer[32]; they offered no means to prevent the exploitation of children in textile mills; they did not say how slums were to be removed, slums in which an illiterate proletariat lived in misery, disease, and vice, unrelieved by any serious attempt at education and sanitation. (Roberts, 1958, p. 324)

The 1834 Act radically changed the system previously entrusted to parishes that allocated subsidies to the needy by levying a specific tax on the landowners. Six hundred territorial unions were formed in which welfare was managed by Boards of Guardians

[32] Writing that the "old poor law pauperized and demoralized the agricultural laborer" in 1958, Roberts remained in the wake of a long interpretative tradition inspired by the Report of the Commission charged with investigating poverty that would lead to the reform of 1834 (Royal Commission into the Operation of the Poor Laws 1832). He could not take into account the subsequent harsh criticisms of that deplorable Report, including those of Mark Blaug (1963). The Report had been based on information that was partly invented, partly distorted, and deserved Blaug's criticisms, even if they were scaled down by James Stephen Taylor (1969). It is not true that "the more the Old Poor Law relieved poverty, the more it encouraged the poverty which it relieved" because by subsidizing the increase in wages of agricultural workers above the subsistence level, "such institutional arrangements lead to a greater total product than would otherwise be available" (Blaug, 1963, pp. 151, 154).

(elected by taxpayers who had a number of votes proportional to their assets), each of which managed its own Workhouse. Subsidies were abolished except for the incapacitated. The poor who were able to work had to take refuge in the Workhouses if they wanted assistance. And there they had to earn their living. The treatment was programmatically punitive: wives were separated from their husbands, the canteen distributed bad and insufficient food, the work was very hard. This corresponded to the principle of "lesser admissibility" that the new law was inspired by applying the indications of the Commission's Report: «Into such a house none will enter voluntarily; work, confinement, and discipline, will deter the indolent and vicious; and nothing but extreme necessity will induce any to accept the comfort which must be obtained by the surrender of their free agency, and the sacrifice of their accustomed habits and gratifications» (Senior & Chadwick, 1834, App. (C.) pp. 164 and 173–174). Opposition to this law was keen on the part of workers, politicians and religious leaders. But it was above all the high costs necessary to build and operate the workhouses that led to a review as early as 1847. A 2019 study concludes thus:

> Over the course of the nineteenth century, hundreds of thousands of the poor in England were subjected to the harsh regime of the workhouse based on the mistaken conclusions of the Political Economists. Parents were separated from each other, and their children, men and women were set to long hours of meaningless make work like breaking stones. The children in labouring families with the misfortune to produce large numbers of surviving children were brought up in conditions of grinding poverty. Yet this deliberately induced suffering gained little for the land and property owners who funded poor relief. Nor did it raise wages for the poor, or free up migration to better opportunities in the cities. One of the first great triumphs of the new discipline of Political Economy, the reform of the Poor Laws, consequently had no effects on economic growth and economic performance in Industrial Revolution England. Political Economy was born in sin. (Clark & Page, 2019, p. 241)

Even the inability to prevent the launching of this unfortunate law can ultimately be considered a legacy of Owenism. Owenian paternalism conceived the central importance of the education of the proletariat, but at the same time was impotent regarding their immediate condition. And it was at the very least ambiguous even on the contents of such education, understood substantially as learning bourgeois culture. This approach influenced the deep soul of British socialism between the nineteenth and twentieth centuries (Diamantopoulos, 2023, p. 13).

5.4.2 *Times and Pace of Industrialization*

English industrialization was the earliest and most regular, capable of avoiding too traumatic structural ruptures, taking 150 years, from 1700 to 1850, to achieve the transition from 50 to 70% of GDP in non-agricultural activities. In Belgium, the "champion" among the pursuers, this structural change occurred in 50 years from 1800 to 1850, 60 (1840–1900) in Germany, 40 (1870–1910) in Italy where it only reached 65%. The case of France is unusual. With a long phase of industrialization already begun in the mid-eighteenth century, even if with ups and downs, France had closely followed England. The process was, however, interrupted by the serious events of the second half of the 1880s (the crisis of the Second Empire and the defeat in the Franco-Prussian War), so that country experienced the fastest subsequent transformation in two decades, between 1870 and 1890 (Fig. 5.8).

The only case of a slow and regular process of industrialization was that of England, from which there was enough time for the process of erosion of traditional popular culture, of appropriation by the proletariat of canons of the dominant culture, but with the decisive grafting of democratic participation. Added to this was the related condition of an early articulation of the working class. In his important work of 1984, Eric Hobsbawm had underlined a notable homogeneity of interests

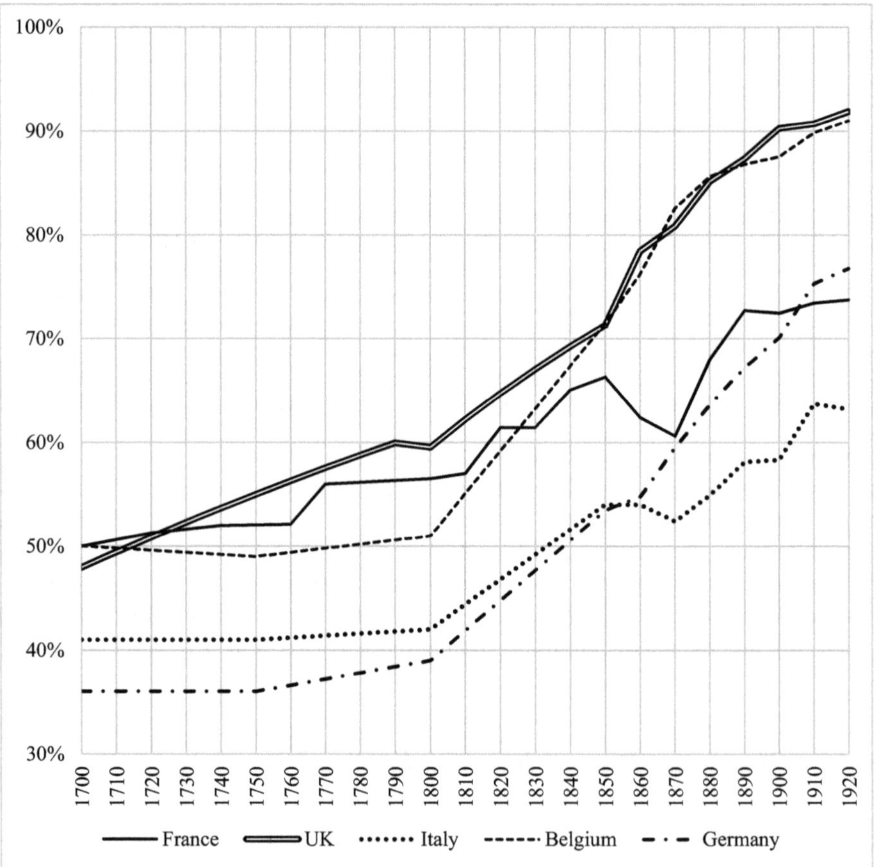

Fig. 5.8 Shares of non-agricultural value added in GDP. *Source* Figure obtained by processing data from University of Groningen database, Saito and Shaw-Taylor (2021), Chilosi and Ciccarelli (2022), Nuvolari and Ricci (2012). *Note*: for the United Kingdom the data are complete; for France the missing data are interpolated: 1710, 1730, 1750, 1780–1790; for Italy 1720–1740, 1760–1790, 1810–1840; as for Belgium and Germany

and ideas among English workers after 1880, that is, after the first industrial revolution which still saw the widespread presence of workers who owned their means of production. But a few years later he accepted the criticisms that several historians addressed to this thesis. In reality, the proletarian movement was far from compact even after the 1980s: «the working class had a more complex internal structure, was in a more continuous process of change, and was less impervious to non-manual worker groups than Hobsbawm supposed» (Reid, 1987, p. 234).

5.4.3 *Chartism's Failure and Culture*

In the vast literature that has examined the history of Chartism, the first organized movement of the subaltern classes in England, which lasted 12 years from 1836 to 1848,[33] the interpretation that very soon attributed the disappointing outcome to a lack of education of the popular masses gained special importance. The movement was supported by educated militants and adherents especially in London, without whose mobilization no movement could succeed.[34] But, also due to a certain elitism, they were not able to drag along the less educated, not as sensitive to the political-institutional program of Chartism.[35] On the other hand, in the districts of the industrial

[33] Chartism was born in 1836 in London where a group of craftsmen developed a "people's charter" entirely oriented toward institutional political claims: universal suffrage (men only), annual election of parliament, secret ballot of deputies, electoral districts for equal territorial representation, abolition of the census to be elected, remuneration of deputies. It ended 12 years later, in 1848, when the economic crisis and the revolutionary movements of central Europe pushed the Chartist movement onto the terrain of overturning the balance of power: it presented a petition to parliament in which it was declared that the wealth of the nation depended solely on work and that therefore the people were the only source of authority. Fearing insurrection, the government mobilized the armed forces under the command of the Duke of Wellington. On 10 April 1848, the leader of the movement, lawyer Feargus Edward O'Connor, convinced the protesters to disband after receiving assurances that Parliament would discuss the petition. When calm returned, Parliament went back on its promise and the movement died. It died, among other things, in ridicule (undeserved throughout its history): the petition was presented saying it had 5.7 million signatures. Once counted, there were in reality only two million and many were double, counterfeit, and humorous like those of the Queen and Mr. Punch, the famous puppet that in England stands in for Italian Pulcinella. Shame overwhelmed O'Connor and was not unrelated to the madness that in a few years destroyed him.

[34] London was important for its size with two million inhabitants in 1841 out of a total of 18.8 million in the whole country. But it was important above all from a political-social point of view. "In the agitation which had led up to the 1832 Reform Act, London had played a considerable part, although being initially slower to act than the provinces. This had, however, been an agitation devised by the middle classes, led by the National Political Union, and it was obvious from the immediate antecedents of London Chartism that most of this enthusiasm had been dissipated" (Rowe, 1968, p. 472). The 1832 law assigned a more adequate number of seats in the House of Commons to the cities that had developed during the industrial revolution and increased the electorate from 400,000 to 650,000 eligible voters out of a population of 14 million: certainly not a "revolution".

[35] "While the more sophisticated and educated artisans [...] were rebelling largely on theoretical grounds, their following among the less educated depended to some extent on economic conditions. This would suggest that 'The Pioneer' was right when it attacked working-class demands

development, especially in the North, where Chartism had greater support from the illiterate workers, its objectives were different, such as the protest against the Poor Law of 1834[36] and for the cost of bread during the famine between the 1830s and 1840s. In this way the movement was weak on the main and national objectives and stronger on objectives intended as subordinate, in reality typical of the territorial rooting that would perhaps have been successful, certainly such as to allow the elaboration of cultural contents alternative to those of the bourgeois class that instead with the defeat of Chartism proved to be superior.

Faced with the grave situation, the League against the Corn Laws, based on the petty bourgeoisie, and the Chartism based on the proletariat were unable to form a common front and manage the popular protest that broke out in 1842 and was harshly repressed despite the fact that the disturbances with damage to property had been few. The Chartist program proposed "a combination of government intervention and community action (collective purchases, cooperatives, boycott of traders hostile

---

for the franchise, without first ensuring the education of its members. [...]. Stonemasons, tailors, shoemakers, hatters and coppersmiths all founded their own Chartist associations in London [...] in order that 'the whole people may be able to give practical effect to their wishes in framing the laws they are called upon to obey'. [...]. London Chartism also had the initial advantage of middle-class support, through such men as Place and Black and the Radical members of parliament and from the Radical Club, although the wider social distinctions than in towns such as Birmingham meant that this relationship was always tenuous. The growing extremism of Chartism soon led to the defection of the middle classes. [...]. It was the failure of Chartism in London that it was unable to devise a programme which could obtain the unflinching support of a large group" (Rowe, 1968, pp. 484–486). The weekly "The Pioneer" was published from September 1833 to July 1834 and was printed in an exceptional 20,000 copies in London as a clandestine organ of the proto-trade union organizations. It is famous in its own way because it contained the 14 "Letters of Senex" which represent, before Pierre-Joseph Proudhon's treatise (Qu'est-ce que la propriété? Recherche sur le principe du droit et du gouvernement, 1840), the earliest articulation of an anti-capitalist political economy.

36 "The New Poor Law [...] was a constant reference point for working-class radicals, particularly because of its impact on the working-class family. Modern scholarship has rightly emphasized the centrality of the domestic within Chartism, and this helps explain Joseph Rayner Stephens's immense popularity in the early years of the movement. In his sermons, Stephens regularly excoriated masters who lorded it over the market as well as the workplace, arguing that the famine that working people currently endured was a sign that the devil ruled the land: 'if there be a hell upon earth comparatively with other nations of the world, it is England'. The food dished up in New Poor Law bastilles was a favorite subject for Stephens as it clearly demonstrated how the poor were stripped of their humanity. Workhouse bread was 'devil's dung', and, he claimed, the thin soup or 'skilly' that formed the staple diet of inmates was laced with resin, a substance fed to pigs to stuff them up and lend a plump appearance: 'Good God! and art Thou merciful, and art Thou just—merciful to those poor whose bodies are lined and pitched with resin, that the skilled may not scour them into the cholera morbus'. Stephens understood that the politics of consumption lay at the center of Chartism, and that is why he referred to it as a 'knife and fork' question. He frequently asserted that the New Poor Law undermined the entitlement of the poor to relief in times of death, widely regarded in the movement as a right grounded in history and Tudor statute. Like many other Chartists, Stephens concluded that even theft and violent resistance were appropriate responses to scarcity" (Gurney, 2009, p. 108). Joseph Rayner Stephens (1805–1879) Methodist minister committed to social reform, active in the Manchester area, elected delegate to the Chartists' National Conference, also suffered imprisonment in 1838 for seditious language.

to the cause) to help poor consumers squeezed by industrial capitalism as well as protectionism" (Gurney, 2009, p. 101). The League advocated the free market and the rigorous separation between economics and politics, which should not interfere with each other. Both Chartism and the League were defeated, while shortly afterward with Gladston (William Ewart), first President of the Board of Trade (1843) then Chancellor of the Exchequer (1852), the government succeeded in a policy of supporting the living conditions of the lower classes through the reform of duties and the tax system. This result demonstrated with facts the "superiority" of the bourgeois culture that had inspired "to balance successfully the interests of all consumers as 'the people' and construct a new moral politics of consumption in the aftermath of the defeat of both Chartist utopianism and League dogmatism" (Gurney, 2009, p. 102).

In essence, it was an excessive articulation of the objectives of Chartism that ended up making their effective impact difficult. And this excessive articulation descended from the mobilization of a composite mass on the cultural level. The lesson that English socialism drew from this was that the class struggle had to be preceded by an increase in the level of education of the proletariat also for tactical reasons, education as learning of normal knowledge more widely shared. All the more so since in the same years among the middle and bourgeois classes there was spreading "the idea that acculturation would cure many of society's ills" (Waters, 1990, p. 4). It was Raymond Williams who demonstrated that in England the times of the emergence of the idea of culture as an ordering factor and of its conception as a "glue" between the classes coincided. This is clear in the extract of a speech by John Frederick Dennison Maurice[37] in Manchester, at the "Ancoats and Salford Working Men's College", in 1859:

> I hear one intelligent man and another confessing «Ten years ago we thought differently. But all of us have acquired since that time, a new sense of our relation to the working-class». It did cause us to fear, I own; but it was not fear for our property and position; it was the fear that we were not discharging the responsibilities, greater than those which rank or property imposes, that our education laid upon us. We believed and felt that unless the classes in this country which had received any degree of knowledge more than their fellows were willing to share it with their fellows, to regard it as precious because it bound them to their fellows, England would fall first under an anarchy, and then under a despotism. [...]. What we wanted, if possible, was to make our teaching a bond of intercourse with the men whom we taught. How that could be, we might never have found out. But the working men themselves had found it out. We heard in 1853 that the people of Sheffield had founded a People's College. The news seemed to us to mark a new era in education. We had belonged to Colleges. They had not merely given us a certain amount of indoctrination in certain subjects; they had not merely prepared us for our particular professions; they had borne witness of a culture which is the highest of all culture. (Williams, 1960, pp. 122–123)

Williams' commentary follows:

> This aspect [...] could hardly be more evident: culture, quite explicitly, is offered as the alternative to anarchy. The need for popular education might be met in a number of ways; the Utilitarians, in particular, had been early in the field. But Maurice's emphasis is that of

[37] F.F.D. Maurice (1805–1872) was an Anglican theologian, prolific author, and one of the founders of English Christian socialism.

> Coleridge and Newman. The general opposition to Utilitarianism, and the alarmed reaction to increasing working-class power, here came together in a most significant way. (Williams, 1960, p. 123)

5.4.4 Conclusion

It was due to the general conditions that in England the clubs, people's houses of the third type, played important roles, including the development of a new culture of democratic participation even if not entirely alternative to that of the dominant classes. The causes were various. The early and regular process of industrial development had an influence, making revolt difficult and of little use and very quickly differentiating the composition of the working class. Secondly, there was paternalism as an issue; an issue originating from the closure of monasteries and lands, brought to the fore by the debates and difficulties of the poor laws, challenged by Owenism on its own ground, from which derived the affirmation of education as the primary lever of emancipation. The third cause of the peculiarities of the English workers' clubs was in the construction of a suitable way of thinking of the socialists, who adhered to the Owenist perspective, were influenced by widespread ideas, were taught by the Chartist failure interpreted as a lack of education of a decisive part of the militants. Local conditions also played a role, acting in the opposite direction toward more demanding "people's houses" and an alternative working-class culture: the clubs were local schools of democratic self-management in which it was demonstrated "that middle-class guidance was necessary to accomplish moral and social improvement seemed the club men to be degrading nonsense". But the general conditions prevailed for the construction of third-type people's houses.

5.5 German Union Houses

An alternative working-class culture, strictly speaking, but also with its own specific characteristics, was developed in Germany, partly by the German socialists, but mostly out of necessity. The ruling classes of imperial Germany, more reactionary than the English, by repressing the proletarian movement, prepared the conditions for a harsh response also on the cultural side. The great historian Wolfang J. Mommsen held a lecture in 1985[38] in which he put forward the thesis according to which "While there has been considerable rivalry, antagonism, and, eventually, open conflict and war between Britain and Germany, it has been rivalry and antagonism between societies which, if measured against the rest of Europe, were in many ways similar rather than different" (Mommsen, 1985, p. 3). He therefore specified the differences in order to demonstrate how they were more than balanced by the similarities. And

[38] It was the "Annual Lecture" of the "German Historical Institute" in London entitled "Great Britain and Germany 1800–1914—Two Paths of Development to Industrial Society".

the greatest difference that he highlighted was precisely the attitude of the dominant classes toward the emerging classes. The case of the bourgeois and intellectual class was different, but in Germany it could not undermine the *Junckertum*'s domination in the government, administration and army,[39] which remained the effective ruling class until their defeat in the First World War.

> Britain followed a more graduated path than Germany towards industrial society and managed to maintain a large degree of political cohesion despite mounting class divisions, with its ruling class gradually giving way to new social forces, although it maintained its privileged social status amazingly well during this process. In Imperial Germany, by contrast, the ruling elites, which on the whole continued to operate from a fairly narrow social base, hardened, and the constitutional system experienced a certain degree of petrification. Germany was heading for a good deal of internal division and domestic strife which would warrant the existence of a strong authoritarian government transcending political parties and social groupings. (Mommsen, 1985, p. 8)

As for the alternative proletarian culture, first of all it must be said that it was certainly not at the center of initiatives that used the term "workers' houses". These were bourgeois and philanthropic initiatives for the integration of the working class.

> To find the first examples of workers' houses [...] we must go back to a time when the modern industrial working class was in its infancy [...]. A group of bourgeois liberals, wealthy and educated, with progressive ideas, as well as various religious circles, interpreted the social crisis that also in Germany was becoming more acute around 1840 [...] as a threat [...]. After the shocking event of the Silesian weavers' uprising in the summer of 1844, they began to form a series of more or less successful organizations, which were supposed to help social discomfort; in these, alongside conservative-restorative attempts, there were also noteworthy progressive and social-reformist aspirations. Alongside all this, the idea of private houses came into play for the first time, as centers of bourgeois influence on the working class. (Reulecke, 1984, p. 131)

One of these initiatives, which had particular importance, was that of Adolf Kolping, realized in 1850 when he was vicar of Cologne Cathedral. Kolping, before becoming a priest, had been a shoemaker. Traveling for work throughout Germany, he had first-hand experience of the "social question" and had understood the importance of a workers' house. Kolping wrote that "they should be useful and comfortable; they should offer various educational opportunities—from the exhibition of books and periodicals to conferences and advanced training courses—and create a climate of familiarity capable of providing the young worker with a substitute for the security of the family and thus giving him a new home". After quoting this Kolping text, Jurgen Reulecke added: «for itinerant workers who found there food and lodging as well as medical care in case of illness, and for the members of the local association, the worker's house was a second paternal home where a head of the family, together

[39] Junkertum, or "junkerism", refers to the Prussian landed aristocracy, especially the noble landowners, known as Junkers. This term evokes a social and political system based on landed property and traditional power. The Junkers exercised considerable influence in Prussia, especially in the army and the bureaucracy. Their prominent position had a significant impact on German history, contributing to the formation of a strong national identity and influencing foreign policy, especially in the period preceding the First World War.

with a spiritual director, led the workers' association like a large family» (Reulecke, 1984, p. 134). More than 50 years after the first house, in 1907 there were 357 built by 1,161 Catholic associations with almost 200,000 members (Reulecke, 1984, p. 135). Although not as significant as the socialist ones, these clerical-bourgeois initiatives prevented the socialists from using the terms "people's house" or "workers' house". And not only to avoid confusion of terminology, but above all to underline differences and distances from a reality that nevertheless constituted a challenge and, for the ruling classes, a reassuring alternative that strengthened their hostility toward socialist initiatives. As will be seen, the alternative proletarian culture was instead at the center of the "union houses", true houses of the people even if not in name. The union houses in Germany were authentic houses of the people according to the definition of Margareth Kohn. As for their characterization, it can be said that they were placed between the fourth and fifth type.

5.5.1 Alternative Proletarian Culture

The history of the German Socialist Party was decisive for the alternative culture. The party was born in 1875 from the merger of the General Workers' Association that Ferdinand Lassalle had founded in 1863 and the Social Democratic Workers' Party founded by August Bebel and Wilhelm Liebknecht in 1869. In 1891 it adopted its current name, the Social Democratic Party of Germany (SPD) and had the collaboration of Friedrich Engels until his death in 1895. The internal conflict between the two factions that had merged, revisionists led by Lassalle and orthodox Marxists by Bebel and Liebknecht, remained heated in the early years, but did not prevent the SPD from becoming the relative majority party in the Reichstag in 1912, despite having been outlawed from 1878 to 1890: just one of the many examples of damage caused by the persecution by the government and its chancellor Otto von Bismarck. Interpreter of the feelings of the German elite, Bismarck considered the mere existence of a socialist party a threat to the security and stability of the newly unified Reich (in 1871). According to several authoritative reconstructions, the basis of the success of the SPD was the need to find a way to overcome this hostility by leveraging the working-class culture: recognized, nurtured and claimed as a superior alternative to that of the ruling classes. Gerhard Ritter reports a passage from the article that appeared in the "Correspondenzblatt" (Number 11, 29 May 1893) by Carl Legien, SPD and trade union leader, member of parliament between 1893 and 1898 and then from 1903 to 1920, in which one can read:

> All sympathetic politicians agreed that within the workers' organization lay a strong moral force and an untamable urge for a higher culture. And whoever seeks to destroy these organizations simultaneously hinders this desire for more humane conditions, for a higher level of education and civilization, and acts against progress» [...] This reflects the belief of the workers' leaders [...] that the task of the movement was not merely to better the economic position of the workers and to gain political power. It was also to be an instrument of cultural and educational emancipation. (Ritter, 1978, pp. 166, 167)

If this formulation seems similar to that of the English clubs, in reality it had a very different meaning. The high culture to which the proletariat had access was not simply that of the dominant classes, but a "translation" of it. This can be seen in the case of the Berlin Workers' School, inaugurated by Liebknecht in 1891, whose "teaching staff came from the group of journalists, writers and intellectuals of the Berlin party [...]. In the period 1898–1899, the teachers were Conrad Schmidt[40] Richard Calwer,[41] Bruno Borchart,[42] Paul Kampffmeyer,[43] Max Schippel,[44] Rudolf Steiner, who later became known as the founder of anthroposophy[45]" (Lidtke, 1985, p. 163). This teaching body, ideologically very diverse, was not supposed to carry out a program of Marxist indoctrination. Liebknecht had made this clear at the inauguration. Nevertheless, it was supposed to carry out a program aimed at the struggle for the emancipation of the workers.

> Addressing some four thousand people in the Brauerei Friedrichshain, Liebknecht set forth the radical goals of the school [...that] was to prepare workers to carry on the struggle for emancipation, not to make them learned specialists filled with superfluous information. For a model he drew heavily on the earlier Workers' Educational Society in Leipzig, in which he had been an active member and which he described as having been a «kind of agitational school». The new Workers' Educational School in Berlin would make up for what workers had missed in the public elementary school and, in addition, would sponsor scholarly lectures

[40] Conrad Schmidt (1863–1932) was a philosopher and journalist, but above all an important Marxist economist known above all for having been the first to identify, according to Eugen von Böhm-Bawerk, the difficulty of transforming values into prices in the labor theory of value that Marx himself then pointed out in the draft of the third book of Capital published posthumously by Engels in 1894. "Either products do actually exchange in the long run in proportion to the labour attaching to them—in which case an equalization of the gains of capital is impossible; or there is an equalization of the gains of capital—in which case it is impossible that products should continue to exchange in proportion to the labour attaching to them. From the Marxian camp the actual incompatibility of these two propositions was first acknowledged a few years ago by Conrad Schmidt. Now we have the authoritative confirmation of the master himself" (Böhm-Bawerk, 1896/1949, p. 28).

[41] Richard Calwer (1868–1927) was one of the best-known representatives of the reformist wing of the SPD before the Great War. He wrote essays on economics and statistics.

[42] Bruno Borchardt (1859–1939) was a physicist but very active in politics. From 1912 he was a member of the provincial parliament of Brandenburg. A staunch opponent of Nazism, he was beaten by the SA in his hometown of Falkensee during the pogrom of November 1938 and died a few months later from his injuries.

[43] Paul Kampffmeyer (1864–1945) journalist, poet, and essayist, founding member of the Garden City Movement. Literary consultant, author, and archivist at the JHW Dietz publishing house in Weimar, he wrote among other things the biographies of Friedrich Ebert, Wilhelm Liebknecht, Ferdinand Lassalle and Georg von Vollmar.

[44] Max Valentin Schippel (1859–1928) journalist of the "Volksblatt" (1886–1887) and then of the "Volkstribune" (1887–1890) and politician, was elected to Parliament in 1890.

[45] Rudolf Joseph Lorenz Steiner (1861–1925), known as the "Master" of anthroposophy, was, however, and before that, a philosopher and man of letters of merit. In 1886 he published a first book on Goethe's philosophy and in 1888 he was invited to work as a curator in the Goethe archives in Weimar, where he remained until 1896, writing introductions and commentaries to the four volumes of Goethe's scientific writings and publishing a second book in 1897: "Goethes Weltanschauung". In 1891 he obtained a doctorate in philosophy at the University of Rostock, with a thesis on the concept of ego in Fichte, later expanded and published under the title "Wahrheit und Wissenschaft". In those years he collaborated on the complete editions of the works of Arthur Schopenhauer.

> [...] to be fashioned so that a Social Democratic victory in the economic realm would be accompanied by vast gains for workers in the intellectual sphere. Workers, he insisted, made the best agitators for the socialist cause because they possessed something that even the most intelligent and committed middle-class socialists lacked. (Lidtke, 1985, p. 162)

The teachers had to carry out this program (1901–1902 edition): History (origins and history of various religions, primitive and ancient literature, history and literature of the Middle Ages), Law (Prussian Constitution and the German imperial state), Economics (Cooperatives, commercial and exchange policies, some topics on banking and the stock exchange), Science (energy theories), Presentation practices (reports and discussions on social, trade union and intellectual life issues, writing and oral presentation practices). The student attendance data are also interesting: History 230, Practices 191, Economics 176, Law 36, Science 23. The topics chosen and their presentation with a "class slant" had the task of selecting the contents taken from the culture of the dominant classes but appropriately "translated" for an alternative proletarian education. The Berlin workers' school thus perfectly represents, according to Vernon Lidtke, all the "ambiguities" of German socialist culture with respect to a Marxist-revolutionary canon, but nevertheless represents its alternative character. So much so that, while he considers the concept of subculture historically forced, at least in the sense attributed to this expression by Guenther Roth in its application to the SPD, he nevertheless uses a term such as "social-cultural milieu of the German labor movement" to affirm its effective alternative nature.

> The social-cultural milieu lacked the tight cohesiveness that is [...] implied in the phrase "Social Democratic subculture." On the other hand, when placed within the context of the larger society, the internal diversity and even the contradictions appear to be less significant than the differences that separated the socialist labor movement from most segments of Imperial Germany. [...]. The evidence does demonstrate that amalgamation and centralization of educational and artistic programs were means by which socialists sought to create a standardized labor movement culture on the national level. Despite the weaknesses and contradictions that those policies may have had [...] the educational and artistic programs constituted an essential part of the overall Social Democratic alternative to existing German society. (Lidtke, 1985, pp. 192–194)

It is in this context that one can see the reasons why in Germany the people's houses were the "union houses". The same persecution that explains the rise of an alternative proletarian culture forced the first German trade unionism into hiding, which gave rise to the need to have houses to host persecuted militants together with itinerant workers, houses that then became basic union headquarters in a center-periphery structure that had to be "rational" precisely because of the lesson learned from that persecution.

5.5.2 *The Union and Its Houses*

Apart from the English one, the recurring story about the birth of the people's houses in Belgium, France, Italy, begins with the serious problem that the socialists had to solve in order to meet, organize literacy schools[46] and reading rooms, meeting sympathizers and proselytizing. They had tried to rent premises, but the homeowners had a thousand difficulties and asked for exaggerated rents. They had tried to use taverns, bars, cafes; but the police had often closed them down so that this solution had proved precarious. There was no hope of solving the problem by using the home of some sympathizer lucky enough to have a large house: there were very few of them, they ran too many risks, many members did not agree. This is why it was necessary to build their own house, namely, the people's house. And this is also why there were so many people's houses.

In the German case, however, the story begins in a completely different way. Since the 1860s, associations between workers, even if banned by law following the revolutionary attempt of 1848,[47] had begun to spread and strengthen in the German states, first clandestinely, and later in an almost legal manner thanks to a relaxation of repression.[48] Then, after two failed attempts to assassinate Kaiser Wilhelm II attributed to socialist propaganda, on 19 October 1878 the "anti-socialist laws" were passed to paralyze the proletarian organization by prohibiting trade union activities and any meeting or publication whose purpose was to spread socialist principles. The laws had a limited duration but were continually renewed until, after Bismarck's

[46] It was not only, as has often been written (Kohn, 2003, p. 95), because illiterates were denied the right to vote. The rule that excluded illiterates from voting existed only in Italy until 1912, having been taken up again in its entirety by the Piedmontese law that allowed voting only to males of at least 25 years of age who were able to read and write and who paid no less than 40 lire in direct taxes. In the first political elections of 1861, there were only 418,696 voters, equal to 1.89% of the population, in 1880 621,896 (2.2%). A first reform, laws of 22 January and 7 May 1882, reduced the minimum age from 25 to 20, still males able to read and write, and introduced the alternative between having passed the second grade exam or having paid at least 19.80 lire in taxes. The electorate increased to two million (6.9% of the population). Universal suffrage, requested above all by radicals, republicans, and socialists, but also by Catholics and right-wing liberals hoping that the vote of illiterate peasants would guarantee the status quo, had been rejected by the Chamber in June 1881. Only in 1912 did a new electoral law, promulgated by Giovanni Giolitti, grant illiterates the right to vote, provided they were 30 years old or had performed military service. In France, the penalization of illiterates was introduced only during the July Monarchy from 1830 to 1848 as a counterweight to the extension of suffrage to those who paid at least 200 francs in income tax, whereas previously the limit was 300. After 1848, this penalization no longer existed, which was introduced in Belgium in 1883, there too, with the reduction of the wealth limits. But it was abolished in 1893, even though the plural vote was introduced, which rewarded, among others, graduates: two or three votes were granted to the 35 year-old married man if he paid at least 5 francs in taxes, to the owner of a house or financial assets worth at least 100 francs, to the graduate.

[47] Born in Berlin, the Workers' Brotherhood in 1848 had about 20,000 members spread across many parts of Germany. Initially composed almost exclusively of apprentice craftsmen, the Brotherhood tried to give itself a comprehensive dimension by addressing all manual workers, connected with the liberal left present in the Frankfurt parliament and was also active in the field of mutual aid and political and cultural education of its members. It represented a bridge between the old craft organizations and modern parties and unions. After the failure of the revolution of 1848, in 1854 the Brotherhood was outlawed in all the states of the German Confederation.

[48] The lifting of the coalition ban that allowed this relaxation occurred first in Saxony in 1861, then in Weimar in 1863, and finally throughout the North German Confederation in 1869. The formation of "interest groups" was not permitted for agricultural and transport workers, however. Trade union activity itself remained subject to many restrictions.

resignation on 25 January 1890, a new proposal for renewal was rejected by a large majority in the Reichstag. In the years between 1878 and 1890, trade union activity was therefore once again clandestine. Trade unionists and members were persecuted in various ways and often lost their jobs. They therefore had to migrate to find another, feeding the mass of itinerant workers, once itinerant artisans now also wage earners, for whom clerical-bourgeois initiatives had already provided workers' homes. It was for this reason that one of the primary initiatives of the union became that of the "pensioners". "They represented the meeting places for members who travelled; here they took care of the formalities for collecting travel contributions, here they found food and lodging and contact with their comrades. The pensioners were located in hotels rented totally or partially [...]. They can be considered as the nucleus of the future houses of the union" (Domansky, 1984, p. 152). In this function, these proto-people's houses were of the three types: meeting places with the purpose of helping and aggregating.

The houses of the union retained this original function, adding others determined by the particularities of the history of the union. After 1895, when German trade unionism began its development in law and in fact,[49] the organization was structured into "cartels" of trade or craft unions. A rather hierarchical structure was thus established with the institution of the "Central General Commission" an expression of the national trade unions established in 1892. This structure coordinated by the center was considered indispensable to have a strong and rational organization, in particular on the issue of striking. The union houses were part of this structure, and this influenced their nature, size, diffusion, and the connection between the people's house and alternative proletarian culture. They were large and expensive, present above all in the major cities, intended for all the functions of the workers' movement to demonstrate its strength. If in 1901 there were 11, in 1913 there were 83 and 184 in 1929 (Robert, 2013, p. 183). The progression was quite rapid, but the numbers remained modest if one considers that the members of the Confederation of German Trade Unions (DGB) were 700,000 in 1901, 2.2 million in 1913, 4.5 million in 1929. But these modest numbers depended only on the fact that the union houses were very large. The construction of the union house in Berlin (1899–1900 for 92 trade union associations) cost almost a million marks, as did the one in Hamburg (1904–1906 for 78 associations), 800,000 in Leipzig (1904–1906 for 40 associations). Eight hundred thousand marks at the time corresponded to 308 years of work of a specialized worker who earned about 2,600 marks a year.[50] As seen, the workers' houses of the Catholic

[49] In the first five years after the end of the anti-socialist legislation, the continuous warnings of Kaiser Wilhelm II about the coup parties, the massive police operations against the strikers and the bitter defeats suffered had induced the unions to be extremely cautious with the consequent loss of members. The membership began to grow again (to reach 2.2 million in 1913) when union action began to produce concrete results: an increase in wages (in 1913 the average worker's wage reached 1,100 marks per year against 650 in 1890 at constant prices) and a reduction in working time to 10 h per day.

[50] In Table A-4 page 336 of the publication edited by Gerhard Bry (1960) for the NBER, it is reported that in Berlin in 1906 a skilled worker earned 75 Pfenning per hour and worked on average 10 h per day. The annual wage, therefore, can be calculated at 2,600 marks.

associations were, in absolute terms and in proportion to the members, many more but they were much smaller, less complete and less complex than those of the DGB unions. These data also indicate that, despite the cost and effort required to build them, the times of setting up the union houses were relatively rapid in Germany. This was not the case in Belgium and France.

> The decision to set up offices, assembly halls, libraries, hostels and refreshment services brought together under one roof the main functions of the workers' movement, namely organizational activity and the care and development of sociality. The concentration of the offices of many different unions in a single building was intended to foster communication and cooperation between the various associations. Furthermore, the possibility of having their own halls and refreshment services was intended to free the associations and their members from bourgeois influences, consequently the houses simultaneously fulfilled the function of boundary walls and defensive walls. (Domansky, 1984, p. 157)

All this happened because a compromise had been reached (Regulation of 1899) on the question of central or local prerogatives in order to decide on strikes. The agreement established that such decisions had to be central, thus sanctioning the sectoral-categorical nature of the union conflict. The task of achieving the unity of workers regardless of their profession was instead delegated to the local level and the cartels were given the task of allowing it concretely and representing it symbolically by setting up union houses. These buildings caused difficulties and conflicts among the unionists themselves because they were too expensive and because they were too "urban" while many would have preferred many small houses on the outskirts. These problems were, however, overcome as it was urgent to strengthen the cohesion of the cartels.

> Some unions demanded that other priorities be established. They argued for a social rather than cultural commitment, calling for the construction of apartments for workers instead of a representative building: «Of what use can a castle be to the worker, if he does not even have a home?» [...]. There were unions that rejected the idea of building a central house [...], as they actually needed many small union houses. [...]. The answer to the question of why the project [Hamburg union house] was adhered to despite numerous arguments against [...] and the enormous financial difficulties is provided by a meeting of cartel delegates in December 1900. At this meeting it was discussed that there had been «a certain opposition» to the cartel's activity [...] so it was decided that «the construction of our house should be undertaken, which will further strengthen the consolidation of the working class». [...This] decision was part of the attempt to reunite the forces that had gradually distanced themselves from it in the cartel, entrusting them with a common commitment. Therefore, the union house should have fulfilled an internal function, before publicly demonstrating the strength of the unions. (Domansky, 1984, pp. 160–161)

The German union houses were people's houses of type four: something more than socio-political containers, but not spaces establishing a true collective agent subjectivity. Just as the local cartel of trade or craft unions was not really a unitary union but only an alliance, so its house basically maintained more the character of a condominium than of a shared home. The construction times were quite short despite the significant cost because the houses were part of a rather hierarchical structure of the union organization which was capable of deciding and acting quickly.

5.5.3 *Conclusion*

The German case presents, compared to the English one, the affirmation of an alternative proletarian culture in the true sense, people's houses called union houses were larger and more important, but not subjective acting units (not type five), a partial welding between actual alternative culture and people's houses. The seats and structures of that proletarian culture (sometimes even considered a subculture in the technical sense) were not primarily but only relatively the union houses. In Germany, unlike in England, two general conditions were favorable: the hostility of the ruling class toward the subaltern for fear that their antagonism threatened the stability of the recent unification of Germany, the flourishing network of moderate Catholic initiatives that could reassure the upper classes and were in competition with the union houses. But they were unfavorable due to the rather centralized organization of the German union, which the local determinants were not able to counterbalance. The settlement in the major cities contributed more to the alienation than to the rooting and interaction in and with the specific territorial realities. The two cases, English and German, therefore, seem to suggest a "model". The people's houses of type five, unitary collective subjects acting and building an alternative proletarian culture in the strict sense, did not fully exist when the general determinants did not act with the local determinants in the direction of territorial rooting. Continuing the analysis of other experiences, one could then find such interaction at the basis of people's houses fully of type five as the main seats of an alternative proletarian culture. This was effectively the case in Belgium and France.

5.6 People's Houses in Belgium

On 5 August 1872, in Jolimont, a district of La Louvière, 60 km south of Brussels, the blacksmith Théophile Massart bought a house on behalf of the workers' societies (La Solidarité, Union Ouvrière, Union des Métiers du Centre). It was the first people's house in Europe that was truly such in name as well as in fact, neither a recreational-educational club as in England nor a union house as in Germany. The initiative lasted 14 years, until 1886 when the costs became unsustainable and would have led to its closure if Massart himself together with Abel Wart had not had the right idea. After a visit to the "Vooruit" cooperative in Ghent, they also promoted a consumer cooperative in Jolimont ("Au Progrès" 20 June 1886) which supported the people's house by transforming it from a meeting-aggregation space (third type) to a container for a plurality of collective actions of the proletariat (fourth type) and finally to a space establishing a collective acting subjectivity (fifth type).

> Most of the people's houses founded before the First World War were built according to a general [...] scheme. [...]. Some workers in a locality decided to break away economically from the capitalist system by creating a bakery [...] and organizing a shop where they sold basic necessities at more advantageous prices and at a more precise weight than in private

> shops. [...]. The beginnings were difficult, often due to bad management and lack of experience [...], the limited number of cooperators and the lack of organizational spirit of the working class [...]. Many cooperatives failed, while others managed to survive. But as time went by, cooperation took on increasingly solid roots. This is how [...] the people's houses gradually emerged within the cooperatives. In 1903 Jules Destrée and Emile Vandervelde noted that «[...] all socialist cooperatives have as their immediate aim the creation of bakeries but also beer shops, with rooms for parties, conferences and meetings, all groups affiliated with the Workers' Party find here a free place, a meeting place where socialist life is concentrated». (Flagothier, 1984, p. 285)

In Belgium, due to the conditions of the proletariat, bread and subsistence goods were the primary needs that the people's houses were called upon to respond to, following the example of the large cooperative "Vooruit" of Ghent, which took the name "Forward" in 1880, but whose origins were earlier. Vooruit was in fact founded in 1873 and was only a bakery[51] made by weavers and spinners at the Zacheus tavern. Members could purchase bread cards to spend the following week, receiving, at the end of the year, a share of the residual[52] proportional to the quantities they had purchased, distributed in the form of vouchers for the purchase of bread and, later, also meat, coffee, blankets, and clothes. The success was remarkable, and the Zacheus tavern became too small. So, the cooperative moved to a former industrial building on the Garenmarkt, its first people's house, which also had a café, a fabric and clothing store, a library with a reading room and a space for parties and meetings. The largest and most magnificent people's house in Ghent was built by the cooperative in 1912.

On the spread of people's houses in Belgium, there is systematic data only for Wallonia and Brussels, but, in addition to the one in Ghent, the people's houses in Antwerp and Bruges are also known. In Flanders, however, there were few of them because they were displaced by the previous social initiative of the parishes in a strongly Catholic region (Lussien-Maisonneuve, 2002). The data for Wallonia show that the people's houses were a very widespread reality, with a number of creations per 100,000 inhabitants similar to that of the less demanding English clubs (Figs. 5.9 and 5.10).

[51] But "the bakery has long been a social institution as powerful as the Church or the factory" (Scascighini, 2009, p. 6).

[52] In cooperatives, or at least in those that respected and, in some cases, still respect true self-management principles, the "operating result" is not profit. Capital is "bought" by workers who pay interest. The capitalist production relationship in which it is capital that buys labor is reversed. The operating result is then called "residual" and belongs to the workers as what remains after the costs have been paid, including the purchase of capital and the salary that they have together decided to pay in a fixed amount. In this way, the remuneration of labor in the self-management company is partly fixed (salary) and partly variable, depending on the performance of business. The variable part of the remuneration of labor is given by the portion of the residual that they collectively decide to distribute minus the part that they decide to set aside for self-financing.

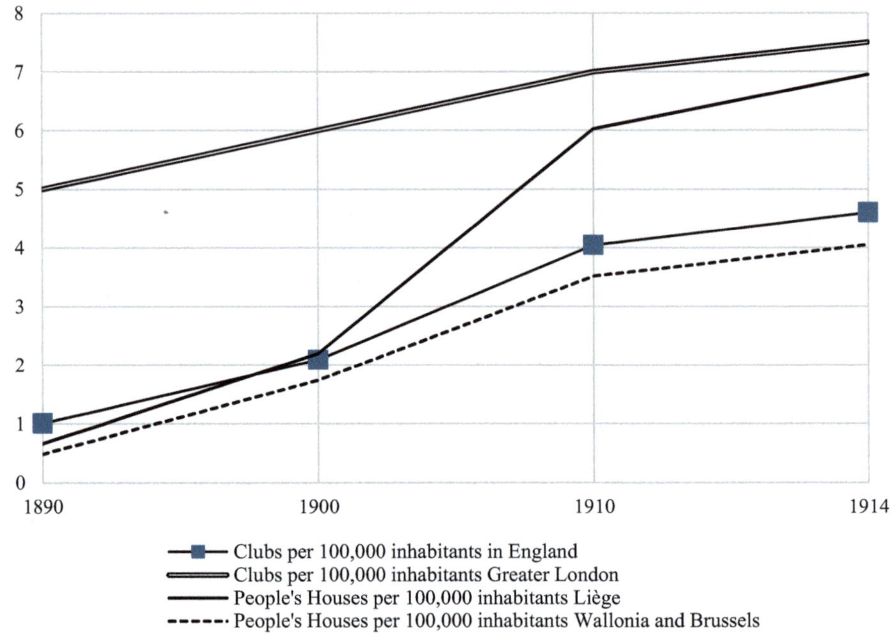

Fig. 5.9 Diffusion of people's houses in Wallonia and Brussels compared to that of English clubs. *Source* Figure obtained by processing data from *La Population de la Belgique* C.I.C.R.E.D. Series 1974 and Flagothier (1984)

5.6.1 Delayed from Industrial Take-Off

These data show that people's houses in Belgium spread between 1900 and 1910–1914, almost 20 years after Belgian industrial takeoff. It is significant, in fact, that the first house of 1872, which was exceptionally early, lived precariously until its rescue in 1886. Similarly, the cooperative "Vooruit" of Ghent, born as a simple bakery in 1873, became a people's house with a prestigious headquarters only much later, in 1912. One will see that in France too, people's houses spread only a certain time after the takeoff of industrial development. Therefore, the most demanding people's houses (of type five), like those of Belgium and France, needed an advanced context of industrial growth. (In comparison, the Italian case appears unusual. In Italy, people's houses had already begun to be built in the early 1890s, almost 10 years before the start of significant industrial growth: an "anomaly" that will be explained).

The delay with respect to the industrial takeoff of the most complete people's houses, with a wide range of services that they made available to the proletariat, families, and their organizations, cannot be justified by considering the needs of the workers. Based on the needs, they would have been useful much earlier since the level of wages was very low. The Belgian development model was of the export-led type supported by low wages: «also citing Coolsaet (2014), Alloul and Auwers

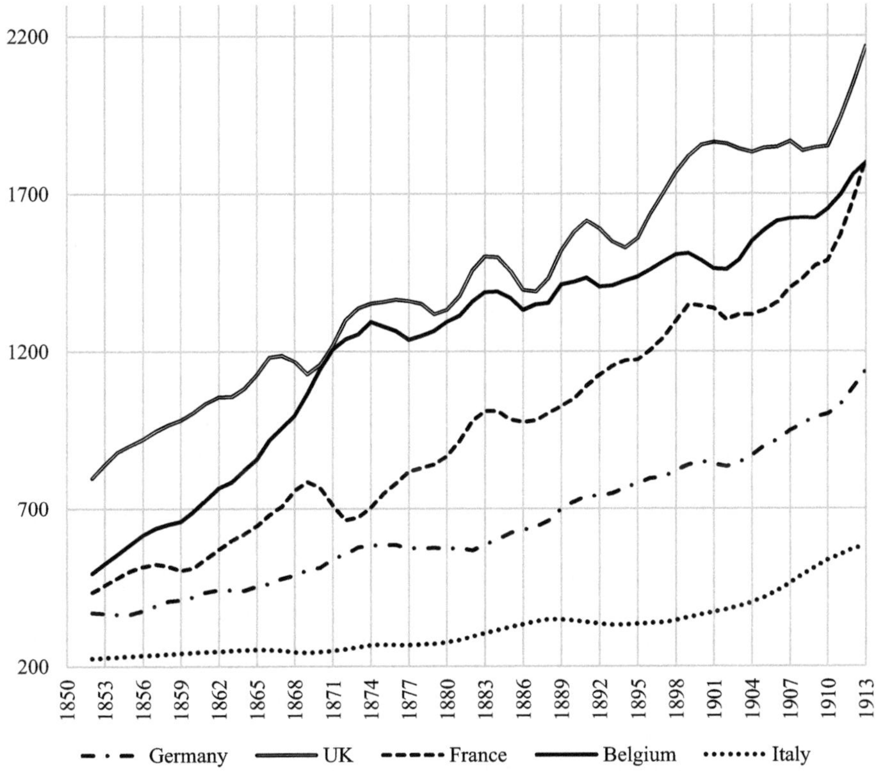

Fig. 5.10 Industrial production per capita at constant prices and purchasing power parity, three-year moving averages. *Source* Figure obtained by processing data from Groningen Growth and Development Centre, *Historical National Accounts Database*

(2018) believe that the Belgian elite has consistently ensured broad consensus for a policy of fiscal moderation, flexible corporate law, and low wages to keep Belgian industry competitive on the international market» (Vandamme, 2019, p. 21). The export-led development model works well if wages are low enough to attract foreign investment from advanced companies already operating on global markets. They know how to move in the international market, which is difficult for inexperienced companies. It can therefore be considered that if the model works, as it did in Belgium, this is proof that wages were so low that it was convenient for foreign companies (especially English ones) to set up production units despite all the higher indirect costs typical of a country that was not yet developed. The low wages in the areas of Belgian industrialization constituted the decisive lever for the purpose of valorising its singular intermediate position between early English development and the relative backwardness of the rest of Europe: «Belgium was the territory which became keyed first and most successfully into such an intermediary role [between advanced England and the large market of other European countries], and Belgian industrial history can be fully understood only within the context of this dual relationship» (Pollard,

Table 5.3 Index of kilograms of bread and meat that could be purchased with the weekly wage of a worker (blacksmith) in 1878, taking 100 as the English quantity

	Germany	Belgium	France	England
Bread	36	48	89	100
Beef for boiling	53	45	56	100

Note The data from the "Letter" allow the reader to see that the price of meat for boiling was representative of that of protein foods of animal origin. The wages of blacksmiths were representative of the average wages of skilled workers: in all the countries indicated, about one and a half times that of unskilled workers
Source Table obtained by processing data from United State Department of State (1879)

1973, pp. 640–641). Considerable English investments flowed into Belgium in search of greater returns from companies that were already substantial and able to take advantage of the first "globalization"[53] when wages at home had already begun to rise. According to Michael Edelstein (1982, pp. 42, 43), between 1860 and 1890, the most important destinations for the emigration of capital and entrepreneurial skills from Great Britain were, in order, Belgium, France, and the United States. But one may ask what the gap in real terms between wages in Belgium and those in England was. An answer can be found in a valuable publication from 1879 taken from the "Reports of the United States Consuls in Relation to Labor in Europe", as a "Letter" from the Secretary of State to Congress and preserved in the Library of the University of Illinois at Urbana-Champaign. With the statistics collected for this publication, Table 5.3 could be compiled.

At the end of the 1870s, when Belgian industrial production had already caught up with English production for 10 years, Belgian wages in terms of purchasing power for consumer goods were a little less than half of English wages. French wages were significantly higher, and German wages were lower if spent on bread but higher if spent on meat. Therefore, Germany could also be an interesting location for English foreign investments, which, in fact, occurred although to a lesser extent than in Belgium. Belgium offered a notable advantage over Germany because it was a smaller country with a weak state and could not threaten the supremacy of Great Britain. The fact remains that the standard of living of Belgian workers was at the limit of subsistence, especially considering the purchasing power for protein consumer goods. In this regard, one can consider the comment that accompanied the statistics in the "Letter". The United States was then subjugated by the unbridled liberalism that characterized its history from the Civil War to the First World War.

> From the close of the Civil War through the first decade of the twentieth century. More [...] the rationale was created [...] to justify the exemption of business enterprise from unwanted government interference. This body of ideas [...] reached full flower in America during those years and was [...] the dominant strain in the contemporary political mentality.

[53] Federico and Tena-Junguito (2019) reconstructed the data on the share of exports in GDP for the 38 largest countries in the world, highlighting that this share increased from 5.5% in 1870 to 7.3% in 1890, reaching 9% on the eve of the First World War. In terms of volumes, from 1870 to 1913 global exports increased fivefold.

> [...] this conservative triumph was facilitated by a degeneration in the liberal democratic tradition [...]. Much that was warm and humanistic in the older tory tradition was swept aside in deference to a cold and sometimes brutal calculus of utility. [...] the devotion to a material ideal which characterizes the thinking of these men helped to exaggerate the extent of their conservatism by releasing it from the inhibitions a different norm might have imposed. It left them free to follow out the logical implications of their postulates. (Green McCloskey, 1951, pp. vi, 169–170)

Well, the State Department of a country like the United States, where absolute freedom of enterprise was the established credo, in reporting on work in Belgium praised the "wisdom, patience, gentleness, and strength of mind" of the Belgian workers who bore the entire burden of sustaining the international competitiveness of their industry.

> The great wisdom displayed by the Belgian workingmen in accepting their peculiar situation is worthy of the highest commendation; whether this has been learned of necessity or whether it has been reached through a more patriotic channel, is of minor consequence. [...] It must not be understood from this pleasing picture that the working people of Belgium are better off than their neighbours. On the contrary, their lives are continual struggles for meagre subsistence, and nothing but that spirit of patience, kindness, and fortitude, which enables them to practice the severest economy, makes it possible for them to subsist themselves and supply the necessaries of life to their families. At the very best, the lot of the workingmen of Belgium is hard and unremitting toil, an unceasing battle with most adverse circumstances, but it would be immeasurably worse were they to resort to strikes and violence to better their condition. (United State Department of State, 1879, p. 2)

Ultimately, if the people's houses in Belgium had been born on the basis of the need for subsistence aid, they would have spread much earlier: at the beginning of industrial development and not 20 years later. But not only that. It can also be observed that the differentiated diffusion in the provinces was positively correlated with the relative level of GDP per capita in 1890. The people's houses spread more in the relatively richer areas and not in the poorer ones (Fig. 5.11).

The need to have good quality bread at low prices often dictated the origin of the houses as social bakeries, but the long times required for them to become real people's houses can only be explained by their huge construction costs and by the difficult and prolonged process of developing the indispensable alternative proletarian culture for the consequent possible development of collective actions.

5.6.2 *Localization*

The localized character of the industrialization areas was the second notable consequence of the export-led development model with the prominence of foreign direct investment. The model, in fact, was not dominated only by macro-systemic variables such as generalized low wages. It was also driven by the localized conveniences that individual multinational companies explored, discovered, and used. In fact, it was the analyses of foreign direct investment (such as that of Pollard) that discovered that in order to explain industrialization in Europe one had to descend to the local level.

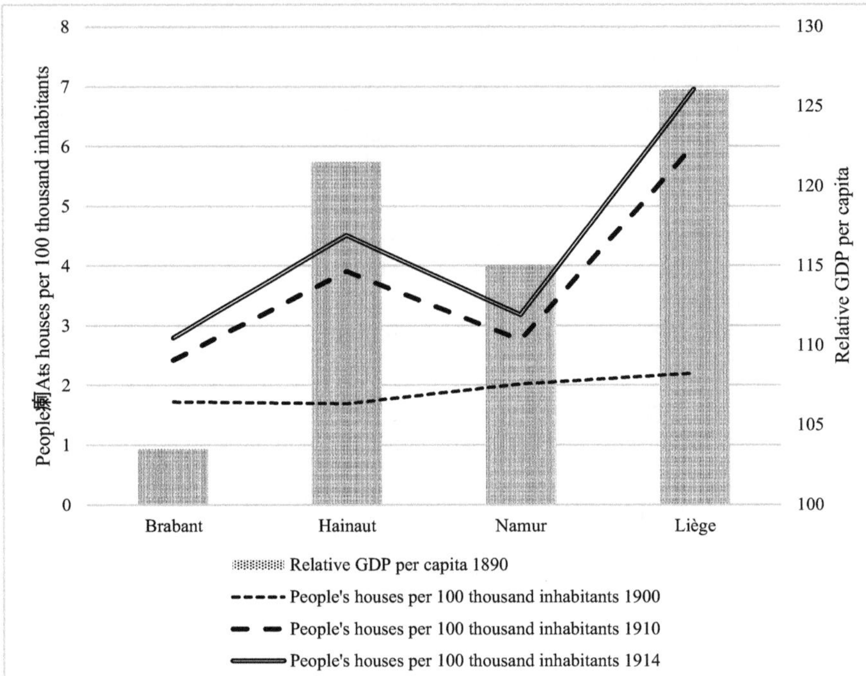

Fig. 5.11 People's houses per 100,000 inhabitants in the provinces of Belgium for which data are available, compared to the level of relative GDP per capita (100 = national average). *Sources* see previous figure and Buyst (2018, p. 78)

Traditionally, the industrialization of Europe has been viewed as a series of separate "industrial revolutions". Each country has been treated as an "economy" and its progress compared separately with some kind of implied model. [...]. There are many good reasons for making the political state, or even a notional country like Germany before 1871, the unit of investigating the process of industrialization. [...]. And in truth many issues of direct relevance to industrialization operated within political boundaries or were affected by political decisions. These included protection, the currency, access to markets and colonies, and poor laws and factory acts. Other important legal and social data, such as serfdom, the status of the businessman, primogeniture, and guild and staple rights, might in some cases coincide with the political frontiers, but as a matter of fact did not so coincide in some of the leading countries of Europe. [...]. This article will argue that the traditional view has reached its limit as a method both of exposition and of analysis, and that further advance must come from a new starting point. It will argue that useful as the "national" approach has been in the past, particularly by evolving testable models, it was based on faulty observation. The industrialization of Europe did not proceed country by country. [...]. What disposed some areas to take more quickly to the new system than others? [...] we see [...] that some solutions proffered on a national scale come off badly [...] when some early industrializing regions differ so widely from others subject to the same legislation, while showing great similarities to their opposite numbers existing under a very different political framework; or the doctrine of a "critical minimum effort" needed to take an economy out of its traditional balance which has little persuasive power in a regional context. [...] we may hope to get some positive aid

> by operating at the micro level in our search for causes, sequences, and the relative weight of factors. (Pollard, 1973, pp. 636, 639)

Joan Rosés and Nikolaus Wolf (2018), citing Pollard, presented the map that the scholar had imagined without being able to compile it due to the lack of complete data, reconstructed only recently (Fig. 5.12).

> On a map of Europe in which industrialization was coloured, say, red, it would by no means be the case that an area corresponding to a country within its boundary would turn uniformly pale pink, dark pink, and so on to deepest crimson. On the contrary, industrialization would appear as red dots, surrounded by areas of lighter red diminishing to white, and with the spread of industrialization these dots would scatter across the map with little reference to the political boundaries. It would also follow that the dynamic of the infection of this rash of red dots, crossing frontiers while by-passing large areas of the home country, must clearly have a largely non-political explanation. (Pollard, 1973, pp. 636–637)

Already in 1900, the "Blue Banana" was taking shape from the North of England to regions of Belgium, Holland, France, Germany, and Switzerland up to Northern Italy, which, not respecting national borders, would characterise the development of the old continent for over a century (Fig. 5.13).

The long duration of this territorial characterization, already present in 1900 and still present 100 years later, shows that the development processes were localized not because of contingent circumstances destined to disappear soon, but for structural reasons. In this way, the processes that led to the birth and development of the most demanding people's houses, strongly anchored to their territory, also responded to structural reasons. To understand this, the best reference is to the famous, celebrated, emblematic people's house in Brussels.

Its history began modestly like that of Jolimont. To stem the unbearable exploitation of the poorest who had to buy poor quality bread at exorbitant prices, a cooperative bakery was founded (spring 1879) which prospered rapidly. In 1886, the cooperative managed to buy a headquarters, in the former synagogue on rue de Bavière. The success was remarkable and cooperative projects multiplied. A larger building was needed. So, in 1895, the Société Coopérative Ouvrière de Bruxelles bought a plot of land between the church of La Chapelle and Place du Sablon. The architect who was entrusted with the project was 34 years old, his name was Victor Horta and he was already considered a master since he was the first, in the construction of the Villa Tassel in 1893, to introduce the canons of Art Nouveau. Horta developed the preliminary design in six months, and in a year, under the direction of the architect Pringers, 15 draftsmen completed it with 8,500 square meters of drawings. Twenty-five bricklayers worked on the construction site for two and a half years and various work cooperatives that installed 600,000 kilos of iron and steel and 2,000 cubic meters of masonry. The Maison du Peuple opened its doors on Sunday, 2 April 1899, exactly 20 years after its humble origins in 1879. Starting from the Gare du Midi and opened by the banner of the Belgian Workers' Party, the procession was a sea of red flags that advanced to the Place du Sablon where 1,000 artists performed

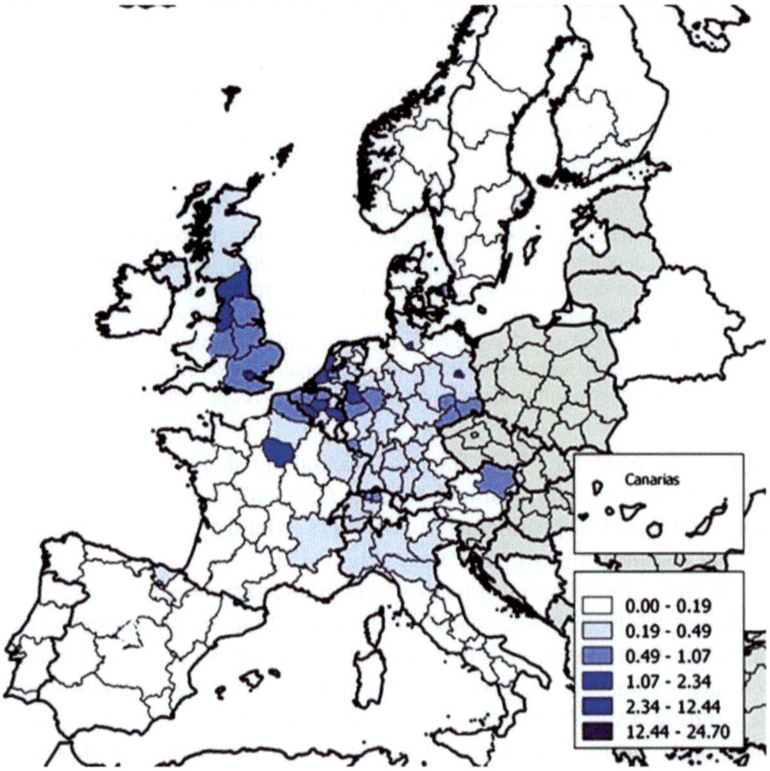

Fig. 5.12 European regional map by GDP density (GDP per square kilometer corrected) in 1900. *Note* Having population as the denominator, the GDP per capita has the drawback of being reduced in regions that have had significant population increases due to their development. The opposite happens to the GDP per square kilometer indicator, which is high when the population density is high even with low GDP per capita. A compromise is used in the figure obtained by correcting the GDP density in the regions with the highest population density. *Source* Figure obtained by processing data from Rosés and Wolf (2018, p. 42)

the inaugural song. There were speeches by Jean Jaurès[54] and Emile Vandervelde (1866–1938, then MP for Charleroi of the Belgian Workers' Party who ended by exclaiming: «Even higher up, above the sea of roofs, the terrace with vast horizons, like the deck of a mighty ship sailing at full steam towards the shores of another world» (Khon, 2003, p. 99) (Fig. 5.14).

The architecture of Victor Horta's people's house, later a model for many others, suggested the antipanopticon to Margareth Khon. "While the Panopticon was structured on the principle of individualization, the People's House on the construction of solidarity. At the heart of the Panopticon was the efficient use of power [...], at the heart of Horta's construction [...] the spaces were [...] organic [...] to the

[54] Jean Jaurès (1859–1914), defeated in the 1898 elections, became involved outside Parliament and became one of the major intellectual champions of socialism.

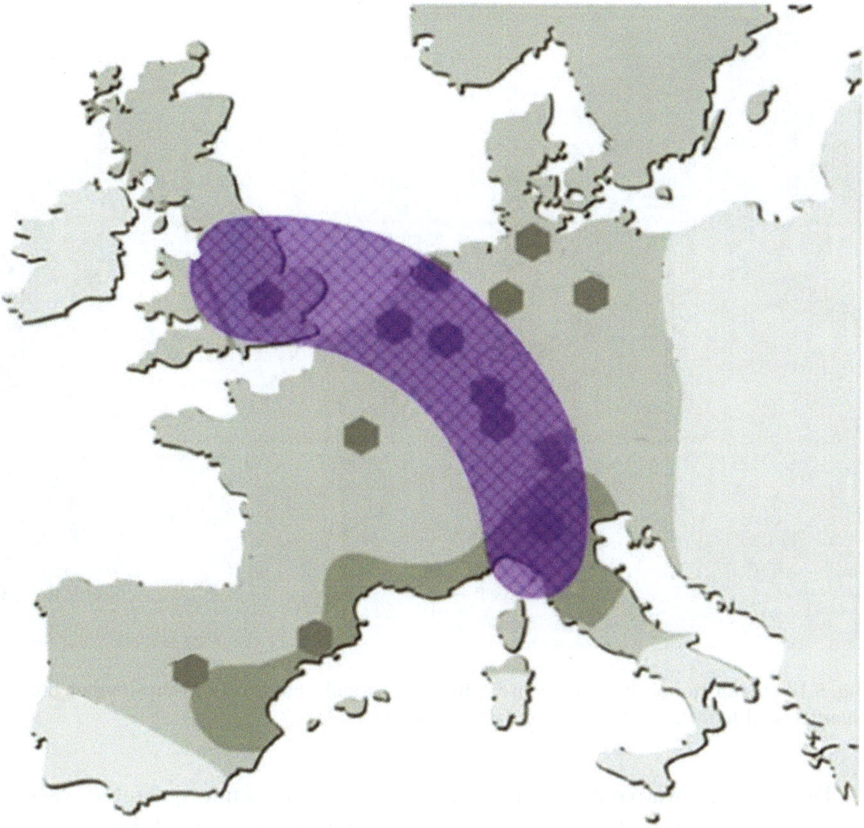

Fig. 5.13 Blue Banana, main development centers and North-Mediterranean development direction, 2000s. *Source* Figure adapted from Reimer (2010)

need for continuous interaction, coordination, cohesion" (Khon, 2003, p. 103).[55] In Horta's people's house, power did not emanate from the inscrutable center. "Power emanates from the peripheral spaces where the various unions, cooperatives, groups, associations are located. [...] and it is totally visible" (Khon, 2023, p. 103). At the center was the large room, where meetings were held, and the confrontation and visibility of all and for all took place, as well as concerts and theatrical performances. It was almost 60 m long (this measurement is significant) and was located on the third floor, an ideal and practical fulcrum to which one converged via a monumental double-circulation staircase that connected all the floors (Fig. 5.15).

[55] Michel Hastings (1991, pp. 117, 352) had also thought of the antipanopticon for the courtyards of Halluin, as one will see, places of basic socialization at a certain point animated and conducted by activists of the people's house.

Fig. 5.14 Victor Horta's People's House in Brussels, virtual reconstruction (https://urban.brussels/en/articles/3d-modeled-virtual-tour-of-the-maison-du-peuple)

The same innovative Art Nouveau canon, with its dynamic syncretism between functional structure and decoration, industrial materials and natural forms, contrasted with the heavily classicizing and static Panopticon, which it therefore contributed to condemn. But one can go even further, noting that the dimensions of the auditorium corresponded to the archetype of the Athenian agora, characterized by a space available to all those admitted,[56] of a measure appropriate to the acts of standing up and speaking intelligibly and responsibly, and to the squares of the medieval cities of the republican government.

> The agora is […] linked to the practice of democracy […], a set of actions. And actions require […] a designated space to be put into action. […]. Showing one's face and making a true speech can only be done in a theatrical space that allows visual contact and within range, as the entire assembly must be able to see and hear the speaker. […]. In Athens, the Theatre

[56] "The agora [between the sixth and fifth centuries] had a complex spatial organization, with different functions clearly recognizable on the ground by means of enclosures, monuments, paths that identified the various parts of which it was composed. […]. There was a special magistracy to define the public spaces in which official meetings and assemblies took place: the peristiarchoi […] who carried a sacrificed pig all around the area and marked the perimeter of the meeting area with blood. The distinction between inside and outside was clearly an act of worship and ensured a scrupulous definition of public functions […]: the peribolos or the enclosure mark the forms and rights of participation and exclusion in the common space" (Lippolis, 2019).

Fig. 5.15 Victor Horta's house of the people in Brussels, the third-floor auditorium, (54 × 16.5 × 10.5 m, could accommodate 1500 people (https://hiddenarchitecture.net/maison-du-peuple-house-of-people)

> of Dionysus [is] the formalization of the agora in a properly theatrical function. [...]. A clear example of the need to have an empty space in the centre of the city that presents a republican institutional form is the development of the centre of Florence [...] from 1115 [...] to 1295 [...] with the demolition of the nobles' towers [...] and the progressive expropriation and demolition of the buildings around the Palazzo Vecchio. [...]. If we compare [its] dimensions with [...] the Theatre of Dionysus, we observe that they are similar and are around 60 metres. This is because 30 meters is approximately the maximum distance at which a man can speak out loud and be heard. Trying to measure other squares in municipal cities [...] you get [...] overlapping areas [...]. Often even the history of their formation is similar, [...] laborious work of creating a void [...] that continues [...] for hundreds of years. To arrive at the vaguely semicircular shape of Piazza del Campo in Siena [...] it took almost two centuries. (Toson, 2018, pp. 145, 150)

The architecture of Victor Horta's Maison du Peuple corresponded to that of the democratic city with the square or the theater at its center, functional to the authorized participation of the diverse, symbols of their unity, places of free critical debate for the common good. There was therefore not only the difficulty and the cost of setting up such a demanding architecture but also the time required and the material-spiritual conditions for the development of a proletarian culture of the "class for itself" and of collective action.

The reason for this time can be explained by resorting to a famous reading by Foucault of the Kantian text (1784) "Was ist Aufklarung?" Between 5 January and 9 March 1983, Foucault held 20 lectures at the Collège de France, later published with the title "Le Gouvernement de soi et des autres", introduced with that "text for me a bit of an emblem and a bit of a fetish […] that today I would like to look at a little more closely" (Foucault, 2009, p. 17). Kantian reading placed at the center of modern critical thought the escape from submission (minority), inferiority, dependence, subjection, tutelage, not only due "to the violence of an authority but […] to ourselves, to a certain relationship with ourselves […]: because men are cowards, because they are lazy, because they live in fear. […]. Consequently, what the Aufklarung will have to achieve […] will be precisely […] the redistribution of the relationships between the government of the self and the government of others" (Foucault, 2009, p. 40). Such escape from submission implied for Kant a responsible, frank and true public discourse, the opposite of "tolerance". "You see that here is the definition of Aufklarung: it is the exact opposite, Kant says, of 'tolerance'. What is tolerance in fact? Well, it is precisely that which excludes reasoning, discussion, the freedom to think in its public form" (Foucault, 2009, p. 43). Foucault started from there and then invited one to discover what the nature of the frank and true responsible discourse in fourth-century Greece was, when parrhesia[57] changed meaning with the crisis of democratic institutions: from the right of free and equal citizens to speak as males and owners, to the right of criticism based on the ethical-moral qualities of those who exercised it. While in conditions of normal functioning of social and political structures the word of those who were appointed to speak was valid, in conditions of crisis and for change this legitimacy had become insufficient.[58] It was no longer enough to have the truth of those who said it convinced that it was

[57] "Parrhesia is a verbal activity in which a speaker expresses his personal relationship with the truth and risks his life because he recognizes that telling the truth is a duty to help other people (or himself) live better. In parrhesia the speaker makes use of his freedom, and chooses frank speaking instead of persuasion, truth instead of falsehood or silence, the risk of death instead of life and safety, judgment instead of flattery, and moral duty instead of personal gain or moral apathy" (Foucault, 2001, pp. 19–20).

[58] "In the fourth century B.C. […] a discussion arose about the relationship between parrhesia and democratic institutions. […]. To us this problem seems obvious and familiar, but to the Greeks its discovery, the identification of a […] antinomy between parrhesia—freedom of speech—and democracy, inaugurated a long and passionate debate specifically about the nature of the relationship […] between democracy, logos, freedom, and truth. […]. For Plato, the main danger of parrhesia is not that it leads to bad decisions in government, or that it provides some ignorant and corrupt leader with the means to gain power and become a tyrant. The main danger of freedom and free speech in a democracy is what happens when everyone lives as he pleases […] which Plato calls kataskeue tou biou (κατασκευε του βιου). In this case there can no longer be a common logos, a possible unity for the city" (Foucault, 2001, pp. 77, 84).

true, so much so that they put their face to it (in Greece at that time even their life). Now the truth had to be really true. This was guaranteed by the ethical-moral qualities of the one who asserted it, that is, if their speech was in accordance with their life which therefore constituted the testimony of it.[59] It turned out that proper and appropriate participation in collective activity required the long-term experience of such testimony. This was true for fourth century Greece. But for Foucault it is true for all Western critical thought despite the "transformation that [starting with Descartes] makes possible the institutionalization of modern science [...] so that I can be immoral and yet know the truth [...], an idea that was rejected by all previous culture" (Polidori, 2005, p. 4). According to Foucault it was not at all a breakthrough: «Needless to say, when I affirm that [...] this link between truth spoken and truth witnessed has been definitively interrupted, I do not believe it one bit. All the interest of the matter derives precisely from the fact that the links have not been [...] severed» (Foucault, 2003, p. 22–23).

5.6.3 Conclusion

The Belgian people's houses of type five, fully-fledged collective entities, could arise and sustain themselves only through long processes, not only because they were large and expensive. Such long processes were also essential to allow the mutual experience of truth in collective confrontation for the common good. And they were created because the general determinants interacted with the local determinants, pushing in the same direction. Accelerated industrial development according to the export-led model driven by foreign direct investments leaped over national borders, building itself on territorial bases. Belgian socialism, in favor of cooperatives and grassroots initiatives by the proletariat to compensate for low wages, was functional to this model, at least partially obviating the social costs it entailed. The strong local initiatives supported each other through the network of cooperatives and the socialist party itself.

[59] "In Euripides' Ion [...] the parrhesiastic role [...] was based on a mythical genealogy [...] parrhesia was the civic right of Athenian citizens of good family. [...]. The problematization of parrhesia involved a play between logos, truth and nomos (law). [...]. With Socrates, the problematization of parrhesia takes the form of a play between logos (truth) and bios (life) in the field of a personal learning relationship [...]. And the truth that the parrhesiastic discourse brings to light is the truth of a person's life, that is, the type of relationship he has with the truth: how he constitutes himself as an individual who must know the truth [...], and how this relationship with the truth is ontologically and ethically manifest in his life" (Foucault, 2001, p. 101).

5.7 Bourses du Travail in France

Even in France, the people's houses were rooted in the territory, even though those born on the Belgian example were few and concentrated in the northern departments. In the rest of the country, there was the important network of the particular "Bourses du Travail", initiatives that had a specific function but also assumed the role had elsewhere by the people's houses. Strictly speaking, one could distinguish between people's houses and Bourses du Travail in the sense that sometimes the latter and the local trade unions that organized them were hosted in the former (when the locations took the name of people's houses which only happened sometimes). What matters, however, is that in any case the center of activity was organized like and around the Bourses du Travail. It was from their origin and from the slow maturation of ideas and related practices, that their functions developed, until they constituted the central institution of a possible federalist socialism, even though after some time it was considered utopian. Only in the north of France, where the people's houses were built following the Belgian example, as will be seen in the case of Halluin, the Bourse du Travail was annexed to the people's house as one of its activities.

5.7.1 The Original Function

The original function was to collect and coordinate information on the supply and demand of labor, a service that may seem like a recent invention but is actually very ancient. English-language literature traces its conception back to 1650 when Henry Robinson (1605–1664), a merchant-essayist (his most famous work was dedicated to liberty of conscience), unsuccessfully presented a draft bill to the English Parliament, which he then illustrated in a publication in which one reads:

> Oh the stupidity of this Nation [...] that boasts it selfe to be Constituted an absolute Tyrant over the whole Creation: Certainly it must be notoriously degenerated, if not besotted, that is become so unable to help it selfe: The very bruit beasts in many respects apprehend better their owne Advantages, and are more dextrous at the practise of them. How many rare discoveries have beene long since made unto this Nation [...] which yet by most men are held Hereticall, and for the most part obstructed because so few are at leisure to search into the depth and glory of them. [...] We find by Experience that Multitudes of people, of all sorts, both Handicrafts, Artificers, Manufactors, and others, are brought to poverty and beggery, because they doe not timely meet with any one to Set and continue description them at Worke; And yet at the very same time, we like wise meete with multitudes of others, both Merchants and Shop-keepers af all Callings, that cannot furnish their Customers so cheape and speedily as were to be desired, because either they cannot presently get Work-folk, or else not at such cheap rates as to make a benefit thereof. [...]. And this great reliefe unto the poore, and advantage to the encrease of Trade, is infallibly secured by this Register of Adresses, this common Center of Intelligence, from whence all persons may forth with be directed, and receive satisfaction, and encounter in whatsoever they can lawfully desire; For although so many severall Arts, Trades, and Callings as are requisite to the Constitution of Cities, and Common-wealths, as so many parts and members of so great a Corporation, are purposely introduced, to be of mutual succour and assistance to each others occurrences; Yet,

since most of them are scituate some distance from one another, oftentimes unknown, & in number infinite; There is more than a seeming want unto the perfection of humane society, that as yet there never was any publique place appointed which might have served as a Treasury, or Abridgment of all Accommodations desireable. (Robinson, 1650, pp. 2–3)

However, it is not true that the idea was English. In reality, the first time a service of this kind was designed was in 1629 in Paris and, thanks to a royal privilege, the following year it was created by the doctor, journalist, and philanthropist Theophrastus Renaudot, a protégé of Richelieu.[60] It was the "Bureau d'adresses et de rencontres" (île de la Cité, between the rue de Calandre and the quai du Marché-neuf) where offers and requests for work were collected "to remedy poverty and vagrancy" by avoiding traditional charity and confinement. In 1633, a king's order obliged all the unemployed to register with the Bureau. Georges Gilles de La Tourette, Renaudot's biographer, wrote:

The wars of religion had ruined France. All the cities of the kingdom had suffered, and the poverty was great. [...]. When the civil war ended after [...] the Edict of Nantes, the wretched [...] were joined by discharged soldiers accustomed to living by plunder [...]. Companies of beggars, brigands, and the sick were formed, who filled the streets but above all infested the capital. [...]. Charity at that time always had an ecclesiastical matrix [...]. But the only ones admitted to the charitable institutions of the capital were those born in the viscounty of Paris [...], foreigners and those able to work were not helped and indeed [...] had to leave the city under penalty of arrest [...]. These ordinances were never really applied. The Hotel-Dieu was overflowing with patients [...], the mortality rate was enormous and the system of putting several patients in the same bed was so harmful that it was necessary to decree [...] that if one was on the point of death the others had to be temporarily moved from that bed [...]. To remedy this state of affairs, it was decided to lock up all the vagrants in hospices or rather workhouses. [...]. Arriving in Paris, Renaudot was struck [...] by this mass of unfortunates who had come with hopes of improvement [...] who had spent everything they had in the vain wait for a job that they thought they would find or that someone had promised them [...], from which came begging, thefts, crimes [...], illnesses [...]. When instead they could [...] have gone an hour after their arrival to the office and immediately seen if there were any opportunities for work and, failing that, gone elsewhere[61]. (La Tourette, 1884, pp. 34–50)

---

[60] The relationship between the Protestant Doctor of Medicine (graduated from the University of Montpellier in 1606) Theophrastus Renaudot, and Armand du Plessis, future Cardinal de Richelieu, then only Bishop of Luçon, dates back to 1610. This relationship bore fruit from 1612 when he was appointed ordinary physician to the king. In 1619 he was also appointed General Commissioner of the Poor of the Kingdom. In 1625, when Richelieu's political rise really began, Renaudot left his town of Loudun to settle in Paris and in 1626 or 1628 he converted to Catholicism, it seems out of conviction, as well as convenience.

[61] If John Harris and Michael Todaro (Massachusetts Institute of Technology) had read La Tourette or at least Montaigne, they would have known that the idea at center of their celebrated "model of rural–urban migration" in developing countries (1970) had already been anticipated three and a half centuries earlier. And they would not have gone to Africa to look for the "curious" empirical evidence from which they started: «Throughout many less developed economies of the world, especially those of tropical Africa, a curious economic phenomenon is presently taking place. Despite the existence of positive marginal products in agriculture and significant levels of urban unemployment, rural–urban labor migration not only continues to exist, but indeed, appears to be accelerating» (Harris & Todaro, 1970, p. 126).

The idea, however, was not even Renaudot's, as he himself acknowledged, but Montaigne's (Michel Eyquem de), or his father's if one is to believe the passage cited by Renaudot[62] which is found at the beginning of chapter 34 of the "Essais".

> My late father, a man whose judgment was very wise for someone who had only the help of experience and his natural gifts, once told me that he would have liked there to be in every city a designated and well-marked place where anyone who needed something could go and register their request […]. For example, «I am trying to sell pearls», or «I am looking for pearls to buy», so and so is looking for someone to accompany him to Paris, another would like to hire someone with that qualification, another […] is looking for an employer. […]. Some this, some that, each according to his needs. (Montaigne, 1588/2009, p. 311)

In the archives there are several issues of the "Feuille du Bureau d'Adresse" that Renaudot published weekly with the list of job offers and requests. They go from 1633 to 1654, a year after his death in 1653. Renaudot's initiative also had another content, which extraordinarily anticipated the broader multifunctional character of the future Bourses du Travail, making them true people's houses in fact if not in name. "If the meeting of offer and demand for work was a service provided by the Address Office, it also had the function of intermediating between those who wanted to do charity and those who needed it, and was also able to provide addresses of doctors, surgeons, apothecaries ready to practice their art for free" (Mazauric, 2019, pp. 29–30).

There is no news of the Bureau after 1654, and more than a century had to pass before the idea was revived. On 2 March 1790, almost a year after the conquest of the Bastille, in the most "peaceful" phase of the Revolution, Lord de Corcelles[63] presented a memorandum to the Constituent Assembly to remake the employment service. The project was welcomed by the Assembly, sent to the Department of Public Works where it was archived, and remained a dead letter, but not through carelessness or laziness. The problem was that the proposal, referring to the Address Office of Renaudot, proposed its inspiration, which stemmed from a lack of confidence in the spontaneous balancing functioning of the labor market, so much so that it was appropriate to be supported by an information service. This concept seemed to go against the liberal spirit dominant in that phase, which would soon register a notable victory with the "Le Chapelier Law"[64] promulgated on 14 June 1791. By outlawing any concertation, this law also introduced a ban on trade union activity.[65] It would

[62] Passage cited in the text: Discours sur l'utilité des Bureaux d'adresse, "Mercure François", Tome XXII anno 1637, p. 65.

[63] This is the news, then repeated again and again, that was written for the first time in the history of the Bourse du Travail by Fernand Pelloutier: «Politically, the Bourse du Travail are a century old, that is, from the day (March 2, 1790) when a report (later untraceable) by M. de Corcelles proposed the project» (Pelloutier, 1921, p. 123). Who this lord of Corcelles was (estate and castle in the municipality of Corcelles-en-Beaujolais, Department of the Rhone) is not specified by Palloutier or by anyone else later.

[64] Isaac Le Chapelier, who presented the bill to the Constituent Assembly, was a lawyer in the Parliament of Brittany and a deputy to the States General since 1789.

[65] This prohibition was repealed only on 25 May 1864 with the law that abolished the crime of coalition and with the subsequent law of 21 March 1884 (Waldeck-Rousseau Law) which legalised trade unions.

take half a century for the idea to reappear in 1843, and on the initiative of a liberal economist, Gustave de Molinari, who saw no violation of free trade in creating a private placement center operating according to the commodity exchange system. A few years later, in 1848, the proposal of Adolphe Leullier, a socialist close to the ideas of Louis Blanc, was added,[66] presented to the Paris city hall starting from the observation that in reality private work exchanges existed but functioned badly.

> The Bourse du Travail is not an innovation, it exists: on the Place de l'Hotel de Ville, bricklayers are waiting to be hired, on the Place du Châtelet, painters. All the construction trades have similar places, and all in complete abandonment and without any organization. The Stock Exchange in the courtyard of the Palais-Royal was once in similar conditions, then on the Place des Petits Frères [...]. Our project is therefore nothing more than a step on the road to progress, and it boils down to this: the improvement of the meeting of supply and demand and its centralization. (https://gallica.bnf.fr/ark:/12148/btv1b53014361z/f1.item.zoom)

Neither the Molinari nor the Leullier proposal was followed up, demonstrating that it was difficult to organize the meeting of supply and demand for work (as if it were a commodity like any other) and at the same time maintain the ban on coalitions and union activity. Work is a "conscious commodity" and the certification of excesses of supply over demand (unemployment) or even of demand over supply (vacant positions) have direct effects on the bargaining power of the parties and on the collective conflict actions that arise from it. The Paris Bourse du Travail was thus born only on 3 February 1887, three years after the abolition of the ban on union activity (almost a century after the project of Mr. de Corcelles), to organize the meeting of supply and demand for work, which remained in name, but also for more complex purposes and on the basis of other circumstances. Fernand Pelloutier, a trade unionist, Secretary of the Federation of Bourses du Travail created in 1892, who held the position from 1895 to 1899 when he retired from all activity due to serious illness, explained this. In his "History of the Bourse du Travail" written in 1902 but published posthumously in 1921, Pelloutier reconstructed the difficult relations between the more or less clandestine trade union organization and the socialist-inspired parties before 1887[67] from which the system of the Bourses du Travail acquired particular significance.

---

[66] Louis Jean Joseph Charles Blanc (1811–1882) was a great historian (he wrote, among other things, a monumental History of the French Revolution in 12 volumes) and an important politician: he was an authoritative member of the provisional government after the February Revolution of 1848 and the fall of Louis-Philippe. His ideas were inspired by sympathy for the proletariat, which "had to be saved from the crushing of the bourgeois economy", urging conscience and reason against social injustice. He proposed the progressive socialization of the means of production in a corporative society, but he stood out above all for his eloquence, moral commitment, and uprightness of character, much less in terms of action. A member of the National Assembly in 1871, he sided against the Paris Commune and in 1876 was one of the founders of the French Radical Socialist Party.

[67] A socialist party was founded in France nine years earlier, in 1878, when the Lyon Workers' Congress formed a party under the name of the Federation of the Socialist Workers' Party of France (FPTSF), which had a troubled life. A first split occurred in 1881, when Édouard Vaillant, of Blanquist inspiration, founded the Central Revolutionary Committee (CRC), later the Revolutionary Socialist Party. Vaillant's abandonment left the two factions of the FPTSF facing each other, that of the reformists of Proudhonian inspiration and that of the Guesdists of Marxist inspiration. The

Pelloutier highlighted a fatal divergence. On one side was the prudent trade union orientation toward concrete conquests, a caution due first to the prohibition of association and then, after 1884, to the fear of new punitive norms, but also due to the urgency of concrete results to improve the condition of workers. On the other side was the progressive revolutionary orientation of French socialism obtained even at the cost of repeated splits. So that, on the eve of 1887, Pelloutier, siding with the trade union associations, harshly criticized the socialists.

> In treating workers' associations with contempt [...], they who affirmed the impossibility of any conciliation between labour and capital under capitalism, they who proclaimed the inevitability of class struggle, did not realize that [...] since the members of the trade unions were sensitive to concrete experiences rather than to party formulas, perhaps it would have been politically appropriate to know how to manage them. So that, on the day they joined socialism, they would strengthen the party's organization through their own organization. As a result of this error, the gap between the Party and the workers' associations widened more and more. From time to time some wise socialist called for an agreement, but the increasingly evident failure of sectarianism and the dissensions introduced into the unions by discussions on electoral action distracted them from a rapprochement [...]. As for the party leaders, they maintained that the unions were subordinate to them, since economic emancipation, they said, should not be the cause, but the consequence of political emancipation. And so the efforts made by the two forms of proletarian organization remained distinct, only to later become antagonistic. (Pelloutier, 1921, pp. 101–102)

The Bourses du Travail system took on the onerous but indispensable task of finding some remedy for such a gap between union and party.

5.7.2 Between Gradualism and Revolution

The lack of synergy between the party and the union resulted in both being rendered impotent: the party, waiting for the conditions for the revolution, was reduced to noting the poor results obtained through parliamentary means, and the union was reduced to noting the poor results of its moderation in demands.

> While the various socialist currents, divided since the Saint-Etienne congress of 1882 until the fragmentation, [...] registered the reformist impotence of parliamentary action, the workers' organizations began to recognize how chimerical their projects of conciliation

---

conflict grew inexorably until the Congress of Saint-Étienne (25–31 September 1882). On Monday 26 September, the 23 delegates of Guesde and Lafargue, who had been subjected to violent criticism, left the hall (where the other 82 delegates remained) and met the same day in Roanne, constituting themselves as the first congress of the Workers' Party (PO). In 1893, the Workers' Party became the French Workers' Party (POF), which merged in 1901 with the Blanquist Revolutionary Socialist Party and the Revolutionary Communist Alliance to form the Revolutionary Socialist Unity, which became the Socialist Party of France (PSdF) in 1902. In 1905, the Socialist Party of France merged with the French Socialist Party led by Jean Jaurès to form the French Section of the Workers' International—SFIO (Second International). The French Communist Party was established in 1920, following the split of a large majority of the SFIO which formed a new party, the French Section of the Communist International—SFIC (Third International) the following year called the Communist Party.

> between worker and employer were. These arbitration boards, on which they had placed so many hopes, what had they produced? Nothing. The bosses refused even to discuss working conditions. Even the strike, which some unions had condemned because it could compromise French industry without benefits for the workers, had returned to being the necessary weapon, and the declaration of strike was not only justified, but even became obligatory since the workers were threatened with wage reductions. (Pelloutier, 1921, p. 103)

This was the condition of the proletarian movement in the 15 years following the repression of the Paris Commune of 1871 carried out by the Thiers government with unprecedented ferocity.[68] After this premise, Fernand Pelloutier described the nature and purposes of the Bourses du Travail that had the task of remedying this impotence. This is the text underlining the decisive passages that represent an effective summary of the historical program of the people's houses of type five. It is all there: the coming together for the common good, the alternative proletarian culture, the collective action, the network of different initiatives so that they support each other. One may note, in particular, the organic local unification of the trade unions operated through the Bourses du Travail, which were very different from the German Union Houses that, as seen, remained only condominiums.

> La Bourse du Travail, a <u>meeting place for workers' organizations</u>, would have the first result of establishing <u>solid and permanent relationships</u> among them, that is, allowing them that <u>understanding</u>, that mutual <u>education</u>, the absence of which has been the insurmountable obstacle to their development and effectiveness up to now. Thanks to Bourse du Travail, workers could <u>unite</u>, first of all <u>by similar professions</u> in order to protect and defend their professional <u>interests, compared with the particular resources</u> of their sector, the duration of their work and the rate of their wages, and if this duration were excessive, if this rate were miserable, discover how much a suspension of work would increase their strength [...]. They could also meet, <u>without distinction of profession</u>, to reflect on their condition, identify the general data of the economic problem, study the mechanism of exchanges, in short, search in the current social system for the elements of a <u>new system</u>, and at the same time avoid the <u>incoherent efforts</u> made up to now that have ended up delivering the disarmed workers to the political, financial and moral power of Capital. The Bourse du Travail therefore legitimized the rosiest hopes and no one doubted that it would bring about a <u>real revolution</u> in the trade union economy. And what ambitions did we conceive when we saw the birth of Bourses du Travail of Béziers, Montpellier, This, Lyon, Marseille, Saint-Etienne, Nîmes, Toulouse, Bordeaux, Toulon, Cholet? [...]. The services provided by the Bourse du Travail can be divided into four classes: (1) the <u>mutuality</u> service, which includes placement, unemployment benefits, assistance for travelling workers, accident assistance, (2) <u>education</u> services: library, information office, social museum, professional courses, general education courses, (3) the <u>propaganda</u> service: statistical and economic studies, creation of new agricultural and maritime industrial union sections, cooperative societies, [...], (4) the "<u>resistance</u>" service: organization of strikes and striker aid funds, as well as demonstrations against bills that could damage economic activity. [...]. The idea of <u>uniting</u>

[68] The Paris Commune of 1871 arose from the uprising of March 18 against the government of Thiers in a last-ditch attempt not to submit to the conditions imposed by victorious Prussia, and then inspired in its government action (credit, cooperatives) by Proudhonian principles. The Commune had little support from the groups adhering to the International, even if Marx later exalted the movement as the first concrete seizure of power by the working class. Thiers, who had taken refuge with the legal government in Versailles, unleashed a repression of unprecedented ferocity: 20,000 of the rebels died during the struggle or were shot. The courts decreed thousands of convictions and deportations. The period from May 21 to 28, 1871 was called the "Bloody Week".

> these Bourse du Travail was inevitable. [...]. The Paris Bourse du Travail sponsored the idea, submitted it to the congress held in Saint-Etienne on February 7, 1892, and obtained the creation of the French Federation of Bourse du Travail. The Federation [...] had all the elements to be successful. It was made up of local entities that combined the attractiveness of novelty with the advantage of responding to a need, and whose administration was personally and directly interested in the development of trade unions and the progress of economic studies. Consequently, not only did it ensure support for local entities, but in turn the Federal Committee found in these local entities a fruitful and incessant collaboration. (Pelloutier, 1921, pp. 113–115, 141)

5.7.3 People's Houses of the Fifth Type

Taking into account, as Pelloutier's preface makes clear, that the system of Bourses du Travail had remained the main if not the only effective organization of the proletarian movement, they were true people's houses of the fifth type: spaces that establish a collective subjectivity, in which users and actors are activists and unionized workers, with their own strategies, for collectively specified, pursued, and obtained objectives. A people's house that takes on symbolic value as an image "of a new system" and that possesses the reality of an acting community. Pelloutier even reports the annual costs: repayment of loans for construction 1,500 francs, heating, lighting, and maintenance 500, personnel expenses 3,000, for a total of 5,000 francs. With the addition of expenses for assistance and help, irregular expenses depending on the circumstances, which could reach an equal amount, or in total about 10,000 francs, which was the equivalent of seven years of work of a worker, with deviations of more or less 20% depending on the size (Pelloutier, 1921, pp. 226, 287). One notes the absence of a "fifth service", that of entertainment which was instead notable in the houses of the people of Belgium (and in Italy). In the period between 1887 and 1901, the Bourses du Travail thus characterized, "through a series of brilliant institutions, reflecting the state of mind of the workers' groups on which they in turn reacted, had given substance to the desire of the workers to shake off all tutelage and to draw from themselves the elements of their emancipation" (Pelloutier, 1921, p 247). Their quantitative development was notable, as is documented by the following data (Fig. 5.16).

In 1901, the maximum development of the Bourses du Travail was recorded: there were 74, one in every industrial center of any importance. The number of registered workers reached over 300 thousand, a share of 62% calculated on the total number of unionized workers, around 80% if calculated on the unionized workers of the centers large enough to support the costs of a Bourse. After 1901, they continued to carry out their functions until 1913, when—absorbed into the CGT—they lost their role as political-union agents in their own right to become a peripheral structure of the General Confederation of Labor. Political-union agents is a term fully authorized by historiography even if fragmentary,[69] which leaves no doubt about it. Although

[69] "Historians who have studied the Bourse du Travail have treated them in a partial way, emphasizing their decisive role in the structuring of the workers' movement, without however making the

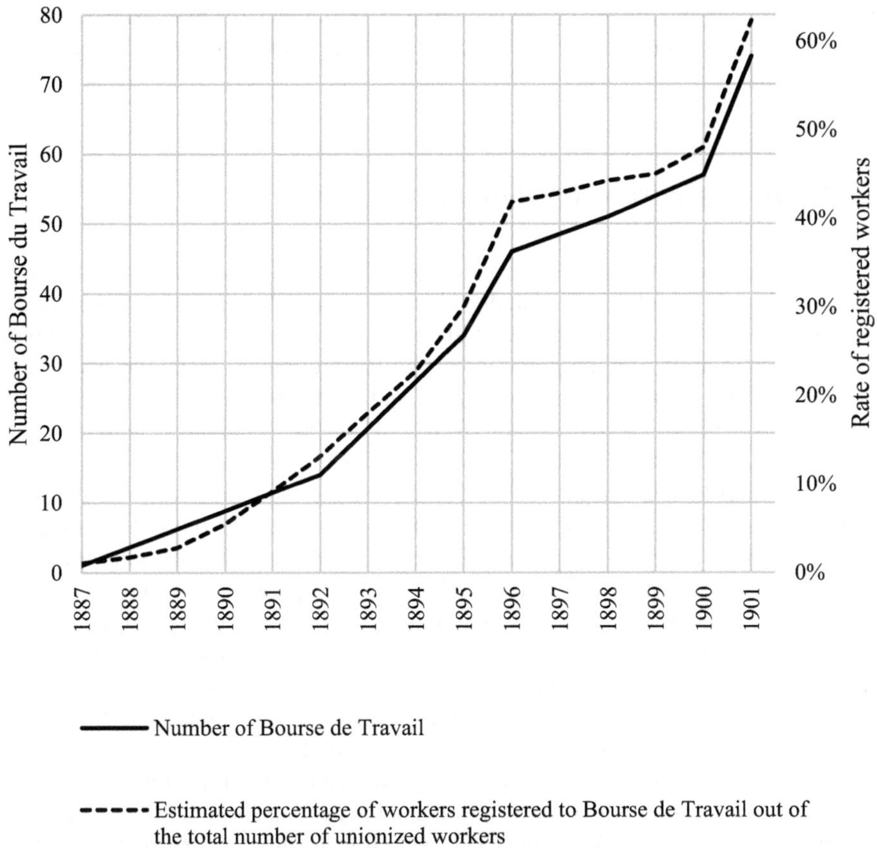

Fig. 5.16 Number of bourses du Travail in France and estimate of the rate of registered workers in the total number of unionized workers. *Source* Figure obtained by processing data from Pelloutier (1921)

in Pelloutier's "History" the trade union-demanding dimension emerges dominant, the political-cultural dimension was equally notable, also indicated by the Secretary of the Federation, albeit in the synthetic but significant terms of "search in the current social system for the elements of a new system" and "mutual education". The deciphering of this formula, permitted by this historiography, brings to the fore the important topic of technical–economic-social and ultimately political "paradigms". But before giving due attention to this topic, it is necessary to remember that the extraordinary growth of the Bourses du Travail took place at the same time in which

history of the National Federation a true object of study. Analyses focused on trade unionism at the micro-social scale [...] are rare [...]. Since the early 1990s, other research has revisited the Bourse du Travail through the prism of economic history and cultural or urban history, but without making it their central object. For this reason, the Bourse, as a collective movement, are still looking for their 'biographer'" (Hamelin, 2011, p. 24).

France was experiencing the fastest economic development, the greatest inequalities and the specific systemic contradictions, a phase that could have been "objectively" revolutionary.

5.7.4 An Objectively Revolutionary Phase

France had reached an unprecedented inequality between a tiny minority of very rich people and everyone else, an inequality that far exceeded even that recorded in the years before the Revolution. By 1910, the richest 1% of the population had come to own 55% of all private property. After the Revolution, in 1800, the percentage was 43%. It then took more than a century, and with other revolutionary uprisings in between (1815, 1830, 1848, 1870–1871, 1905–1906),[70] but the system managed to "betray the Revolution", to use Piketty's expression, or—from the rich's point of view—to repair its egalitarian wound. But it had gone too far. So much so that then the share of the rich began to decline, with strong accentuation from 1912, during the First World War, the post-war period and the Second World War: the minimum was reached in 1990 with 16% while today it is 23%. As regards income, the scenario is similar, even if less marked. The income of the 1% of the wealthiest had reached the highest share in 1910 with 22% (18% in 1800), it fell to 9% in 1990.[71]

The level of inequality reached in 1910 demonstrated the manifest dysfunctionality of the political-social structure, in particular with respect to the greater distributive balance claimed in vain with the strike wave of 1906. In that year there were 1300 strikes with a total of 438 thousand participants and an average duration of 19 days for each strike. The demonstration and the general strike for the eight hours, carefully prepared for weeks by the CGT, were transformed in Paris by the Minister of the Interior Georges Clemenceau into a battle: 20,000 soldiers, including 5,000 on horseback, 36,000 policemen, two dead, hundreds wounded, 800 arrests. The strong development of proletarian organizations was underway, emblematically represented by the First of May and the "Charter of Amiens", 13 October 1906, the manifesto of

---

[70] Charles Tilly distinguished between "revolutions" and "rebellions", the former as a refusal of the subalterns to integrate into the system, the latter as a sometimes serious malaise in the process of integration. According to Tilly, the uprisings of 1789 1815 1830 1848, 1870–1871 have generally been considered revolutionary, those that took place between the end of the nineteenth century and the first two decades of the twentieth century have been considered rebellions. But he added: «the period 1905–1907 does not have such a reputation as a phase of crisis in national politics [...]. However, those years saw the definitive end of the state religion, the arrival of the Socialist Party, the attempted general strike of May Day, [...], the open confrontation between union leaders and the government, a vast mobilization of winemakers in the South. [...]. The North played a central role in the wave of strikes of 1906: miners, weavers, dockers, mechanics all united. [...]. The demonstrations of 1906 appeared to demonstrate the revolutionary solidarity of the working class» (Tilly 1986, pp. 306–307).

[71] http://piketty.pse.ens.fr/files/ideology/ppt.

revolutionary syndicalism[72] of the CGT Congress. There was also a precise syndrome of the ruling class as "fear of the people" in a society in full transformation.

> Faced with the growing influence of the CGT, which worried them, Clemenceau and the republicans forcibly broke the strikes and amnestied the condemned in a politically cynical way, [...] which testifies to the fear they had of the people, not new, but which was confirmed and reconfigured precisely at the moment when the social movement was structuring itself and industrialization was accelerating. (Gacon, 2015, p. 19)

But the level of inequality was also dysfunctional for the strategic objectives of the ruling classes themselves. It was accompanied by an exceptional increase in foreign investments, the fund of which was already a high 9% of the national wealth in 1900 and reached 15% in 1914 (Nouailhat, 1979, p. 40). The share of foreign investments in savings, a comparable figure for different countries, between 1905 and 1914 was on average 49% for the United Kingdom at the height of its imperial power, 7% for Germany and 17% for France (Daudin et al., 2010, p. 10). In 1914, in terms of foreign assets minus domestic assets of foreign holders, the shares in GDP were, 191% in the United Kingdom, 125% in France, 58% in Germany, −10% in the United States. The rich, who had become very rich, were anything but patriotic. They invested a lot abroad, despite paying little tax: the marginal tax rate on the incomes of the richest French was zero in 1914 (UK 9%, Germany 3%, Japan 22%, USA 8%). Low taxes paid by the rich in the face of the explosive growth of the overall tax due to the construction of an increasingly imposing public apparatus, meant heavy taxation on the middle and lower classes. In 1800 the total tax corresponded to just 100 h of work per capita, but it reached 330 in 1914 and then stabilized at that level, surpassed only

[72] The text of the motion approved with 834 votes in favor, 8 against, one blank ballot, is this. "The Confederal Congress of Amiens, in confirming Article 2 of the CGT Statute, states: The CGT brings together, beyond any political school, all workers conscious of the need to fight for the disappearance of wage earners and employers. The Congress believes that this declaration constitutes a recognition of the class struggle, which pits workers in revolt on economic grounds against all forms of exploitation and oppression, both material and moral, implemented by the capitalist class to the detriment of the working class. The Congress specifies this theoretical statement through the following points. In the daily work of making demands, trade unionism pursues the coordination of workers' efforts, the increase in workers' well-being through the implementation of immediate improvements, such as the reduction of working hours, the increase of wages, etc. But this commitment is only one aspect of the practice of trade unionism, which prepares the integral emancipation that can only be achieved through the expropriation of the capitalists, advocates the general strike as a means of action, and believes that the trade union, today an organism of resistance, will be, in the future, the grouping responsible for production and distribution, the basis of social reorganization. The Congress declares that this double commitment, in the present and for the future, arises from the condition of wage earners that weighs on the working class and that makes it a duty for all workers, whatever their opinions or their political or philosophical tendencies, to belong to the essential grouping constituted by the trade union. Consequently, as regards individuals, the Congress affirms that, outside the corporate grouping, trade union members are totally free to participate in the forms of struggle corresponding to their philosophical or political conceptions and limits itself to demanding, in exchange, that opinions professed outside are not introduced into the trade union. As regards the organizations, the Congress declares that, in order for trade unionism to achieve the maximum result, economic action must be directed directly against the employers, since the confederated organizations, as trade union groupings, do not have to worry about the parties and sects that, externally and collaterally, can freely pursue social transformation".

in the 1960s (Tilly, 1986, p. 62). And this was precisely the problem. On the one hand, much capital was exported and caused a lack of jobs that would have been useful for providing answers to the social question; on the other hand, to also keep together an increasingly divided country, it was necessary to strengthen the public apparatus, the cost of which, however, was not supported by those who were or felt threatened by the social conflict. The solution, which was reached after two wars and 2 million dead proletarians, could only be one, that is, a new structure for France in which "the conflict ended with the partial admission of organized workers within the confines of the national power structure" (Tilly, 1986, p. 388).

5.7.5 "Federalist" Socialism

The development of the Bourses du Travail was part of this scenario of a real structural crisis in full accelerated growth from an economic point of view. They were the central element of those particular institutions that were supposed to allow a realistic and desirable new system in a short time that was considered "utopian" due to a series of circumstances that were anything but inevitable. It was the system hoped for by Pierre-Joseph Proudhon, the French philosopher who supported a social revolution that transcended individualism but not statist collectivism. Several protagonists of French "revolutionary syndicalism" and of the French section of the First International were inspired by Proudhon.[73]

> Unlike Smith or Marx, these men were enmeshed in the lives of the working classes of their day: Proudhon, trained as a typographer, was thoroughly familiar with and clearly influenced by the semi-clandestine world of trade fraternities and mutual aid societies that survived the Revolution and flourished in France in the decades before 1848. [...] In contrast to Marx and Engels, who had little popular following until late in the century, their ideas often inspired

[73] Among the socialist leaders, one can mention the first three correspondents for France of the Socialist International: Henri Tolain (1828–1897), Ernest Édouard Fribourg (1834–1903), Charles Mathieu Limousin (1840–1909). Tolain was a bronze engraver, active in workers' societies. In 1864 he drafted the Manifesto of the Sixty, a program of social and political demands. In the same year, on 28 September, he participated in the founding congress of the First International in London and assumed an important role in the French section (January 1865, Paris, rue des Gravilliers 44). At the Geneva congress of 1867 he presented the "Mémoire français des délégués". At the Brussels Congress (6–13 September 1868, Belgian, English, Swiss, German, French, an Italian and a Spanish delegates) he defended the Proudhonian positions on mutualism which were defeated and approved the thesis on the socialization of the means of production proposed by Marx (absent). Ernest Fribourg, an embroidery designer, was a correspondent for the periodical "La Mutualité Revue du Travail", for the cooperative and mutual aid societies directed by Jules Vinçard. Charles Limousin, a typographer, one of the signatories of the Manifesto of the Sixty, was director of the "Tribune Ouvrière", editor of the "International Bulletin of Cooperative Societies", monthly and then weekly, of "La Liberté" and of the "Journal of the International Workingmen's Association" of Geneva. Among the trade unionists, one can at least remember Leon Jouhaux, a worker in a match factory, who joined the union at the age of 16 and became national secretary of the CGT on 12 July 1909. There he defended the theses of revolutionary trade unionism and was the protagonist of the subsequent evolution of the Confederation toward a more "pragmatic" trade unionism.

> or precipitated projects of co-operative production. Yet precisely because of this attachment to particular communities and epochs, the work of all [...them] presupposes knowledge of a context of political idioms and conditions of production which the writings of the well-schooled theoreticians of mass production do not. (Sabel & Zeitlin, 1985, pp. 142–143)

The new system of mutual education, as a "republic of independent craftsmen linked by dependence on one another's skills" (Sabel & Zeitlin, 1985, p. 142) could only be born with a revolution. But not necessarily only after the system of large enterprises had exhausted itself due to its contradictions. This was the Marxist idea which, however, did not agree very well with the reality of the observed facts, for example, in the United States.

> [The Marxist idea was that] changes in markets and innovations in special machine design continually reinforced each other [...]. [...However] the chief problem for the narrow-track idea [...] in that from the 1840s, successive waves of immigration made labour more abundant than in the preceding decades. Yet this influx of cheap hands did not, as the notion of market determination would suggest, provoke, any substitution of labour for capital in the organization of production. It seems more plausible to argue, in fact, that in industries such as steel or shoes, the technology shaped the use of labour, not vice versa. [...And] it is politics and not the immanent characteristics of the technologies which will decide how the new machines are designed. And if that is so, then a deeper understanding of the historical alternatives to mass production is one way to ensure that current possibilities are not unwittingly dismissed as utopian simply because they did not win out in the past. (Sabel & Zeitlin, 1985, pp. 171–172, 176)

In fact, it was not only large-scale enterprise and mass production that enabled technological innovation.

> It is a habit of classical political thought and a lesson of experience that mechanization had as its precondition capitalism, and as its consequence mass production. But our account of an alternative form of industrial organization is evidence that this chain is a restatement of what happened, not the summary expression of an inevitable logic of interest and efficiency. Even within the western European capitalist property regime surveyed here, technology appears to be more malleable and its connection to politics far more complex than the pervasively influential writings of classical political economy allow. A broader survey of abandoned alternatives to Anglo-American industrialization would likely reveal [...] units of production [...] that are typically small and meet differentiated demand by use of flexible technologies. Workers and employers [...] form a collective of producers which controls machines and institutions that realize economies of scale. This collective provides credit and insurance to firms and workers to cushion them against reverses in fluctuating markets; and it polices competition to ensure respect for the rules of continual innovation. [...] If Proudhon's claims that competition and productive association were complementary, not mutually exclusive, forms of economic behaviour and that machinery could extend the range of human skill rather than expedite its decomposition seemed to Marx [...] Just those conditions Proudhon could take so much for granted that he felt no need to elaborate his understanding of them, and Marx regarded as contradictions in terms. (Sabel & Zeitlin, 1985, pp. 174–175, 143–144)

Already in the 1910s, the strength of industry in the United States managed to enchant the capitalists and then also the trade unionists of all the industrialized countries. But there were no reasons for technical and organizational superiority compared to the model of collaboration between small businesses. Instead, it was the victory of mass production in an era in which mass consumption took on an irresistible symbolic and ideological value.

> By the 1920s [...], the sheer material success of mass production in practice made it almost irresistible as a paradigm. Leading industrialists the world over were mesmerized by it. But the true measure of its attractive power was not the fascination it held for those to whom it promised wealth and power, but rather its attraction to those schooled to detest mass production: workers raised in the craft tradition. Thus, few demonstrations of the appeal of American ideas are so convincing as the story of a leader of the reformist French socialists, a skilled metalworker by trade and a mutualist by political profession, who visited Detroit in the inter-war years, worked in automobile factories, and returned to France a convinced believer in Fordist techniques. It was almost as if Proudhon himself had awoken from a sleep of fifty years to discover not only that the world had enacted the ideas of his opponents, but that he approved of what they had done. Sabel & Zeitlin, 1985, pp. 173–174)

These considerations of Sabel and Zeitlin were not and are not their particular points of view. On the contrary. One can read in the celebrated work of Kenneth Tucker published eleven years later:

> Sabel and Zeitlin, in their influential article "Historical Alternatives to Mass Production," discussed the triumph in twentieth-century Europe of a vision of the future based on mass production and corporate economics rather than small-scale economic organization. Echoing the view of a growing number of historians, they argued that capitalism did not follow necessary laws of development. The belief in the inevitability and superiority of mass production represented only an ideological and factual victory. (Tucker, 1996, p. 3)

5.7.6 *Affirmation of Mass Production*

All this fascination failed to consider that another powerful reason had made mass production more efficient in the specific conditions of the United States. Ford in Detroit had used Taylor and not vice versa. He had introduced the standardization and ease of assembly of automobile components making the assembly line and the division of tasks possible because: (1) he had a workforce that, speaking 50 different languages, could not be coordinated by themselves because they did not understand each other,[74] (2) because he wanted to produce a car (the Model T) that a worker

[74] "A 1915 survey revealed that Highland Park [10 km north of downtown Detroit, where there was the Ford plant with 14,000 workers that produced 400,000 cars a year, 45% of all cars produced in the United States] workers spoke more than fifty languages and that many of them could barely speak English. How could this army of strangers cooperate to produce a greater volume of a complex product (the Model T) than any company had previously imagined—and do it with consistent accuracy. The answer lay in taking the idea of the division of labor to its ultimate extreme. The skilled fitter in Ford's craft-production plant of 1908 had gathered all the necessary parts, obtained tools from the tool room, repaired them if necessary, performed the complex fitting and assembly job for the entire vehicle, then checked over his work before sending the completed vehicle to the shipping department. In stark contrast, the assembler on Ford's mass-production line had only one task—to put two nuts on two bolts or perhaps to attach one wheel to each car. He didn't order parts, procure his tools, repair his equipment, inspect for quality, or even understand what the workers on either side of him were doing. Rather, he kept his head down and thought about other things. The fact that he might not even speak the same language as his fellow assemblers or the foreman was irrelevant to the success of Ford's system. [...]. Someone, of course, did have to think about how all the parts came together and just what each assembler should do. This was the task for a newly

with a good salary could buy,[75] to be produced in an enormous number of units, (3) because he wanted it to be simple enough to allow farmers to repair it using only the skills they already had for the maintenance of farm machinery.[76] These were specific conditions in the United States. So much so that when Toyota went to Detroit to visit the factory, upon returning home he concluded with his collaborators that the Ford system in Japan could not work, hence "Toyotism" as a new production system.

> In the spring of 1950, a young Japanese engineer, Eiji Toyoda, set out on a three-month pilgrimage to Ford's Rouge plant in Detroit. [...]. Eiji was not an average engineer, either in ability or ambition. After carefully studying every inch of the vast Rouge, then the largest and most efficient manufacturing facility in the world, Eiji wrote back to headquarters that he «thought there were some possibilities to improve the production system». But simply copying and improving the Rouge proved to be hard work. Back at home in Nagoya, Eiji Toyoda and his production genius, Taiichi Ohno, soon concluded [...] that mass production could never work in Japan. From this tentative beginning were born what Toyota came to call the Toyota Production System and, ultimately, lean production. (Womack et al., 1990, pp. 47–48)

Toyotism is characterized, compared to Fordism, by the reduction of manufacturing defects during assembly and not delegated to a specialized department located downstream of the assembly line, by the drastic reduction of warehouse costs for parts and components, by the drastic reduction of design times for new models, and by a different subcontracting system based on concentric circles and not on horizontal organization. To achieve these objectives, the organization of work abandons fragmentation, instead valorizing versatility, autonomy, and degree of responsibility of each worker. The reason for the introduction of this new system was that in Japan: "(1)

---

created professional, the industrial engineer. Similarly, someone had to arrange for the delivery of parts to the line, usually a production engineer who designed conveyor belts or chutes to do the job. Housecleaning workers were sent around. With this separation of labor, the assembler required only a few minutes of training. Moreover, he was relentlessly disciplined by the pace of the line, which speeded up the slow and slowed down the speedy. The foreman—formerly the head of a whole area of the factory with wide-ranging duties and responsibilities but now reduced to a semiskilled checker—could spot immediately any slacking off or failure to perform the assigned task. As a result, the workers on the line were as replaceable as the parts on the car. [...] In 1908, on the eve of the introduction of the Model T, a Ford assembler's average task cycle—the amount of time he worked before repeating the same operations—totaled 514 min, or 8.56 h. [...]. By August of 1913, just before the moving assembly line was introduced, the task cycle for the average Ford assembler had been reduced from 514 to 2.3 min" (Womack et al., 1990, pp. 29–30, 25–26).

[75] In 1920, a car cost $300, and a Ford worker was paid $5–6 a day. The competition was making $2,000 cars and paying workers $3–4 a day (working an hour more than Ford). Higher wages and shorter hours were Ford's solution in early 1914 to avoid what he saw as the risk of unionization of his workforce as well as his very high turnover due to the repetitive, intense, and alienating work on the assembly lines. He had a sharp drop in turnover and kept unions from gaining a foothold in the Ford Company until 1941.

[76] "To appeal to his target market of average consumers, Ford had also designed unprecedented ease of operation and maintainability into his car. He assumed that his buyer would be a farmer with a modest tool kit and the kinds of mechanical skills needed for fixing farm machinery. So the Model T's owner's manual, which was written in question-and-answer form, explained in sixty-four pages how owners could use simple tools to solve any of the 140 problems likely to crop up with the car" (Womack et al., 1990, p. 28).

The war-ravaged Japanese economy was starved for capital and for foreign exchange, meaning that massive purchases of the latest Western production technology were quite impossible; (2) The outside world was full of huge motor-vehicle producers [...] ready to defend their established markets against Japanese exports; (3) The domestic market was tiny and demanded a wide range of vehicles; (4) The native Japanese workforce, as Toyota and other firms soon learned, was no longer willing to be treated as a variable cost or as interchangeable parts. Furthermore, in Japan there were no 'guest workers' that is immigrants willing to put up with substandard working conditions in return for high pay, or minorities with limited occupational choice" (Womack et al., 1990, pp. 48–49).

The causes of Fordism-Taylorism and in Japan of the different Toyotism were therefore not technical but geopolitical: in the United States the large size of the country and the internal market, agricultural mechanization and the large multi-ethnic industrial cities; in Japan the small size of the country and the market and the tradition of "human respect". Geopolitical also in the sense underlined by Stefan Link (2020), that is, in the context of international economic and political competition coinciding with the decline of Great Britain as the center of the global system. Without the contribution of the United States to the defeat of the Central Empires in the First World War, Fordism would probably not have had the strength to impose itself as a paradigm of industrialism in Europe.

Having thus clarified the theoretical and factual background, it is clear that with the Bourses du Travail the proletarian movement in France between the nineteenth and twentieth centuries also posed the question of workers' education and culture in a particular way. Not yet misled by the ideology of alleged scientistic determinism, they were well aware that it was not just a question of forces and structures, but also, if not above all, of knowledge and conviction. Proletarian education could therefore not be the learning of contents and canons of the dominant culture, as in part in England, and not its "translation" and selection as in Germany, but a real new construction directly drawn from the experience of work and struggle. David Hamelin (2011), who has long dealt with this theme, has written:

> Overall, what emerges from my research is that [in historiography] there has long been [...] a simplification of the role and activities of the Bourse du Travail [...]. On the education and instruction of workers, the analysis has often privileged the texts of theorists to the detriment of concrete achievements [...]. Studies have only partially taken into account the historical depth, the progress, the numerous and sometimes lively debates, and the concrete achievements [...]. Instead, these were processes that contributed to building the foundations of an integral education, combining adult and child education, without any intermediation other than that of the workers themselves and without losing the perspective aimed at establishing a new social order. Processes to be evaluated in the light of a context characterized by the rebirth of a marginalized social movement after the fall of the Paris Commune and by the competition between socialisms, but also in the light of the ability of these labour exchanges to demonstrate flexibility, inventiveness and depth in their educational approach. (Hamelin, 2011, pp. 24–25)

In this sense, the term used for that phase, "revolutionary syndicalism", is fully justified. As is the thesis of its defeat on ideological and factual grounds. This defeat was not inevitable, however. In France, a revolutionary perspective of a "federalist socialism of professionalized workers" between the nineteenth and twentieth centuries, was a real possibility. And it was inscribed in the proletarian culture of the Bourses du Travail. It was defeated by the ideology of large-scale Fordist industry through the support of European capitalism but also of the workers' organizations themselves. A singular paradox actually occurred. In this regard, it is necessary to return to the weaknesses of the union and the party that have been mentioned, and the crisis of the revolutionary perspective after the repression of the Commune. The Bourse du Travail system had responded to these weaknesses on the concrete terrain of facts, but not enough on the theoretical-ideological terrain. Thus, when the union had got back on its feet by overcoming its weaknesses, in fact, its ideological weaknesses that had not been overcome led it to essentially renounce the ideas and culture of the Bourse du Travail that had saved it.

> These widespread ideas, combined with the weakness of its revolutionary theory [...] helped lead the CGT to gradually replace the vision of a federalist socialism of skilled workers with an image of industrial society like that of many elites. [...]. An integral component of this outlook, shared by syndicalists and many republican and capitalist elites, was that positivistic science offered an insight into the natural order of production, and could lead to a healthier and more productive workplace. Syndicalists' adoption of this vocabulary was not simply imposed on them, but derived in large part from an elaboration of their own labour-based discourse in the context of a crisis of revolutionary ideology and belief. The experience of World War I reinforced this productivist doctrine. (Tucker, 1996, p. 10)

5.7.7 Conclusion

The case of France, after those of England, Germany, and Belgium, seems to provide confirmation of the "model" of the people's houses—alternative proletarian culture. The general determinants, in particular the singular times of French industrial development, not unrelated to the internal divisions of the workers' movement, had ambiguous effects on the formation of an alternative proletarian culture. After the devastating crisis of the 1870s, the Paris Commune and its repression, the party was reduced to noting the poor results obtained through parliamentary means and the union the equally poor results of its moderation in demands. The spread of the Bourses du Travail can be considered a remedy to this impotence, in a context of accelerated economic growth and a strong increase in inequalities that were dysfunctional for the interests of the ruling class itself. The local determinants interacted to the point of giving rise to a potentially revolutionary perspective from below for a "federalist socialism". In the years of their growth and up until the eve of the First World War, the Bourses du Travail were fully-fledged collective agents and places for the development of a true alternative proletarian culture, as they were integrated or meshed with the social, economic, and political reality of their specific territory. This meshing was inscribed in the long elaboration and realization of their original function as employment services, objectively and absolutely linked to the local labor market. It was from this origin and the slow maturation of related ideas and practices

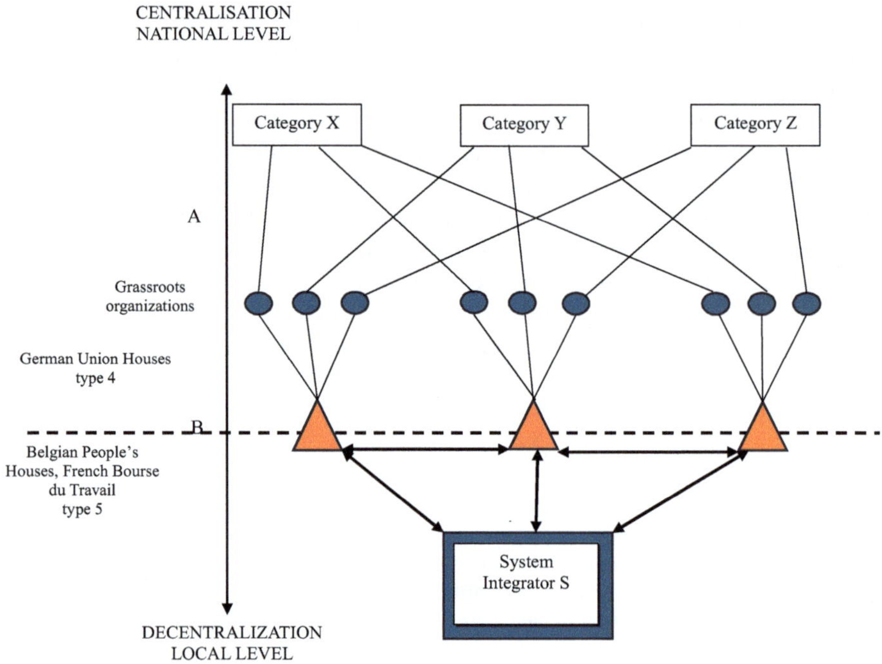

Fig. 5.17 Systems of proletarian organizations

that their functions developed, until they constituted the central institution of that possible federalist socialism, even if it was later considered utopian. Central institutions, like the Bourses du Travail, supported each other, forming a "system" through their Federation.

To fix in a scheme what emerged in the German, Belgian, and French cases, a graphic representation is useful (Fig. 5.17).

The meso-situation of the Belgian People's Houses and the French Bourses du Travail was defined by the fact that they were nodes of an integrated system, while for the German Trade Union Houses it could be said that the system was only composite. The difference was also linked to a stronger meshing in the territorial realities in the Belgian and French cases. In the German case, the Trade Union Houses, as a rule larger and above all located in large cities, did not have the same meshing. In terms of strength from the point of view of the elaboration of an alternative proletarian culture and of the social and political impact, it could be said that in the case of the German Trade Union Houses the system had the strength of the sum of its components. In the case of the Belgian People's Houses and the French Bourses du Travail, this strength of the system, once a threshold was exceeded, was instead greater than the sum of its components. A threshold demonstrated by the fact that the times were long due to the complicated process of political-social maturation that was at its basis. Instead, the German hierarchical system had allowed the setting up of Union Houses quite quickly, even though they were large and expensive.

The place of the meso-systemic location of collective action is, therefore, the territory when the emancipation of the subaltern is a question, as Pelloutier writes, of acting within a complex of people who must understand and educate each other, between jobs or professions that must reflect on their condition, in a network that supports their organization. In the Fordist-Taylorist structure the "place" was instead the factory on one side and the nation on the other. Also from this point of view, the experience of the people's houses can be useful today, when the need to become aware of the precarious, dispersed, destructured condition of the great majority emerges again. The synergy between people and work and the synergy between grassroots organizations and "integrator" from the network probably require the territory again: for face-to-face dialogue and for "the reciprocal experience of truth in collective confrontation for the common good".

5.8 People's Houses in Italy

It has already been said that the people's houses in Italy were ahead of their time, being born at the beginning of the industrial takeoff and not 20 years later, as in Belgium and France. Reading the numerous monographs available gives the impression that the ideas and creations were imitated, establishing themselves in Italy despite the delay in development compared to that of Northern Europe. This importation of ideas and practices in conditions different from those of the copied "models" accentuated the eclecticism of the people's houses in Italy.

5.8.1 Imitation Adaptation Differentiation

In Italy, a double idea was particularly evident at the basis of the people's houses, even though they were two apparently irreconcilable ideas: seats of the revolutionary organization, homes of "non-integrated integration".[77] Returning to Rinaldo Rigola's autobiography, one reads that in Piedmont, still in the last years of the nineteenth century, for activists and executives "on the doctrine that questions property [...] there was no possibility of misunderstanding. [...] they all agreed on the anti-proprietor

[77] "The functional problem of the proletariat that is oriented towards integration is probably the following: integrated, it will not be revolutionary, but not being able to feel at home within capitalist society and being oriented towards qualitative values, community values, it will be necessary to create within bourgeois society a sort of society of its own where it can feel at home. In fact, the working class cannot feel at ease like the small shopkeeper or like the capitalist, and it will integrate much more easily if it can do so on the political and economic level, but by possessing a small world all for itself that, on the ideological level, opposes this bourgeois society" (Goldman, 1978, p. 175).

plan. [...]. Who could have resisted such a seductive theory?" (Rigola, 1930, pp. 84, 85). On the other hand, such "seductive theory" seemed indispensable to the activists because "the workers' struggles with the related defeats [of the 1860s and 1870s] had [...] led the majority of the people I lived in contact with to believe [...] that there was an iron law, according to which the workers would always break their horns every time they tried to do differently from what the bosses wanted—the rich are made to command and the poor to serve" (Rigola, 1930, p. 69). In this way Rigola established a cause-effect relationship between workers' resignation and activists' revolutionism, with dominant emotional postures on both sides: "seductive theory" and "iron law". Vigorous contradictions or ambiguities have been seen in various contexts, even those that were more advanced overall. But in Italy they were particularly accentuated precisely because of the late nature of industrial development: between integration and revolution as between backwardness and advancement. The delay favors the "followers", who can imitate consolidated experiences of others that have already demonstrated their merits. But it forces them to graft them onto a backward reality, giving rise to hybrids: sometimes bad copies but sometimes real "inventions".

Imitation without the conditions of advanced development gave rise in Italy to people's houses built even in rural contexts often with strong, sometimes happy, adaptations. The celebrated "first people's house of Massenzatico" a hamlet of Reggio Emilia[78] was born in 1893 when there were already 25 houses in Belgium and 20 Bourses du Travail in France. It was born in an absolutely rural environment, although it explicitly referred to the different Belgian experience, which it reproduced as being of socialist and cooperative inspiration, without claiming to represent any "grandeur".

> On Saturday afternoon, the congressmen and socialist militants were invited to the inauguration of the Consumer Cooperative in Massenzatico, where they arrived with a service of garden carriages, at a very reduced price, for a drink with a frugal snack, at the cost of one lira. The intent was clearly to show how in Prampolini's Reggio they were oriented towards promoting consumer cooperation, according to the model of the Belgian people's houses. Enrico Ferri, Camillo Prampolini, Giuseppe Croce, Filippo Turati and the prophet of the cooperative Vooruit Emile Vandervelde spoke at the toasts and banquet in the Cooperative. The participants took it for granted that this was the start of a movement for the construction of workers' headquarters, on the model of the People's Houses of Jolimont and Ghent. From then on, it became common to consider the Massenzatico Consumer Cooperative the first Italian People's House, aimed at imitating the organizational model of the Vooruit, while Reggio began to be considered the Italian Ghent, not so much as an industrial center, but rather on the cooperative level». (Fincardi, 2012, p. 309)

The notable differences of the transplant were pointed out by Vandervelde himself (together with the common socialist inspiration) present at the inauguration of the people's house in Massenzatico.

---

[78] The mother of the socialist leader Camillo Prampolini was born in that "Villa" in Massenzatico, he donated his land to build the headquarters of the cooperative. The inauguration took place on Saturday 9 September during the days of the second national congress of the Italian Socialist Workers' Party which was held in Reggio Emilia from 8 to 10 September 1893 (the founding congress had been held in Genoa on 14 and 15 August 1892). There were 250 delegates representing 262 associations) (Canovi et al., 2012, p. 19).

> Thus we felt […] this homeland without borders, which is always expanding as socialism grows, that beautiful evening when, in the Emilian countryside, among fig trees and vineyards, we inaugurated the Casa del Popolo of Massenzatico. Poor peasants had built it, after their day's work, with materials found almost everywhere, without spending a cent, nor spending a penny for labour. And, in this Casa del Popolo – built in conditions so different from ours – in the cooperative form of their association, in the inauguration speeches that were given there, we found the dominant idea of Belgian socialism, cooperation considered as a means, as an end, the Workers' Party, sitting in solidarity on brick foundations. (Fincardi, 2012, p. 235)

The case of the people's houses in industrial environments was very different, such as that of Crocemosso, which without hesitation took inspiration directly from the prestigious people's house in Brussels (2 April 1899).[79] But it took a long time and many resources to build it. The one in Massenzatico was completed "in record time" (Canovi et al., 2012, p. 260). Instead, in Crocemosso, from the first appearance in the press of the "people's house issue" (Corriere Biellese, 29 August 1900) until its inauguration on 30 April 1911, eleven years of planning and discussions were necessary (Moranino, 1992). But 14 years passed from the beginning of the first fundraising. "The first idea of building the People's House in Crocemosso dates back to February 1897, when the Mutual Aid and Education Society between weavers and workers began to organize itself to find the funds to start the works" (https://primabiella.it/eventi-e-cultura/casa-del-popolo-oggi-valle-mosso-111). If the one in Massenzatico cost very little apart from the voluntary work,[80] the people's house of Crocemosso cost more than 35 years of work by a worker, always in addition to the voluntary work of members and supporters. This figure can be reached with a conservative estimate: at the inauguration the debts to be paid to companies in addition to the voluntary work amounted to 17,400 lire. 19,600 lire had already been paid between the purchase of the building and the first renovations, which makes a total of 37,000 lire "a sum that is to be considered lower than the real one, the amount of which I have not been able to ascertain" (Moranino, 1992, pp. 35, 38, 43,

[79] "The 'Corriere Biellese' is the sounding board for all the problems inherent in the construction and use of this and other people's houses [in the Biella wool industry area], the circulation of which […] already required a print run of three thousand copies at the beginning of the century. It will be this very newspaper, with information on the inauguration of the new People's House of Belgium, which took place on 2 April 1899, that will introduce the discussion on people's houses. In August 1900, the one to propose again from its pages to build the 'People's House of Biella' is 'Solitario' [Vitale Viola, maestro], who states with certainty that his idea is shared by many" (Moranino, 1992, p. 17).

[80] "At all hours, especially on holidays, bricklayers, labourers, artisans, farmers volunteered for the 'Mother House', the house of all; and they were continually entertained by songs, music and whatever else was needed […]. The carters and farmers who had a horse […] gathered with carts […] well cleaned and decorated […] and in single file they went partly to the furnace to get the bricks and partly to the Crostolo [a river] to get gravel and sand. Some worked on site and others left and arrived with the materials needed for the construction site. It was a spectacle […] that cannot be forgotten" (From an article in "La Giustizia" of 15 January 1893, cited by Canovi et. al. 2012, pp. 260–261). According to this story, the construction cost almost nothing. It is difficult to think, however, that the furnace had given the bricks for free, and then there were the fixtures and the systems.

54). It can be taken into account that an average worker's wage could be estimated at an excess of 1.8 lire per day in 1903. The total funds spent on the house of Crocemosso therefore corresponded to a minimum of 20,600 days, or 60 years of work by a worker. Assuming that voluntary work had added another 40 years of equivalent work, to obtain the cost of building the Leipzig trade union house it is necessary to multiply by three, for the Roubaix people's house one will see that it is necessary to multiply by two. But for Italy the cost of the Crocemosso people's house was still huge. In the same first decade of the twentieth century, of the 65 people's houses built or renovated in rural areas in the Emilia and Romagna plains surveyed by Marco Fincardi "only 23—just over a third—had estimated costs equal to or above 5 thousand lire, with peaks of two […]: San Giorgio, cost 10 thousand lire, Voghenza […] cost 12 thousand lire and voluntary work estimated at 2,000 days" (Fincardi, 2012, p. 369). If the average wage in this predominantly agricultural region was estimated at about half the wage in the wool district,[81] the people's house of Voghenza (in the countryside 15 kms south-east of Ferrara) would have cost 45 years of equivalent total work, about half of that of Crocemosso. If the one in Massenzatico had "eight rooms […] which in February 1902 will increase to twelve, always on three floors […with another annexed] building for the 'Teatro Artigiano' […] of 336 m^2 of covered surface" (Canovi, 2012, p. 266), the one in Crocemosso

> stands majestic and beautiful […], a large building surrounded […] by a long and vast terrace […]. In it, the Textile League of the Strona and Ponzone Valleys, with over two thousand members, which owns the house, the Strona-Ponzone-Sessera Textile Union, the Mutual Aid Society […] of Crocemosso, which has a rich and valuable library, the Leagues of stokers, machinists, mechanics, sawyers […], the Federation of Consumer Cooperatives, the Socialist Section, the café-restaurant with accommodation, the Dramatic Society, […] a large, elegant, modern hall for the theatre in which the large organisations hold their meetings and weekly performances of music, singing, dramatic and cinematographic performances and conferences are held. (Archive sheets of the Textile Arts League of the Strona and Ponzone Valleys dated 20 April 1911 cited by Moranino, 1992, p. 42)

The reference to the Belgian experience is well documented and testifies that ideas were circulating and the name was "dragging" toward something organic capable of giving new form and functionality to

> associative structures typical of the first workers' movement [...which had] other names: wine club, with the initial aim of reducing the price of wine by eliminating operating costs and of encouraging [...] meetings between workers; club [...], educational club; family club; resistance society, league, bundle, group, recreational centre [...]; cultural association [...]. Each organisation is named after either personalities of the international and Italian workers' movement, or emblematic dates of this, or the district in which they arise, or principles and concepts typical of the socialist movement, such as Freedom, Redemption, Equality, Awakening, Redemption, Future. (Fincardi, 2012, p. 296)

[81] Data for the early twentieth century for the Ferrarese and Biella areas are not available. However, it can be considered that for the Ferrarese area there are data on the wages of workers in the agricultural sector with reference to 1875. A manzolaro, a fairly well-paid figure, earned 1 lira a day while there were maximum wages of 1.25 lira and minimum wages of 40 cents (Nani, 2017, p. 15). For the average of "some factories" probably Piedmontese, Federico Chessa (1909, p. 19) reports a statistic according to which the daily wage, in the same year 1875, was 1.94 lira.

But another important push came from specific needs, very different in different contexts, which further contributed to the extreme variety of creations to be considered a particular characteristic of Italian people's houses. Giuseppe Garibotti (1865–1930)[82] a socialist from Cremona, a supporter of cooperation, wrote in 1902:

> In the face of the enthusiasm and certainty of success of some socialists for the People's Houses, we find others who do not believe it is possible or useful for the party to venture to imitate Belgian cooperativism. And if it were a question [...] of getting down to work, just by eye, to establish People's Houses, only because they are developing successfully in Brussels, Liège, Ghent, Jolimont, etc., I would not hesitate for a moment to align myself with the opponents. But, in fact, no one thinks of establishing People's Houses just for the sake of creating new cooperative organisms and only because such institutions were successful in Belgium. We return – and more insistently – to thinking about establishing People's Houses in Italy, because we are convinced that they can satisfy the needs of the proletariat, because [...] we are led to judge this form of cooperation to be very useful, which can integrate the function and effectiveness of political organization. [...] If generalized, they would not divide workers into two classes, one cooperating and the other excluded from the benefits that cooperation can give, but would instead establish a new means of brotherhood and beneficial solidarity. (Fincardi, 2012, p. 354)

From the very beginning, the people's houses in Northern Italy had such varied characteristics that they corresponded to almost all the types of classification. Often, they were simple places of socialization, alternative to parishes, and in any case, often capable of "modernizing" the associative fabric already available.

> In the Po Valley countryside, modern lay association circuits occupied and made modernly dynamic those spaces and mechanisms of social communication that until a few decades earlier had been the prerogative of parishes, whose traditional ties and normative capacity on collective morality had been disintegrating, being now unsuitable to represent a mobile labourer society with a culture similar to that of the urban or industrial proletariat. It was evidently not the socialist circles that determined these changes, but rather the multifaceted associative fabric available at the end of the 19th century that was guided by socialist intellectuality, as previously it had been influenced by republican and radical intellectuality, now inadequate to push the conflict with the landowners and the moderate or clerical rural bourgeoisie beyond a certain degree. (Fincardi, 2012, p. 330)

They were meeting places for the leagues and for socialist propaganda.

> Both in Grontardo and in Pieve S. Giacomo the workers then think of procuring small tracts of land to build communal houses, where it is possible to meet both to discuss the interests of the Resistance League, and to explain the socialist propaganda action. But these constructions need money. So, let's see, these farmers say, how we can put together a little money. Let everyone contribute twelve lire to be paid as soon as possible. The contributions of a hundred

[82] Garibotti helped found the Camera del Lavoro (CGIL local branch and headquarters) of Cremona in 1893, one of the first in Italy, of which he was the first president, a position he would hold until 1914, when he entered the municipal council of the first socialist mayor of Cremona, Attilio Botti. As a young man, Garibotti had attended technical schools until he obtained the license of municipal secretary. Many years later this was written about him: «When in June 1914 the Socialist Party conquered the Municipality of Cremona, the only comrade who had a strong administrative preparation was Giuseppe Garibotti. Led and trained by him, the socialists held the municipal administration for six years, victoriously overcoming multiple obstacles, despite the sometimes disloyal and unjust opposition of all the other parties» ("Eco del Popolo" 15 December 2015).

> or more Members for each municipality are enough for the purchase of the land and for the beginning of the modest house. (Giuseppe Garibotti 1906, cited by Fincardi, 2012, p. 352)

They could have been headquarters of cooperatives.

> In Buscoldo, only two years later [1909], they began to collect funds to aggregate the local cooperatives in the Casa del popolo. During the popular celebrations of a "proletarian carnival", [...] a local worker, skilled as a buffoon, performed a show in which he comically mimed the inadequacies of the headquarters of the workers' associations in the village and the pressing need to start a completely new headquarters. (Fincardi, 2012, p. 358)

They were sometimes also faithful to the more demanding model "prescribed" by Camillo Prampolini at the inauguration of the one in Correggio (1906), "strategic from an institutional, economic [...] cultural point of view" (Canovi, 2012, p. 292).

> The People's House must be like the hub around which all the cooperative institutions of a municipality or a specific area live and prosper; it must be the driving force of the entire progressive movement of the proletariat; the asylum of all the underprivileged and the enlightened guide in the fight against every kind of speculation, dishonesty and inhuman parasitism of which the less well-off classes are victims in today's society. All forms of welfare and assistance must be included in it: from consumer and production organizations to mutual aid, to evening school, to the secretariat of the poor. In short, it must be an element of order and a peaceful, progressive and very valid instrument of material and civil elevation for the proletariat. ("Risveglio Democratico", 21 January 1906. Canovi, 2012, p. 292)

In 1906, with reference to the rural reality of Cremona and Mantua, Garibotti could still speak of "modest houses" while in 1913 in the hamlet of Buscosoldo the new people's house had 45 rooms. This extreme variety, then preserved over time, also explains the very notable diffusion of people's houses in Italy between the end of the nineteenth century and the first two decades of the twentieth century.

5.8.2 *Widespread Diffusion*

Luigi Arbizzani, consulting the archives of the "Almanacco Socialista Italiano" 1918 and 1919, extracted a sample of 164 municipalities distributed throughout Italy, finding "49 worker-owned premises: 29 people's houses, [...] 15 socialist houses, one worker's house, 4 cooperative premises" (Arbizzani, 1984, p. 110). Margareth Khon (2003, p. 100), citing the same data, did not hesitate to calculate that, since in Italy there were "8 thousand municipalities [...], there were 1500 people's houses" (the exact calculation would give 1,414, and 2,390 considering all 49 worker-owned premises). In reality, in 1919 there were 9,195 Municipalities and therefore the people's houses thus named would have been 1,625 and the workers' owned premises would have been 2,747, seven per 100,000 inhabitants: exactly like in 1914 in the province of Liège, the largest number in all of Belgium, and like the English clubs in the London metropolitan area. This calculation is undoubtedly risky because Arbizzani does not provide information on the formation criteria of his sample of 164 Municipalities. However, considering the exhaustive census carried out for Forlì,

Cesena, Rimini, Ravenna (Menzani & Morgagni, 2020), the people's houses built before 1922 were 208 out of 600,000 inhabitants (1921 Census), that is, an impressive number of 35 per 100,000 inhabitants. It must be taken into account that Romagna must be considered a special case, given that each of the two political forces of the left (socialists and republicans) wanted their own. Of the 570 people's houses surveyed (208 built before 1922, 362 after 1944), 330 were socialist/communist in orientation, 223 republican, and only 12 unitary (Menzani & Morgagni, 2020, pp. 115–116). But even dividing the total by two, there would still be 17.5 people's houses per 100,000 inhabitants: still an exceptional number. For the Florentine area, Antonio Fanelli (2014) did not present any census; however, he wrote about a continuity of the people's houses over time:

> In Italy, after the fascist dictatorship that expropriated the structures of left-wing associations [...], an autonomous and grassroots movement was reborn [...] during the Liberation and then [...] with the fight against the evictions of the Scelba government in the mid-1950s, when the government decided to return the assets of the dissolved PNF and, among these, many people's houses into the hands of the State. [...]. One figure is enough [...]: in the implementation phase of the Scelba decrees [...] 23 people's houses were evicted; in many cases there were agreements, compromises, such as the purchase of the structure by the members. (Fanelli, 2014, p. 4)

A figure like this is certainly not "enough", however, a calculation can be made: if the people's houses before 1922 had been double those evicted by Scelba, the number per 100,000 inhabitants (386 thousand in the 1921 Census) would be 12, while considering only the evicted it would be 6, a very high number in any case. All these numbers suggest that the creations were very different in the different contexts: in rural areas often as the only meeting place or congregation space alternative to parishes and the old associationism, elsewhere with more complex purposes. They were also very different over time, often a long time. As collective property, often by right, however considered so having been made with collective resources, many strenuously opposed their closure, sometimes successfully even after defeats, distortions and abandonments. The data of the 507 people's houses surveyed in Romagna demonstrate that 21% people's houses built before 1923, less those destroyed by the fascists and not reopened, are still used for social activities today.

5.8.3 Conclusion

In conclusion, it is precisely the Italian people's houses that show, in their history (though the case of Halluin will be examined shortly), the application of the formula faith against science and science against faith. Faith in their own abilities and resources, however poor and small they might appear compared to the needs of "disinherited victims of every kind of speculation, dishonesty and inhuman parasitism of which the less well-off classes are victims in today's society". Against science, to quote Garibotti, who "in the face of the enthusiasm and certainty of success of certain socialists" warned to realistically consider "neither possible nor useful to venture" into such difficult enterprises. But then, for their life, application of science against faith. The science of socialist doctrine and of the experiences of others that explained, to quote Prampolini, the importance of a "fulcrum around which to make all the institutions of the proletarian movement live and prosper, an element of order and a peaceful progressive instrument of its material and civil elevation". Against faith, or rather the desperate belief, to use Rigola's words, "that there was an iron law, according to which the rich are made to command and the poor to serve". Faith against science and then science against faith that gave rise in a very characteristic way to achievements that conformed, on the basis of specific resources, to local realities responding to specific needs.

The case of the Italian people's houses suggests that the formula applies in collective action especially when the need for *inclusive innovation* is acute. In Italy, industrial development was backward, while the teaching that came from the experiences of the proletariat in more advanced realities was known and available. Therefore, the perception of a very accentuated and evident distance between needs—desires and reality was widespread. From there came the urgency of innovation and inclusion, that is, of a collective action of emancipation of the subaltern classes which expanded. It expanded in its locations, adapting it to specific needs, so as to be able to serve and involve the greatest possible number. It expanded also as a multiplication of locations in many realities, even very different from each other. In the last chapter, one will see in detail the application of this scheme in the most documented and most famous case of "Halluin the Red": the town in the industrial North of France on the border with Belgium and the people's house of the proverbial proletarian recovery.

References

Alekseeva, E. V., & Kazakova-Apkarimova, E. Y. (2020). People's houses as answers to the challenges of modernity in Europe and Russia. *RUDN Journal of Russian History, 19*(4), 952–964.

Allen, R. C. (2000). Economic structure and agricultural productivity in Europe, 1300–1800. *European Review of Economic History, 4*(1), 1–26.

Allen, R. C. (2009). *The British industrial revolution in global perspective.* Cambridge University Press.

Alloul, H., & Auwers, M. (2018). What is (new in) new diplomatic history? *BTNG-RBHC, 48*(4).

Arbizzani, L. (1984). Case del popolo e associazionismo in Italia dopo la Prima guerra mondiale. In M. Degl'Innocenti, *Le case del popolo in Europa* (pp. 109–128). Sansoni.

Arkell, T. (2006). Illuminations and distortions: Gregory King's scheme calculated for the year 1688 and the social structure of later Stuart England. *The Economic History Review New Series, 59*(1), 32–69.

Belchem, J. (1991). *Industrialization and the working class: The English experience, 1750–1900.* Scolar Press.

Berg, M. (1990). *Markets and manufacture in early industrial Europe.* Routledge.

Bermani, C. (1981–1982). Breve storia del Proletkul't italiano. *Primo Maggio*, autunno-inverno, 27–40.

Blaug, M. (1963). The myth of the old poor law and the making of the new. *The Journal of Economic History, XXIII*(2), 151–184.

Böhm-Bawerk (von), E. R. (1896/1949). *Zum Abschluss des Marxschen Systems in Staatswissenschaftliche Arbeiten. Festgaben für Karl Knies zur fünfundsiebzigsten Wiederkehr seines Geburtstages in dankbaren Vehehring.* Otto v. Boenigk (Hrsg.) O. Haering, 1896, S. 87–205. Paul M. Sweezy (ed.): Karl Marx and the Close of his System by Eugen von Böhm-Bawerk & Bom-Bawaerk's Criticism of Karl Marx by Rudolf Hilferding Together with an Appendix consisting of an Article by Ladislaus von Bortkiewicz on the Transformation of Values into Prices of Production in the Marxian System. Augustus S.M. Kelley 1949.

Brown, J. W. (1986). Alimentary discourse in nineteenth-century social theory: Pierre Leroux, Etienne Cabet and Charles Fourier. *Dalhousie French Studies, 11*, 72–96.

Bry, G. (1960). *Wages in Germany 1871–1945.* NBER.

Buyst, E. (2018). The causes of growth during Belgium's industrial revolution. *Journal of Interdisciplinary History, XLIX*(1), 71–92.

Cabet, E. (1842). *Voyage en Icarie: Roman philosophique et social.* Mallet.

Canovi, A., Fincardi, M., Pavarini, R., Poletti, M., & Testi, R. (2012). *Di nuovo a Massenzatico Storie e geografie della cooperazione e delle case del popolo.* Rubbettino.

Canovi, A. (2012). La ricerca - Le case del popolo tra XIX e XX secolo. In A. Canovi, M. Fincardi, R. Pavarini, M. Poletti, & R. Testi, *Di nuovo a Massenzatico Storie e geografie della cooperazione e delle case del popolo* (pp. 231–269). Rubbettino.

Chilosi, D., & Ciccarelli, C. (2022). Evolving gaps: Occupational structure in southern and northern Italy 1400–1861. *The Economic History Review, 75*, 1349–1378.

Cirese, A. M. (1976). Le Osservazioni sul folclore e l'edizione critica dei Quaderni gramsciani. In *Intellettuali, folclore, istinto di classe—Note su Verga, Deledda, Scotellaro, Gramsci* (pp. 145–147). Einaudi.

Clark, G., & Page, M. E. (2019). Welfare reform, 1834: Did the new poor law in England produce significant economic gains? *Cliometrica, 13*(2), 221–244.

Chessa, F. (1909). La statistica dei salari in Italia. *Rivista Internazionale di Scienze Sociali e Discipline Ausiliarie., 50*(197), 18–34.

Coolsaet, R. (2014). *België en zijn buitenlandse politiek (1830–2015).* Van Halewyck.

Daudin, G., Morys, M., & O'Rourke, K. H. (2010). Globalization, 1870–1914. In S. Broadberry & K. O'Rourke (Eds.), *The Cambridge economic history of modern Europe—Volume 2. 1870 to the present.* Cambridge University Press.

De Martino, E. (1949). Intorno a una storia del mondo popolare subalterno. *Società, V*(3), 411–435.

Degl'Innocenti, M. (1984). *Le case del popolo in Europa.* Sansoni.

Diamantopoulos, M. (2023). A legacy of 'propagandist action': Robert owen, the paradox of working-class pedagogy, and the making of Britain's co-operative movement. *Journal of Co-Operative Studies, 56*(3), 13–24.

Domansky, E. (1984). Le origini e lo sviluppo delle case del sindacato in Germania dalla fine del XIX secolo alla Prima guerra mondiale. In M. Degl'Innocenti, *Le case del popolo in Europa* (pp. 149–166). Sansoni.

Edelstein M. (1982). Overseas Investment in the Age of High Imperialism—The United Kingdom 1850–1914. New York: Columbia University Press.

Engels, F. (1880). *Socialisme utopique et socialisme scientifique.* Derveaux.

Engels, F. (1885, November) Zur Geschichte des Bundes der Kommunisten. *Sozialdemokrat.*

Fanelli, A. (2014). *A casa del popolo—Antropologia e storia dell'associazionismo ricreativo.* Donzelli.

Federico, G., A. Tena-Junguito. (2019). World trade, 1800–1938: a new synthesis. *Revista de Historia Económica—Journal of Iberian and Latin America Economic History, 37*(1), pp. 9–41.

Feinstein, C. H. (1998). Pessimism perpetuated: Real wages and the standard of living in Britain during and after the industrial revolution. *The Journal of Economic History, 58*(3), 625–658.

Fincardi, M. (2012). Case del popolo della belle époque nella pianura padana. In A. Canovi, M. Fincardi, R. Pavarini, M. Poletti, & R. Testi (a cura), *Di nuovo a Massenzatico Storie e geografie della cooperazione e delle case del popolo* (pp. 295–455). Rubbettino.

Flagothier, R. (1984). Contributo allo studio delle case del popolo in Vallonia e a Bruxelles (1872–1982). In M. Degl'Innocenti, *Le case del popolo in Europa*. Sansoni.
Foucault, M. (1984/2010). *Eterotopia*. Trad. it. Des espaces autres, "Architecture, Mouvement, Continuité", n. 5, octobre 1984. Mimesis 2010.
Foucault, M. (2001). *Il soggetto e il potere*, in: Dits et Écrits, vol. 2: 1976–1988. Quarto Gallimard.
Foucault, M. (2003). *L'ermeneutica del soggetto. Corso al Collège de France (1981–1982)*. Edizione stabilita da F. Gros, trad. di M. Bertani. Feltrinelli.
Foucault, M. (2009). *Il governo di sé e degli altri – Corso al Collège de France 1982–1983*. Milano: Feltrinelli. Prima edizione: Le Gouvernement de soi et des autres: Cours au College de France, 1982–1983. Seuil/Gallimard 2008.
Fourier, C. (1829). Le nouveau monde industriel ou l'agriculture combinée. *Le nouveau monde industriel et sociétaire ou Invention du procédé d'industrie attrayante at naturelle distribuée en séries passionnées* (pp. 577–664). Bossange Père.
Gacon, S. (2015). La République briseuse de grèves et l'amnistie (1905–1914) - Une tentative de régulation politique du conflit social en France, Vingtième Siècle. *Revue D'histoire, 125*, 17–31.
Gay, E. F. (1903). Inclosures in England in the sixteenth century. *The Quarterly Journal of Economics, 17*(4), 576–597.
Geisser, A., & Magrini, E. (1904). *Contribuzione alla storia e statistica dei salari industriali in Italia nella seconda metà del secolo XIX*. Roux & Viarengo.
Ghetti, N., & Iacarella, A. (2021). Tra Russia e Italia, da Bogdanov a Gramsci, la via culturale alla rivoluzione. *Pandora* 21 Aprile. https://www.pandorarivista.it/articoli/tra-russia-e-italia-da-bogdanov-a-gramsci-la-via-culturale-alla-rivoluzione
Glass, D. V. (1950). Gregory King's estimate of the population of England and Wales 1695. *Population Studies, 3*, 338–374.
Goldman, L. (1978). Révolution et bureaucratie. In L. Goldmann, *Pour une théorie de la liberté - Épistémologie et philosophie politique*. Denoël/Gonthier.
Gramsci, A. (1916). Socialismo e cultura. *Il Grido del Popolo*, 29 gennaio (Firmato ALFA GAMMA).
Gramsci, A. (1935/1977). *Quaderno 27 Osservazioni sul folclore § 1*. In Gerratana V. (a cura) Quaderni del Carcere vol. 3. Einaudi 1977.
Green, M. R. (1951). *American conservatism in the age of enterprise 1865–1910*. Harper Torchbooks.
Griffin, E. (2018). Diets, hunger and living standards during the British industrial revolution. *Past and Present, 239*(1), 71–111.
Groh, D. (1973). *Negative Integration und revolutionärer Attentismus. Die deutsche Sozialdemokratie am Vorabend des Ersten Weltkrieges*. Propyläen.
Gurney, P. J. (2009). Rejoicing in Potatoes: The politics of consumption in England during the hungry forties. *Past & Present, 203*, 99–136.
Guzzone, G. (2020). Tra marxismo senza Capitale e post-operaismo negativo: Un dilemma (in)evitabile? *Syzetesis, VII*, 437–468.
Hamelin, D. (2011, avril–juin). Les Bourses du travail entre éducation politique et formation professionnelle. *Le Mouvement Social*, 23–37.
Harris, J. R., & Todaro, M. P. (1970). Migration, unemployment and development: A two-sector analysis. *American Economic Review, 60*(1), 126–142.
Harrison, J. F. C. (1969). *Robert owen and the owenites in Britain and America—The quest of a new moral world*. Routledge.
Hastings, M. (1991). *Halluin-la-Rouge 1919–1939—Aspects d'un communisme identitaire*. Lille: Presse universitaire de Lille.
Horrell, S., & Humphries, J. (2019). Children's work and wages in Britain, 1280–1860. *Explorations in Economic History, 73*(101272), 1–25.
Humphries, J. (2013). Childhood and child labour in the British industrial revolution. *The Economic History Review, 66*(2), 395–418.
Jossa, B. (2015). Socialism today, utopian and scientific. *Open Access Library Journal, 2*, 1–13.

King, S., & Tomkins, A. (Eds.). (2003). *The poor in England 1700–1850: An economy of makeshifts*. Manchester University Press.
Kohn, M. (2003). *Radical space—Building the house of the people*. Cornell University Press.
Lafontaine, A. (1911). *Charles fourier*. Librairie Bloud & C.
La Tourette (de), G. G. (1884). *Théophraste Renaudot d'après des documents inédits - Un essai de Faculté libre au XVIIe siècle: Bureau d'adresses, Monts de piété, Consultations charitables*. Librairie Plon.
Lee, R. D., & Schofield, R. S. (1981). British population in the eighteenth century. In R. Floud & D. McCloskey, *The economic history of Britain since 1700 volume I 1700–1860* (pp. 17–35). Cambridge University Press.
Leroux, P. (1834/1850). *De l'individualisme et du socialisme* (Revue Encyclopédique tome LX 1934). In *Oeuvres de Pierre Leroux 1825–1850*. Société Typographique, 1850.
Lidtke, V. L. (1985). *The alternative culture—Socialist labor in imperial Germany*. Oxford University Press.
Lindert, H. (1986). Unequal English wealth since 1670. *The Journal of Political Economy, 94*(6), 1127–1162.
Link, S. J. (2020). *Forging global fordism. Nazi Germany, Soviet Russia, and the Contest over the industrial order*. Princeton University Press.
Lippolis, E. (2019). Riunioni, operazioni di voto e agoni nell'agorà di Atene. In Aldo Borlenghi et al. (a cura), *Voter en Grèce, à Rome et en Gaule*. MOM Éditions. https://doi.org/10.4000/books.momeditions.6432
Lussien-Maisonneuve, M.-J. (2002). Groupes paroissiaux catholiques et maisons du peuple socialistes: Des instruments concurrents d'éducation populaire à la fin du xixe siècle et dans la première moitié du xxe siècle. In P. Guignet (Ed.), *Le peuple des villes dans l'Europe du Nord-Ouest (fin du Moyen Âge-1945)* (Vol. 1, pp. 471–486). Publications de l'Institut de recherches historiques du Septentrion.
Maler, E. (2024). *La vocation révolutionnaire du prolétariat selon Karl Marx (1843–1848)*. Convoiter l'impossible. http://athena.henri-maler.fr.
Marlow, L. (1984). Progresso e impegno civico: temi dell'attività educativa dei club operai 1862–1912. In M. Degl'Innocenti, *Le case del popolo in Europa* (pp. 311–338). Sansoni.
Marx, K., & Engels, F. (1848/1974). *Manifest der Kommunistischen Partei*. Werke, Band 4, S. 459–493. Dietz Verlag 1974.
Marx, K. (1844/1976). Kritische Randglossen zu dem Artikel Der König von Preußen und die Sozialreform. Von einem Preußen (Vorwärts! Nr. 60). In *Karl Marx/ Friedrich Engels - Werke Band 1*, S. 392–409. Dietz Verlag, 1976.
Marx, K. (1846/1972). Zirkular gegen Kriege. In *Karl Marx, Friedrich Engels Werke*, Band 4, S. 3 – 17. Dietz Verlag, 1972. Written on May 11, 1846, distributed as a lithographic circular in May 1846.
Mazauric, S. (2019). *Savoirs et philosophie à Paris dans la première moitié du XVIIe siècle - Les conférences du bureau d'adresse de Théophraste Renaudot (1633–1642)*. Éditions de la Sorbonne.
Menzani, T., & Morgagni, F. (2020). *Nel cuore della comunità – Storia delle case del popolo in Romagna*. Franco Angeli.
Mommsen, W. J. (1985). *Britain and Germany 1800 to 1914 two developmental paths towards industrial society*. German Historical Institute.
Montaigne (de), M. E. (1588/2009). *Les Essais*. Pernon Editions.
Moranino, L. (1992). *La casa del popolo di Crocemosso*. Edizioni Leone & Griffa.
Mulgan, G., & Worpole, K. (1986). *Saturday night or Sunday morning? Fron arts to industry—New forms of cultural policy. Old waking*. The Gresham Press.
Nani, M. (2017). Fattori, caporali e capisquadra. Note su mediatori e mercato del lavoro agricolo nel Ferrarese dell'Ottocento. *Mélanges de l'École française de Rome - Italie et Méditerranée modernes et contemporaines, 129*(1), 1–38 [Online].

Nardinelli, C. (1980). Child labor and the factory acts. *The Journal of Economic History, 40*(4), 739–755.
Nouailhat, Y.-H. (1979). *France et États-Unis Aut 1914 - Avril 1917*. Publications de la Sorbonne.
Nuvolari, A., & Ricci, M. (2012). *Economic growth in England 1250–1850: Some new estimates using a demand side approach* (LEM Working Paper 2011/22).
Owen, R. (1857). *The life of robert owen written by himself: With selections from his writings and correspondence* (Vol. 1). Effingham Wilson.
Owen, R. D. (1873, April). Thomas Clarkson and Nicholas of Russia: A chapter of autobiography, *The Atlantic*. (https://www.theatlantic.com/magazine/archive/1873/04/thomas-clarkson-and-nicholas-of-russia-a-chapter-of-autobiography/630939/).
Pelloutier, F. (1921). *Histoire des Bourses du Travail: Origine Institutions Avenir - Ouvrage posthume*. Alfred Costes Éditeur.
Pizza, G. (2013). Gramsci e de Martino. Appunti per una riflessione. *Quaderni di Teoria Sociale, 13*, 75–119.
Polidori, F. (2005). Le verità di Foucault. *Etica & Politica, 1*, 1–13.
Pollard, S. (1973). Industrialization and the European economy. *The Economic History Review, 26*(4), 636–648.
Price, R. N. (1971). The working men's club movement and Victorian social reform ideology. *Victorian Studies, 15*(2), 117–147.
Reid, A. (1987), Class and Organization Reviewed Work: Worlds of Labour: Further Studies in the History of Labour by E. J. Hobsbawm, *The Historical Journal, 30*(1), pp. 225–238.
Reimer, A. (2010). Understanding chromatic diagrams: Towards a taxonomy. *The Cartographic Journal, 47*(4), 330–350.
Reulecke, J. (1984). Gesellenheim, casa degli operai, casa operaia. Iniziative borghesi per la crescita spirituale delle classi inferiori in Germania prima della Prima guerra mondiale. In M. Degl'Innocenti, *Le case del popolo in Europa* (pp. 130–147). Sansoni.
Rigola, R. (1930). *Saggio sulla storia del movimento operaio – Rinaldo Rigola e il movimento operaio nel Biellese – Autobiografia*. Giuseppe Laterza & Figli.
Ritter, G. A. (1978). Workers' culture in imperial Germany: Problems and points of departure for research. *Journal of Contemporary History, 13*(2), 165–189.
Robert, L. (2013). *Gewerkschaftsdämmerung: Geschichte und Perspektiven deutscher Gewerkschaften*. Studien des Göttinger Instituts für Demokratieforschung zur Geschichte politischer und gesellschaftlicher Kontroversen n. 6, transcript Verlag, Bielefeld.
Roberts, F. D. (1958). Tory Paternalism and social reform in early Victorian England. *The American Historical Review, 63*(2), 323–337.
Roberts, F. D. (1979). *Paternalism in early Victorian England*. Routledge.
Robinson, E. (1650). *The office of adresses and encounters*. Matthew Simmons.
Rosés, J. R., & Wolf, N. (2018). *Regional economic development in Europe, 1900–2010: A Description of the Patterns* (CESifo Working Paper Series n. 6952).
Roth, G. (1963). *The social democrats in imperial Germany*. Bedminster Press.
Rowe, D. J. (1968). The failure of London Chartism. *The Historical Journal, 11*(3), 472–487.
Rule, J. (2014). *The labouring classes in early industrial England 1750–1850*. Routledge.
Sabel, C., & Zeitlin, J. (1985). Historical alternatives to mass production: Politics, markets and technology in nineteenth century industrialization. *Past & Present, 108*, 133–176.
Saint-Simon C.H. de Rouvroy. (1820/1869). *Œuvres*. E. Dentu Editeur 1869. First Edition 1820.
Saito, O., & Shaw-Taylor, L. (2021). Comparative history of occupational structure. In A. Litvine (Ed.), *French occupational structure, industrialisation and economic growth, France 1695 to the Present*. Cambridge University Press.
Scascighini, M. (2009). La Maison du peuple. Auto-émancipation ou mise sous tutelle? *Art+Architecture, 1*, 6–11.
Schierup, C.-U., Ålund, A., & Kellecioglu, I. (2021). Reinventing the people's house: Time, space and activism in multiethnic stockholm. *Critical Sociology, 47*(6), 907–922.

Senior, N., & Chadwick, E. (1834). *Poor law commissioners' report 1834 copy of the report made in 1834 by the commissioners for inquiring into the administration and practical operation of the poor laws. Presented to both houses of parliament by command of his majesty*. HM Stationery Office.

Shipley, S. (1984). I club operai londinesi e la virile arte del pugilato nell'ultimo decennio del XIX secolo. In M. Degl'Innocenti, *Le case del popolo in Europa* (pp. 311–337). Sansoni.

Siméon, O. (2012, December 10). Robert owen: The father of British socialism? *Books and Ideas.*

Stein (von), L. (1850/1964). *The history of social movement in France 1789–1850*. The Bedminster Press. First edition: Geschichte der socialen Bewegung in Frankreich von 1789 bis auf unsere Tage. Leipzig: Wigand, 1850.

Taylor, J. S. (1969). The mythology of the old poor law. *The Journal of Economic History, 29*(2), 292–297.

Tholfsen, T. R. (1961). The transition to democracy in Victorian England. *International Review of Social History, 6*(2), 226–248.

Thompson, E. P. (1964). *The making of the English working class*. Victor Gollancz Ltd.

Thompson, E. P. (1971). The Moral Economy of the English Crowd in the Eighteenth Century, *Past & Present, 50*, pp. 76–136.

Tilly, C. (1986). *The contentious France*. Harvard.

Toson, C. (2018). L'agorà e la piazza civica, spazi teatrali per la parrhesia - La città costruita intorno allo spazio vuoto. In F. Fava, E. Monaci, & C. Toson, *Vuoto/pieno - I caratteri della Venezia che cambia Rivista di Engram* (pp. 155, 141–162).

Tristan, F. (1843). *Union Ouvrière*. Paris: Libraire Prévot.

Tucker, K. H. (1996). *French revolutionary syndicalism and the public sphere*. Cambridge University Press.

United State Department of State. (1879). *State of labour in Europe, 1878*. Government Printing Office.

Vandamme, T. (2019). *Beyond Belgium—The business empire of Edouard Empain in the First Global Economy (1880–1914)*. Universiteit Gent.

Waters, C. (1990). *British socialists and the politics of popular culture*. Stanford University Press.

Williams, R. (1960). *Culture and society 1780–1950*. Anchor Books.

Womack, J. P., Jones, D. T., & Roos, D. (1990). *The machine that changed the world*. Free Press.

Chapter 6
Halluin "La Rouge"

6.1 Introduction

If the Franco-Belgian border continued straight south-east following the initial Dunkirk-Armentières trajectory, the north-eastern half of the Arrondissement of Lille would be Belgian: Roubaix, Tourcoing, Halluin. But this region formed by the deviation of the border toward the north-east, which at Armentières begins to follow the Lys before returning south-east precisely at Halluin, was definitively assigned to France in 1713. Thus, Halluin is at the northern tip of a French bridgehead toward Belgium, and Menin or Menen, the Belgian town opposite, could be one of its districts, or vice versa. This territory tormented by wars but always industrious and then intensely industrial, has had considerable importance for the mobility of men and ideas. In Lille there was the crossroads of the ancient Roman road which, coming from Arras, went east toward Maastricht, west toward the sea. It was there that the Carolingian Road to Bruges began. Their geographical position has had a great influence on the history of these places (Fig. 6.1).

The development of the fundamental textile industry, first in Roubaix then in Halluin, was linked to its earlier development in Flanders, whose origins dated back to the widespread cultivation of flax and its weaving at home throughout the eighteenth century.[1] This activity favored a long period (1750–1810) of high incomes, higher than the already high agricultural incomes,[2] and the spread of a particular figure, the

[1] This emerges in several works that were intended to discuss Franklin F. Mendels's (1972) thesis according to which the case of Flanders demonstrated a link between the reduction of the marriageable age and proto industrialization. Such a link has been found to be very dubious, but incidentally it has been demonstrated that "at the end of the *ancien régime*, almost half of the Flemish population was employed, at least part-time, in the rural linen industry" (Devos, 1999, p. 104).

[2] "Dérival, a French nobleman travelling through the Netherlands in 1782–1783, noted: all the inhabitants of the cities of the Netherlands live if not in opulence at least in great abundance: but this is even more noticeable in the countryside than in the cities" (Devos, 1999, p. 104).

G. Seravalli, *Collective Action in the Age of Polycrisis*, Contributions to Economics,
https://doi.org/10.1007/978-3-032-12653-5_6

Fig. 6.1 Map 1914. Cropping from Bartholomew's Map of North-Eastern France, Belgium, and the Rhine. The Edinburgh Geographical Institute 1914—Wikimedia Commons. *Note* The red stars indicate the fortresses

personally landless agricultural assistant: a wage earner with considerable weaving skills.

That happy age ended because of the competition from English cotton fabrics while the more expensive domestic linen was no longer protected by traditional protectionist policies, much accentuated under Napoleon.[3] There was then a mass

[3] To the traditional high customs tariffs strengthened by Napoleon to support industrialization in the territories annexed to France (including Flanders, later lost after Waterloo), was added the "continental blockade" decided in 1806 to isolate England just at the beginning of the rapid process of mechanization of the English cotton industry. Once the blockade was lifted in 1814, this advanced industry demonstrated all its strength to a degree that astonished the European producers who were ruined by it. Its strength came from the mechanical loom powered by steam which had originated in England (1787 Cartwright model) and improvements (1802 Radcliffe, 1803 Todd, 1806 Horrocks and Marsland, 1810 Cotton) that would lead in 1822 to the Roberts model. The ruin of the European producers had devastating social effects. In Ghent, for example, the 6,000 weavers of 1800 were reduced to a few hundred in 1817, almost all of whom had to emigrate after having fought in vain through demonstrations that had gone as far as "demolishing shops selling English products"

emigration of Flemish workers beyond the Lys where, in Roubaix especially,[4] a new textile industry which received a decisive boost from that emigration of low-cost expert workers, was emerging. Then emigration from Belgium favored Halluin when, shortly before the mid-nineteenth century, in Roubaix the consolidated textile industry no longer absorbed work and actually expelled it[5] while in West Flanders the crisis continued: a crisis that is remembered as particularly tragic. The combination of three misfortunes overturned the previous prosperity: the previously mentioned competition from cotton that hit the proto-linen industry, the potato blight that jeopardized the livelihoods already at risk due to the unemployment of the weavers which depressed wages, and a series of disastrous cereal harvests that delivered the final blow.

> In 1835 the crisis of rural industry was in full swing [...]. The fragmentation of agricultural property supported increases in rents and land prices in Flanders, while wages remained stationary and even began to decline from 1840 onwards due to competition from the unemployed in the linen industry. The food crisis hit the linen districts in particular. In his study of pauperism in Flanders, Jacquemyns noted that the paupers and beggars, whose bands reached Brussels, even causing a bloody riot on 17 May 1847, and also invading the North of France, were particularly numerous in the districts of Courtrai, Roulers, Thielt for West Flanders [in the immediate vicinity of Halluin], Ghent and Audenarde, for East Flanders, which were then most affected by epidemics, such as the "hunger disease" or the "Flanders disease". Hence, from 1845 to 1850, a frightening demographic decline in the flax districts. (Leuilliot, 1929, p. 626)

(Scholliers, 2001, p. 3). Throughout West Flanders, the linen industry went into serious crisis, beaten by the competition of the less valuable but much more affordable English cotton.

[4] Roubaix was a town of 9,000 inhabitants in 1800 (by the end of the century it would reach 100,000), the center of a modest system of home-based work spread throughout the countryside for wool dyeing and to a lesser extent for cotton weaving, modest in comparison to Lille, the center of linen, and Tourcoing, the center of wool. The modesty of this small industry was, however, an advantage at the beginning of the nineteenth century because, without a heavy tradition and heavy technical immobilizations, it was possible to rapidly build a new sector, that of mixed cotton-wool-silk fabrics dyed according to fashion, favored by connections with Lille and Tourcoing. This made Roubaix's fortune in years of tough competition from the English who offered good quality products at reduced prices but of traditional conception (Fohlen, 1951).

[5] The decline in employment in Roubaix was due to the increase in productivity caused by the increase in the size of production units following mechanization. "The crisis [1846–1849] accelerated the process of technical concentration that had begun in 1840: thus the Delannoy Frères wool spinning mill alone employed seven hundred workers (it was one of four that employed more than two hundred workers and absorbed more than half of the wool workers). Cotton spinning was dominated by the gigantic Motte-Bossut factory: founded in 1843 and equipped with self-winding looms, it had twenty thousand spindles; after the fire of 1845 it was rebuilt with forty thousand spindles. The tendency towards concentration is identical in weaving: in 1845, three of the one hundred and fifty-seven weaving mills employed more than five hundred workers: these were the Lagache weaving mill (500 workers), Veuve Lefebvre (580) and above all Wibaux-Florin (955)" (Petillon, 2006, p. 25).

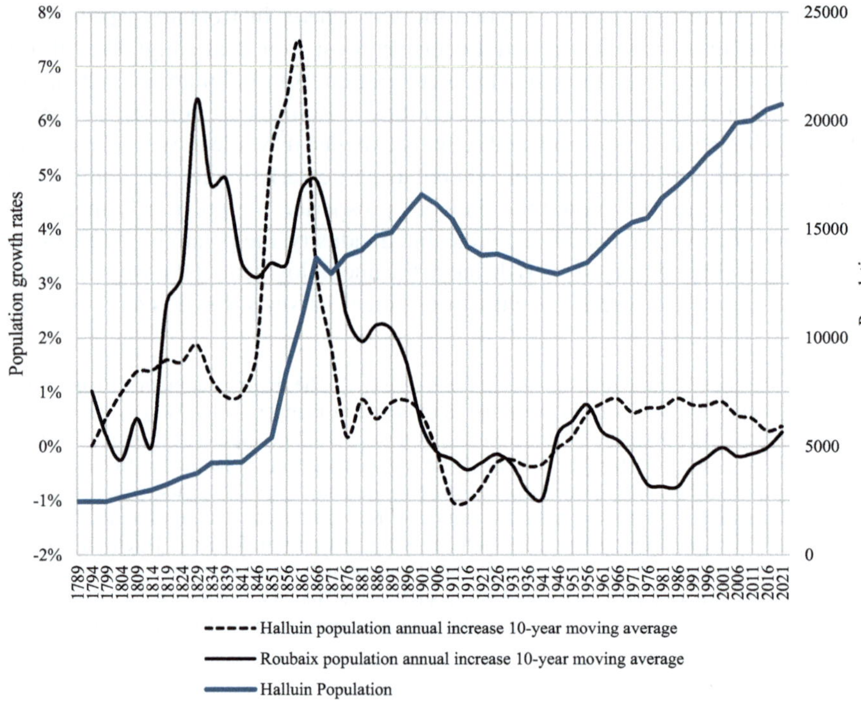

Fig. 6.2 Population trend in Halluin and increases in Halluin and Roubaix. *Source* Figure obtained by processing data from Hastings (1991) and INSEE

The "hunger disease" refers to the consequences of the *Phytophthora infestans* of 1845–1848 and the three consecutive poor grain harvests, the tragic combination that caused 40,000 deaths in Flanders out of 200,000 inhabitants.[6]

6.2 First Roubaix then Halluin

These events left a clear mark on the population trends of Roubaix and Halluin. The population of Halluin grew very slowly from the last decade of the eighteenth century to the 1830s. Then, between the 1840s and 1860s, the turning point came when the number of inhabitants increased from 4,000 to 14,000. This turning point occurred in conjunction with the collapse of increases in Roubaix after the peak recorded at the beginning of the 1830s (Fig. 6.2).

[6] The potato blight, which arrived from Mexico, affected all of Europe, but had devastating effects especially in Ireland due to the specific conditions of the rural population. In Ireland between 1845 and 1849, there were one million deaths from hunger and one million emigrants abroad out of eight million inhabitants.

At the end of the 1960s, the rate of population growth in Roubaix recovered in conjunction with the recovery of the deeply restructured industry. The introduction of mechanical wool combing allowed the rapid development of what was a small medium–high quality wool sector already present in Roubaix since the end of the eighteenth century. Wool, a more expensive and profitable product, almost entirely replaced cotton. Other development factors also contributed, such as the expansion of the railway and canal network that allowed the supply of coal at a lower cost and the spread of steam engines. Finally, there was the creation of important local banks that allowed industrialists to overcome the chronic lack of capital that had held back development until the 1950s (Fohlen, 1951, pp. 100–102).

The migrants from Flanders sought landing places no further than three or four-days' walk: they all began with seasonal migration and even later, despite knowing its lack of realism, they always cultivated the hope of returning home. "They came from a triangle formed by the cities of Menin, Bruges and Ghent, a distance that does not exceed 50 km" (Hastings, 1991, p. 32). Furthermore, they tried to go "to places where there was home-based flax processing in rural families. The Flemish is reluctant to leave the land, he clings to it, he remains a peasant who is difficult to uproot" (Hastings, 1991, p. 28). But the migratory flow of the Flemish was first oriented toward Roubaix, which was more distant and where there was no home-based flax weaving, and only 20 years later toward the closer Halluin, where there was flax processing. The reason for this anomaly is that Halluin was very backward until the 1840s. "Compared to the dynamism and creativity of the producers of Roubaix and Tourcoing, the linen employers of Halluin appear [...] stuck in antiquated structures" (Hastings, 1991, pp. 46, 48). Two consequences arose from this backwardness of the productive structures in Halluin. One was the singular and persistent mental traditionalism of the employers, unrestrained by any counter-power of the workers.

> In the mid-nineteenth century, Halluin employers were [...] a rising bourgeoisie coming from artisan work in an agricultural environment [...]: from the farm to the shop, from the workshop to the factory [...]. Despite a wealth that was clearly inferior to that of the masters of Lille, Roubaix or Tourcoing, the master of Halluin liked to demonstrate his social level through a certain lifestyle that kept the working people at a distance. [...]. At the beginning of the twentieth century, the merchant-producers of Halluin rented 2/3 of the real estate and urban space but lived in the remaining third [...in] very few streets where they were all gathered. [...]. Religious loyalty, the cult of work, a sense of belonging to the caste outline the contours of the employer mentality. [...]. The feeling of belonging to the same environment is accompanied by the awareness of one's own identity [...] «We made Halluin». [...] But the affirmation of identity also means the exclusion of others [...], the erection of social barriers, the desire for distance and difference in level. The employers' reflection on the condition of the workers is the most significant example. «The Halluin worker [...] is a good-natured boy but he is slow. It must be said that he shows a lot of negligence. You always have to keep up with him». An infantilizing representation that at the turn of the century the workers, overwhelmed by poverty, were less and less willing to accept. (Hastings, 1991, pp. 55–66)

The second consequence was the workers' lessons from the experiences that their compatriots had lived and were living in Roubaix, more advanced experiences corresponding to a more dynamic capitalism. The exchange of information was not difficult. The example of the Belgian socialists and of Roubaix was important, and their direct role was also decisive. It was they who directed the first important social conflict in Halluin, and they provided the immaterial and material structures including the people's house.

The exchange of information was based on the common Belgian nationality, which was also retained by children born in France until the new citizenship rules of 26 June 1889[7] and on the common language, Flemish.[8] In 1886, after 60 years in Roubaix and 30 in Halluin since the peaks of immigration, the share of Belgians in the total population was 77% in Halluin and 54% in Roubaix (Hastings, 1991, p. 32). Finally, proximity was important because at that time traveling was expensive. The railway to the Belgian border was opened in 1842, and the 12 kms from Roubaix to Halluin could be covered in half an hour, at the end of the century in no more than 20 mins. The cost of a return ticket in third class was 1.2 francs in 1900 (Le Mouel, 2003), when a kilo of bread cost 0.38 francs and the daily wage (for 10 h of work) of a weaver was 2.50 francs (Benoist, 1904). Thus, a worker from Halluin could not go to Roubaix more than once a month, but it was enough for union meetings and for the cooperative assemblies in which he could therefore be an active member.

The experience of the workers' movement in Roubaix was "from another world", but it was useful, even if not in a short time. "At the end of the [19th] century, Halluin was a 'white city', subservient to the clerical conservatism of its notables. [...]. In this unfavourable terrain, the emergence of socialist ideas was slow. And it was through the double filiation from the Belgian workers' movement and from Roubaisian Guesdism which would define the structures and the operational methods of the first organisations in Halluin" (Hastings, 1991, p. 133).

The Belgian cooperative movement emerged earlier (and proved more resilient) than the French one and supported the creation of cooperatives in France through a cross-border transfer of social innovation. Thus, by the end of the nineteenth century, Roubaix had become both a central node of the French cooperative system and a laboratory of the rapidly growing socialist movement. The socialists had already gained control of the municipality in 1892, a

[7] The 1889 law established for the first time that French nationality was to be recognized to foreigners born in France and domiciled upon reaching the age of majority, unless they expressly renounced it. Previously, on the basis of the 1851 law, the "double ius soli" was valid: the child born in France of foreigners who were in turn born in France was French unless they renounced it.

[8] "Belgian speakers, regularly invited to meetings of La Paix [the Roubaix cooperative based in the People's House], gave speeches in Flemish. In 1899, the administrator of the people's house in Ghent [...] was invited to a meeting. He spoke in Flemish, a police observer noted: 'The floor was then given to citizen Schaw, from Ghent, who spoke in Flemish about socialism and cooperation'" (Cossart & Talpin, 2012, p. 602).

> triumph personified by the elected socialist mayor Henri Carrette[9] [...] and by Jules Guesde[10] who was elected member of parliament there in 1893. (Cossar & Talpin, 2012, p. 585)

Halluin's political situation was so backward that it struck the few observers who spoke about it in hindsight as incredible that at the beginning of the century there was not only a trace of socialism, but even a trace of republican radicalism. In 1903, Halluin still appeared "out of time and on the margins of the national territory. [...]. There is no dissent in the City Council, whose members are all against the Republic" (Hastings, 1991, p. 133). For Halluin's first few vanguards, relying on their comrades from Roubaix and Belgium was therefore inevitable. A police report from 1882 reported a new socialist group, "almost entirely made up of workers from Halluin", which, however, met on the other side of the border, in Menin. During the meeting—the report continues—"the newspapers Le Forçat from Roubaix and L'Avenir from Ghent were distributed free of charge [...] and the meeting took place at the Eperon d'Or, a disreputable venue, in front of an assembly of 20 people". This attempt "does not seem serious to me"—wrote the commissioner—"The Halluin worker is lazy, even vicious, but above all indifferent. Anyone who commits himself to a drink today will not remember tomorrow the commitment he made the day before". Hastings comments: "Despite the increasingly tight surveillance and repression by the bosses, despite the working conditions that leave little time or energy to participate in these political meetings, a handful of activists gather to receive instructions and advice from the Belgian leaders" (Hastings, 1991, p. 138). A pioneering strike in Halluin

---

9 Henri Carrette, born in Roubaix in 1846, the son of a weaver who left school at 11 and then became a weaver himself, was then a tavern keeper and newsagent. A member of the French Workers' Party founded in 1882, he directed "Le Forçat", a newspaper of the Socialist Federation of the North region, from 1882 to 1883. He was the first Socialist mayor of Roubaix, serving uninterruptedly for almost 10 years from 1892 to 1901. He is buried in the Roubaix cemetery, and his tomb bears the epitaph: Arise, wretched of the earth.

10 Pseudonym of Jules Bazile (1845–1922) taken from the name of his mother Eléonor Guesde, he was employed at the Ministry of the Interior when in 1863 he joined the Republican Party, later approaching the followers of Auguste Blanqui, intransigent supporters of the war against the capitalist order. After various events, convictions, prison, exile, following a series of conferences, in 1879 he founded the worker's party with Paul Lafargue, of which he drew up the program. Because of his intransigence, he soon found himself in conflict with the faction of Jean Jaurès, which was oriented toward obtaining immediate improvements in the conditions of the workers also through collaboration with the capitalist governments; and the contrast became more acute when, elected deputy for the department of Roubaix in 1893, he fought bitter parliamentary battles against the "possibilists". At the Reims congress (1903) the intransigence of the Guesdists allowed Jaurès to win. This intransigence also contrasted with the revolutionary syndicalism of the CGT on the question of the respective roles of the union and the party. Guesde tried for a long time to subordinate the union but never succeeded, while the French Communist Party succeeded by promoting the union split with the creation of the CGTU at the Saint-Étienne congress of 25 June-1 July 1922: Confédération Générale du Travail Unitaire which lasted until 1936 when it merged again with the CGT.

had to wait until the winter of 1895–96 (Gratry conflict),[11] a good 13 years after this police report on the first socialists. This uprising, which was successful,

> surprised observers of the time and can be considered the founding act of the workers' movement in Halluin [...], it reveals the decisive role played by the Belgians. The leaders of the conflict are almost all external to the municipality of Halluin. The strike committee was set up in Les Baraques [...] on Belgian territory between Menin and Halluin. [...]. The only people from Halluin mentioned in the police reports have no leading role in the development of the strike: Jules Massel, Vanoverbeck, Verstraete, all arrested for assault. [...]. This strike confirms the debt that the local workers' movement has towards the Flemish socialists. (Hastings, 1991, p. 83)

On 1 January 1896, about 30 weavers gathered in the tavern "A la Brousse d'Or" and founded the Halluin section of the Roubaix textile workers' union. "Before this date, union activity seems to have been practically non-existent. [...]. When the Gratry conflict broke out, there were only about twenty members of the socialist unions in Halluin" (Hastings, 1991, p. 86). It is in this context that the fundamental role played by the cooperative La Paix of Roubaix and its people's house for "Halluin la Rouge" must be placed.

6.3 The People's House of Roubaix

Founded in 1885 by Belgian workers following the example of the "Vooruit" in Ghent, "La Paix" was initially a small cooperative for bread and wholesale purchases of coal and foodstuffs. Members made their daily purchases there at low prices and, based on the decisions of the assembly, any surplus was partly set aside and partly distributed to the members in proportion to their purchases. The cooperative functioned democratically (one person, one vote), and the members of the Board of Directors had to be only workers[12]. Almost immediately, La Paix became openly socialist by tying itself to the Workers' Party founded by Guesde and Paul Lafargue in 1882. But it was not until 1899 that the cooperative was consolidated, with a beautiful headquarters,[13] but not yet a House of the People. This opened in 1901,

---

[11] "On November 15, 1895, thirty Gratry weavers went on strike to get their wages aligned with those of other employers. Jules Gratry [...], who had a reputation for absolute intransigence, responded on November 21 by firing the strikers and also their wives and children if they were his employees, a total of about a hundred people. This brutal decision provoked a reaction of solidarity that spread [...]. At the end of the month, there were 1,500 strikers [...]. The demands [...] multiplied (increase in wages, elimination of work on two looms, moderation of fines) [...]. The strike lasted three months. Some employers gave in fairly quickly. Others, like Gratry, refused to negotiate. It took the mediation of the Prefect to find an agreement on the new wages. The weavers resumed work on February 10, 1896" (Hastings, 1991, pp. 82–83).

[12] From the 1887 Statute: «In order to maintain full and complete independence, members who were team leaders, department heads, etc., may not be part of the Board of Directors» (Cossart & Talpin, 2012, p. 600).

[13] In the newspaper "L'Égalité" of 9 August 1899, one could read: "Anyone who has not been at La Paix for a few months would no longer recognize the place. Everything has been restored. The coffee room has been painted very nicely. It will soon be decorated with portraits of the world's

built by the Parisian architect of Swiss origin Albert Buhrer (Knight of the Legion of Honor). This is stated in a pamphlet distributed in view of the General Assembly of 1906:

> Members of the cooperative, you must never forget that with us everything belongs to everyone. [...]. We own buildings that cost about half a million; [...] we host: the Socialist Party, the Textile Union, the Mutual Aid Societies, the Freethinkers Groups; [...] we maintain a brass band, a trumpet group and a choir[14] (Cossart & Talpin, 2012, p. 589)

The construction and especially the successful management in balanced conditions of the people's house in Roubaix surprised many at the time and still surprises today. To understand it, it is necessary to know the living conditions of the working-class families that this initiative was intended to make less precarious. Hastings (1991, p. 75) discovered the documents of an investigation, extraordinary for the time, conducted by Dr. Verhaeghe through a questionnaire on 1,485 workers from Lille, Roubaix, and Armentières between 1903 and 1904. The investigation revealed that one worker in two at the age of 35 was in poor health, the longer they had worked in the textile industry, the worse their health. They suffered above all from respiratory problems (68% of the sick): chronic cough affected 8% of the workers who had worked less than three years and 40% of those with more than 20 years of work; 20% were tubercular patients. The causes were partly the unhealthiness of the places and the work but above all the excessive fatigue of the weavers; the cleaners were less ill and did a less healthy but lighter job. These difficult conditions of the workers resulted in high costs for the welfare and social security activities arranged by the people's house. If around 1900 the contributions to the strikers,[15] the party, and trade union activities cost 1.2% of the turnover, as did the assistance to sick or injured workers, free medical and pharmaceutical services, and social security insurance in the event of a serious accident or death. Now, "even Catholic cooperatives[16] provided

leading socialist activists. [...]. The large ballroom is splendid [...]. In the painted inserts on the walls, there are the names of Guesde, Jaurès, Liebknecht, Marx". In 1915, Karl Liebknecht founded the International Group, later the Spartacist League, with Rosa Luxembourg, and in 1919, during the "January Uprising", they were kidnapped and murdered by paramilitary groups employed to repress the movement by the same social democratic government then in power.

[14] The Bourse du Travail is not included in this list because the brochure wanted to draw attention to less obvious realities and initiatives, while it was obvious that the Bourse du Travail was there. "Dans le Nord [...] le modèle [...] unifie dans la Maison du peuple tous les piliers du mouvement ouvrier, parti, syndicat, coopération, mutuelle, Bourse du travail" (Morin, 2007, p. 47).

[15] "During the great March–April 1904 textile strike in Roubaix, which involved nearly 25,000 workers in 150 factories, La Paix organized soup kitchens for which [...] 5,000 francs were spent on meat, and bread was distributed free of charge. In addition, it guaranteed an allowance of 15 francs per week to its striking members. It defended them in court and paid all legal costs" (Cossart & Talpin, 2012, p. 591).

[16] The "Social Catholics" movement was particularly strong in this part of France after Rerum Novarum of 5 May 1891, the Encyclical of Pope Leo XIII that encouraged Catholics to deal with the "social question" by condemning socialist ideas of abolition of private property but also individualistic liberalism indifferent to the common good. It was in Roubaix in 1893 that the Catholic union was born at the instigation of Father Jules Bataille. Parish priest of Saint-Joseph in Wattrelos, he had already organized workers' meetings in 1892 and on 9 May he founded,

medical care, and even interest-free loans, but they never had relief funds for sick or injured members, and certainly no strike assistance or contributions to political parties or the union" (Cossart & Talpin, 2012, p. 590). For this reason, the Catholic cooperatives had a significant advantage over the people's house: they provided bread at lower prices. "From the beginning of the twentieth century, [...] La Paix was at a loss, and it was noted that the number of members was no longer increasing, [... the cause] was the price of bread, which was lower in the non-socialist cooperatives that did not spend on propaganda and solidarity" (Cossart & Talpin, 2012, p. 590). In fact, although the mature and elderly members might be interested in the exchange between more expensive bread and medical care, the young were less interested, as can be understood on the basis of the results obtained by Dr. Verhaeghe. Hence, the question is how it was possible to go on with the strong competition of the Catholic cooperatives. "The competition between the organizations was then fierce within the cooperative field" (Cossart & Talpin, 2012, p. 590). Trying to answer this question, one will understand that according to the "science" acquired with the example of Roubaix, no one would have seriously thought that a people's house in Halluin was possible.

The budget of the cooperative and the management of the people's house in Roubaix were balanced only thanks to the "self-financing" activities; parties, meetings, paid entertainment and cultural initiatives that, due to their popularity and attendance, provided considerable financial contributions. Often the witnesses spoke of their value for sociality and politics "beyond the financial aspect", thus taking for granted their importance from the resource side (Cossart & Talpin, 2012, p. 594). But the success of these activities came *after* the success of the people's house explained by the early political maturation, as Cossart and Talpin have shown. What emerges from their work is that there was certainly a mutual contamination between politics and sociality: «there is a mutual contamination [...]. The practices of the entrepreneurs of socialist politicization, in La Paix, far from neutralizing social affiliations, insert politics into everyday life. Traditional sociality is colored by politics and politics borrows its forms of organization from sociality» (Cossart & Talpin, 2012, p. 596). But it was politicization that allowed the people's house to take off and not vice versa (Cossart & Talpin, pp. 597–599). This also emerges in another writing by Cossart and Talpin (2012) dedicated to investigating the position of Guesde and the Workers' Party. Precisely because on the level of revolutionary theory they regarded cooperation with hostility, their contradictory support stood out: Guesde

---

with Florentin Wagnon and Louis Vienne, the "Union of the true workers of the textile industry of Roubaix" whose flag had the motto "For God and for the people". The new organization published a manifesto addressed to the working class, emphasizing independence from any socialist or employer influence. The Catholic union soon reached 1,200 members and was at the origin of the "Union des Syndicats libres de Roubaix-Tourcoing" in 1919. As for cooperatives, it is enough to note that in 1900, if La Paix had a baking room of 350 m^2, that of the Union was 1,000 (Jarrige, 2020), a cooperative born on the initiative of the Catholic union and some bourgeois in 1892, explicitly to compete with the socialist cooperative. In 1893, the Union's bread production was 832 tons, which became 6,104 in 1902. In 1904, it moved to larger premises, and its activities now included all those of the socialist cooperative with the exception of political activities (https://ateliers-memoire.com/roubaix/centre/la-boulangerie-de-lunion/).

himself inaugurated the new premises of La Paix in 1887. Concrete conveniences were valid: the politicized cooperative gave important support to the Workers' Party as well as to the parties that continued its action. Therefore, if the Belgian socialists[17] and the French socialists of Jaurès[18] were in favor of the development of the Roubaix cooperative for ideal and theoretical reasons, for practical reasons the Guesdists were also in favor, so that in the proletarian front everyone was in favor without exception. This was the lesson that came from the Roubaix experience: the people's house is the result of a process that can be set in motion and supported only by the *previous* political maturation. Therefore, the extremely backward state of the proletarian politicization of Halluin[19] made it clear to anyone with a sense of logic that it was impossible to transplant initiatives like the people's house to achieve this maturation: it would have been like reversing the cause-effect relationship.

6.4 Faith Against Science

But the improbable turned out to be possible and was achieved. While in Roubaix the Workers' Party won the municipal elections in 1892 and the people's house was inaugurated in 1901, in Halluin the socialists won them in 1919, and the people's house had already been there since 1907. While in Roubaix class consciousness and political action were the center and lever of social restructuring, from which followed the development of the cooperative and the people's house, in Halluin it was the people's house at the center of social restructuring. For this reason, to make it come into being it was necessary to use faith against science. That faith was used against science does not come only by deduction, that is, from the argument according to which for science the people's house of Halluin could not have been born in 1907. In fact, it is possible to trace the precise elements of the fideistic process of its birth whose reasons could have remained sterile without a "Moses"—Vandervelde who pushed and guided the proletarians of Halluin who were faced with the dramatic question of "to be or not to be". To be there as a counter-power as the comrades of Roubaix had shown they could be. A dramatic question since the alternative "not being there" was unbearable as a very serious distance widely perceived between desires and needs considered vital and reality.

[17] "One of the salient features of socialism in the North lies in the contrast between its two main inspirations: the orthodox Marxism of Guesde and the pragmatic Belgian tradition of cooperative and communitarian socialism. [...]. Belgian workers' activism is in fact characterised by the close relationship between party, cooperative and trade union" (Cossart & Talpin, 2012, pp. 168–169).

[18] In this regard, one can cite Jaurès' article in l'Humanité on 23 July 1910 entitled "At Work", in which he reaffirmed that socialist transformation is built with the "combined effects of cooperative action, trade union action and the political action of workers".

[19] "The centuries-old rule of conservative notables [...] was based on a close collaboration between industrial employers and the Catholic Church: an alliance [...] whose effectiveness lay in the effective implementation of a paternalistic system of mass control of workers" (Hastings, 1991, p. 264).

In 1899, Philippe Dannely[20] sent an "open letter to the senators and deputies of the North" "in which he painted a dark portrait of Halluin 'who exudes poverty from every pore' while Menin 'a city without factories is full of splendid shops'" (Hastings, 1991, p. 87). Philippe Dannely was the promoter of the "League for the Defense of National Labor" which proposed taxing non-resident workers who "weaken local trade" (Hastings, 1991, p. 87). By 1899, 10 years had passed since the first application of the law that gave French citizenship to the many Belgian workers who thus found themselves having to deal with the competition of their fellow countrymen as cross-border workers. "Placed in a situation of competition [...], the workers of Halluin and cross-border workers, despite their common origins, show profound divergences of interests" (Hastings, 1991, p. 88). The persistence of cross-border movements weakened the bargaining power of Belgians who had become French and worked in the same factories. It weakened it because life was cheaper in Belgium. And this happened "in the entire Lys valley [...where] trade union conflicts reveal xenophobic undertones. The suspicion, if not hostility, that exists in French factories towards workers who are not resident in France, accused of accepting low wages, of interrupting strikes or, on the contrary, of starting them thoughtlessly, finds strong support in public opinion" (Hastings, 1991, p. 88).

In 1903, out of 16,000 inhabitants, the number of workers in Halluin was 7,800 in 61 production units, 6,300 in textiles (5,500 weavers), 70% male, 80% over 18 years old, 54% worked in production units with 100 to 500 workers. There were 4,000 cross-border commuters, who came and went every day from Menin and the surrounding area. The members of some trade unions (socialist or Catholic) were 1,000 (Hastings, 1991, pp. 67–70). With half of them being cross-border workers, also mostly heads of families, with half of them being weavers in medium-small enterprises with high labor intensity (the mechanization of weaving had begun very late, only from 1872[21]), the resulting wage depression and low unionization[22] caused serious poverty among the population, both material and moral. Uncontrolled explosions of discontent followed, but they were short-lived and often led to the resistance front breaking during the strikes.

> At 3:30 p.m. on October 5, 1903, the strike was total [...] nearly 7,000 workers were out. For several days, an atmosphere of violence enveloped the city. Barricades were erected [...] at the corners of rue Neuve and rue des Ecoles. Clashes broke out between strikers and police.

[20] Foundry worker and vice-president of the Chamber of Trade Union of Metalworkers of the Maubeuge basin, 90 kms south-east of Halluin, still close to the Belgian border.

[21] "Renowned for their manual skill, less demanding in terms of wages than their French companions, these thousands of workers of rural origin will constitute a powerful brake on the mechanization of linen weaving which will appear in Halluin only around 1872. Such a low-cost workforce strengthened the local employers in their conservative attitude and absolute loyalty to a traditional, safe, profitable and undemanding system of production" (Hastings, 1991, p. 49).

[22] "In Halluin, workers' demands are organized around a very limited number of themes. Requests for wage increases represent 60% of the reasons. This over-representation of the wage aspect (43% in Saint-Denis, an industrial area in the northern suburbs of Paris) is the sign of archaic social relations, dominated by piecework, the individualism of the employer and the weight of the foreign workforce. Only one strike in five concerns the improvement of working conditions, defective raw materials or excessive fines" (Hastings, 1991, p. 97).

> 2,000 soldiers arrived. The brutal cavalry charges were met with the throwing of beetroots and broken bottles. The road from Halluin to Roncq was blocked by uprooted trees and torn up paving stones. Telegraph wires were cut, gas burners broken. [...]. But the strike evolved rapidly. Work resumed on October 19. [...]. This brief but rarely intense conflict is rich in lessons. [...] did not the workers on this occasion show the extent of their weaknesses, of their total disorganization, to the point that the riots swept away the young local union which, due to lack of resources, had to suspend its functioning until November? (Hastings, 1991, p. 102)

On the side of negotiations and the conduct of struggles, the poor unionization constituted a very serious problem that the accusations of strikebreaking launched by the few members against the many non-members did not help to resolve. All this and the strike of 1903 demonstrated that the issue was simple to understand and difficult to resolve: putting a stop to the powerful anarchic drift that made the Halluin workers structurally dependent on external organization but at the same time and for the same reason considered unreliable. This reality would have, in fact, required adequate consideration by the Roubaix Syndicalist Chamber on which the Halluin section depended, and, in general, by the socialist organization. Instead, this was lacking. Not only that, but on the occasion of the strike of 1903, Roubaix's aid to the Halluin strikers was actually reduced, a serious act which was justified by disagreements on the conduct of the strike, which, however, demonstrated total incomprehension on the part of the trade unionists and socialists of Roubaix. The events of 1903 demonstrated to the activists of Halluin, and to the population, their inferiority, dependence, subjection, tutelage, their "minority".

The solution was reached fairly quickly with the decision to set up an autonomous textile organization in Halluin and three subsequent years of a real attitude of dissidence toward the Guesdist-leaning National Federation of the Textile Industry (Hastings, 1991, p. 88). But the dissidence was not ideological. "If it is true that the 'dissidence' of Halluin took place in a context of clashes between Guesdists and Cégétists on the issue of the union function, [...] Victor Vandeputte's attitude, his concern for independence, testify above all to the determination of a man to understand and defend the unique reality of the city where he was born, and which the leaders of Roubaix do not understand" (Hastings, 1991, p. 88). But there was not only the front of dissidence; there was also that of action. In January 1904, a group of activists under the direction of Vandeputte himself began to develop the project for a cooperative bakery which, despite considerable difficulties in raising the initial capital of 500 francs, opened its doors in June of the same year under the name "La Fraternelle",[23] which at its foundation had about 60 members. After six months, there were 150 and the turnover was 39,000 francs. In 1907, there were 550 members, and the turnover was 100,000 francs. In that same year, La Fraternelle managed to open the Maison du Peuple, "rue de Saint André, a new place of worship" (Hastings, 1991, p. 91). Michel Hastings interviewed a dozen communist militants who were active between

---

[23] The initiative had considerable practical importance for the reduction of the price of bread, but it also had a symbolic meaning as a definitive detachment from the oppressive paternalism of the bosses. "At the beginning of the century there existed a small consumer cooperative, the 'Epicerie économique' [...] linked to the paternalism of the employers" (Hastings, 1991, p. 89).

the two wars, asking what they knew about those times in which Halluin's "red" identity was beginning to emerge. After reporting their testimony, in addition to the archive documentation he had collected, Hastings draws this summary.

> To be born or not to be born, that seemed to be the question […]. Collective emergence, first of all, of a working-class community that had been marginalized for too long […]. But also individual awareness of the unacceptable and the unbearable. […] Our interviews revealed this double question that structures the entire adventure of Halluin the Red, and that invariably runs through the theme of social revenge. […]. Local memory returns fragments of this process. «With the Party, I think, we made them pay… it was a fight to the death… One day there had to be justice» (Emilio V.). This desire to say what is right and true gives the action of the Maison du Peuple that additional legitimacy that is essential for any missionary enterprise. […]. «Every day we had to convince people… tell them what we were doing» (Gustave Casier). (Hastings, 1991, pp. 425–426)

One can note: «saying what is right and true», a singular coincidence, unless Hastings had listened to Foucault's lectures or read the transcripts that were circulating, but he does not cite him, and it is not possible that he read the printed text which was published only in 2008. It means that that argument and its precise expression impose themselves on reality for their strength that is thus testified. One must then note "one day there had to be justice", this is the faith that allowed the people's house of Halluin to be born. Then, "if in 1907 the comrades had the satisfaction of having a small People's House, they soon needed an adequate Temple, large enough to organize meetings and celebrations […] whose inauguration, on 26 July 1914, will take on the aspect of a consecration" (Hastings, 1991, p. 91) (Fig. 6.3).

Fig. 6.3 The People's House of Halluin (https://pagnerre.blogspot.com/2000/02/la-maison-du-peuple-halluin.html)

6.5 Polycrisis

The years that saw the maturation of the idea in Halluin, then the realization, and then the consolidation of the people's house were times of structural crisis that would be further aggravated by the war. It was a season of exhaustion of the consolidated forms of social organization, and the local dimension was inserted into a critical scenario at the national level. The explicit and implicit rules that governed the distribution of social and political roles, of power, income, and wealth had come to demonstrate results that were now intolerable. Added to all this, in the departments of Northern France, there was a problem of weakening of the productive structure. The fundamental textile sector was in difficulty and constituted 35% of the French industrial added value, concentrated in the North apart from the relatively minor silk sector in Lyon. The production quantity index, which had risen from 100 in 1890 to 135 in 1907, stopped at this level (Lévy-Leboyer, 1968) because, except for silk, it had lost competitiveness (Bécuwe & Blancheton, 2020).

This complex of structural exhaustions in Halluin manifested itself together with the now unbearable anachronism of the traditionalist employers loyal to religion (but also firmly opposed to the first social openings of the Church) who continued to say, as already reported: the Halluin worker is "a good-natured but slow boy who shows a lot of negligence, an infantilizing representation that the workers, overwhelmed by poverty, were less and less willing to accept". They were those workers who "lived in unhealthy houses (still in 1968 only 19% had a toilet in the house) with two or three rooms per family, rented, with the main consolation of having a dive for every 11 houses" (Tilly, 1986, pp. 367–368). Furthermore, the regime of low wages in relation to the cost of subsistence had become unbearable, an element of serious frustration that had almost ceased to exist in France for over 40 years. The rudimentary workers' organization was unable to remedy the situation, also because it was little understood and little helped by the union and party headquarters, and the absenteeism of militants was serious[24] both because, having to extend their working hours to earn a living, they had little free time, and because their mental space was reserved solely for the struggle for bread.

The war added a further serious trauma to this state of crisis. It began in France on August 3, 1914, and the entire region of Lille-Roubaix-Halluin was occupied from 13 October when the Germans, after the first battle of the Marne, retreated toward the sea, leaving only on 14 October 1918, after exactly four long years of occupation. The damage they caused was enormous. The loss of inhabitants (11% between the censuses of 1911 and 1921), greater than that which occurred in Lille,

[24] "The meeting of March 31, 1907 brought together only ten people, barely one sixth of the number of members. On October 28, 1906, the financial situation could not be checked. Only one of the five members of the commission was present. The lack of attendance also affected the executive committee: only three members out of twelve attended the meeting of February 10, 1909. Faced with what he called desertions, Vandeputte decided a few days later, despite the contrary opinion of the treasurer Villers, to establish a system of attendance fees of 25 cents in exchange for a fine of 10 cents for each delay, regretting 'that we have to play the carrot and stick to hope to be able to walk more or less regularly'" (Hastings, 1991, p. 145).

Roubaix, and Tourcoing (5–7%), triggered a demographic crisis that continued into the post-war period. While at the end of the conflict in other urban centers the decline in population stopped and then increased, in Halluin the negative balances continued. There had been the forced evacuation of 6,000 people in June 1917 and the deportation to Germany of able-bodied men who were not employed in the requisitioned factories. The direct damage can also be quantified: 417 victims and 1,000 wounded, 10 million francs (1914 currency) for 700 houses completely razed to the ground (20% of the existing total) and another 1,200 damaged, 20 million (4 million in 1914 currency) of debt of the Municipality which would be a very heavy legacy for the communists when they came to government in 1919, 280 million (56 million in 1914 currency) of damage to the production system. "The war presents itself to Halluin as the traumatic event par excellence, the detonator of the social cataclysm to come" (Hastings, 1991, p. 181). Therefore, the years from 1907 onwards saw serious cracks in all the supporting structures of local society. The people's house found itself born and growing.

> in the midst of a demographic, social, cultural transformation. [...]. The identity remains [...], but the wear and tear of its various defining elements transforms the old coat of arms of recognition into a stigma of the past, obsolete and fragile. On the other hand, there is a slow-paced industrial change [...] and the strengthening of the traditional textile mono-industry [...] which makes Halluin vulnerable to the slightest jolt of crisis. The community freezes, closes in on itself. After having been a place of adoption and welcome, Halluin becomes an immobile society and rediscovers, in these times of industrial rationalization, the autarchic languor of rural cities» (Hastings, 1991, p. 189)

In such conditions, the birth of the people's house due to the exercise of faith against science was followed by growth for which the exercise of science against faith was essential.

6.6 Science Against Faith

Science was a "theorem" learned from the Roubaix experience. Statement: *the people's house is the place of proletarian self-emancipation.* Demonstration: *the people's house gains credit by solving workers' problems; therefore, an interactive relationship is established between the social and political body, which uses traditional forms of social interaction, from which further consensus and the ability to solve problems as well as the ability to progressively modify such forms of social interaction.*

Solving workers' problems:

> The people's house provides bread, coal, medicine, unemployment insurance and health insurance. In this way the interest in participation goes far beyond the simple pleasure of sociality. [...] it is because local socialism solves the daily problems of workers that militants have been able to enjoy almost constant electoral loyalty. (Cossart & Talpin, 2012, p. 607)

Interaction between social and political body.

> The socialist vote [...becomes] a gesture of social affirmation, a testimony of loyalty to a group. [...]. The Maison du Peuple [...] constitutes a space in which this group can form, become aware of itself through the work of the entrepreneurs of politicization. [...]. It is therefore a question of placing oneself in a perspective that is attentive to the way in which the party – through the mediation of the Maison du Peuple – constitutes the group that will support the party (Cossart & Talpin, 2012, p. 599).

Further consensus and problem-solving ability.

> By building an appreciated and glorious image of the workers, of which the Maison du Peuple is the incarnation, and by penetrating the forms of traditional sociality, [...it] has contributed decisively to the formation of a working-class consciousness. (Cossart & Talpin, 2012, p. 599)

This science was in clear contradiction with the faith of the revolutionary trade union and then of the Communist Party of the Third International: believing that prosperity for the proletariat would come only after the destruction of bourgeois power. It was a condition similar to that faced by Moses, who, in order to lead the people to new structures, did not neglect tradition, and "from the imagination of the people" drew new institutions not too much in contrast with their habits. As in the example of the Jewish people, the theorem of the people's house also presents innovation and inclusion. Innovation because it solves the problems of the proletariat, inclusion because it is a device open even in the process of politicization, with the interaction between social group and party. In the theorem of the people's house, one can also recognize a synthesis of the "model" coming from the literature on collective action. It was said that the commitment is renewed provided that there are adequate resources, the valorization of all the contributions to the design and implementation of collective action, good results. Good results are the solution of workers' problems, adequate resources come from the interactive relationship between the social and political body, the valorization of all the contributions to the design and implementation of collective action lies in the use of traditional forms of social interaction that valorize contributions, even apparently eccentric ones, from which further consensus and the ability to solve problems emerge.

The "people's house theorem" was truly a science. One can even recognize in it the analogy with the Structure–Conduct–Performance paradigm conceived in the 1930s and formalized by Joe Staten Bain of the University of Berkeley in 1959: the first «positive theory of strategic corporate management that attributed a scientific dimension to questions of industrial organization, until then considered only from a normative point of view, of the efficiency of different forms of the market» (Teece, 1984, p. 94). According to this paradigm, the results of the company depend on the use that it makes of its resources to adapt and take advantage of the technical–economic structure in which it operates, with feedback effects from the results to the resources and the ability to influence the structure. Thus configured, the paradigm concerns a basic question that is found in every organizational reality, that of the relationship between "agency" and "structure". For this reason, the analogy between business and the people's house is not inappropriate, even though they are devices located in very different worlds, that of private profit and that of the collective good. The people's house, a device for producing utilities that are greater than costs (solving workers' problems) is analogous to a business that aims for a positive balance of the economic account. The traditional forms of social interaction in the people's house (usual forms of exchange and communicative relations through presence, gesture, and word) are analogous to the technical–economic structure in which the business's relations are located. The resources obtained from the interactive relationship between the social and political body also on the basis of problem solving are analogous to the business's resources obtained on the basis of profits. The return effects on the technical–economic structure are analogous to the return effects on the transformation of social interaction forms.

6.7 Outcomes

The services provided by the people's house and "La Fraternelle" (1,000 members in 1914, almost double 10 years later) were similar to those in Roubaix. But other initiatives, specifically aimed at assisting striking and unemployed workers, were particularly important in Halluin: a work cooperative "Emancipation ouvrière", a mutual aid society, and above all a specific "educational" action. It has been seen that in Halluin the problem of inconclusive rebellion was acute. From 1903 to 1914 there were about 100 strikes lasting an average of 25 days, almost double that of other industrial areas in Northern France, while the number of strikers far exceeded that of union members. From a condition of resigned social peace, the "earthquake of 1903" had given rise to a season of revolts. But the costs outweighed the benefits. It was the weight of the missed wages in the face of disappointing outcomes of the disputes, it was the layoffs that inexorably followed every defeat of the workers, it was the weakening or lack of strengthening of the union due to a mechanism set in motion by the strike that was not fully understood.

> The strike was often intended not as a means to open a negotiation with the aim of improving a concrete condition, but as a way of gesturing […] against tyranny. […]. The socialists were "used" by the workers for blackmail […] if you force us, the weavers told the bosses, we will follow the enemies of property. This threat produced some concessions [but also] the persistent panic of the bosses in front of the union and the refusal to recognize it […] contributing to maintaining the worker in the status of "deferential worker". […]. Every lost dispute ended with a load of dismissals […] and with the order given to the industrialists of the region adhering to the Consortium, to refuse any hiring of "hotheads". (Hastings, 1991, pp. 108, 228)

For this reason, assistance activities for the unemployed and strikers were crucial, but also "an intense educational effort" aimed at unionization as discipline "to limit the number of strikes and, above all, to avoid their sudden outbreak" starting from the "Resolution" which stated: «The strike is a dangerous weapon if used badly, every strike that breaks out suddenly can harm the interests of workers, it can have its true effect only when it is used as a last resort» (Hastings, 1991, p. 99). On 28 March 1909, the leaders of Halluin founded a "Union of Trade Unions" which was transformed on

20 June 1910 into the Bourse du Travail with its headquarters in the People's House. The Bourse quickly brought together five unions. To those of textiles (1903) and wood (1905) were added those of construction (4 July 1909), carters and transport (5 May 1910), and food workers (11 December 1910). From the 1,000 members of the textile union in 1900, this organizational development favored the increase in unionization and in 1913 the number of members reached 3,000(of which more than 2,000 were textile workers).

The first fruits of this "educational effort" were recorded as early as 1912 by Victor Vandeputte: «We see that [...] our union method has given good results. We are not strikers to the bitter end» ("L'Union Syndicale" 52, 1912). The results of the educational effort were seen in the discipline that led to the success of the 1920 dispute. Faced with rising prices without wage adjustments, the union delegates of the Lys Valley and Roubaix had sent a letter to the employers' organization, the Textile Consortium, to start negotiations, but had received an arrogant refusal. On March 10, the work stoppage was decided, and it had a very large turnout (65,000 strikers), so much so that, five days later, the Consortium offered to triple the value of the cost-of-living allowance. The CGT considered the offer insufficient and ordered the struggle to continue. The arbitration of the Minister of Labor Jourdaine intervened and on 30 March the agreement was signed. "Ultimately, this textile strike [...] was a triple victory: material victory thanks to the economic advantages obtained [quadrupling of the allowance], moral because the determination and cohesion of the workers had been demonstrated, [...political] because they had been recognised by the public authority" (Hastings, 1991, p. 208). This result, which certainly did not solve all the problems but undoubtedly constituted an important step forward, translated into new consensus for the organizations established in the people's house. The party doubled its members (from 109 to 231), the union went from 2,700 to 3,200 members out of 9,700 workers. This consensus supported a virtuous mechanism of reciprocal relations between the party and the social group of the people's house.

6.8 Interactive Relationship

Political and trade union organizations conceived the strategies and tactics of proletarian emancipation in very different ways. Jules Guesde himself and the Guesdists attempted in various ways to unify them under the leadership of the Party: first the People's Party, then the Socialist Party of France, then the SFIO (French Section of the Workers' International—Second International). The objective was finally achieved—at least formally—by the Communist Party of the Third International which, after the Tours Congress (25–30 December 1920), took the place of the SFIO.[25] These efforts of overall political direction by the party resulted in a

[25] At the Tours Congress, the motion to join the Third International was approved by 3,209 delegates (76%) and rejected by 1,022 (24.2%) out of a total of 4,231. On 1 October 11,921, the new "Section Française de l'Internationale Communiste" (SFIC), later "Parti Communiste" had 109,391 members

process of selection of militants. Many members joined but after a short time they left "silently" (Kriegel, 1966a, 1966b, p. 11; Kriegel, 1966b, p. 1250) both because militancy entailed concrete dangers (up to arrest), and because it was not easy to ensure the dedication required by the party and, after 1920, the Third Internationalist orthodoxy. Traces of this selection by exclusion can be found in the trend of members compared to union members in France. In fact, it can be noted that, although with ups and downs, there was a tendency for this ratio to reduce, as the complex history of the party unfolded, first with a growing number of members until the 1920s, then in decline, and then again on the rise until the Second World War (Fig. 6.4).

In Halluin too, at least since 1906,[26] there were efforts to unify the political line, indeed particularly intense efforts due to the delay in the birth of workers' organizations. In fact, the comparison between Halluin's data and the national data is surprising, with an opposite trend in the ratio between party and union members, which was increasing in Halluin in the presence of a no less complex history: there too the number of members first increased until the mid-1920s, then decreased until the mid-1930s and then increased again (Fig. 6.5).

This comparison is only a clue, but a significant one, of the difference between the characteristics of the evolution of the proletarian party nationally and in the local reality of Halluin: nationally through selection of militants by exclusion, locally by avoiding it. Perhaps this is because in Halluin the organization of the party was less demanding, so that the relative absence of selection by exclusion came from a "lighter" militancy. The answer to this hypothesis can only be negative due to the strictly working-class character of Halluin's socialism and then communism. In this regard, Bernard Pudal's interpretation is valid, according to which the practice of "trials" within the party, always attributed to impositions from above later exacerbated by Stalinism, had, in reality, happened previously. It responded to a logic of self-valorization of the militants who imposed demanding conditions to exorcise the fear of remaining "nothing but stooges". Even in Halluin such political processes were practiced for a vast repertoire of shortcomings, not only those stirred up by sectarianism after 1920, which also claimed its victims.[27]

(Kriegel, 1966a, 1966b, p. 18), a loss of about 20,000 members from the previous year. At the Congress of the Federation of the North in Lille on 19 December, six days before the start of the National Congress in Tours, support for the majority motion had been 63%, significantly lower than the 76% it would have in Tours, and this was due to the greater weight of the revolutionary socialists displaced by the Bolsheviks. In Halluin the membership was unanimous but in an assembly that brought together only half of the members (Hastings, 1991, p. 205), demonstrating a subtle but real distance between official discipline and the actual feelings of the members.

[26] "The date [...] of the creation of a socialist group in Halluin has long remained uncertain. [...]. A real structure [...] was created on 8 April 1900 by Jean Goerland, Victor Vandeputte, Achille Huysentruit and Cyrille Dumoulin. [...]. In reality, like trade unionism, socialism in Halluin would extend its prehistory until 1903–1904, dates in which the local workers' movement first asserted its true autonomy" (Hastings, 1991, pp. 142–143).

[27] "The Party pays a high price for its sectarianism: marginalization of its most popular figure, ousting and demotion of two of its most active leaders, resignations of activists from the PC, the CGTU and Free Thought (the figure of 80 is cited). The acceptance of this bloodshed seals the

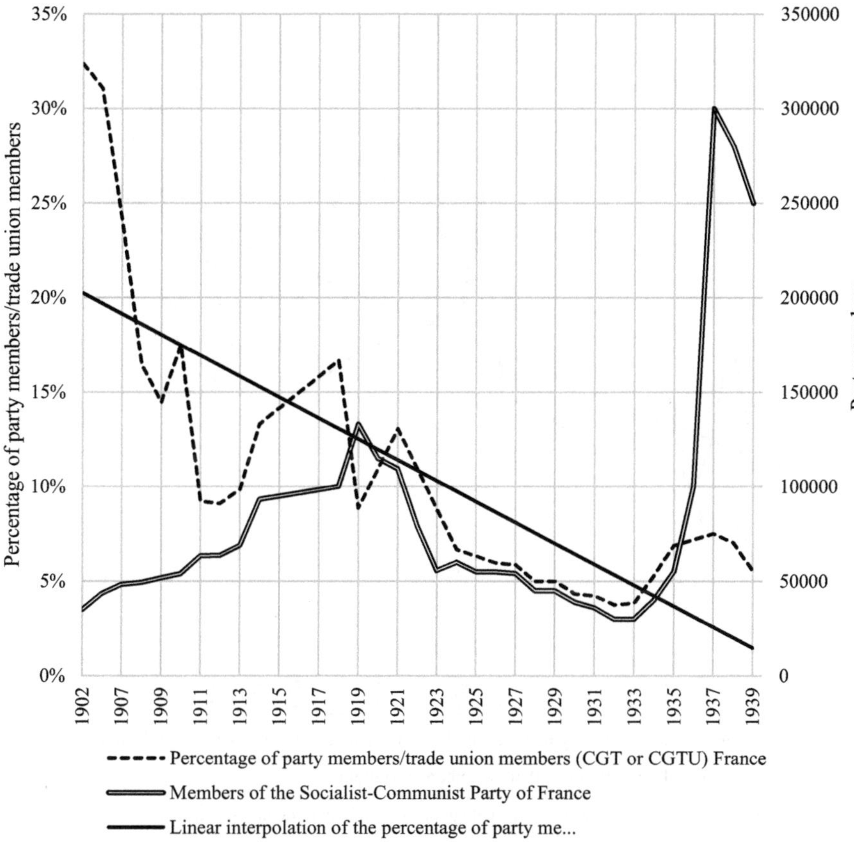

Fig. 6.4 Socialist-Communist Party members and share in relation to trade union members (CGT-CGTU) in France excluding overseas territories (interpolated missing data 1915–1918, 1922–1923). *Source* Figure obtained by processing data from Dreyfus (1995), Cépède (2008), Kriegel (1966a, 1966b), Azéma et al. (1986); when different figures were found in different sources for the same year, the average was taken

The different character assumed by the militancy in Halluin, certainly not facilitated and certainly not protected from losses and defections, must therefore be explained differently. In the face of losses and defections, there was a continuous strong feeding of the members for the interactive relationship between the *open* social group and the party, an interaction which was possible thanks to the strength of the people's house. This interaction was achieved, paradoxically and therefore very effectively, precisely at the instigation of the Guesdist leaders who in principle were wary of cooperation (but also wary of trade union autonomy).

---

victory of a militant ethic on which Stalinism will anchor its doctrine, in Halluin as elsewhere" (Hasting, 1991, p. 233).

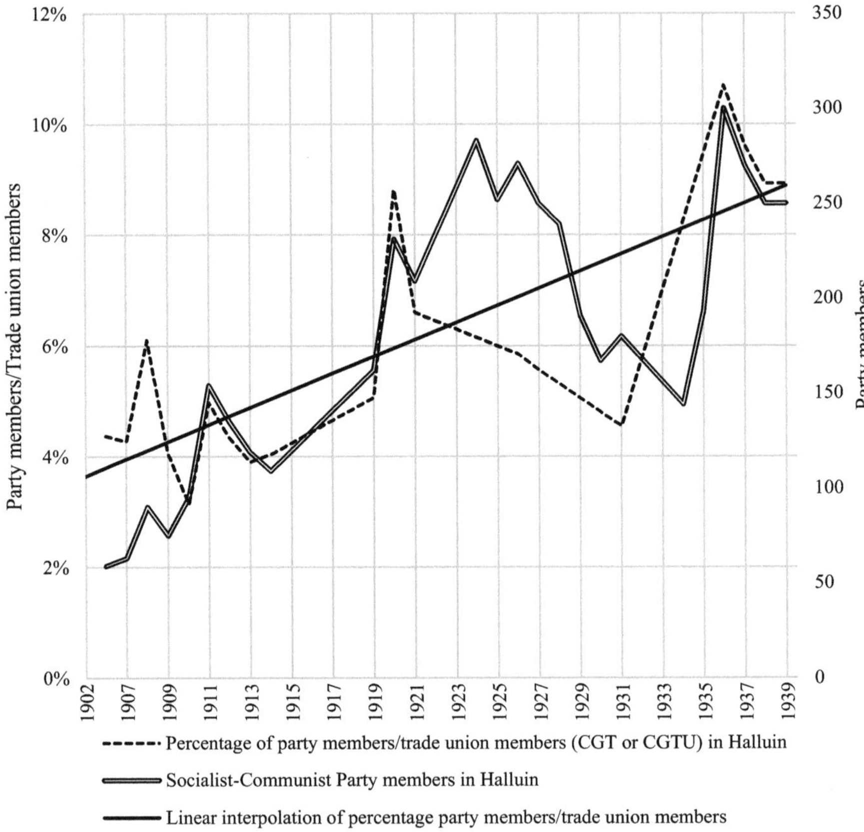

Fig. 6.5 Socialist-Communist Party members and share in relation to trade union members (CGT-CGTU) in Halluin (interpolated missing data 1915–1918, 1922–1925, 1932–1934). *Source* Figure obtained by processing data from Hastings (1991) various pages

> The Guesdists of Halluin did not limit themselves to accepting cooperative societies as a means of financing political activities, but they admitted the idea that they could be transformed into places of socialization in which feelings of solidarity would be strengthened through contact with a dense network of different activities. The associative framework [...] constitutes the antechamber of the socialist movement [...where] one soon finds oneself surrounded on all sides by a beneficial network of solidarity works so that the member, initially not very convinced, appreciates more and more the group to which he belongs and remains permanently tied to it. (Hastings, 1991, pp. 90–91)

The reason for this position of the Guesdists in Halluin can be understood by considering the value of the percentage of party members in relation to union members, on average a meager 5% until 1919, while at the national level it was more than double. With the aim of putting the union under control, it was therefore a question of using the cooperation and the people's house not only for financial contributions but also to increase party members in order to counterbalance the preponderant strength of the union.

But, beside this side of the relationship between the open social group of the people's house and the party, beside this propulsion of militancy, there was also the other side, which went from the party to the nourishment of the social group. This second side of the interactive relationship concerned the forms of communication and socialization promoted by the party in favor of the people's house. Especially in contexts with a dominant working-class base and dominant bourgeois hegemony, as emblematically in Halluin, political propaganda and information certainly used newspapers, magazines, and meetings, but next to these usual forms,

> considered most of the time boring by the workers, the Guesdists developed and perfected forms of propaganda of a festive nature [...]: cavalcades, games and competitions, dances and concerts; supporting recreational and sports societies [...], a parallel sociality, on the margins of the associative fabric controlled by the conservative notables [...]: the competition that begins between the socialist party and the employers, whose stake is the conquest and the use of entertainment and popular customs. (Hastings, 1991, p. 148)

From there it was a rather short step toward investing in traditional forms of social interaction to make them forms of "progressive folklore".

> Halluin la Rouge [...]: twenty years of a formidable revolutionary epic during which a small frontier town in the Nord department became the holy city of communism [...]. How can we explain the total conquest by the CP in 1920 of a town that had until then been completely conservative? Shouldn't one of the keys to the adventure of the weavers of Halluin la Rouge be sought in the nature of local communism? [...]. Local communism does not appear as a set of normative solutions produced by elites [...] that would gradually spread throughout the social body through militant dynamics, the ability to convince and mobilize. To permeate the political and social fabric of the town, communism had to become something other than itself, far beyond what it said. Not just a systematic project of power distribution but a vector of identity. Joining the PCF, through voting and activism, allowed the Halluin community to renew its distinctive loyalties at a time when the community fabric was fraying [...]: a collective personality to [...] be proud of. The success of this transmutation, the foundation of identity, can only be understood on condition that Halluin communism is not confused with a theoretical corpus or a political line [...] defined by the Congresses [...], but as a form of popular culture, which had become the mirror in which the inhabitants of Halluin looked at themselves and expected to be recognized. (Hastings, 1991, pp. 2, 430)

6.9 "Progressive" Folklore

This "local communism vector of identity" was born and grew in the people's house, the "machine" whose eclectic generative capacity was truly surprising. It was being built, remembering the lesson of Ernesto De Martino, the progression between the use of traditional forms of mythical articulation of chaos (the drama of being rejected) and the reparative action, to arrive at representing and realizing the articulation of the passage from the old clerical-bourgeois order to the new lay-proletarian.

6.9.1 Identity Spaces and Mythical Figures

The first and basic piece of community regeneration was in the town's "courtyards". These were spaces enclosed between a group of houses built by the masters of Halluin without any urban plan just for reasons of pure building speculation, so much so that they were then counterproductive for the control of the subordinates. In other contexts of nineteenth-twentieth century industrialization in the urban planning of the workers' citadels of the paternalism of the capitalists, the spaces were open and distributed to exclude places of subversion and favor their control from the outside. The courtyards of Halluin were, on the contrary, places closed toward the outside and open toward the inside. They were paradoxical anti-panoptic devices, paradoxical because they were built by the capitalists: small agoras of visibility and participation of the proletarians and their families in their daily lives. Well, in these spaces of community life the natural leaders were activists of the people's house in the 1920s and 1930s.

> The court represents a microcosm of total transparency. [...]. In these spaces where everything is done, everything is seen and everything is heard, a reference personality ends up emerging. Oral testimonies have confirmed that it was often an activist of the Maison du peuple. These "leaders" ensure the cohesion of the community by exercising a sort of permanent social pressure where the apparent absence of political ideology nevertheless imposes a framework of conduct. (Hastings, 1991, p. 350)

In the communist newspaper "Le Travailleur" of October 1929 one could read: «We must work to ensure that the courtyards of Halluin become healthy places. But we do not want to erase them. For the residents who live there they represent a family spirit that must be protected». A strange and significant contradiction: the courtyards and the family spirit yes, the cells of the Bolshevik party no. The newspaper "Cahiers du Bolchevisme", which had already returned several times to the merely formal Bolshevism in Halluin, would in fact denounce the following year: «Despite numerous textile companies, despite a major strike, despite but perhaps because of a communist municipality, [...] in 1930 there was no company cell» (Hastings, 1991, p. 365).

From micro to macro, from the existing to the utopian, one can change perspective and consider what was the representation of the future ideal city proposed by the people's house. With some surprises. In fact, the paradoxical operation, nevertheless affirmed, of making a radically new, but also ancient, proletarian city, capable of not excluding anyone, was proposed. On the one hand, initiatives to build the image of Halluin "The Red" multiplied, even with the change of street names[28] and the boycott of the construction (with private money) of the monument to the fallen of the First World War, "bourgeois and imperialist war". Thus, the Police Commissioner wrote to the Prefect on 20 August 1924: «since the arrival of the revolutionaries at the town

[28] "The new nomenclature loses its battlefields (Alma, Austerlitz, Jemmapes) and its intercessors (Saint-Jean, Saint-Roch, Saint Hilaire) to celebrate science (Darwin, Champollion, Galileo), social literature (Emile Zola, Eugène Sue), the pioneers of the workers' and republican movement (Jules Guesde, Louise Michel, Blanqui)" (Hastings, 1991, p. 356).

hall, Halluin has lived far from everything and against everyone» (Hastings, 1991, p. 364). But, on the other hand, in the "manifesto" of the future city of November 1919, alongside ecumenical beauty, brotherhood appears, and, at the center, there is the people's house which becomes "the House of All", exactly the opposite of the biased opinion of the Police Commissioner.

> Halluin, a workers' citadel placed at the vanguard of the socialist troops [...] will awaken pride in the souls of its inhabitants. Let us imagine the city of tomorrow, tree-lined, cleaned, with wide streets, embellished with lush gardens and public monuments. Whose architectural simplicity will be an inspiration of brotherhood, with the House of All at its center. ("Le Réveil Socialiste", n. 52, 30 November 1919)

After the articulation of places, one must consider the figures made mythical by the communist narrative produced in Halluin: the smuggler and the migrant weaver. Both are singularly connected to the places of solidarity and struggle (the courtyards for the smugglers, the factory and the people's house for the weaver who came from Flanders in search of dignity), but also mythical figures of local tradition. It was once again "Le Travailleur" (26 August 1924) that reports the story of Emilio, one of the many characters who were periodically evoked in interviews, which may or may not have been true, but were in any case absolutely plausible: «I have been working since I was 9, I am 77 and I still have no pension while many of the bosses I worked for now have large factories. When I was young, I had to leave my hometown, I was put on the black list by the priest and the notables of the town because I dared to defend my rights as a worker». As for the smugglers, who had always been active in this border region, they found refuge and assistance in the courtyards, first when they transported food and "comfort" goods, then when they began to transport subversive ideas and propaganda materials.

> By protecting the smugglers' subculture, the courtyards gradually transform into environments of ferment of opposition ideas. A clan organization reigns [...] so significant that it later influences the modes of political expression of workers' protest. [...] Well, the smugglers and the migrant weavers were the social stereotypes from which the activists of the Casa del Popolo extract the heroes of a mythical discourse. [...] A sort of popular exemplum that converts local singularities [...] into a true "chanson de geste", which knows how to speak to the inhabitants of Halluin [...] who recognize themselves in the smuggler, in the migrant weaver, these slices of life that the Party spreads liberally in its newspapers, their names populate the local legend and impose themselves as references of identity. The social imaginary of the city feeds on these recognized figures that time idealizes and that communist hagiography transfigures. (Hastings, 1991, pp. 351, 370, 374)

Finally, one must consider the true apotheosis of investment in traditional forms of social interaction, revisited by the people's house to serve the generative proletarian narrative: the "funeral" of Désiré Ley. It will be an important lesson for understanding the long labor of developing an alternative proletarian culture and, perhaps, also for grasping a utility for the present. In Ley's funeral one can examine the economy of the process intended to build "progressive folklore", an irreplaceable piece of the application of science against faith. Science as a theorem: the people's house gains credit by solving workers' problems, therefore an interactive relationship is established between the social and political body, which uses traditional forms of social interaction, from which a further consensus and the ability to solve problems, as well as the ability to modify such forms of social interaction. Against faith, according to which prosperity for the proletariat would come only after the destruction of bourgeois power without having to demonstrate improvements in the process that led to the conquest of power. Indeed, the "funeral" shows that using traditional forms of social interaction in order to obtain consensus and the ability to modify them is a difficult task that requires sophisticated attention to cultivate a singular "ambiguity" between conservation and innovation.

6.9.2 Désiré Ley and the "Consortium"

Désiré Ley, a former worker, became Secretary of the Roubaix-Tourcoing Textile Consortium in 1919[29] which included Halluin. Some data relating to the Textile Consortium are available which allow the following table to be compiled (Table 6.1).

The absolute importance of the Consortium can be seen. In 1924, out of a total population of 209,000 people (115, 000 in Roubaix, 80,000 in Tourcoing, 14,000 in Halluin), the workers working in member companies were 57,000 and their families included 145,000 people: seven out of ten inhabitants of the district lived on wages paid by Consortium companies. Five years later, in 1929, the population had increased slightly, reaching 212,000 inhabitants, while the workers of the member companies had reached 73,000 and the proportion of people living on their wages had reached 8.7 out of 10. But it was not only the wage bill that determined the dependence of the entire population on the Consortium companies. There was also a system of "surplus wages"[30] inherited from the previous Catholic-inspired employer initiative ("Familia"[31]) which had adopted it, so it was stated, to comply with the

[29] In an eight-page pamphlet entitled "To the workers subjected to the yoke of the Consortium under the dictatorship of Ley" printed in Lille by the Communist Party in 1927, one reads: «The Consortium Textiles was created in 1919 [actually on April 1, 1920] by an industrialist from Roubaix, Mr. Eugène Mathon, a member of 'Action Française', and by Désiré Ley. At the beginning it included only thirty or so employers, but today there are 347 industrialists who are members of the Consortium». "Action Française" was the right-wing nationalist movement born during the "Dreyfus Affair" which, after his rehabilitation in 1906, denied the innocence of the Jewish captain, although it had been clearly established, and continued a campaign of extreme violence so much so that it received heavy sentences following the denunciations of Alfred Dreyfus himself. Between the two wars, Action Française, while remaining fundamentally anti-Semitic, on the social question adopted positions close to those of the Social Doctrine of the Church in favor of the integration of the proletariat into a legal and political society but rejecting the class struggle.

[30] Family allowances in the amounts (1926) of 2.4 to 3.6 francs per day for each child under the age of 14 (the lowest amount for a single child and then increasing as the number of children increased), equal to something more than 10% in relation to the average daily wage. There was also a bonus of 240 francs at the birth of each child and reimbursement (50 francs) for a prenatal medical visit. Finally, there were payments in the event of illness.

[31] Already during the German occupation, Eugène Mathon had gathered some members of the dormant "Catholic Association of Employers of the North" around the Reverend Ernest Lebeau, spiritual assistant of this association, with the aim of "reviving an organization based on faith,

Table 6.1 Consortium of the Roubaix-Tourcoing textile industry (which included Halluin), wages, working hours, and employees in all the member firms

	1922	1923	1924	1925	1926	1927	1928	1929
Wages (millions of francs) textile activity only	272	296	335	375	489	516	575	596
Wages (millions of francs) all activities (*)	288	314	355	398	518	548	610	632
Working hours (millions) textile activity only	128	137	142	149	168	162	175	182
Working hours (millions) all activities	135	146	151	158	178	172	186	193
Working days (8 h) all activities (millions)	16,9	18,2	18,8	19,7	22,2	21,5	23,2	24,1
Daily wage all activities (francs)	17	17	19	20	23	25	26	26
Workers (330 working days per year) all activities (thousands)	51	55	57	60	67	65	70	73

(*)Estimates based on 1926 data; (**)Estimates based on wages
Source Figures obtained by processing data from Denuc (1930, p. 956), Ley (1927)

recommendations of the social doctrine of the Church.[32] In fact, the system, which was rapidly adopted in the main industrial centers throughout France in the two-year period 1918–1920,[33] responded only to a minor extent to these recommendations, as well as to a general pro-natalist concern of employers who saw large families

intended to develop a triple action in businesses: social, moral and religious" (Caudron, 1991, p. 411). Nothing came of it also because Mathon did not want to give space to intentions, such as that of an authoritative participant in these meetings, Dr. Jules Vanneuf Ville of Tourcoing, who wanted to associate workers' organizations if available. Thus, on 15 March 1919, the association of only employers, "Familia", was born, which had a short life, replaced on the initiative of Mathon himself on 1 April 1920, by the "Consortium" without references to spiritual values. During its short existence, Familia nevertheless had time to formalise the "surplus wage" already applied since the summer of 1917 in some companies in Roubaix and shortly before in Grenoble.

[32] "The worker and the employer may form the agreement by mutual consent, and specifically to establish the amount of the wages; but there always enters into it an element of natural justice, prior and superior to the free will of the contracting parties, and that is that the amount of the wages must not be less than the subsistence of the worker, frugal of course and of upright morals. If the latter, forced by necessity or fear of worse, accepts harsher agreements which, because they are imposed by the owner or the employer, must be accepted willingly or unwillingly, it is clear that he suffers violence, against which justice protests" (Rerum Novarum 15 May 1891, Encyclical Letter of Leo XIII, point 34).

[33] In 1920 Pierre Richemond, President of the Compensation Fund (see below) in the Paris area, wrote: «these last two years have seen the birth and development, with extraordinary speed, of a very interesting movement tending to include the consideration of the family situation of workers in the determination of wages» (Richemond, 1920, p. 590). An investigation by the Ministry of Labor led to the estimate that in the whole of France about two million private sector employees were receiving family allowances in the spring of 1920 (Richemond, 1920, p. 601). In truth, this movement in the private sector was a late follower of initiatives by some public administrations and large railway companies that had adopted a system of family allowances since the end of the nineteenth century.

as a good antidote to the "revolutionary" ambitions of workers. The main purpose of the system was another: «the narrative [...] of family allowances established on the initiative of social Catholicism and for a specific conception of wages and the family of benevolent employers, does not stand up to an analysis of the facts» (Math, 2023, p. 166). The main purpose was to contain wage pressures. Granting something to those who were on the edge of subsistence before they were forced to claim it was "a way of stemming the continuous pursuit of wages and thus fighting inflation" (Math, 2023, p. 168). This had also been demonstrated by the case of the road workers between 1896 and 1913.[34] Paying an over-wage based on family responsibilities was the morally acceptable way to avoid the cost of equal wage increases for all while also avoiding the less accepted unequal increases. So employers[35] too considered them as a part (usually half) of the increases due to the increase in the cost of living (allocation de vie chèr). Since wage bargaining almost always took place to obtain adjustments to the prices of pure subsistence, it was immediately unclear who actually paid the family allowances. Whether employers paid them as a true overpayment for "an element of natural justice". Or instead, workers paid them, because they were forced to give up parts of the salary due, a "round trip" transaction for those who received them, with the aggravating factor of penalizing young people who contributed with lower salaries and did not receive the allowances. This justified question makes one understand why the socialist union was against family allowances unlike the Catholic one, which was more sensitive to the teachings of the Church on social and family matters. And it also makes one understand why the "Compensation Funds" were born, that is, funds financed by all or almost all local businesses, so that they would contribute to the collective good given by the containment of wage demands: the much-feared general strike. These Funds could also have increased the effective over-wage nature of the allowances if, as recommended by independent experts, they had been autonomous and therefore not also wage authorities. This was not the case of the Textile Consortium which, having established the fund in February 1920, a few months later opened a dispute on its own initiative to

[34] When in France a great national effort to improve the state of the roads, which had become pitiful, could no longer be postponed, the increase in wages for road workers seemed inevitable. But the contributions made by the central government in favor of the departments were given as a total amount, so that what they spent on personnel they could not spend on materials. They thus sought a way to give wage increases that were accepted and considered fair but not equal for all. Hence the choice to graduate them on the basis of family responsibilities, which was done since 1896 (Montes, 1999).

[35] In Grenoble, it was the industrial manager Émile Romanet who in 1916 began to pay 20 cents per day for each child under 13. Since the average daily wage was 5.5 francs, this was less than 4% for each child (Romanet, 1922). The very modest sum was obtained, as Romanet himself recounted, through a survey of the workers after they had coldly accepted the requests to subscribe to the war loan while the terrible battle of Verdun was underway (October 1916). It emerged that a family with two dependent children needed 6.6 francs per day to live. This was a sum of 1.1 francs more than the average individual wage paid in the factory: 55 cents per child. The sum of 0.2 francs, a third, was established considering that wives also often worked, albeit irregularly and always at lower-than-average wages. Thus the "enlightened" Romanet had introduced checks less than half of those that the "reviled" Ley Textile Consortium would pay four years later. But, as will be seen, in the case of the Consortium it was not a question of benevolence.

reduce wages, while the right to allowances was subordinated, month by month, to actual presence at work except for justified absences. In this way, anyone who went on strike for even just one day lost family allowances for the entire month. It seems clear, therefore, that if the sums paid out for this system were substantial (on average 5% of the total wages paid by the Consortium firms in the 1920s) it was because they had to be a fairly powerful tool for containing ordinary wages.

Then there was the "Social Secretariat". Financed by contributions from companies, with the aim, according to the official reports, of "helping companies, associations, committees, etc., which carry out activities of general interest (choral, musical, sports, educational groups, etc.)" (Ley, 1927, p. 242); according to the communist pamphlet, to: «subsidize choral, musical, sports, gymnastics and military training societies to distract the youth from the fight to defend their wages and make them good 'patriots' for the defense of the bosses' safes». Furthermore, the pamphlet continues:

> it is at the Social Secretariat that the famous Boulin, a former labor inspector who has gone over to the service of Capital, and the filthy Richelmy, a former policeman, work, as well as a whole host of other unscrupulous individuals for whom money buys everything [...also involved] in the filing system by which every worker is classified according to political opinion. It is the Social Secretariat that buys the silence of the Combatants' Association [...], which created the association of leaders and supervisors [...] to which it pays 80 francs a month to always have strikebreakers available in the event of a strike, [...] which has secret funds to support partisan newspapers [...] and buy the silence of the so-called independent ones.

Finally, there was the central activity of the Consortium, financed by the member companies with a contribution equal to 5.5% of the total wages (28.5 million in 1926) which covered, in addition to the general expenses and those of the Social Secretariat, a strong and decisive aid to employers in the event of a strike: a guarantee for the prices of immobilized raw materials and the supply of as many meters of fabric or as many kilos of wool as those normally produced, plus an indemnity equal to 150% of the wages paid. The communists' pamphlet commented: "and it is precisely because this employer system exists that Ley was able to say with ferocious joy, at a banquet recently held in Paris: 'Strikes are opposed with the most absolute resistance' and, raising his glass of champagne, exclaim, to the applause of his audience of industrialists and reactionary deputies: 'in our factories you march or you die!'". Désiré Ley was the absolute leader and unhesitating operator of this "war machine" which was effective against the power that the proletariat was laboriously building for its own defense (Fig. 6.6).

> Public enemy number one of the working class, eminence grise, evil genius, Beelzebub, damned soul [...], he compensated for his humble origins with an extraordinary activity [...] apparently at the service of the masters [...] in reality dictator of the region disguised as a false humble [...] his back obsequiously bent. But suddenly a glance that darts out from his glasses, a cutting gesture, a short word, warns you that this boor who disguises himself as a faithful servant [...] is in reality the boss of the bosses. (Hastings, 1991, p. 322)

Fig. 6.6 Désiré Ley. ("La Bataille"[36]: "Sous le pressoir du consortium", 13 July 1920)

[36] "La Bataille", a socialist weekly from Roubaix, was published from 1909 to 1914 on four pages with many illustrations. After the interruption of the war, it resumed as "La Bataille Journal du peuple" (1918–1920), to become from January 1921 "La Bataille—Organe officiel de la Fédération du Nord du Parti socialiste SFIO".

6.9.3 *Ley's "Funeral"*

But Désiré Ley did not only record successes. He also suffered a resounding failure between 1923 and 1924.

> On March 22, 1923, determined to put an end to the "communist tyranny", a group of Halluin employers formed a local Industrial Union, affiliated with the famous Textile Consortium directed by Désiré Ley.[37] Taking advantage of a strike [winter 1923], he decided to close the factories two days a week. But the intransigent firmness of the Secretary contrasted with a certain coldness of the Halluin employers, individualistic and fearful after the loss of municipal power in 1919. On February 10, 1924, Pierre Defretin, the main representative of the Union, capitulated and agreed to increase wages as requested by the strikers. This defection sabotaged employer solidarity and the dissolution of the Union followed on February 14. «On February 14, 1924 at 5:35 p.m., Désiré Ley died. Pride killed him. The working class of Halluin is preparing a grandiose funeral for him», was the headline in the Party newspaper on February 25. The organization of this symbolic burial mobilized the militants for three weeks, arriving on Sunday March 9, 1924 at a true carnivalesque syncretism that combined the Catholic ritual with the scenes of medieval theatre. (Hasting, 1991, p. 403)

The last sentence, "arriving at a carnivalesque syncretism that united Catholic ritual with the scenes of medieval theatre", rather than an interpretation introduces the theme, which is also the problem, of deciphering Ley's "funeral". In the intention of the Halluin communists, the staging was to perform a double operation: to celebrate the defeat of Ley and his clerical-bourgeois order, to preach the superiority of the new lay-proletarian order, both experienced through an understood and shared ritual, drawn in appropriate ways from tradition. The goal was achieved, but - as will be shown - the actual unfolding of the "funeral" does not offer clear elements to suggest the identification of which rite was used among three possibilities: the carnival procession of Shrove Tuesday of Flemish folklore; the rites of Celtic folklore dedicated to spring renewal; or the "living corpse" of ancient Mediterranean rituals. The interpretative problem is also made difficult because it is necessary, first of all, to understand what could and should have been an adequate drawing from tradition. After having clarified this, it will be seen that the solution to the interpretative problem is not the indication of one rite or the other, but of all three together: a formal ambiguity and inconsistency that, instead of constituting a limit, were the strength of Halluin's "folklorized" communism.

6.9.3.1 Appropriate Use of Tradition

Ley's "funeral" was conceived "playing with the flexibility of popular festivals to say something else" (Hastings, 1991, p. 404). That is, using an ancient rite that indicated the end of a time and the beginning of a new time to say the end of the clerical-bourgeois order and the beginning of a new order of proletarian emancipation. It

---

[37] As the proletarians had done, in this way the industrialists of Halluin, who were and remained affiliated to the Consortium, intended to acquire a greater capacity to exercise their power over the workers of Halluin by better calibrating their action on the specific local reality.

was an operation methodologically similar to that, studied and explored by many historians and ethnologists, codified since the seventh century in the Christianization of the still "barbarian" populations of Northern Europe.[38] It was intended to use pagan religiosity to affirm the new Christian religion of the one Almighty God. There is a kind of "guide" in this regard, whose citation is found continuously throughout the centuries so that it must be considered known to a vast public, not only to scholars. It was the letter, written in 601, by Gregory the Great for Bishop Mellitus with suggestions to be transmitted to Augustine (of Canterbury) sent in 597 on a mission to Christianize the "Angles".[39]

> This wonderful text [...] constitutes a testimony, among others, of beliefs and customs that medieval literature of the 12th or thirteenth century will continue to use with candor or

[38] Christianization in Europe occurred in two ways: an institutional one based on urban churches and parishes, and an "individual" one through the evangelizing action of monks and missionaries. After Constantine's edict of 313, the first way, ordered toward a more rigorous orthodoxy, was the one generally followed in the territories that were organically under the empire. The missionary way was instead typical of the Christianization of the "barbarians", populations that were never truly Romanized or who were no longer totally so, as in the case of Britain after its abandonment by the legions (between the end of the fourth century and the early fifth century). If the evangelization of the Angles by missionary means was the aim to which the letter to Mellitus contributed (see shortly), the Christianization of the populations of Belgium and the Roubaix-Tourcoing-Halluin territory north of the great road that went from Lille to Maastricht, must not have been different. "In the sixth and seventh centuries the greater part of the Belgae [who were north of this road] were still barbarians and pagans [...] and carefully preserved the customs and religion of their Germanic ancestors. The cause of this obstinacy of the Belgae [...] in spite of the edicts of Theodosius and the Frankish kings [...] is that they were never directly under the empire as were the Gauls [...] but retained their chiefs and their traditional constitutions by serving as auxiliaries in the army and also in the Emperor's guard in Rome" (Schayez, 1834, pp. 25–26).

[39] "Gregory to Mellitus Abbot. [...] When [...] Almighty God has brought you to that most reverend man and our brother, Bishop Augustine, tell him what I have concluded after having meditated at length on the question of the Angles, namely that the temples of the idols of that people must not be destroyed [...]. Let holy water be produced, let it be sprinkled in those temples, let altars be built, let relics be placed in them, because if those temples are well built they must be converted from the worship of demons to the worship of the true God, so that that people, seeing that their temples are not destroyed, will remove error from their hearts and, knowing and adoring the true God, will gather with greater confidence in their accustomed places. And I have concluded that on this occasion some solemnity should be changed, as on the day of dedication or on the day of the birth of the holy martyrs whose relics are deposited there, and that huts should be built with the branches of trees around those same churches that have been transformed from the old temples, and that the solemnity should be celebrated with pious banquets. And no longer should animals be sacrificed to the devil, but animals should be killed to be eaten for the praise of God [...]. Thus the Lord manifested himself to the people of Israel in Egypt: but he preserved for his own worship the use of sacrifices that they were accustomed to offer to the devil, commanding them to immolate animals as a sacrifice for himself; so that, by changing their hearts, they might lose something of the sacrifice, but retain something, so that, even if they were the same animals that they were accustomed to offer, immolating them to God and not to idols, they were no longer the same sacrifices. You must therefore tell the said brother [Augustine] this decision so that he, who is now placed there [in England as bishop], may consider how he should organize everything. God save you, most beloved son" (Translation by Alberto Schena from the Latin text published in Ludovicus M. Hartman Gregorii I Papae Registrum Epistolarum Tomi II Pars II Libri X-XIV. Berolini Apud Weimannos 1895, p. 331).

> skepticism but with touching insistence [...and] explains the slow process of conquest that Christianity had to develop in a region of the world not previously acquired. [...]. If there is one point on which historians of religion now agree, after so many useless disputes, it is precisely the fact that Christianity was not invented [...], built from nothing in the West. This imported religion had to include its doctrine and its commemorations in the preceding pagan calendar in order to better assimilate it. It reached an authentic religious compromise where the part of Christian orthodoxy and that of the apocryphal traditions could not be easily separated. (Walter, 2010, pp. 10–11)

But "the wonderful text" was not a discovery of Philip Walter since Antoine Guillaume Bernard Schayes cited the same letter of Gregory the Great in 1834 (on page 26 of his "Essay on the customs, beliefs, traditions, ceremonies and religious and civil practices of the ancient and modern Belgians"), which in turn he had found in the "History of the Decline and Fall of the Roman Empire" by Edward Gibbon published between 1776 and 1789, taken from the "Historia ecclesiastica gentis Anglorum" of 731 by the Venerable Bede, who reports it in full in chapter 30. And it is precisely by commenting on the passage in which Bede reports the Pope's letter that Lesley Abrams specifies a very relevant point.

> Some modern commentators have seen Gregory recommendations as motivated by a balanced pragmatism; others have found them cynically opportunistic. These judgments, though different in their emphasis, stem from the same idea (often distasteful to modern sensibilities) that the pope's concept of what to do was materialistic [exploit existing materials and resources without beating around the bush]. In fact, Gregory's advice represents an attitude that must have been deeply rooted in the experience of those who lived in the Mediterranean world of the sixth and seventh centuries, where the presence of past civilization continued, reinterpreted, monumental [...]. And such advice was not merely materialistic. It was highly intellectual. It exemplified the academic practice of hermeneutic thought [...], which distinguished between internal and external meaning and recognized layered meanings [...]. Sites were reinterpreted, animals became offerings to God [...]. Idols were strictly forbidden, but finding God in what had been elements of pagan practice: sites, festivals, the eating of animals was not. Gregory offered two things: a way of thinking about traditional religion and a practical program for his missionaries. (Abrams, 2013, p. 5)

Gregory's motives were not opportunistic if one considers that "it was the Angles and not the Pope who moved Augustine's mission [...], and the reason why in 590 a barbarian people sought Christianization is that such a request came from the court" (Wood, 1994, pp. 9–10).[40] The Pope's advice was not to remove obstacles to the Christianization of the Angles, who were actually seeking it, but was related to Gregory's theology: «The letters of Gregory the Great continue to provide an opportunity to reevaluate the context in which mission must be understood [... and it is] some aspects of Gregory's theology that allow us to better understand Augustine's

---

[40] Faced with fears that Kent would fall under the rule of the Merovingians, it was appropriate to remove their religious motivation by converting to Christianity before being forced to do so. "It has sometimes been said that the English feared Merovingian domination and therefore waited to become Christians until the papal mission arrived to avoid subordination to the French church and state. Such an interpretation is untenable in the face of the facts. [...]. The Angles attempted to obtain missionaries from France. It was the unwillingness of the Franks [...] that ensured that it was the mission from Rome that was the source of the Christianisation of Kent" (Wood, 1994, p. 10).

approach to mission» (Wood, 1994, p. 1). And according to this theology, evangelization had to conquer the "hearts" of the people whose previous beliefs therefore had to be treated with respect.

In the face of all this, it can be said that the communists of Halluin could not have been less wise men than the Christian missionaries of the seventh and eighth centuries. For the "new evangelization" according to socialist values, their operation, far from being purely opportunistic, had to offer "a way of thinking about tradition" and a "practical program".

6.9.3.2 Carnival Rite

In the processions of Shrove Tuesday typical of Flemish folklore, figures, in the strangest costumes of the dying carnival, accompany, with torches and to the sound of drums, the puppet placed on the cart exclaiming "he's dead, he's dead", up to the square where the pyre burns the simulacrum (van Gennep, 1935). Understood in this way, the question was whether Ley's "funeral" really used and respected the traditional rite. The answer cannot be yes because it would have implied a double inversion: the proletarian order against the bosses' order and the victory of carnival against Lent. Making Ley's "funeral" as a carnival would have been as if Gregory had recommended not only replacing the pagan idols with Almighty God but also razing the ancient temples and using the stones to build new ones. The use of the rites of Shrove Tuesday (the dying carnival) would have been difficult to understand. One wonders what dies. The consolidated social and moral codes should die, but in traditional rites their temporary suspension dies instead.

> At carnival, everything is allowed. [...] Social and moral codes lose strength. Other logics assert themselves. The usual norms and consolidated hierarchies are replaced by a new order, the roles are reversed. A disobedience and an irreverence punctuate the event with a load of violence that symbolically compensates for its temporariness. [...]. Playing their role as spectator-actor, the people of Halluin make the plot of everyday life fall, go beyond the ordinarily insurmountable limits of their social space. They break the barriers of their cultural ghetto by saying today what tomorrow they will have to keep quiet. (Hastings, 1991, p. 405)

Brueghel's painting "Dispute between Carnival and Lent", also mentioned by Hastings (1991), eloquently expresses the material superiority of the carnival but its moral inferiority destined to lose it.[41] One may ask how the welding of the new order and

---

[41] The painting reflects the idea of the Christianized carnival, as it appeared at the beginning of the second millennium. "In 1091 the Council of Benevento set the beginning of Lent on Ash Wednesday, and from then on, the carnival began to develop as an explosion of joy and license, a logical antithesis to the constraints that would be imposed until Easter. Carnival is a final paganizing debauchery before the asceticism of Lent, and in this way, it is an anti-Lent, but it is also a pre-Lent [...]. Emphasizing the Christian character of carnival is essential for its understanding. This statement is a presupposition that must however be expanded through the search for pre-Christian antecedents. Carnival, in fact, a negative product of Lent, did not appear spontaneously, coming from nowhere; it was the extension and the receptacle of previous traditions. Carnival, a non-canonical

elements of traditional identity could take place if the consolidated order was overturned, but the rite was that of the carnival, which was destined to succumb to Lent, that is, to the restoration of the established order after a temporary vacation.

6.9.3.3 Spring Renewal

In the ancestral carnival, prior not only to its Christianization, but also to the traditions used by it, the celebration revolved around the end of winter. It celebrated the rhythms of Nature and not those of institutions. And it was a "totemic" celebration with explicit reference to blood and the killing of the sacrificial victim.

> What [...was] the original role of carnival? Undoubtedly to ensure the passage between winter and spring by acting on two registers: that of the circulation of souls and that of purification. These religious ideas were very early associated with the bear, an animal god known since prehistoric times. We do not really know the religious thought of our troglodyte ancestors on death, but what we are certain is that there was one, and undoubtedly a very elaborate one. Historical times, those that have left us more tangible testimonies, have subsequently updated and adapted this thought to the point of establishing a mythological system around the redistribution of life, in the image of Nature that becomes green again, and of purification [...]. The whole world then seems to be reborn, man remains alone [...]. Excluded from relief [...], he is reduced to inventing his own rites to get in touch with the gods to also seek divinity through a path of purification. (Coussée, 1989, p. 145)

Since prehistoric times and in places of the world even very far from each other, the bear-God may have even been the first divinity associated with the idea of strength and fertility as well as with the idea of the passage. Because of its resemblance to man, the bear has been considered the double animal of man, a tutelary ancestor. In Celtic myths, the life cycle of the bear, which includes wintering, puts it in close connection with a symbolism of renewal and strength. Thus, the many celebrations that recall the ancient rites are organized in ways that highlight these aspects.

> For the Balkans and the Carpathians, the work of ethnologists has mainly focused on the late winter rituals with the bear [...]. Their main function is to hasten the return of spring and fertility by bringing the bear out of hibernation. The animal, in fact, embodies the spirit of vegetation and presides over the growth of cereals. For this purpose, it is carried in procession [a disguised man or a puppet], decorated with straw, branches or leaves; it is offered seeds and fruits, it is cajoled, it is made to spin and dance, [... others] jump on its back. [...]. Sometimes, when it is a straw dummy, it becomes a victim, it is symbolically put to death and then burned. Similar agrarian rites, all linked to fertility, are attested in all parts of the Slavic and Germanic world. [...]. The most unbridled of these practices consisted in drinking the animal's blood and eating its flesh, a sort of ritual meal, with a strongly totemic essence

---

festival in the Christian calendar, is the extension of practices that predate Christianity, and at the same time it was involuntarily strengthened and defined by the Church" (Feuillet, 1991, pp. 20–21). But the tradition was much older. In Babylon in the third century BC there was a festival called Sacaea, during which the servants were served by their masters and one of the slaves was elected as king, "he wore the insignia of power, exhibited himself on the throne, ate at the king's table, slept with his women, before being put to death on the fifth day" (Fabre, 1992, p. 14) when the real king resumed his place for the reconfirmed security of the people, who sacrificed there the temporary joyful liberation from slavery.

> [...] which symbolically contributed to transforming the warrior into a bear, to endowing him with the strength of the beast and, thus, to making him invincible. (Pastoureau, 2007, pp. 64, 144, 318)

One could question whether this really would have been the meaning to be attributed to Ley's "funeral". It would have been as if Gregory had recommended using the pagan gods to draw from them the strength of the new God, who, thus, would not have been the Almighty at all. Hence, the question becomes whether it was Ley's strength that the proletarians wanted to absorb by sacrificing him. It does not seem so, if one considers the "funeral notice" printed and posted everywhere in Halluin and the neighboring villages in view of the "funeral" of "ignoble" Ley.

> In memory of Mr. Désiré Ley husband of the Lady Industrial Union of Halluin, born in an unspecified country in an unknown era and morally dead in Halluin on February 14, 1924 at 5:35 p.m. Founder of the Consortium of the starvers, member of the Brotherhood of the memory of Von Tessin and companions. As soon as he appeared, he took it upon himself to give relief to the workers by reducing their wages to prevent them from overindulging at the table. He never stopped at anything to punish the poor fathers of families guilty of union action and other acts against his good friends the Bosses. On several occasions he went so far as to provoke riots to serve his blood drinkers. He was one of the most faithful servants of inhumanity that the North has ever known, always on the move to defend the rights of the strongest against those of the weakest. He did everything possible to accelerate the triumph of the bosses' dictatorship. Unfortunately, although he was still young, illness took him away. His stomach was greedy for communists, and despite the pressing recommendations of the famous doctor YOU-MUST-STOP-IT-NOW from Courtrai, to abstain from them for several months, badly advised by friends, temptation won and the last one he swallowed, a communist from Halluin, was so hard to digest that he died. He left this world taking with him the contempt, the antipathy and the repudiation of everyone. All workers will remember him. A Deutschland Uber Alles. Plenary indulgence (https://alarecherchedupasse-halluin.net/index.php/evenement/evenements-politiques-et-sociaux-majeurs/desire-ley-parodie-de-funerailles).[42]

[42] The reference to Von Tessin concerns the German general Baron von Tessin who was commander of the Tourcoing and Halluin area during the occupation in the First World War (Heinrich commander in Lille, Hofmann in Roubaix), all three engaged in the ferocious requisitions and above all in the forced labor of civilians. This reference also allows the reader to understand the ending where, instead of the usual "a prayer" we find "Un Deutschland Uber Alles", that is, the reference to the third stanza of the "Song of the Germans" written by August Heinrich Hoffmann von Fallersleben on 26 August 1841 in Helgoland against French territorial claims on the Rhineland during the Rhine crisis. The famous doctor NOW-YOU-MUST-STOP of Courtrai, translates célèbre Docteur "TES-ZOO-LATE" de Courtrai. The expression TES-ZOO-LATE, in the West Flanders dialect, can have two meanings depending on the word on which the accent falls. If it is on LATE it means "it's so late", if it is on ZOO it means "it's too much". It was therefore thought to translate "NOW-YOU-MUST-STOP-IT-NOW" coherent with the text. Courtrai is in Belgium not far from Halluin where there was a famous hospital. I owe this precious information to my long-time friend Eddy De Beir ("of the Bear", interestingly) from Louvain.

6.9.3.4 The "Living Corpse"

A funeral rite capable of authorizing the funeral for the death of the "political body" of a powerful person was available in tradition. One can start from some pages by Ernesto De Martino.

> The loss of a loved one is, in the most prominent way, the experience of what happens without and against us: and in correspondence with this suffering we are called in the most peremptory way to the harsh effort of courageously becoming procurators of death, in us and with us, of our dead, lifting ourselves from the torment [...] to that ability to cry which, through objectification, dries up the tears and reopens us to life and value. [...]. The crisis of presence on the occasion of mourning can take on the forms of a delirium of denial of the mournful event: without carrying out the necessary work of internalizing the dead and transcending the event, the sick presence tries to establish a behavior as if the dead were still alive, perhaps concentrating the organization of its own delirium on any surrogate. To a certain extent this can also happen in the normal work of mourning, as demonstrated by the infinite expedients used to erase or attenuate the harshness of the unacceptable "never again" and to gain the time necessary to complete the detachment [...]. But if the work of mourning succeeds, these expedients are part of the dynamics of the mourning period [...] as techniques of readjustment to historical reality. [...]. In ancient Mediterranean religious civilizations [...] one of the most important cultural forces for combating the crisis of mourning was the institution of the ritual funeral lament. [...But] the ancient funeral lament is only one moment of the corresponding funerary rituals [...which] move within mythical horizons defined [...] dominated by that important [...] ideology of the living corpse [...], an intermediate phase of passage between the condition of the living and that of the dead, between this side and the hereafter, however individual religious civilizations then configure both this intermediate phase and the terminal condition of the souls in the realm of the dead. The intermediate phase of the living corpse [...] is supported and determined by ritual behavior [...], so that if the rites are not performed [...] the kingdom of the dead is not reached. (De Martino 1958/2000, pp. 42, 47, 53–54, 192–193)

By clarifying the central role assumed in the ancient funeral rite by the "living corpse", to represent a prolonged phase of passage between this world and the other, these pages by De Martino allow one to understand the matrix of elaborate rites, which appeared in France in the first two decades of the fifteenth century: the exposure of the corpse of nobles (Beaune, 1975) and of the king prolonged using an effigy while the physical body was rapidly inhumed. Rapidly inhumed because the embalming techniques that were progressing, were not able to allow a long exposure of the body; prolonged, to allow the dilation of the "intermediate phase" proportional to the importance of the deceased and to the complex "passing of power" according to the principle *Dignitas non moritur* already canonically established after 1059 (Walters, 2001).

> Dignitas non moritur, that is, the continuity of Dignitas despite the death of the holder, the unity between the predecessor and the successor, the binding power to social obligations [...] in the name of dignity [...] were practiced for [...] centuries in connection with the Quonian abbas decree [of Pope Alexander III]. Only in one respect did the legal jargon [...] deviate from the original notion of Dignity, replaced by "political body". [...]. And where, especially in France, the tendency was so strong as to read in the life of the king the life of the "ideal person" it was to be expected that [...] sooner or later the phrase «the king never dies» would arise [...]. The cry «the king is dead, long live the king» [...] made its first appearance at the funeral of Louis XII in 1515. (Kantorowicz, 1957, pp. 408, 411)

On this basis, the inversion in the funeral of Ley's political body, which had been defeated without *Dignitas*, was therefore understandable. The text of the funeral notice clearly sets out the reasons justifying the death of Désiré Ley's political body as being devoid of *Dignitas* and indeed ignoble, indecent, sordid: (i) "born in an unspecified country in an unknown era", i.e. foreign, alien; (ii) "founder of the Consortium of the starvers, member of the Brotherhood of the memory of Von Tessin and companions", i.e. architect of the war machine against the proletariat, as was the German occupier who forced them into forced labor; (iii) so much so that "as soon as he appeared, he took it upon himself to give relief to the workers by reducing their wages to prevent them from overindulging at the table. He never stopped at anything to punish the poor fathers of families guilty of union action and other acts against his good friends the Masters. He was one of the most faithful servants of inhumanity that the North has ever known, always on the move to defend the rights of the strongest against those of the weakest. He did everything possible to accelerate the triumph of the dictatorship of the masters" and this requires no comment; (iv) "his stomach was greedy for communists, on several occasions he went so far as to provoke riots to serve his blood drinkers", that is, while the Dignitas of the "noble" was worthy of never dying because it was tied to the "eternal" task of feeding the people, the ignoble dies because, on the contrary, he drinks the blood of the people; (v) "and despite the pressing recommendations of the famous doctor YOU-MUST-STOP-IT-NOW of Courtrai, to abstain from it for several months, badly advised by friends, temptation won and the last one he swallowed, a communist from Halluin, was so hard to digest that he died", that is, the death of the ignoble is inevitably caused by his behavior which is against nature, as anyone who knows its laws, like the doctor from Courtrai, knows and warns; (vi) his death therefore deserves "the contempt, the antipathy and the repudiation of everyone" which cannot be forgotten: "all workers will remember him"; (vii) and finally, if praying for the noble whose *Dignitas* survives him is meritorious ("plenary indulgence"), so it is meritorious to recite for the ignoble the verse "Deuschland uber alles" remembering the oppression of the foreigner.

6.9.3.5 Fertile Ambiguity

But one cannot conclude in this way with the funeral of the political body of Ley, against the other hypotheses of the Christianized carnival or the ancestral rites of spring. Reporting from articles published in local newspapers (right-wing "La Croix du Nord" 12 March 1924, left-wing "L'Enchaîné" 15 March 1924), Hastings transcribes the adjectives that recurred there: «ridiculous, grotesque, hateful, degrading and incoherent, a farce»; and on the other hand: «courageous initiative, unforgettable and grandiose day, Halluin in celebration» (Hastings, 1991, p. 403). And then he describes the procession: «The procession opens with fifes and drums preceding the funeral convoy pulled by two donkeys. Wreath bearers follow a priest […] in disguise, and a group of mourners with onions on their faces entertain the spectators by simulating pain. Then comes in strict order […] a dozen triads: workers' fanfare, delegation from a nearby municipality, float» (Hastings, 1991, p. 410). The local Catholic newspaper wrote: «this farce of the vigil of the dead, this coffin and this puppet, this funeral procession [...] were truly a grotesque parody» (Hastings, 1991, p. 412). On the other hand: «the mental structure of Halluin, despite everything imbued with multi-secular religiosity, [...] prevents the local Communist Party from an openly anticlerical discourse. Anticlericalism exists [...] but takes refuge [...] in an ambiguity that the leaders themselves seem to cultivate» (Hastings, 1991, p. 412). In the ceremony for Ley there was therefore *everything*: the seriousness of the funeral of the political body, the Christian funeral mocked but not too much, the ancestral carnival, the reversal of the Christianized carnival. Hastings concludes:

> This association of Flemish festive orthodoxy and communist eschatology suggests the hypothesis that a cultural heritage is made to survive the disappearance of the community's village structures, when an actor, in a position of hegemony, recovers to his own advantage the collective heritage of local beliefs and traditions. By accepting the rules of the game, Halluin the Red imposes the image of a communism adapted to local conditions and cultural sedimentations. A folklorized communism. (Hastings, 1991, p. 414)

Halluin's "folklorized" communism was founded on a profound ambiguity, which constituted its strength, not unlike what Gramsci noted in his "Observations on Folklore" in which it is included in the list of world conceptions.

> The enormous latitude that Gramsci in fact assigns to his notion of worldview, that is, his dilating it to include even the most bizarre, disintegrated and occasional combinations of heterogeneous and indigestible elements, retains an undoubted aggressive charge towards traditional conceptions that identify culture with its own culture and reduce history to the history of the vertices. [...]. Thus, Gramsci's use of the notion of worldview, at least when it concerns spontaneous conceptions, is continually supported by a dense network of references to concrete social situations, even if very humble, of which the cultural jumble examined from time to time constitutes the «way of seeing and operating». And therefore the judgement on the formal qualities or contents of those agglomerates is accompanied by the observation that that particular co-presence of cultural elements, whatever their origin or level, constitutes the intellectual heritage of a certain social group, which lives and enjoys it from within without perceiving its contradictory nature, or at least not perceiving it in the ways that are typical of those who look from the outside. Thus each combination of cultural elements that forms the product of a social group, however identifiable, comes to constitute a sort of "unity of fact", which can be looked at from the point of view of the group that recognizes itself in it and which can therefore be legitimately called a conception of the world because, even if it is not for us, it is for them. (Cirese, 2008, p. 497)

Ley's "funeral" really represented the condemnation and the overcoming of a system, affirming an opposite one, but not through formal coherence, but rather through the complex and ambiguous combination of the disorganized and fragmentary reference to tradition on the one hand, and on the other, as a cultured, explicit, original, active discourse, in tension toward the hegemonic. It was the combination brought back to "unity" as it meshed with the social group, with the community of Halluin "The Red", through the gesture of staging the event and the symbol.

But one may question whether such an ambiguous and formally incoherent practice was not foreign to "science" and how it could remain an element of the "theorem" capable of relaunching the interactive process between the social and political body that one is accustomed to conceiving as established by explicit coherences contained in canons, manifestos, statutes. The answer can be given by recalling the "science without a name" whose foundation and concrete practice Giorgio Agamben attributed to the great art historian (but not only) Aby Warburg (1866–1929). In Warburg's science without a name, an analytical tool as a mirror of applied science in the formation of Western culture, heterogeneous and apparently incoherent symbols and images of the past play a central role precisely for this reason as an energetic charge and inherited emotional experience.

> The symbol, the image perform for Warburg the same function that, according to Semon, the engram performs in the central nervous system of the individual: in them an energetic charge and an emotional experience are crystallized that survive as a legacy transmitted by social memory and that [...] become effective through contact with the selective will of a given era. [...] Only from this perspective is it possible to appreciate the meaning and importance of the project to which Warburg devoted his last years and for which he had chosen the name [...]: Mnemosyne. [...]. Of the unfinished project [...] there remain about forty black canvas screens on which are pinned about a thousand photographs, in which it is possible to recognize his favourite iconographic themes, but whose material extends to include the advertising poster of a shipping company, the photo of a golf player, that of the Pope and Mussolini signing the Concordat. But Mnemosyne is something more [...]. He defined it [...] «a ghost story for truly adult people» [...]. His "atlas" was a sort of gigantic condenser in which all the energetic currents that had animated and continued to animate the memory of Europe were collected, taking shape in its ghosts. [...]. Perhaps the least unfaithful way of characterizing his "science without a name" is to insert it into the project of a future "anthropology of Western culture" in which philology, ethnology, history, and biology converge with an "iconology of the interval" in which the incessant symbolic labour of social memory operates. (Agamben, 1975, pp. 56.57, 58, 64)

6.10 And Faith

The formula "faith against science, science against faith", however, suggests a circuit that continues. As seen in other examples, especially in that of Silicon Valley, after the implementation of science, faith must intervene again. The question is when. It is to this question that the case of Halluin suggests a significant final answer in illustrating the fatal error made during the great strike of 1928–1929. In this circumstance, the communists of the people's house were not careful enough to evaluate their own forces and suffered a serious defeat in October 1928. In the new bitter conflict with the Consortium, they did not stop in time when they found themselves isolated. Allowing themselves to be tempted by the faith of their origins, they believed they could win in an unequal confrontation that they lost. The defeat certainly did not destroy Halluin's communism and the people's house, but it certainly weakened them greatly. Thus, when the time of faith really came, they did not seize it because they had failed in the time of science, with serious and long-lasting consequences. The Halluin case therefore allows one to add two clarifications, one to the "people's house theorem", the other to the collective action formula, as will be seen in the conclusions.

Table 6.2 Halluin 122–1936: Unionization and Communist Militancy

	CGTU members	CGTU and CFTC members	Population	CGTU members on population %	CGTU members on total CGTU + CFTC %	% share of Communist Party activists in electoral votes
1922	3.160	4.660	13.780	22,9	67,8	16
1926	4.635	6.435	13.844	33,5	72,0	17
1930	2.285	5.285	13.800	16,6	43,2	9
1936	2.805	6.105	13.278	21,1	45,9	11

Source Figures obtained by processing data from Hastings (1991, pp. 222, 317). *Note*: CFTC is the Catholic union; CGTU (Confédération générale du travail unitaire) was a trade union confederation that soon became aligned with the French Communist Party. It was founded in 1922 as a confederation that had left the socialist-dominated General Confederation of Labor (CGT), and in late 1936 merged back into the CGT

The conflict of 1928 was of exceptional severity and duration: 200 days of confrontation between workers and employers and, in the most participated phase, 70,000 workers on strike throughout the district. Due to its conclusion with the defeat of the communist union, the event was periodizing. Following the defeat, the union and communist party members were halved from 1926 to 1930 (Table 6.2).

By the spring of 1928 the wage issue had already worsened. At the end of May, a proposal for a dispute and a united front was presented and discussed by the union leaders at the Tours congress on 8 July and then at the second congress on 2 September. In the meantime, since 30 July, the union organization was overtaken by the base: metalworkers had been on the move with work stoppages to demand a raise of 50 cents an hour: ten sous, from which the name that was later given to the entire struggle, called the "dix sous". On 11 September, Gilbert Declercq[43] of the Communist regional, delegated by the Party to the political direction of the strike, sent a telegram to the CGTU National Secretariat: «Serious situation—Halluin—Send a CGTU delegate—Urgent—Workers threaten a general strike» (Hastings, 1991, p. 337). On 17 September the general strike was proclaimed by CGTU. On 20 September the workers who downed their tools in Halluin were 6,500 and 20,000 in the whole Lys

[43] Gilbert Declercq, born on 15 August 1896 in Halluin, died in tragic circumstances in September 1944 near Nîmes. From a very poor family after the death of his father, a weaver, Gilbert was an apprentice weaver in 1909 and then a specialized weaver when, two years later, he joined the Socialist Youth, of which he became secretary in Halluin in 1913. During the German occupation, he was imprisoned several times for refusing to work for the enemy. In 1921, he was elected secretary of the People's House and participated in the creation of the local structures of the Communist Party. Elected city councilor in May 1925, designated second deputy mayor, he immediately became a target of the police. Sentenced to 15 days in prison in 1921 for "provoking soldiers to disobey", in June 1926 he was again sentenced to six months. On 3 September 1927, he was elected for the Communist Party in the supplementary elections for the district council of the canton of Carnières. Already at the end of 1926, in agreement with the regional leadership of the PC of which he was a member, he left the management of the People's House of Halluin to devote himself to organizing strikes in the textile centers of the Lille area, also as vice-secretary of the Textile-Clothing Federation CGTU.

valley. The Catholic union CFTC, which had said it was against the general strike with political significance, after having tried "in every way" to avoid it, ended up joining. The CFTC Secretary Artur Houte wrote on 21 September in the "Journal de Roubaix": «We are faced with a political strike, but the underlying reason is correct. We are in the mechanism, and we must move forward» (Hastings, 1991 p. 337). By the end of the month, almost all of the Consortium's workers had joined the strike.

However, already in the first week of October, defections were recorded in Armatiers and then also in Lille, Roubaix and Tourcoing due to three causes (Hastings, 1991, pp. 337–338): (1) the notable impact of the Consortium's recourse to "scabs" (*briseurs de grève*); (2) a certain bureaucratization of the struggle: «the strike committee was transformed into a small parliament, decisions were not always taken with the necessary speed, its composition was lacking being formed largely by union officials and to a minimal extent by strikers» (Hastings, 1991, pp. 337–338); (3) the perception of a provocation by the employers: the employers had rejected the inexpensive concession to the metalworkers and then any negotiation; a provocation even perceived by the Police Commissioner who wrote in a Report: «the mechanics' strike takes a turn unexpected by the leaders of the Halluin people's house due to a maneuver by the employers. Ley tries to exhaust the workers with successive strikes so that they are not able to sustain the struggle with the bosses» (Hastings, 1991, p. 338).

In mid-October it was necessary to make the crucial decision. And it was Gilbert Declercq who had to make it, he who had perceived "with a certain panic, that he would be 'caught in the middle' [...] in the test of strength that the Consortium intended to engage in [...] anxious to defeat the proletariat of the red city" (Hastings, 1991, p. 338). The decision was to go ahead in Halluin even alone. Hastings does not inform us about the reasons that pushed Declercq to make a decision that with hindsight turned out to be wrong. He reports another phrase of his that does not hide concern together with confidence: «now for Halluin it is a question of holding on at all costs» (Hastings, 1991, p. 338). However, it also reports a passage from the circular "Northern Region—French Communist Party" sent to all cell secretaries: «If the Consortium wins, it will increase its audacity and it will be the signal for an even stronger general offensive against all categories of workers. If the Halluin strikers are victorious, the employers of the entire region will suffer a hard blow» (Hastings, 1991, pp. 338–339). It is not known whether the circular was sent *before* or *after* Declercq's decision, but it certainly reveals the climate and perhaps direct pressure on the Halluin delegate, which influenced his decision to go ahead with the strike "in the besieged citadel" (Hastings, 1991, p. 339). It was, in fact, by thinking about this circular that he defended himself (at first) in the "trial" that the Party set up against him after the defeat, accusing him of "opportunism", writing "if we have made mistakes, the Party Centre and the confederal office have also made them" (Hastings, 1991, p. 343).

But the clash was unequal. It was not possible for the 5,000 members of the Halluin union and its 15,000–20,000 workers, who had to bring home results for 70,000 employees of the Consortium companies throughout the district, to win. The resistance lasted until the end of February 1929, and the people's house went into heavy debt to support the strikers. These debts were one of the causes that explain a notable reduction in the activities and capacities of the people's house after 1929. It all ended with 1,800 dismissals, many workers arrested, the resignation of Declercq, a notable weakening of the communist union and the party: the end of an era. It was truly the end of an era, as can be seen by considering the results of the elections for Parliament, which for the French electoral system (single-member ballot with two rounds[44]), constitute a representative indicator of political pre-eminence in a given territory. As can be seen in the following figure, the percentage of votes in Halluin for the elected communists had contributed decisively, from 1924 to 1928, to supporting the results of the left (communists and socialists): 10 points more than the national average. But the progression stopped and actually underwent a reversal of the trend with the elections of 1932. The small recovery of 1936 achieved reconnection with the national average which had grown in the meantime. But it was only temporary. Subsequently, there was a real collapse in the percentage of communists, in clear contrast to the national average. Thus, in Halluin the left did not experience at all the exceptional growth that it had in France from the Second World War, indeed it always remained lower, except in the 1970s, but at that point not due to the merit of the communists (Fig. 6.7).

One may ask what happened that was so negative and important in the elections of 1932. What happened is that the candidate presented by the Communist Party was not the historical protagonist of Halluin's peculiar social interaction communism, Gustave Desmettre, mayor of the turning point of 1919. Gilbert Declercq, who at the end of the "trial" had made a full self-criticism, was preferred to him: «Declercq had returned to the odor of 'sanctity' after his self-criticism of 1929» (Hastings, 1991, p. 282). Desmettre, on the other hand, was not forgiven for the guilt of having defended Albert Cornette (former secretary of the people's house), accused of Trotskyism for having criticized the organization by cells and expelled on 21 June 1930 (Hastings, 1991, p. 232). There was no faith in the great results achieved by Halluin's community communism. Having believed in it and having lost during the 1928 struggle, it was deemed necessary to resort to other resources, those of the organization of the Party as such regardless of its local configuration. Therefore, the logic of the apparatus prevailed: those who had given proof of submission as good "*apparatčiki*" had to be offered the opportunity for redemption "after the mistakes he had made" in leading the strike in 1928. Those who had shown autonomy had to be taught a lesson. Lack of faith led to closing oneself off, to not including in order to innovate.

> On the evening of the second round, despite the efforts of all political formations, voter turnout dropped by one percentage point. Henri-Constant Groussau [an eighty-year-old

[44] After various vicissitudes, the two-round single-member constituency system, initially with one deputy for every 70,000 inhabitants, gradually increased as the population grew, was adopted by the Third Republic (1870–1940) except for the elections of 1871, 1885, 1919, 1924, in which a mixed system was used. After the Second World War, de Gaulle imposed proportional representation to limit the influence of the Communist Party and to distance himself from the Third Republic. The two-round single-member constituency system was reinstated in 1958 (Fifth Republic) and used until 1982.

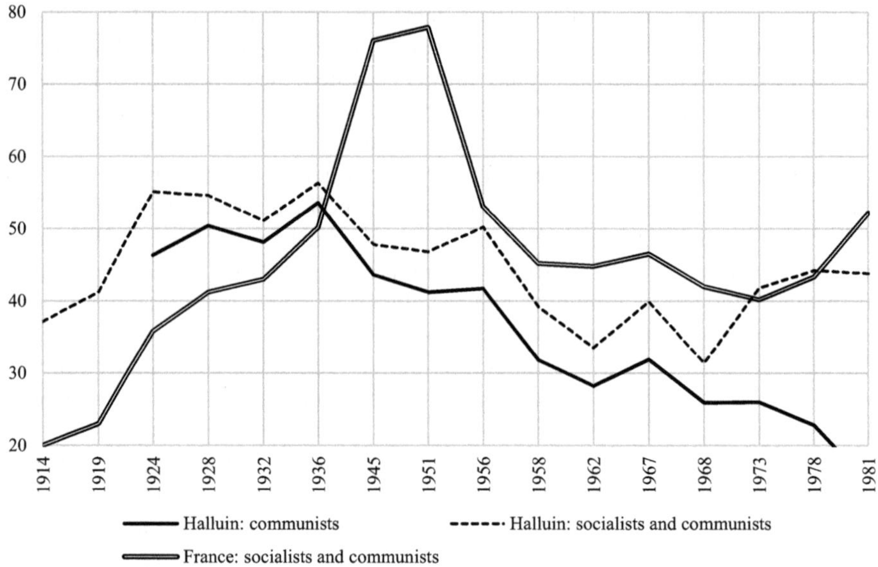

Fig. 6.7 Percentages in the national elections to the Parliament obtained by the Communist Party and the Socialist Party in Halluin and comparison with the results at the national level. *Source* Figure obtained by processing data from Thiébault and Wallon-Leducq (1982, p. 633); for France: Wikipedia French legislative elections several years

> historic right-wing MP] retains his seat [...] with a ten-point advantage over Declercq [...]. One can see the perverse effects [...] of the sectarian drift of the PCF» (Hastings, 1991, p. 284)

Finally, the long-term effects of this defeat due to "lack of faith" took a turn with implications that also had tragic aspects. Declercq was again a candidate in 1936. The Party had done an "analysis of the vote" of 1932 and had concluded that the defeat was of a technical nature largely attributable to the poor quality of the propaganda. Therefore, the blame lay with the candidate and his team certainly not with the choices of the party: «weak action of the network and poor involvement [...]; the drafting of the propaganda material by one or two militants explains the gaps [...], most of it was incomprehensible to the workers» (Hastings, 1991, p. 285). Declercq's re-candidacy, instead of restoring faith in social interaction communism and recalling Desmettre, therefore had the meaning of reaffirming that individuals can make mistakes, but the Party does not.

Declercq won but for a series of particular circumstances: Groussau had retired from politics, and the new right-wing candidate, Jean Bataille, a 40-year-old lawyer, was weak and proposed with less authority the usual defense of family, religious, and employer values; for the first time a candidate of Christian Democrat inspiration was presented, Jules Suys, who weakened the right-wing candidate; a few months earlier the Popular Front had been born, giving the left an extra edge; and between the first and second rounds there was a perfect desistance on both sides of the political spectrum with the result of reducing voter turnout. The Popular Front won: in Halluin 2,513 votes for Declercq and 1,257 for Bataille. It was a clear and strong victory. Too clear and strong. The result had the effect of "imprisoning" the deputy Gilbert Declercq, whose election was interpreted as being solely due to the Party, a condition that in the long run became unbearable for him. So much so that, with a subversive decision, he resigned from the parliamentary group on 4 October 1939. It was said that he had done so in disagreement with the non-aggression treaty between the German Reich and the Union of Soviet Socialist Republics (Molotov-Ribbentrop Pact, 23 August 1939). In reality, he expressed some reservations about the Party line in relation to the Soviet Union only after his resignation and not before (Hastings, 1991, p. 235). According to Hastings, who reports the various hypotheses explored to explain the disruptive gesture, all unlikely, the most convincing remains that "after his election as Deputy in 1936, Declercq had become a 'desocialized' person. Breaking away from the Party ethics, he no longer respected its code of conduct" (Hastings, 1991, p. 235). During the war he joined the Resistance as an independent. In 1944, he disappeared in the region of Nîmes, he was said to have been arrested and killed by the Gestapo, in reality he was probably "taken and murdered by communist partisans" (Hastings, 1991, p. 235).

6.11 Conclusion

The case of Halluin allows one to clarify the "theorem" of the people's house, reiterating, first of all, the importance of evaluating the results achieved over time, one of the crucial needs of innovative and inclusive collective action. This evaluation encourages effort and dedication, but now one understands that it also serves to propose objectives which are commensurate with the forces. The "theorem" can therefore be rewritten. The people's house is the place of proletarian self-emancipation as it acquires credit by solving workers' problems; therefore, an interactive relationship is established between the social and political body, which uses the traditional forms of social interaction, from which further consensus and ability to solve problems, as well as the ability to modify such forms of social interaction, *exercising a continuous accurate evaluation of the results gradually measuring the objectives to the capacities.*

The case also allows one to clarify two points regarding the formula "faith against science and science against faith". Science must dictate the configuration of the objectives by measuring them to the resources. At a certain point, however, a leap of faith is needed to overcome obstacles that may seem insurmountable based on resources. The wrong choice of moment can always be made, as there is no recipe for identifying it correctly. But if one makes a mistake, one must not lose faith. When faced with failure, the temptation to believe that one's abilities and resources are inferior to what they actually are can be great. In this case, one mistake would be compounded by another, and the consequences could be serious. Secondly, it is necessary to clarify the nature of "science". It will not be the science of formal coherences but rather that of meshing with the social group, Warburg's nameless science. Indeed, the ultimate mistake could be precisely that of giving it up, believing it to be lacking, in order to resort to formal science that would be extraneous, unproductive, even destructive in view of collective action for innovation and inclusion.

References

Abrams L. (2013). *Bede, gregory, and strategies of conversion in Anglo-Saxon England and the Spanish New World. Jarrow Lecture 2013.* Bealim Signs Ltd.

Agamben G. (1975/1984). Aby Warburg e la scienza senza nome. *Prospettive Settanta* 1(2) 1975. Ripubblicato in *Aut Aut* 199–200, 1984, pp. 51–66.

Azéma, J.-P., Prost, A., & Rioux, J.-P. (1986). *Le Parti communiste français des années sombres (1938–1941).* Seuil.

Beaune, C. (1975). Mourir noblement à la fin du Moyen Âge. *Actes des Congrès de la Société des historiens médiévistes de l'enseignement supérieur public, 6*, 125–144.

Bécuwe, S., & Blancheton, B. (2020). French textile specialisation in long run perspective (1836–1938): Trade policy as industrial policy. *Business History, 62*(6), 891–914.

Benoist, C. (1904). Le travail dans la grande industrie. La filature et le tissage. *Revue des Deux Mondes, 22*(3), 667–696.

Caudron, A. (1991). Du Consortium à la Bourgeoisie Chrétienne. *Revue du Nord, 73*(290–291), 411–415.

Cépède, F. (2008). La SFIO des années 1905–1914: Construire le parti. *Cahiers Jaurès, 1*(187–188), 29–45.

Cirese, A. M. (2008). Concezioni del mondo, filosofia spontanea e istinto di classe nelle "Osservazioni sul folclore" di Antonio Gramsci. *Lares, 74*(2), 467–498.

Coussée B. (1989). *Sacré carnaval.* Chez l'Auteur.

Cossart, P., & Talpin, J. (2012). Les Maisons du Peuple comme espaces de politisation—Étude de la coopérative ouvrière La Paix à Roubaix (1885–1914). *Revue française de science politique, 4*(62), 583–610.

Denuc, J. (1930). Les Salaires. *Revue d'économie politique, 44*(3), 948–959.

Devos I. (1999). Marriage and economic conditions since 1700: the Belgian case. In Isabelle Devos & Liam Kennedy (Eds.), *Marriage and Rural Economy: Western Europe Since 1400.* Brepols.

Dreyfus, M. (1995). *Histoire De La Cgt. Cent Ans De Syndicalisme En France.* Editions Complexe.

Fabre, D. (1992). *Carnaval ou la fête à l'envers.* Gallimard.

Fohlen, C. (1951). Esquisse d'une évolution industrielle—Roubaix au XIXe siècle. *Revue du Nord, 33*(130–131), 92–102.

Hastings, M. (1991). *Halluin-la-Rouge 1919–1939—Aspects d'un communisme identitaire.* Presse universitaire de Lille.

Jarrige F. (2020). Ils n'auront plus à suer sang et eau. Les boulangeries coopératives et la modernisation du pétrissage (France, 1860–1914). In Alexia Blin, Stéphane Gacon, François Jarrige et Xavier Vigna (Eds.), *L'utopie au jour le jour. Une histoire de la coopération.* Editions L'arbre bleu.

Kantorowicz, E. H. (1957). *The King's two bodies: A study in mediaeval political theology.* Princeton University Press.

Kriegel A. (1966a). Le Parti communiste français sous la Troisième République (1920–1939). Évolution de ses effectifs. *Revue française de science politique, 16*(1), 5–35.

Kriegel, A. (1966b). Le Parti communiste français et la question du pouvoir (1920–1939). *Annales Economies, Sociétés, Civilisations, 21*(6), 1245–1258.

Le Mouel G. (2003). *Le Chemin de fer dèpartementel du Morbihan, de Lorient à Plouay 1902–1948*. Conférence du 6 décembre 2003, Archives départementales du Morbihan.
Leuilliot P. (1929). Mr G. Jacquemyns, Histoire de la crise économique des Flandres (1845–1850). *Annales d'histoire économique et sociale, 1*(4), 624–627.
Lévy-Leboyer M. (1968). La croissance économique en France au XIXe siècle - Résultats préliminaires. *Annales. Economies, Sociétés, Civilisations, 23*(4), 788–807.
Ley, D. (1927). L'œuvre sociale du consortium de l'industrie textile de Roubaix-Tourcoing en 1926. *Journal de la société statistique de Paris, 68*, 241–243.
Math, A. (2023). Les prestations familiales et leur financement jusqu'aux années 1940: Construction d'une assurance sociale singulière. *La Revue de l'Ires, 110–111*(2–3), 159–187.
Mendels, F. (1972). Proto industrialization: The first phase of the industrialization process. *Journal of Economic History, 32*, 241–261.
Montes, J.-F. (1999). Les allocations familiales aux cantonniers Une expérience catégorielle menée entre 1896 et 1920. *Recherches et Prévisions, 56*, 67–77.
Morin, G. (2007). Les socialistes et la société française Réseaux et milieux (1905–1981). *Vingtième Siècle Revue d'histoire, 96*, 47–62.
Pastoureau, M. (2007). *L'ours: Histoire d'un roi déchu*. Seuil.
Petillon, C. (2006). Roubaix, une ville industrielle nourrie d'immigration belge. In David Michel, et al. Editeurs: *Roubaix* (pp. 23–39). Presses universitaires du Septentrion.
Richemond, P. (1920). Allocations pour charges de famille et caisses de compensation. *Revue d'économie politique, 34*(5), 590–606.
Romanet, É. (1922). *Les allocations familiales: Origines, fonctionnement, situation actuelle, renseignements pratiques*. Chronique Sociale de France.
Schayez, A. G. B. (1834). Essai historique sur les usages, les croyances, les traditions, les cérémonies, et pratiques religieuses et civiles des Belges anciens et modernes. Chez l'Auteur.
Scholliers, P. (2001). Mots et pratiques. L'industrie cotonnière gantoise, les crises et la perception patronale de la concurrence internationale 1790–1914. *Revue d'histoire du XIXe siècle, 23*, 1–22.
Teece, D. J. (1984). Economic analysis and strategic management. *California Management Review, 26*(3), 87–110.
Thiébault,.J-L., & Wallon-Leducq, C.-M. (1982). Trois aspects des comportements politiques septentrionaux. *Revue du Nord* LXIV, (253), 603–635.
Tilly, C. (1986). *The Contentious France*. Harvard.
Van Gennep, A. (1935). *Le folklore de la Flandre et du Hainaut français (département du Nord). Tome I, Du berceau à la tombe. Les cérémonies périodiques. Le culte des saints: avec une étude sur la répartition géographique des Géants processionnels et 6 cartes et planches hors-texte*. Paris: G.-P. Maisonneuve.
Walter, P. (2010). *Mythologie chrétienne—Fêtes, rites et mythes du Moyen Age*. Imago.
Walters, D. (2001). Sede vacante—Dignitas nunquam perit: Alexander III (1159–1181)'s decretal Quoniam abbas and its consequences in canon and secular law. *Cahiers du CRHiDI. Histoire, droit, institutions, société, 15*, 39–54.
Wood, I. (1994). The mission of Augustine of Canterbury to the English. *Speculum, 69*(1), 1–17.

MIX
Papier aus verantwortungsvollen Quellen
Paper from responsible sources
FSC® C105338

If you have any concerns about our products,
you can contact us on
ProductSafety@springernature.com

In case Publisher is established outside the EU,
the EU authorized representative is:
Springer Nature Customer Service Center GmbH
Europaplatz 3, 69115 Heidelberg, Germany

Printed by Libri Plureos GmbH
in Hamburg, Germany